South Asian Pornographies

South Asian Pornographies is the first consolidated volume that explores the relationships between pornography, obscenity, law, and desire in South Asia. Focusing on case studies from India, Sri Lanka, and Bangladesh while gesturing towards other countries in South Asia, the authors of this volume come from fields as varied as history, literature, media and communication, and the visual arts. This book proposes that as a geo-political location, South Asia has a unique relationship to pornography, given the multiplicity of cultural and legal-censorial regimes that define the obscene and the permissible. South Asian case studies can demonstrate how pornography in the region is often defined in oblique terms, finding reflection in various modes of popular (and sometimes underground) culture, bypassing legal and censorial constraints. Like questions of identity that can only be answered in the plural (identities rather than identity), this book demonstrates how a range of pornographies constitutes the force field of sexualized media in South Asia. It will be of interest to researchers and advanced students of Communication Studies, Cultural Studies, Film Studies, History, Sociology, and Social and Cultural Anthropology. The chapters in this book were originally published in the journal *Porn Studies*.

Darshana Sreedhar Mini is Assistant Professor at the Department of Communication Arts at the University of Wisconsin-Madison, USA. Supported by the Social Science Research Council (SSRC) and American Institute of Indian Studies (AIIS), her book titled *Rated A: Soft-Porn Cinema and Mediations of Desire in India* (UC Press, 2024) explores the media-ecology produced by Malayalam soft-porn films by mapping their transnational journeys. Her research interests broadly include South Asian Cinema, Feminist Media, Global Media Cultures, and Migrant media. Her work has been published in *Feminist Media Histories, Film History, Porn Studies, Bioscope: South Asian Screen Studies, South Asian Popular Culture, South Asian Film and Media, Journal for Ritual Studies*, and *International Journal for Digital Television.*

Anirban K. Baishya is Assistant Professor at the Department of Communication Arts at the University of Wisconsin-Madison, USA. He is currently working on a book project tentatively titled *Viral Selves: Selfies, Platforms and Digital Image Culture in India.* His research interests include new media and digital cultures, social media and political culture, media aesthetics, surveillance studies, and global media. His work has been published in the *International Journal of Communication, Communication, Culture & Critique, South Asian Popular Culture, Porn Studies, South Asia: Journal of South Asian Studies*, and *Media, Culture & Society.*

South Asian Pornographies

Vernacular Formations of the Permissible and the Obscene

Edited by
Darshana Sreedhar Mini
and Anirban K. Baishya

Routledge
Taylor & Francis Group
LONDON AND NEW YORK

First published 2024
by Routledge
4 Park Square, Milton Park, Abingdon, Oxon, OX14 4RN

and by Routledge
605 Third Avenue, New York, NY 10158

Routledge is an imprint of the Taylor & Francis Group, an informa business

British Library Cataloguing-in-Publication Data
A catalogue record for this book is available from the British Library

ISBN13: 978-1-032-41787-5 (hbk)
ISBN13: 978-1-032-41788-2 (pbk)
ISBN13: 978-1-003-35970-8 (ebk)

DOI: 10.4324/9781003359708

Typeset in Myriad Pro
by codeMantra

Publisher's Note
The publisher accepts responsibility for any inconsistencies that may have arisen during the conversion of this book from journal articles to book chapters, namely the inclusion of journal terminology.

Contents

Citation Information

The following chapters were originally published in various volumes and issues of the journal *Porn Studies*. When citing this material, please use the original page numbering for each article, as follows:

Chapter 1
Cast(e)ing and translating sex in the vernacular: the writings of Santram BA in Hindi
Charu Gupta
Porn Studies, volume 7, issue 1 (2020), pp. 19–35

Chapter 2
Purging the pornographic, disciplining the sexual, and edifying the public: pornography, sex education, and class in early to mid-twentieth century colonial Bengal
Arnav Bhattacharya
Porn Studies, volume 9, issue 3 (2022), pp. 273–291

Chapter 3
A short history of the 'Blue-Photo': Bengali sex magazines and the visual empire of printed images (1940–1970)
Bijleeraj Patra
Porn Studies, volume 9, issue 3 (2022), pp. 312–323

Chapter 4
Reading Anandalok*: obscenity, cinema and other 'prohibitive' pleasures in 1970s–1990s Bengali print culture*
Spandan Bhattacharya
Porn Studies, volume 7, issue 1 (2020), pp. 13–18

Chapter 5
Pornography and Indian miniature painting: the case of Avadh, India
Natalia Di Pietrantonio
Porn Studies, volume 7, issue 1 (2020), pp. 36–60

Chapter 6
'Raped, outraged, ravaged': race, desire, and sex in the Indian empire
Anubhav Pradhan
Porn Studies, volume 7, issue 1 (2020), pp. 61–75

Chapter 7

Between aunties: sexual futures and queer South Asian aunty porn
Kareem Khubchandani
Porn Studies, volume 9, issue 3 (2022), pp. 346–364

Chapter 8

The X factors of sex: hijras, Victorian law, and digital porn in postcolonial India
Rahul K. Gairola
Porn Studies, volume 7, issue 1 (2020), pp. 76–96

Chapter 9

Pleasure, bodies and risk: women's viewership of pornography in urban India
Ketaki Chowkhani
Porn Studies, volume 3, issue 4 (2016), pp. 443–452

Chapter 10

When celluloid pornography went digital: class and race in the Bangladeshi cut-piece online
Lotte Hoek
Porn Studies, volume 7, issue 1 (2020), pp. 97–114

Chapter 11

Transgressions in Toonland: Savita Bhabhi, Velamma *and the Indian adult comic*
Darshana Sreedhar Mini and Anirban K. Baishya
Porn Studies, volume 7, issue 1 (2020), pp. 115–131

Chapter 12

Capitalizing on desire: (re)producing and consuming class in Indian 'gay' pornography
Michiel Baas
Porn Studies, volume 9, issue 3 (2022), pp. 324–338

Chapter 13

'Grindr is basically interactive porn': ethnographic observations from Kolkata on queer intimacies and 'pic exchange' on Grindr and PlanetRomeo
Rohit K. Dasgupta
Porn Studies, volume 9, issue 3 (2022), pp. 339–345

Chapter 14

#Patriarchykapackup: mediating sexual discourse and the casteless feminist subject in Indian performance poetry
Pallavi Rao
Porn Studies, volume 9, issue 3 (2022), pp. 365–383

Chapter 15

'I am a porn star!" Sex and Sunny Leone unlimited in Bollywood
Tupur Chatterjee
Porn Studies, volume 4, issue 1 (2017), pp. 50–66

Chapter 16

'We give sex a good name': an interview with Paromita Vohra
Darshana Sreedhar Mini and Anirban K. Baishya
Porn Studies, volume 9, issue 3 (2022), pp. 384–399

Chapter 17

Confluences: of war porn and nationalism, at the limits of memory
Ricky Varghese
Porn Studies, volume 7, issue 1 (2020), pp. 132–137

Chapter 18

Porn, sexuality and expression in Sri Lanka: feminist debates and interventions
Subha Wijesiriwardena
Porn Studies, volume 9, issue 3 (2022), pp. 400–410

Notes on Contributors

Michiel Baas is a senior research fellow with the Max Planck Institute for Social Anthropology, Halle, Germany. He has published extensively on the topic of men, masculinities, and sexualities in India. His most recent book is titled *Muscular India: Masculinity, Mobility and the New Middle Class* (2020). In earlier scholarly work he investigated questions of migration from India to Australia and Singapore while in his most recent project he is developing an anthropological approach to artificial intelligence.

Anirban K. Baishya is Assistant Professor at the Department of Communication Arts at the University of Wisconsin-Madison, USA. He is currently working on a book project tentatively titled *Viral Selves: Selfies, Platforms and Digital Image Culture in India*. His research interests include new media and digital cultures, social media and political culture, media aesthetics, surveillance studies, and global media. His work has been published in the *International Journal of Communication, Communication, Culture & Critique, South Asian Popular Culture, Porn Studies, South Asia: Journal of South Asian Studies*, and *Media, Culture & Society*.

Arnav Bhattacharya is a PhD candidate at the Department of History and Sociology of Science. His dissertation tentatively titled *From the Kamasutra to Scientia Sexualis: A History of Sexual Science and Medicine in Twentieth Century India* explores the history of the production, consolidation, and dissemination of medical and scientific knowledge on sex and sexuality in colonial and post-colonial India. His project interrogates how the history of Indian sexology through the course of the 20th century came to be increasingly intertwined with myriad issues such as medico-legal jurisprudence, social and sexual hygiene, public health initiatives, and sex education. He situates his scholarship among larger global histories of sexology and argues that factors like racism, Orientalism, and colonialism were not only instrumental for sexological knowledge production in India and also influenced Euro-American histories of sexology. His research has been funded by various research bodies and institutions within the University of Pennsylvania, as well as the American Institute of India Studies (AIIS) and the Huntington Library, USA.

Spandan Bhattacharya is Assistant Professor at the Department of Humanities and Social Sciences at BITS Pilani, Hyderabad, India. He holds a PhD in Cinema Studies from the School of Arts and Aesthetics at Jawaharlal Nehru University, New Delhi. His co-authored book on Bengali cinema, *Tollygunge to Tollywood: The Bengali Film Industry Reimagined* (2021), provides a study of the contemporary Bengali film industry and the larger media landscape from which it emerged. His co-edited volume, *Film Studies: An Introduction* (2022), brings together discussions on film elements, global film histories, critical and theoretical debates in Cinema Studies and Indian cinematic forms, aesthetics, and histories.

Tupur Chatterjee is Assistant Professor in Global Film and Media at the School of English, Drama, and Film at University College Dublin, Ireland. Her research interests include global media cultures, media industries, media architectures, streaming platforms, and feminist media studies. Her work has been published in journals like the *International Journal of Cultural Studies*, *Feminist Media Studies*, *South Asian Popular Culture*, *Porn Studies*, and *Synoptique*.

Ketaki Chowkhani is Assistant Professor of Sociology at Manipal Centre for Humanities at the Manipal Academy of Higher Education, India, where she teaches India's first ever course on Singles Studies. Her writing on gender, sexuality and singlehood has appeared in the *Indian Journal of Medical Ethics*, *Journal of Porn Studies*, The New York Times, Square Peg, The Hindu, and in edited volumes published by Routledge and Cambridge University Press. Dr Chowkhani has a PhD in Women's Studies from the Tata Institute of Social Sciences, Mumbai, India, where she researched sexuality education and adolescent masculinities in urban India.

Rohit K. Dasgupta is Senior Lecturer in Cultural Industries at the University of Glasgow, UK. He is the author of *Digital Queer Cultures in India* (2017).

Rahul K. Gairola, PhD (University of Washington, Seattle, USA) is The Krishna Somers Senior Lecturer in English & Postcolonial Literature and a fellow of the Asia Research Centre at Murdoch University, Greater Perth, Western Australia. He is the co-editor and author/co-author of five books including *South Asian Digital Humanities: Postcolonial Mediations across Technology's Cultural Canon* (2020); *Migration, Gender and Home Economics in Rural North India* (2019); and *Homelandings: Postcolonial Diasporas and Transatlantic Belonging* (2016). He is the co-editor of special issues of the *Journal of Intercultural Studies*, *Journal of Postcolonial Writing*, *South Asian Review*, and *Asiascape: Digital Asia* and previously taught at the Indian Institute of Technology Roorkee, India, and Queens College and York College, The City University of New York, and Seattle University, USA. He was appointed Digital Champion for the State of Western Australia by The Digital Studio at the University of Melbourne, Australia, and is a lifetime member of Pembroke College at the University of Cambridge, UK. He is Editor of the Routledge/Asian Studies Association of Australia (ASAA) South Asian Book Series and is currently working on two book projects with Routledge, a book project with Oxford University Press, and several research essays for blind peer-reviewed journals.

Charu Gupta is Professor at the Department of History at the University of Delhi, India. The focus of her work is gender, sexuality, masculinity, caste, religious identities, and vernacular literatures in early twentieth-century north India. Her publications include *Sexuality, Obscenity, Community: Women, Muslims and the Hindu Public in Colonial India* (2002); *The Gender of Caste: Representing Dalits in Print* (2017); and *Contested Coastlines: Fisherfolk, Nations and Borders in South Asia* (2008, 2018). She is presently working on social histories of particular genres and subjects through life narratives in Hindi in early twentieth century north India.

Lotte Hoek is a media anthropologist whose research is situated at the intersection of anthropology and film studies. She is the author of *Cut-Pieces: Celluloid Obscenity and Popular Cinema in Bangladesh* (2014) and the co-editor of *Forms of the Left in Postcolonial South Asia: Aesthetics, Networks and Connected Histories* (2021). She is one of the editors of the journal *BioScope: South Asian Screen Studies*. She is Senior Lecturer in Social Anthropology at the University of Edinburgh, UK.

Kareem Khubchandani is Associate Professor in theater, dance, and performance studies at Tufts University, Medford, USA. He is the author of *Ishtyle: Accenting Gay Indian Nightlife* (2020), co-editor of *Queer Nightlife* (2021), and guest editor of "Critical Aunty Studies," a special issue of *Text and Performance Quarterly*.

Darshana Sreedhar Mini is Assistant Professor at the Department of Communication Arts at the University of Wisconsin-Madison, USA. Supported by the Social Science Research Council (SSRC) and American Institute of Indian Studies (AIIS), her book titled *Rated A: Soft-Porn Cinema and Mediations of Desire in India* (UC Press 2024) explores the media-ecology produced by mapping the transnational circuits traversed by Malayalam soft-porn cinema. Her research interests broadly include South Asian Cinema, Feminist Media, Global Media Cultures, and Migrant media. Her work has been published in *Feminist Media Histories, Film History, Porn Studies, Bioscope: South Asian Screen Studies, South Asian Popular Culture, South Asian Film and Media, Journal for Ritual Studies,* and *International Journal for Digital Television*.

Bijleeraj Patra is pursuing his PhD on book history from Jadavpur University, Kolkata, India, and has completed M.Phil. from CSSSC. His research interests include book history, visual culture, Bengali literature, sexuality, pornography, and manuscript culture.

Natalia Di Pietrantonio is the inaugural curator of South Asian art at the Seattle Art Museum and an affiliate faculty member for the School of Art + Art History + Design at the University of Washington, Seattle, USA. Previously, she was a postdoctoral fellow at Scripps College and at the Bard Graduate Center.

Anubhav Pradhan is Assistant Professor with the Department of Liberal Arts at the Indian Institute of Technology Bhilai, India. His work straddles urban planning, heritage, history, and writing as well as colonial cultural contact and the intersections of empire and modernity. He is Deputy Editor of *South Asia Research*, Council Member of the Committee for Publication Ethics, and Board Member of the Association for Literary Urban Studies. His major publications include *Articulating Urbanity: Writing the South Asian City* (forthcoming, 2023); *Literature, Language, and the Classroom: Essays for Promodini Varma* (2021); and *Kipling and Yeats at 150: Retrospectives/Perspectives* (2019). He has designed and anchored elective workshops on South Asian urbanisms at the Indian Institute for Human Settlements, Bangalore, CEPT University, Ahmedabad, and the School of Environment & Architecture, Mumbai, India, and has previously taught at Ambedkar University Delhi, South Asian University, Delhi, Jamia Millia Islamia, Delhi, and the University of Delhi, India. He also served Primus Books, Delhi, as their Senior Marketing Editor.

Pallavi Rao is Assistant Professor at the University of Virginia, Charlottesville, USA. Her research interests include cultural studies, the political economy of media, contemporary South Asian media industries, and anti-caste and feminist media studies. She has also published her research in the *Journal of Communication Inquiry, South Asian Film and Media*, and *Communication and Critical/Cultural Studies* on caste and patriarchy, popular Hindi film, and India's digital media and entertainment culture.

Ricky Varghese is a psychoanalyst and psychotherapist based in Toronto. Currently, he is also a senior research associate at the Toronto Metropolitan University, Canada. He is the editor of *Raw: PrEP, Pedagogy, and the Politics of Barebacking* (2019) and *Porn on the Couch: Sex, Psychoanalysis, and Screen Cultures/Memories* (2023) and the forthcoming *Sex and the Pandemic* (2024).

Subha Wijesiriwardena is a feminist activist and researcher from Colombo, Sri Lanka. Subha works with CREA, a global feminist human rights organization led by feminists in the Global South. Subha works on CREA's strategic objective in fostering the collective resilience of feminist movements to anti-gender and anti-democracy forces. This includes coordinating a global cross-movement challenging criminalization strategy. Subha is the co-founder of a "Collective for Feminist Conversations", a group dedicated to creating online and on-ground spaces for conversation, to bring broader audiences into the fold of feminist histories, theories, and practices through campaigns and events. She is the co-author of 'Not Traditionally Technical: Lesbian Women in Sri Lanka and Their Use of The Internet' published by the Association for Progressive Communications and Women and Media Collective, 2018, and the lead author of 'Acts of Agency: Exploring a feminist approach to abortion research in Sri Lanka' published by SAGE in South Asian Survey, 2020. Most recently, she has contributed to the journals *Porn Studies* and *Anti-Trafficking Review*.

Introduction—Towards an incomplete repertoire of South Asian pornographies: challenges, potentials and futures

Darshana Sreedhar Mini and Anirban K. Baishya

Why South Asia?

South Asia as a geo-political location has a unique relationship to pornography, given the multiplicity of legal-censorial regimes that define the obscene and the permissible. One of this book's central assumptions is that what we now call 'South Asia' is a region that has been produced by such encounters with the colonial 'Other' and the tectonic aftereffects of such encounters. In conceptualizing South Asia this way, we draw on what Kelly Pemberton and Michael Nijhawan, writing in the field of religion and ritual, call the 'shared idioms' and 'vital elements of identity formation' in South Asia – an 'ongoing process and the historical product of creative human interventions' (2009, 8). It is in such historically situated interventions that the chapters in this book locate the work of the pornographic and the obscene. It is important to note here that Pemberton and Nijhawan's use of 'idioms' denotes a plurality – there is no singular idea of South Asia or South Asian-ness, even as we note commonalities. To push it even further, we must be wary of imposing a predetermined, monolithic idea of sexual culture even in any one of the individual South Asian countries. Rather, much like its languages, religions, cuisines and people, the sexual cultures and erotic artefacts of South Asia are multifarious and diverse. As Purnima Mankekar points out in the context of India, 'There is no singular "Indian" discourse on erotics. At the close of the twentieth century, discourses of the erotic proliferating in the Indian public sphere drew upon [...] preexisting genealogies or existed in uneasy tension with them' (2012, 175 and 177). Like Mankekar we are keen to note continuities and breaks, mutations and radically new enunciations. Such a scholarly exercise must plot its steps on both temporal and spatial axes.

In tracing the intersection between porn studies and South Asia as a constantly evolving relationship, this book addresses why attempts to study localized erotic regimes in global contexts need to grapple with the contingent histories, regional variations and overlapping conventions contained under the label of the pornographic. While one of the critiques against the use of the regional label of 'South Asia' is its provenance in Cold war alliances and the corollary emergence of area studies as an approach to the non-West from a securitization paradigm, we use South Asia with the awareness of its double origins in colonial expansion and post-war bipolar power structures. Instead of mapping geopolitical stereotypes onto pornographic cultures, we turn our attention to South Asia taking a cue from Anjali Arondekar and Geeta Patel's introduction to a special issue of *GLQ* published in 2016.

Writing about the intersection of queer studies and area studies, Arondekar and Patel assert that such scholarly glance at area studies' Other is 'no longer a simple effect of ventures [...] into terrain whose purchase was in objects routed through ethnographic avidity or fervor or the bona fides of local habitations' (2016, 153). To be sure, no reader will find in the pages of this book, an 'A–Z' compendium of each and every particularity of pornographic cultures and practices in every nation in the South Asian region. The term 'nation' is crucial here – area studies as an approach is rooted in processes of imperial expansion, processes that were replicated in the organization of nation-states in the twentieth century. Indeed, any use of the term 'South Asia' invokes this fraught history and the attendant national constituents – Bangladesh, Pakistan, India, Sri Lanka, and so on – that resulted from it.

Readers will of course encounter these national taxonomies and particularities in this book – particularities that inform area studies as well. But our use of 'South Asia' does not resonate with the same configurations of space and time as those that inform area studies-based approaches. It would serve readers well here to pay heed to Anne Murphy's pronouncement that 'such divisions must be construed in heuristic terms, not as instantiating enduring boundaries or categories of meaning' (2017, 91). While recognizing the loaded criticisms of area studies, Murphy still finds in the term South Asia some 'utility as a way of conceptualizing space and culture' (91). Similarly, writing about incidents of official and unofficial censorship of media in South Asia, Raminder Kaur and William Mazzarella note that the frame of South Asia allows them to:

> explore the commonalities that result from their shared history of colonial subjugation, to account for their different locations in distinct national polities, and finally to examine the more recent connections and contestations brought about by regional liberalization in the 1990s and beyond. (2009, 2–3)

Consider, for instance, the following scenarios. In Pakistan, the sale of video pornography is an offence under Section 292 of the Pakistan Penal Code. In 2011, a hacker claiming to be from Pakistan defaced the official website of the Supreme Court of Pakistan and Pakistan Telecommunication Authority with demands for a blanket ban on all websites containing explicit material (Popalzai 2011). This led to a ban on pornographic websites in Pakistan by the Pakistan Telecommunication Authority in 2011, which instead improved the sales of porn CDs and DVDs (Hasan 2012).

In October 2018, the Indian government's telecom department issued a notification to internet service providers to ban 827 websites for hosting pornographic content including Pornhub, Tube8 and YouPorn (Singh 2018). This was not the first time that the Indian government tried to ban and regulate pornography. For instance, the Information Technology (Guidelines for Cyber Café) Rules 2011 required cyber-café owners to equip computers with filtering software to avoid access to pornography (Ministry of Communications and Information Technology 2011, 5). They were also required to keep a log of all websites accessed by the customers for at least a year (2011, 3–4). Furthermore, café owners were also asked not to build cubicles with a height of more than four and half feet. Computers had to be placed with screens facing outwards so as to reduce privacy, and minors were not allowed inside cubicles if not accompanied by their guardians and parents (2011, 4). In the absence of legitimate ID, the internet user could be photographed through a webcam (2011, 3). In 2013, lawyer Kamlesh Vaswani petitioned the Indian Supreme Court for a ban on pornography, following a 2012 Delhi rape case. Vaswani declared porn to be 'worse than Hitler, worse than Aids, cancer or any epidemic. It is more catastrophic than nuclear holocaust, and must be stopped' (Biswas 2015). This culminated in the government instituting the Cyber Regulation Advisory Committee chaired by the then Telecom and IT minister Ravi Shankar Prasad. Steps were taken by the committee to authorize the Internet and Mobile Association of India to compile a list of sites that host pornography (Jayadevan and Alawadhi 2014). In retaliation, Pornhub announced that they were launching a new site with an altered URL 'in response to Pornhub getting censored and blocked in India' (India Today Tech 2018). In 2015, the government attempted a ban after the supreme court verdict that blamed pornographic content for having promoted instances of sexual assault – the ban was recalled after public outcry.

In Bangladesh, carrying, selling and distributing pornography are prohibited under the Pornography Control Act of 2012, unless it is meant for educational or artistic purposes (Jillani 2012). In Nepal, the Ministry of Communication and Information Technology issued a notice in September 2018 banning digital pornography. The immediate reason for the ban was, as in the Indian instance from 2013, protests against the increase in sexual assault against women. Harsh fines of up to $4200 and prison sentences were imposed on perpetrators and internet service providers who refuse to comply (French 2018). The list of banned websites numbers 24,000, including sex-positive websites, queer platforms and educational websites (Kayastha 2018). Media rights groups were at the forefront in demanding that the distinction between obscene and pornographic is blurred and any ban on these websites is curtailing people's options to choose and explore their sexuality.

It is clear from such instances that the battle over the pornographic landscape remains deeply fraught across several, if not all, South Asian countries. Perhaps the rise of internet-based pornography has accentuated these tensions, but they are definitely not new. As Charu Gupta points out, the genesis of such laws and regulations can be traced back to nineteenth-century colonial India, when obscenity laws first began to appear, with Sections 292, 293 and 294 of the Indian Penal Code being 'explicitly designed for the prevention of any form of obscenity [...] any visual or written material that was "lascivious or appealed to the prurient interest"' (2001, 30–31). She further points out that British India was also a signatory of the agreement for the suppression of obscene publications in 1910 as well as part of a 1923 conference in Geneva that culminated in the Obscene Publications Act, 1925 (2001, 31). The shadows of such colonial-era regulatory effects linger on in the penal codes of contemporary India, Pakistan and Bangladesh, which were all part of the Empire's dominion. In contemporary South Asia, new problems and tensions in digital pornography fuse with earlier, deeply entrenched, colonial-era attitudes. Not everything related to pornography in South Asia needs to be seen through the lens of censorship and its subversion, but it is a major force to reckon with. The cartography of South Asian pornographies would remain incomplete without cognizance of the productive aspects of power – the fact that power 'traverses and produces things, it induces pleasure, forms knowledge, produces discourse' (Foucault 1980, 119). In charting the territory, we must scale the layered vertices of time and the expanses of space. Thus, echoing the work of Murphy, Kaur and Mazzarella, the regional category of South Asia that is at work in this book invokes multiple temporal and spatial registers – of now separate geopolitical entities and nations that are tied together by longer histories of colonialism and fractured modernities.

Why 'South Asian' porn studies?

Conversations on sex, let alone pornography, remain constricted in the South Asian context. Not only are academic studies of pornography stuck between the 'extremes of pro and anti standpoints' (Attwood, Maina and Smith 2018, 1), but porn work – even academic work – in South Asia carries actual risks, both legal and otherwise. Thus, the thrust of this book can be said to be two-fold: first, a sustained attempt at looking at the origins, effects, affordances and formal properties of South Asian pornographic forms; and, second, to move away from what David Church calls 'the broadly Eurocentric contours of current research on porn studies' (2017, 261). We do not presume to have provided the 'global canon' (2017, 261) that Church hopes for (or even a regional one), but we do hope that this book will provide a methodological breadcrumb trail, if not a new path for interrogating pornographic forms from different cultures. This hope is not the sign of a paradigm shift but one of translation – the hope that the discipline itself, and not just its texts, is rendered relevant for those situated at its frontiers.

In many ways, this book deals with the problem of how to speak about sex and sexuality in the South Asian context – and by speech, here, we refer to not only linguistic utterances but also legal, moral and censorial ones. Consider that almost none of the chapters in this book deal with the porn *industry*, strictly defined. Now compare that to the industrial focus of a number of books in the area of porn studies. For instance, Linda Williams' (2004) edited collection *Porn Studies* begins by claiming that it is markedly different from earlier studies of pornography that were predominantly embroiled in the pro-versus-anti-porn debates. In the introduction, Williams points out the status of still and moving image pornography as 'fully recognizable fixtures of popular culture' (2004, 1). The grounds for such an observation, for Williams, lies in the sheer overabundance of pornographic films as compared to the volume of films produced in Hollywood, which makes them 'emphatically part of American culture' (2004, 1–2). Similarly, in *The Pornography Industry*, Shira Tarrant outlines one of the goals of her book as the explanation of 'industry basics – who works in porn; how much they earn; rapid technological changes that are shaping production distribution, and user access; along with often-elusive revenue data' (2016, 1–2). Consider also the predominance of the United States (and perhaps, to a lesser extent, Europe) in such studies. To turn again to Williams' (2004, 2) introduction to *Porn Studies*, part of the rationale for the book lies in the centrality of porn in American culture. Such rationalizations are repeated in the invocation of Justice Potter Stewart's famous pronouncement about pornography – 'I know it when I see it' during the 1964 Jacobellis v. Ohio case (Tarrant 2016, 3; Gorfinkel 2017, 36 and 153) and the First Amendment (Strossen 1999, 13; Harchuck 2015, 9; Tarrant 2016, 3; Gorfinkel 2017, 72) – in many studies of pornography, almost as if these constitute the primal scene for the discipline of porn studies. While these rulings and laws are crucial, as is their investigation, we point towards them to emphasize that they too are rooted in historical and cultural specificities. This again is a question of scale – of the fraught negotiations between the universal and the particular – of codification and vernacularization. If issues such as the Potter ruling and the First Amendment are also spatially and temporally specific, then their predominance in porn studies must be translated, if not questioned. For researchers of pornographic cultures located elsewhere, they become important for their conceptual offerings (the interplay between legal codification, morality and ethics, the concept of freedom of speech, etc.) and not necessarily for the specificities of their social location.

So, what would the primal scene (if at all we can think of one) of South Asian pornographies look like? What would be the historical ramifications of such a scene, and of what use would it be to researchers of pornography located outside that region? In the pages of this book, readers will find conceptual wisdom along with the particularities of the region. In terms of the question of the porn industry that we raised earlier, we must stress that it is not as if there is no porn industry in South Asia. But one would be hard pressed to find translations of equal value for terms such as 'porn industry', 'porn-star' or 'hardcore/softcore porn'. Note that there is no previous work on pornography in South Asia – Bhrigupati Singh's (2008) essay on the soft-porn morning show in Delhi; Namita Malhotra's (2011) monograph on porn, law and technology in India; Lotte Hoek's (2014) book on cut-pieces in Bangladesh; Darshana Sreedhar Mini's (2016, 2019) work on Malayalam soft-porn; Anirban Baishya's (2017) essay on cellphone pornography in India; Ketaki Chowkhani's (2016) essay on women's porn use in urban India and Tupur Chatterjee's (2017) essay on Sunny Leone (both now subsumed in this volume), to name a few. But in each of these cases, readers will notice that the infrastructures and the circuits of the pornographic are not as easily translatable to the image of the 'porn industry' or its alternatives drummed up, for instance, by AVN, Naughty America, *Deep Throat* and Candida Royalle (and there are immense internal variations within these as well). At the same time, we would also like to caution against exoticizing South Asian pornographic cultures – these are places of contact, exchange, adaptation and influence. But these are also, in the spirit of Miriam Hansen's definition, arenas of the vernacular, and as Luzia Savary points out in the context of colonial-era reproduction manuals, such South Asian vernaculars must be 'understood as a new creation, linked to the specific historical and linguistic context in which it was forged' (2014, 383). Or to introduce a specifically porn studies pun to the issue – one definitely does not know 'it' when one sees it. Translating porn studies for each historical and cultural location, then, must start from places of contact and exchange, mutations and borrowings. The authors featured in this book may be working on very specific themes and areas, each specialized within their own disciplines – but collectively they translate the porn studies 'code', providing a methodological extension for the field.

In the process of editing this book, we have also come to the conclusion that a 'full' representation of South Asia is never going to be possible – not only for logistical reasons but for the very nature of the field. By virtue of commonalities forged through colonial subjugation and similar patterns of economic liberalization in South Asia in the 1990s, the pornographic in South Asia is mediated via material cultures, infrastructures and digital exchanges. Colonial regulatory structures seep into the post-colonial idealization of reproductive sexuality, positing this as the norm. On the other hand, the private sphere is cultivated as the dedicated realm for conjugal intimacy and is forever perched on the precipice between obscenity and transgression. Thus, speaking about pornography in the South Asian context brings up more absences than voices, and where we did find representation from spaces outside India, there were also withdrawals. These were often because of where our authors (or their subjects) were located. Thus, legal and censorial factors have impacted the shape of this book in more ways than one. The conflicts and tensions between censorship and obscenity and between permissibility and speech (even research) have only intensified in the last ten years, while we worked on the special issues of the *Porn Studies* journal (2019, 2022), that eventually took the form of the book. So, while this book does feature a bevy of fantastic chapters which we outline later in this introduction, we also want to use this space to talk about such issues not as mere absences but to hold up a methodological mirror for future work. The case of Pakistan as it pertains to this issue is illustrative. For a time, we did have a chapter based on the experiences of obscenity laws and para-pornographic cultures in Pakistan. The author wanted to track the making of a film on *mujra* dancers – a form of sexually suggestive and expressive dance found in India and Pakistan, with the latter having become the hub of this form in the last few years. However, the paper did not take off because the author and the filmmakers were concerned about the security of their subjects. That film turned out to be *Showgirls of Pakistan* – a 2020 documentary by Saad Khan and Joey Chriqui that we have since watched with great interest. Thus, while Pakistan continues to remain an absence in terms of a dedicated chapter from the region, *Showgirls of Pakistan* provides us with an opportunity to explore what is specific about the Pakistani context as well as its greater resonances for studies of South Asian pornographic cultures.

While not strictly pornographic, *mujra* as it exists today – in between the stage and the web – is often framed as such. *Mujra* emerged as a court dance during the Mughal period and was performed by courtesans called *tawaifs* (Syeda 2015). But as is often the case in the South Asian context, British colonial intervention criminalized the dancers, who were then forced to the margins of society to survive. This is the historical context that the film directs our attention to and especially the problem of labelling erotic performance with the category of pornography using a Western lens. *Showgirls of Pakistan* shows the negotiations that performers make while they partake in such erotically charged dance movements. The filmmakers follow three performers – Afreen Khan, Uzma and Reema Jaan – as they go about their daily lives. The narrative is creatively interspersed with sequences from Pakistani films, and the documentary also relies on existing footage of the dancers including interviews they have given on television shows. Performing for an all-male audience, the dancers are constantly monitored by different government departments who send their officials undercover to check whether there are any violations. The instructions for the lessee and owners of the performance space include ensuring provisions for full censor rehearsal, compliance to the script and the prevention of any additional dance moves or music other than what has been permitted. This often means that recordings of the performances are kept for safekeeping and any minute violation can lead to bans and cancellations that prevent the dancers from performing in big theaters for a while. This level of scrutiny is captured in an exchange Afreen has with her dress-maker, who advises her that a body suit with a plunging neckline might land her in trouble and promises to make a dress that can give her the look she wants without any objection from the censor. Further, the film showcases how the women support each other as they fight the moral police and patriarchal structures and navigate an unsafe workspace in which a number of dancers have been shot at, sometimes with fatal consequences.

The practices underlying *mujra* in Pakistan are thus calibrated to accommodate risks and to perform in immersive, often erotically charged performances under restrictions that foreclose physical contact between dancers, insist on mandatory full-body suits and forbid see-through dresses. We see the dancers daringly expose the hypocrisies and moral compunctions that frame *mujra* dancers as sex workers. For instance, to a reporter who refers to *mujra* performance as vulgar, one of the performers says, 'If the upper-class women dance on television, it is performance, when we do, it is *mujra'*. When a cleric claims that moral values are destroyed because of *mujra*, she asks him whether he has ever seen her dance. In the backdrop of their performances are the arbitrary arrests of dancers like Anjuman Shehzadi for 'vulgar dancing'. The documentary centerstages the voices of the performers amidst the pushback they face from hosts of programmes such as the *Hum Log* telecast on Samaa TV and Azadi News. *Mujra*, as it appears in its contemporary form, stands between performative tradition and a global, modern culture – an in-between-ness that is a site of tension between the desire and the law. The film is also testament to changing patterns of media consumption in Pakistani society. Hira Nabi has noted that, alongside *totas* [pornographic bits], the early 1990s saw the outpouring of Pashto films in the CD-R market which were not specifically pornographic but included 'very, very sexually explicit, or very suggestive dances' (2017, 276). And, as Farida Batool Syeda has observed, 'The 90's in Pakistan saw the widespread use of hands-on and user-friendly digital technology, which helped evolve the mujra dance genre into a low-cost and speedy informal industry' (2015, 17–18). Syeda (2015, 127 and 137) also noted the extensive use of mobile phones for the digital life of mujra and its circulation. We see some of this reflected in *Showgirls of Pakistan*, albeit in more 'updated' forms.

Much of the film's footage is drawn from social media videos and recordings taken by the documentary's subjects, showing how digital media offer performers the potential to connect their offline performances with the micro-celebrity status afforded by social media platforms. In fact, the film starts with footage of Afreen as she interacts with her fans online, reading their comments live while updating them on her life as a dancer. The camera is focused on her feet, as she interacts with the audience in the soundtrack, asking them what they would like to see her upload on social media. The soundtrack of Afreen speaking with fans in a dark space without revealing her face allows the transgressive pleasures associated with engaging in stranger intimacy, as in camming, although without the visual as the main frame of reference. We then move to the all-male patrons of *mujra* as they watch Afreen gyrate her hips and the camera focuses on her breasts. The relative freedom that Afreen enjoys is possible only because she is in Lahore, unlike the other two performers we encounter in the documentary. However, in all of the vignettes, the digital modern world is at odds with conservative morality. What we encounter is a neoliberal assemblage of competing forces, some erotic and aspirational (Afreen, for instance, wants to make a music video like Rihanna's), others repressive and censorial. It is in the thick of this tangle that discussions of porn also enter the film.

When rumors emerge of porn clips of her circulating in public, Afreen says, 'Why would anyone want to make porn in Pakistan where wearing sleeveless dress can take your life?' Showcasing one of the clips, she jokes with her friends that the only similarity between herself and the performer in the clip is that they are both blond and that even if it was of her, she does not find it a big deal. In the ensuing exchange, Afreen's choreographer finds ways to prove that the clip is not of her – it shows a performer with breast implants before Afreen had these. The vignette aligns with Syeda's observations about mujra's multiple sites of production, distribution and consumption as well as innovative (and sometimes exploitative) practices such as compensating for the lack of Pakistani men in the videos 'by juxtaposing the images of white heterosexual porn stars, acquired from the net or VCDs in the market, with exposed Pakistani women dancers' (2015, 19) – also reminiscent of practices in Bangladesh and India (Hoek 2014; Mini 2016).

It is intriguing how discussions of porn attach themselves to the film outside the narrative text. Selected by VICE for its non-fiction collection, *Show Girls of Pakistan* was referred to as 'Pak porn' during the 17th Annual Hot Docs Forum by BBC's Nick Fraser – the film's director, Saad Khan, responding that this was equivalent to slut-shaming the film's performers (Mallett 2016). The film offers a case study to discuss not only pornography and obscenity in Pakistan but also the ways in which 'porn' becomes a catch-all term that supports many different claims – those of moral conservatives, Western critics and the filmmakers themselves. What we encounter in the form of *mujra* and in *Showgirls of Pakistan*, then, is a microcosm of what we have been calling South Asian pornographies. *Mujra* today is simultaneously specific to the legal and censorial conditions in Pakistan as well as symptomatic of the nature of pornography, obscenity and sexual cultures in contemporary South Asia. As a novel disciplinary formation, South Asian porn studies must contend with the multiple entanglements of obscenity, desire, sexuality, morality and the law.

The range of chapters in this book attests to these long – and wide – genealogies of any imagined South Asian-ness. Like questions of identity that can only be answered in the plural (identities rather than identity), the chapters in this book demonstrate how a range of pornographies constitutes the force field of sexualized media in South Asia. In fact, the term 'South Asia' in this book points towards a larger, shared ethos more than strict geopolitical boundaries. What would a South Asian 'ethos' of the pornographic look like? If porn studies – itself a relatively nascent field – have now begun to coalesce around certain shared ideas or directions of research, what might a focus on the region offer us as researchers of erotic cultures and practices? Erotic material from the South Asian region can demonstrate how pornography is often defined in oblique terms, finding reflection in various modes of popular (and sometimes underground) culture, bypassing legal and censorial constraints; in other words, social censure and state censorship outline the limits of the obscene and the permissible. While this is not unique to only South Asia, it highlights the fact that understanding the pornographic in this regional context is impossible without accounting for censorship and obscenity. Obscenity is key here. 'Asheelta' (Hindi), as it is called in many Indian languages (including phonetic equivalents such as 'oshlilota' [Bengali], 'ashleelatha' [Malayalam] and 'osleelota' [Assamese]), is a broad term that, as Lotte Hoek points out, 'indicates social distinction and sexual mores within a single term, *combining the English terms vulgarity and obscenity*' (2014, 3; original emphases).

While not all directly censored or banned, much of the kind of material that is examined in this book reveals a kind of a pornographic unconscious, which in turn is directly related to what Kaur and Mazzarella term 'cultural regulation' – 'the performative, the productive, and the affective aspects of public culture' (2009, 9). Censorship understood thus is a 'relentless proliferation of discourses on normative modes of desiring, of acting, of being in the world' (2009, 5). The work of censorship (and subversion of censorship) might be a general feature of media forms across cultures, but in the particularity of South Asia they reveal the edges of the elastic pornographic spectrum. Edges allow us to observe and test the limits of any phenomenon – if centres are where phenomena cohere and norms become apparent, edges are where we can observe them dissolving into other forms, activating resonant energies with their magnetic charge. Obscenity/asheelta with its conceptual elasticity performs this dynamic work in the South Asian context. Such edge-work is not a symptom of the weakness of the phenomenon but rather an invitation to extend scholarly vision to its outer limits. 'South Asian Pornographies' with a focus on erotic forms across the spectrum, including ones that may not immediately register as pornographic to the unsituated eye, is such an invitation. This is as much a disciplinary issue as it is the general understanding of erotic cultures. In fact, we would go on to say that the 'Utility of South Asia' (to echo the title of Anne Murphy's article) is to extend the disciplinary boundaries of porn studies.

This play between porn and not porn is also where we locate the other focus of this book – that of the vernacular. Asheelta is one such vernacular that does the work of the 'shared idiom' of cultural life in South Asia, à la Pemberton and Nijhawan. But the vernacular for us is not just a lexical issue but one of everyday lived reality and practice. Language contextualizes the world of ideas in the material conditions of the world that it emerges in. In that sense, language itself is practice, and the term 'vernacular' describes this aspect of language in praxis. The vernacular is the grey untranslatable area that appears when we move from one cultural context to another. For Barbara Cassin (2014), the untranslatable is not that which cannot be translated but that which is continuously translated. Hoek (2014) points towards this when she treats the Bengali 'oshleel' as an additive word-form that in the English points towards both the obscene and the vulgar. But this lack of fixity in meaning also creates a problem, which according to Cassin is 'a sign of the way in which, from one language to another, neither the words nor the conceptual networks can simply be superimposed' (2014, xvii). Seen through this frame, the vernacular is the surplus in the abstract idea of language but becomes language through practical usage. As Cassin points out, language is 'not a fact of nature, an object, but an effect caught up in history and culture, and that ceaselessly invents itself' (2014, xix). In that sense, all language is vernacular, and being seen as formal or normative language instead of vernacular is only an historical effect of power.

We pay attention to language here primarily because in the South Asian context the category of 'vernacular languages' reverberates with the timbre of the colonial encounter. One only needs to turn to the school system in South Asia where students are educated either in 'English' or in 'vernacular' mediums (meaning education in any of the indigenous Indian languages). This immediately raises the ghost of the colonial past which, as Ragini Tharoor Srinivasan points out, posits 'English as a literary and cultural system' against which 'vernacular, bhasha and language literatures' are in a perennial contest (2018, 314). While we do not intend to plot pornographic cultures on the same scale as linguistic ones, the ramifications of this contention are deeper. In this, we come very close to Miriam Hansen's postulation that the vernacular describes the 'dimension of the quotidian, of everyday usage, with connotations of discourse, idiom, and dialect, with circulation, promiscuity, and translatability' (1999, 60). If language is a kind of practice, can other forms of practice be subjected to the same tests and codes as language? Can we say that pornographic and erotic cultures in South Asia are also untranslatable vernaculars that require us to constantly recontextualize the meanings of pornography in its historical and cultural particularities? The chapters of this book and the clusters they are divided into aim to answer such questions.

South Asian pornographies: plan of the work

Section I – "Before Pornography: Sexology and Popular Sexual Discourses" – traces the popular histories of sexuality with a focus on vernacular publication practices. These chapters demonstrate how the regional dynamics of 'South Asia' inflect pornographic cultures outside Euro-American contexts. Sexological and sex-educational discourses – both past and present – emerge as strong concerns in this section. Sexology, as it was practiced in South Asia in the early half of the twentieth century, took the shape of an elite bourgeoise project to cleanse the sexual by circumscribing it within a disciplinary paradigm.[1] In the pages of the inaugural issue of the Bombay-based *International Journal of Sexology* (1947–1955), the editor A. P. Pillay explored debates around the way female frigidity and 'ideal' orgasmic feminine subjects came to be discussed. Through the global network of knowledge sharing that Pillay forged through the *International Journal of Sexology*, channels of contact and communication were opened between sexologists and contributors from around the world, as well as the English-language readers from Berlin, Switzerland, Sydney, and Tel-Aviv (Ahluwalia 2018). As Sanjam Ahluwalia has pointed out, the journal's reference to Western sexologists like Havelock Ellis, Margaret Sanger and Margus Hirschfeld was compounded by a significant absence of contributions from Pillay's contemporaries in India like R. D. Karve, G. S. Ghurye and Sitaram Phadke. Magnus Hirschfeld's visit to Bombay drew significant interest from the middle class and was widely reported (Fuechtner 2013). Yet global connections and the intermixing of ideas from Hindu scriptural texts, Ayurveda, *bazaar* [street] literature, social reform and *santati sastra* [science of progeny], literature made sexology an eclectic space.[2]

This was often counterposed to the cheap literature that was available in the bazaar and meant for the masses. Through a normative, reproduction-oriented framing and the use of medico-scientific language to steer the attention of the reader to the pedagogical handling of information, sexology provided a strong anchor by which to incorporate scientific discourse on sexuality into the otherwise popular consumption of erotic media (Gupta 2002; Ahluwalia 2018). This worked to reinsert middle-class respectability, stressing a scientific approach to sexuality as a knowledge system, although in an oblique way presenting the same pleasures and anxieties in the guise of science. Sexological tracts were a crucial part of the landscape of global and local connections that democratized sex in popular discourses. These developments are tracked in two chapters of this book: Charu Gupta's 'Cast(e)ing and Translating Sex in the Vernacular: The Writings of Santram BA in Hindi' and Arnav Bhattacharya's 'Purging the Pornographic, Disciplining the Sexual, and Edifying the Public: Pornography, Sex Education, and Class in Colonial Bengal (1930–1950s)'.

In her chapter Gupta explores the work of Santram BA, a caste reformer who also wrote widely on the topics of sex and birth control. Gupta emphasizes that Santram's writings on sex cannot be separated from his anti-caste writings, and they must be read as 'metaphors for the churning going on in caste and gender relations in late colonial India'. For Gupta, then, vernacular language print media offered a vibrant space for conversations on sexual health and eroticism – themes that were often clubbed along with pornography by colonial-era obscenity laws. As Charu Gupta points out in her chapter, the vernacular offers 'a corporeal presence and nearness of lived experience' that is key to the study of sex and sexuality. While Gupta's observation is made in the specific context of Hindi sex-manuals, she draws attention to the cruciality of lived experience, which, when read alongside Hansen's insistence on aspects such as idioms, dialects and translatability, outlines the conceptual spine of this book. Elsewhere, Gupta (2002) has argued that the categorization of sexological tracts and erotic media with the sex advice literature often became blurry as it morphed through various layers of translations and cultural mediations. A. Bhattacharya's chapter expand on this.

A. Bhattacharya tracks the relationship between pornography and sexology by analyzing the works of the Bengali sexologists Abdul Hasanat and Nripendra Kumar Basu. As he points out, sexology gave way to a range of positionalities on sexual science among local sexologists that often varied significantly in the way they approached conjugal sexuality, class and respectability. Among those sexologists who advocated birth control and sex education in Western India, R. D. Karve highlighted the supremacy of Western sexological tracts and a rational approach steeped in European sexology (Botre and Haynes 2018). Karve's contributions included books such as *Adhunik Kamashatra* [Modern Kama-sastra] and editing the journal *Samaj Swastya* [Social Health], one of the first magazines in India to feature a sex advice column (Botre and Haynes 2017). As a critic of marriage, which he found to be constraining for both men and women, Karve supported the legalization of prostitution, while *Samaj Swastya* featured female nudes on the front cover and male nudes on the back to emphasize the relevance of nudity in promoting physical health (Heath 2010). Karve's ideas were radical for the time and different from other sexologists like Abul Hasanat, A. P. Pillay and Nripendra Kumar Basu. A. Bhattacharya shows how Basu's lack of a moral stance on pornography was influenced by his view that the popularity of the erotic literature stemmed from the cheap accessibility of these printed materials. In fact, one imperative that united these varied sentiments among sexologists was the realization of the difficulties in maintaining a ban on erotic material.

The expansiveness of the sexual and the pornographic is something that also structures Section II of this book – 'Art, Print Culture and Literature at the Edges of the Pornographic'.

Bijleeraj Patra's chapter 'A Short History of the "Blue-Photo": Bengali Sex Magazines and the Visual Empire of Printed Images (1940–1970)' shifts the focus away from sexological tracts but sticks with print culture. Patra discusses sex magazines such as *Nara-Nari* (1938–1950s), edited by Sukanta Kumar Halder, and *Natun Jiban* (1944), using these to chart the vernacularization of desire mediated via print technology in the early twentieth century. 'Blue-photos' captured women in a nude or semi-nude fashion, in side-poses and long shots which diluted their immediate identification. Patra also traces the circulation of 'blue-photos' in the way male bodybuilders ['*Sharircharchakari*'] doubled-up as semi-nude models for sex magazines, while the 'blue-photo' tradition can also be glimpsed in the practice of nude models working with art students – art education itself being part of the matrix of colonial modernity. Photographs of the female form used in art education also became part of photo-series in sex magazines. Unlike the exhibition of the face to individualize muscular male bodies, female nudes often had their faces occluded from public view. The facialization of the muscular male body and the facelessness of the 'arty' female nude can be mapped to the gendered politics of respectability in modern Bengal.

Print culture also remains a concern in Spandan Bhattacharya's 'Reading Anandalok: Obscenity, Cinema and Other "Prohibitive" Pleasures in 1970s–1990s Bengali Print Culture'. His chapter explores how the infrastructures of cheap print technology caused the North

Calcutta region of Battla to emerge as the hub for the erotic literature in the early nineteenth century, including a range of material that drew from contemporary sex scandals in the form of novels and farces. Similar to the point about obscenity (*ashleelata*) being a structuring principle for the pornographic, S. Bhattacharya undertakes a practical unpacking of the term *'apasanskriti'* – roughly translated as 'crass/bad/ decaying culture' – as it relates to the illicit undertones in Bengali print culture between the 1970s to the 1990s. Curiously, however, the material he examines in his chapter would not be considered pornographic at first look – the magazine *Anandalok* is owned by a major mainstream press and carries articles and images related to mainstream Bengali cinema. However, as S. Bhattacharya astutely demonstrates, the magazine's tabooed status as *'apasanskriti'* drew on a longer history of print culture including the publication of erotic stories, gossip, mysteries and scandals.

Perhaps the best example of the concerns with South Asian pornography's long durée in this book can be seen in Natalia Di Pietrantonio's 'Pornography and Indian Miniature Painting: The Case of Avadh, India'. Her chapter locates how the practices of eighteenth-century European collectors shaped the taxonomy used to classify the indigenous Rāgamālā miniature paintings produced in Avadh. Taking the instance of Richard Johnson's collection of Rāgamālā images, Di Pietrantonio argues how they were seen as obscene and pornographic at different points in time, contingent on the demands of archival processes and institutional locations. As Di Pietrantonio astutely points out, 'Obscenity and pornography were legal categories imported to India from British imperial policies'.

The last two chapters in this section turn us towards the written word and the circulation of literary texts. Anubhav Pradhan's '"Raped, Outraged, Ravaged": Race, Desire, and Sex in the Indian Empire' undertakes a close reading of August Brancart's nineteenth-century erotic novel, *Venus in India* or *Love Adventures in Hindustan*, that narrativizes the sexual exploits of a British army officer stationed in India. Pradhan calls the novel a 'watershed in South Asian pornography' for its awareness of racial and geopolitical realities of the time, including anxieties of miscegenation and the presence of British women in the midst of native men. In doing so he locates how interracial desire is manifested in the text and the curious ways through which India emerges as a site of deviance that can lead British men in the line of duty. Di Pietrantonio and Pradhan's chapters deal with completely different objects and techniques – the former focusing on visual artefacts, the latter on the written word. But, taken together, both authors offer us useful insights into the erotic frisson produced by the colonial encounter. The Avadhi miniatures and the pornographic text that are the subjects of Di Pietrantonio and Pradhan's chapters, respectively, have their provenance in different circumstances at the hands of different creators. But they are also each other's obverse – one rendered pornographic by the imposition of Victorian attitudes on already existing objects, the other generated by 'the imaginative space of the colony' – what Anjali Arondekar describes as 'an imagined breeding ground for a spectrum of imagined sexual vices that in turn vivify the rhetoric of an evangelical civilizing mission' (2009, 105).

Finally, Kareem Khubchandani's 'Between aunties: sexual futures and queer South Asian aunty porn' explores a selection of South Asian diasporic novels, suggesting that in these, desire is encoded as a continuum coexisting with aunty attributes such as cooking and gossip. Khubchandani's chapter, in many ways, is in conversation with his project on Critical Aunty Studies, a collaboration that brings together scholars working in this area, and two special issues (*Text & Performance &Quarterly* 2022; *South Asia: Journal of South Asian Studies*, 2023) that draw on a colloquium organized in 2021.[3] Exploring the genre of 'aunty porn' and also using the figure of the aunty as a 'method', in alignment with the broader Critical Aunty Studies project, Khubchandani locates how gossip and the surreptitious intimacies that emerge through erotic embodiment are woven into the mundane aspects of interactions between aunties. Tapping into literature film and visual art – what he calls a 'promiscuous archive of aunty representation' – Khubchandani forces us to rethink pornography in the South Asian context, not just as a form of representation but as a form of lived intimacy between aunties that allows queer desires to manifest in otherwise stringent social structures. He provides us with a framework for disentangling the queer erotic realms that allow aunties to 'invent pleasure, play and autonomy beyond the sexual scripts prescribed to them'.

Section III – 'South Asian Porn and the Digital Turn' – is the first section of the book strictly based in the contemporary. Sections I and II cohere around different timelines – Section I focused more or less on the period of twentieth-century print modernity, while Section II is more cross historical. This structuring, while aware of historical specificities, is ultimately concerned with the thematics of sexual cultures that are more analytically productive when examined outside of a strict linear, chronological unfolding. The digital turn, however, is a thematic that is more historically concentrated by its very nature. Even so, the focus on historicity does not disappear altogether in this section, because clearly the tussle between an imagined erotic space and civilizing mission did not disappear with the end of the colonial rule. Vestiges of the colonial era lingered on and continued to shape both legal and moral attitudes towards gender and sexuality in post-colonial nation-states. Rahul Gairola's 'The X Factors of Sex: Hijras, Victorian Law, and Digital Porn in Postcolonial India' begins with this premise in his exploration of the interconnections between colonial-era laws and the current landscape of digital pornography as it relates to *hijras*.[4] As subjects that did not fit the neat binaries of male/female, *hijras* challenged the 'British biopolitical order' and were subsequently pathologized by both 'the British Raj and the postcolonial elite'. Such attitudes, Gairola notes, 'inaugurated a historical precedent for pathologizing transgender' people in contemporary India. Gairola builds upon this complex history of colonial pathologization codified as law and examines how it reverberates in the landscape of digital pornography. Although 'Digital India' might seem far removed from this history of colonialism and colonial-era laws, Gairola's study of digital pornography offers us a much-needed diachronic view that can bridge our understanding of older and newer articulations of law, sex and pornography.

Ketaki Chowkhani's chapter, 'Pleasure, Bodies and Risk: Women's Viewership of Pornography in Urban India' examines the absence of women's experiences in narratives of porn consumption in urban India. Chowkhani's focus is on the pleasures and risks that women negotiate as they watch female bodies in intimate postures. While the risks women navigate include being seen as sexually available and loss of reputation, Chowkhani shows that women also actively reimagine what they want to hold on to in the material they have watched. Many of the respondents Chowkhani interviews mention how watching pornography was tied to space, where one can then set aside time to engage with the material in a safe zone. There are different measures of safety used to ensure that their consumption of porn is not flagged – this includes constantly be on guard to ensure that the internet history is always deleted, use of proxy servers, and that parallel windows are used while browsing material in public computers so that the porn site is not visible to anyone sitting close to you. Thus, many women associated access to pornography itself as a way to locate desire outside monogamous relationships, and the practices that they employ are very much a product of the digital habitus.

Lotte Hoek's 'When Celluloid Pornography Went Digital: Class and Race in the Bangladeshi Cut-Piece Online' examines what happens to celluloid pornography in Bangladesh when it transitions into online digital platforms. In what can be read as an extended epilogue to her book *Cut-Pieces: Celluloid Obscenity and Popular Cinema in Bangladesh* (Hoek 2014), Hoek zeroes in on the digital afterlife of Bangladeshi cut-pieces (sexually explicit 'bits' spliced into the film-reel during exhibition) that were produced illegally by Bangladeshi action filmmakers. An interesting question Hoek raises in her chapter is how traces of locality are addressed and marked in spaces of digital consumption. For instance, in the case of VCDs it is quite common to find 'Pakistani mujra or scenes from Pashto cinema, South Indian soft-porn clips, and music videos from across South Asia' alongside Bangladeshi cut-pieces. Hoek notes that despite certain 'national' characteristics, there are formal affinities between such pornographic bits from various parts of South Asia, emerging from the conditions of cinema production and distribution in the region. In formulating cut-piece pornography this way, Hoek argues for a '*pornographic* region, which is associated with particularities of narrative, aesthetic and, significantly, particular types of bodies' (original emphasis).

These questions re-emerge in Darshana Mini and Anirban Baishya's 'Transgressions in Toonland: Savita Bhabhi, Velamma and the Indian Adult Comic', albeit in relation to pornographic comics. Focusing on two adult comics, Mini and Baishya explore the dynamics of class, gender and taboo as they relate to the figure of the 'bhabhi' (sister-in-law) and 'aunty' – both short-hand notations for married women who form the centre of the comics' sexual fantasy. While part of their argument is formal, related to the affordances of the digital comic book that circulates online, their chapter also focuses on the idea of the region in the Indian imagination and how it operates through matrices of language and visual cues.

Patra's focus on muscularity in the previous section is also echoed in this section on the digital, in Michiel Baas' chapter 'Capitalizing on Desire: (Re)Producing and Consuming Class in Indian "Gay" Pornography'. Baas interrogates gay pornographic expression through an ethnographic exploration of the practices and experiences of fitness trainers and bodybuilders as they fashion their identities to capitalize on their erotic and sexual potential in order to cater to an all-male clientele. Expanding on his previous work (Baas 2020) that locates the space of the gymnasium and use of bodily capital by fitness trainers as a way of moving beyond limited social and cultural capital, Baas shows how fitness trainers occasionally move to porn, explicit photoshoots and sex work to utilize muscular capital, working with and through their bodies. This, as Baas shows, is underlined through patterns of (homo)erotic layering found in photographs featuring muscular men as well as consumption models that open up a range of options – an example being OnlyFans – to explore the possibilities of partaking in a continuum of bodily practices.

Overlaps between homoerotic (self-)representation and digital platforms are also the subject of Rohit Dasgupta's discussion, '"Grindr is basically interactive porn": Ethnographic Observations from Kolkata on Queer Intimacies and "Pic-exchange" on Grindr and PlanetRomeo'. Dasgupta uses digital ethnography to map social media use by young queer men in Kolkata, in order to interrogate porn consumption practices. Training his lens on the queer networks forged through the sharing of self-made explicit images, he locates affective encounters that allow for an interactive exchange of intimacy. By sharing explicit pictures and digital footprints in the form of animated images, users explore variations of phatic communication in order to engage in fleeting intimate encounters that border platformed intimacies and porno-cultures. Together, the chapters in this section explore how such regionality operates within the space of the internet through various registers including linguistic indices manifested as tags, search terms and comments.

The final cluster of chapters in this book are collected in Section IV, 'Feminist and Minor Approaches to South Asian Pornographies'. In some ways the nomenclature here is a bit of a misnomer – all the authors in this volume are attuned to queer and feminist approaches as well as minoritarian concerns. Nonetheless, the chapters in this section more directly address the intersections of gender, class, ethnicity and caste, and/or debates about them. In '#PatriarchyKaPackup: Mediating Sexual Discourse and the Casteless Feminist Subject in Indian Performance Poetry' Pallavi Rao addresses how performances touching upon the erotic require a balancing act whereby any traces of pornographic have to be suppressed while simultaneously directing attention towards questions of desire and pleasure. Focusing on female slam poets utilizing urban performance spaces, Rao examines the erasure of identity categories including caste and class in their performance as they narrate instances of sexual violence and pleasure. Rao juxtaposes the castelessness embodying the universality of experiences in upper-caste female subjects' performances with the politicization of identities of Dalitbahujan women.[5] In doing so, she demonstrates how performance poetry's 'localized articulations of mediated erotics' allow for a kind of sexual confession where sexual action is displaced offstage and reinserted through the soundscape, supplanting the visuality of the sexual act with an aural component.

In what seems like a sharp U-turn from slam poetry, the next chapter, Tupur Chatterjee's "'I am a porn star!' Sex and Sunny Leone unlimited in Bollywood" explores the transnational stardom of Sunny Leone, an Indo-Canadian actress with a former career in porn, whose entry into Bollywood set off a series of debates and readjustments in the India media sphere. Leone's initial stint was in the reality TV show *Bigg Boss* (the Indian equivalent of *Big Brother*), which set off a moral panic about the mainstreaming of pornography. However, Leone has been able to negotiate such hurdles by carving out a space for female stardom that does not necessarily fit into the template of the chaste female star of Bollywood. Rather, as Chatterjee demonstrates, while Leone no longer works in the pornographic industry, she also doesn't disavow her pornographic career as an object of shame. Instead, Leone presents a unique case in which porn works in some ways as a form of capital – at least in the sense that it allows Leone to build on (albeit with modifications) her star image. Drawing on Linda Williams' work, Chatterjee suggests that Leone is a mascot of

> transnational onscenity [that] brings to the fore the centrality of porn in the economies of global cross-cultural exchange and forces us to rethink previous paradigms of both 'pornography' and stardom, two domains that have more or less remained mutually exclusive in the sub-continent.

Recalibrating South Asian attitudes towards sex and pornography continues in '"We give sex a good name": An Interview with Paromita Vohra' – an extensive conversation between filmmaker and sex-educator Paromita Vohra and the editors of this volume. The interview covers a range of topics pertaining to Vohra's experience as an artist, filmmaker, sex educator and creator of the multimedia portal Agents of Ishq (AoI). Vohra walks us through her journey as a curator and the stakes involved in understanding sexual pleasure and desire through a feminist lens. The conversation takes the reader through the messy realities that stall, condition and discipline bodies, making sexual violence the dominant paradigm in understanding the body in the South Asian context. Vohra's work instead directs us towards the multisensory aspects of love and sexual pleasure, as seen in her installation 'A Love Latika', which she describes as 'an electronic forest of erotic poems'. As an exploration of 'public privacy', the installation invited visitors to collectively partake in what they would otherwise consider deeply private moments of listening to erotic poems. The same sense of collectivity is also seen in AoI, both in user-submitted columns and in collaborative multimedia pieces. Of special note is a fascinating collaboration on the idea of consent in which AoI produced a series of videos with *lavani* artists (*lavani* is a Maharashtrian song and dance performed by women and using sexual innuendos). These videos work through different relationship scenarios to explore what counts as consent and the conditions which can signify violation. As Vohra states, the basic premise for AoI is to normalize conversations about sex, using popular culture as a reference point for initiating discussion about sex. This includes conversations on porn and porn-adjacent forms. The eclectic material that is presented by AoI in essays, images and videos envisages an intersectional space, which doubles up as a platform for sex education in India.

Ricky Varghese's 'Confluences: Of War Porn and Nationalism, at the Limits of Memory' takes us to the edges of the pornographic in South Asia. Our earlier invocation of this book as a kind of scholarly 'edge-work' is stretched to its limits in this chapter focusing on questions of violence and brutality. Varghese's meditations, to use a sexual pun, push edge-work to the realm of edge-play. They build on Prabha Manuratne's (2014) work on war porn that explores how wartime violence 'becomes consumed, sexualized, and talked about, primarily by subscribers and users in the Global North/West'. In the process, Varghese interrogates the prevalence of videos of caste and religion-based violence in contemporary India. Comparing the aesthetic of such videos to Multimedia Messaging Service (MMS) pornography in India, Varghese notes that there is a 'voyeuristic quality to the aesthetics' of both lynching and MMS porn videos. Thus, Varghese raises questions that extend into the arena of nationalism and right-wing violence and how the enactment of such violence on screen raises deep-rooted memories of historical trauma and the politics of otherness in South Asia. Varghese's immediate point may not be about pornography proper (sex-films, magazines and the like), but it allows us to draw an important link between the power of virtual mediation and the viral nature of online circulation. If the 'pornographic unconscious' has to do with the limits of 'cultural regulation', Varghese's chapter offers us a chance to understand how the pornographic unconscious operates in images of violence as well – despite contextual differences, objects such as those explored by Gairola, Hoek and Baishya and Mini, it would seem, have something in common with the kind of images Varghese writes about. Blood, semen, the digital apparatus and the space of the internet itself emerge as the objects (and perhaps objective) of the climax.

Sticking with the themes of sex education and feminist intervention, the final chapter in this book, 'Porn, Sexuality and Expression in Sri Lanka: Feminist Debates and Interventions' by Subha Wijersiriwardena, locates the fault lines within which sexuality and erotic media operate in Sri Lanka amidst state sanctions on pornography. Wijersiriwardena points out the residual legacies of colonial legal regulation that define the strictures within which obscenity laws are used in Sri Lanka as they do in India and Pakistan. The Obscene Publications Ordinance No. 4 of 1927 restricts the possession, production, import and export of obscene publications.[6] In the absence of a clear-cut definition of what constitutes obscenity, this Act is used to prosecute same-sex relations as well as sex work, alongside free expression. Wijersiriwardena tracks the various feminist interventions pertaining to regulations on pornography pitched from the rights perspective and how they bring in questions around pleasure and consent. As with the Indian scenario described by Vohra, the absence of a comprehensive sex education policy and strict regulations on obscenity in Sri Lanka makes digital porn an important supplementary avenue for sexual exploration among the country's youth. With platforms such as Jillhub aggregating local content, performers such as Kuweni Devi, Shani Akka and Princess Alekhshi gather a massive following and the regional markers of Sri Lankan erotic media are used in the tags that accompany the content description. Analogous to the anonymization of the face in Patra's discussion of erotic female nude art models in Bengal, Wijersiriwardena showcases strategies of 'home-made' porn where the face of the female performer is deliberately obscured using emojis. Wijersiriwardena points out that the amateur home-made format and the informal regime of production put porn performers out of the realm of visibility. This means that even if there are violations of consent among porn performers, the chances of them coming out in the open are rare.

Such structural factors impact the way research on explicit media takes a different shape in Sri Lanka and more broadly in South Asia, where the safety of respondents is often a cause of worry because of informal work patterns. This aligns with what we observed in the case of *Showgirls of Pakistan* earlier in this Introduction. Research on the pornographic in South Asia often requires modulating between representation, affect, desire and law. As seen in *Showgirls of Pakistan* and as demonstrated by the chapters in this book, this has as much to do with media infrastructures in a rapidly globalizing world as it does with ethics, morality and free expression.

In both Pakistani *mujra* and the case of porn in India, a range of technological changes since the 1970s has led to a reimagination of explicit media and its modes of production and consumption as well as a series of frictions between infrastructure, desire and the law. With the importing of VHS tapes and VCR players to India and Pakistan in the 1990s, adult content could easily be transferred and duplicated. The importing of tapes also boosted transnational underground media production based in the Gulf and Hong Kong. As many scholars have noted, the period of economic liberalization in the 1990s and the opening up of the skies also gave way to anxieties about the importing of sexualized content (Mazzarella 2006; Shah 2007).

In the contemporary moment, those anxieties have moved from the satellite channel and the VHS tape to other spaces – particularly the internet. In the Indian context, these developments are indicative of new discourses about digitally mediated communication in which pornography stands in for an array of anxieties. Take, for instance, the case of

Raj Kundra, a businessman arrested for making pornographic films in 2021. Kundra, who was widely publicized as the mastermind of an adult film racket, had formed a company named Arms Prime Media Limited in February 2019 and developed an app named 'Hotshots', which was later sold to a UK-based company, Kenrin. Indian law enforcement acted on complaints that young actresses were forced into porn films with the promise of roles in web series, and the content was then uploaded on subscription-based OTT platforms meant for adult films. Allegedly, the day-long shoots were carried out in rented bungalows in the outskirts of Bombay like Madh Island, with a limited crew who would 'double up as directors, dialogue writers, location scouters and web app developers' (Thaver 2021).

In some ways, concerns around these developments are similar to the imagining of a criminal underground of porn production in the celluloid era, encapsulated in films such as *Miss Lovely* (dir. Ashim Ahluwalia, 2012), *The Dirty Picture* (dir. Milan Luthria, 2011) and *Kanyaka Talkies* (dir. K. R. Manoj, 2013). Yet they also point towards new sites of anxiety, desire and pleasure that have emerged with the ubiquitous uptake of the internet and cell phones and a porno assemblage. Here, the fear of leaked videos from CCTVs and cell phones exists alongside the potentialities of self-expression and sexual experimentation. Whether it is Pakistani *mujra* as reflected in *Showgirls of Pakistan*, new developments in adult OTT offerings in India, the remediation of Bangladeshi celluloid porn and cut-pieces on the web or the many instances of amateur homemade porn in India, Pakistan, Sri Lanka and Bangladesh, it is clear that South Asian pornography is a transitioning discursive field. Much of the old persists in the new, yet the new must also be studied for its novel offerings. The topics explored by the authors in this book present exactly this blend of continuities and disjunctures.

Notes:

1. For more on sexology in the Indian context, see Ishita Pande (2020).
2. For more on Santati-sastra, see Luzia Savary (2014).
3. See https://www.criticalauntystudies.com/
4. *Hijra* is a difficult term to translate to English. Colonial regimes branded the *Hijra* community as eunuchs, but the term and identity are broader. Today, the term can generally be used to refer to someone who is part of alternative kinship systems formed by gender non conforming communities and asserts a feminine gender identity for usually (but not always) male-born persons.
5. The composite term Dalit-Bahujan is often used in anti-caste movements to broadly refer to marginalized lower-caste groups categorized constitutionally as OBCs, Dalits or Scheduled Castes, and Scheduled Tribes (Rao 2021).
6. See http://www.mediareform.lk/wp-content/uploads/2020/03/164-Obscene-Publications-Ordinance-No.04-of-1927.pdf

References

Ahluwalia, Sanjam. 2018. 'Tyranny of Orgasm: Global Governance of Sexuality from Bombay, 1930s–1950s.' In *A Global History of Sexual Science, 1880–1960*, edited by Veronika Fuechtner, Douglas E. Haynes and Ryan M. Jones, 353–373. Oakland: University of California Press.

Arondekar, Anjali. 2009. *For the Record: On Sexuality and the Colonial Archive in India*. Durham and London: Duke University Press.

Arondekar, Anjali and Geeta Patel. 2016. 'Area Impossible: Notes Towards an Introduction.' *GLQ: A Journal of Lesbian and Gay Studies* 22 (2): 151–171.

Attwood, Feona, Giovanna Maina and Clarissa Smith. 2018. 'Conceptualizing, Researching and Writing About Pornography.' *Porn Studies* 5 (1): 1–5.

Baas, Michiel. 2020. *Muscular India: Masculinity, Mobility and the New Middle Class*. Delhi: Context (Westland).

Baishya, Anirban K. 2017. 'Pornography of Place: Location, Leaks and Obscenity in the Indian MMS Porn Video.' *South Asian Popular Culture* 15 (1): 57–71.

Biswas, Soutik. 2015. 'The Men Waging War Against Pornography.' *BBC*. Accessed April 13 2019. https://www.bbc.com/news/world-asia-india-33955916.

Bortre, Shrikant and Douglas E. Haynes. 2017. 'Sexual Knowledge, Sexual Anxieties: Middle-Class Males in Western India and the Correspondence in Samaj Swasthya 1927–53.' *Modern Asian Studies* 51 (4): 991–1034.

Botre, Shrikant and Douglas E. Haynes. 2018. 'Understanding R.D. Karve: Brahmacharya, Modernity, and the Appropriation of Global Sexual Science in Western India.' In *A Global History of Sexual Science, 1880-1960*, edited by Veronika Fuechtner, Douglas E. Haynes and Ryan M. Jones, 163–185. Oakland: University of California Press.

Cassin, Barbara, ed. 2014. *Dictionary of Untranslatables: A Philosophical Lexicon*. Princeton and Oxford: Princeton University Press.

Chatterjee, Tupur. 2017. ''I am a Porn Star!' Sex and Sunny Leone Unlimited in Bollywood.' *Porn Studies* 4 (1): 50–66.

Chowkhani, Ketaki. 2016. 'Pleasure, Bodies and Risk: Women's Viewership of Pornography in Urban India.' *Porn Studies* 3 (4): 443–452.

Church, David. 2017. 'Introduction (Canon Fodder: Reappraising Adult Cinema's Neglected Texts).' *Porn Studies* 4 (3): 257–262.

French, Michael. 2018. 'Nepal Cracks Down on Porn, Govt Claims 25,000 Sites Banned so Far.' *AVN*. Accessed May 18 2019. https://avn.com/business/articles/legal/nepal-cracks-down-on-porn- govt -claims-25000-sites-banned-so-far-803013.html.

Foucault, Michel. 1980. 'Truth and Power.' In *Power/Knowledge: Selected Interviews and Other Writings 1972–1977*, edited by Colin Gordon, 109–133. New York: Pantheon Books.

Fuechtner, Veronika. 2013. 'Indians, Jews and Sex: Magnus Hirschfeld and Indian Sexology.' In *Imagining Germany, Imagining Asia: Essays in Asian-German Studies*, edited by V. Fuechtner and M. Rhiel, 111–130. New York: Camden House.

Gorfinkel, Elena. 2017. *Lewd Looks: American Sexploitation Cinema in the 1960s*. Minneapolis and London: University of Minnesota Press.

Gupta, Charu. 2001. *Sexuality, Obscenity, Community: Women, Muslims, and the Hindu Public in Colonial India*. New York: Palgrave.

Gupta, Charu. 2002. *Sexuality, Obscenity and Community: Women, Muslims, and the Hindu Public in Colonial India*. New York: Palgrave Macmillan.

Hansen, Miriam. 1999. 'The Mass Production of the Senses: Classical Cinema as Vernacular Modernism.' *Modernism/Modernity* 6 (2): 55–97.

Harchuck, Kimberly A. 2015. 'Pornography and the First Amendment Right to Free Speech.' In *New Views on Pornography Sexuality, Politics, and the Law*, edited by Lynn Comella and Shira Tarrant, 9–36. Santa Barbara, Denver and Oxford: Praeger.

Hasan, Saad. 2012. 'Smutty DVD Sales Go Up as Porn Sites Go Down.' *The Express Tribune*. Accessed January 8 2019. https://tribune.com.pk/story/318155/smutty-dvd-sales-go-up-as-porn-sites-go-down/.

Heath, Diana. 2010. *Purifying Empire: Obscenity and the Politics of Moral Regulation in Britain, India and Australia*, 1st South Asian edn. New Delhi: Cambridge University Press.

Hoek, Lotte. 2014. *Cut-Pieces: Celluloid Obscenity and Popular Cinema in Bangladesh*. New York: Columbia University Press.

India Today Tech. 2018. 'Jio Bans Porn, Pornhub Circumvents Block by Changing Its Website Address.' *India Today*. Accessed May 10 2019. https://www.indiatoday.in/technology/news/story/jio-bans- porn-pornhub-changing-website-address-1377716-2018-10-29.

Jayadevan, P. K. and Neha Alawadhi. 2014. 'Government Asks Internet Service Companies to Block Pornography Sites, Upgrade Systems.' *Economic Times*. Accessed March 6 2019.https://economictimes.indiatimes.com/tech/internet/government-asks-internet-service-companies-to-block-pornography-sites-upgrade-systems/articleshow/45103758.cms.

Jillani, Shahzeb. 2012. 'Bangladesh Cabinet Approves Anti-Pornography Law.' *BBC*. Accessed January 2 2019. https://www.bbc.com/news/world-asia-16385812.

Kaur, Reminder and William Mazzarella. 2009. *Censorship in South Asia: Cultural Regulation from Sedition to Seduction*. Bloomington and Indianapolis: Indiana University Press.

Kayastha, Shubha. 2018. 'The Problem with Nepal's Porn Ban.'*theRECORD*. Accessed October 15 2018. https://www.recordnepal.com/perspective/policing-sexuality-porn-ban-in-nepal/.

Malhotra, Namita A. 2011. Porn: Law, Video, Technology. Bengaluru: The Center for Internet & Society, Researchers @ Work: Histories of the Internet in India.

Mallett, Whitney. 2016. 'The Changing Face of Documentary Distribution: The 17th Annual Hot Docs. Forum.' *Filmmaker Magazine*. May 5, 2016, https://!lmmakermagazine.com/98417-the-changing-face-documentary-distribution-the-17th-annual-hot-docs-forum/#.YtAYGuxByhc.

Mankekar, Purnima. 2012. 'Dangerous Desires: Erotics, Public Culture, and Identity in Late Twentieth-Century India.' In *Media, Erotics, and Transnational Asia*, edited by Purnima Mankekar, and Louisa Schein, 173–202. Durham and London: Duke University Press.

Manuratne, Prabha. 2014. 'Parody of War: Pleasure at the Limits of Pornography.' In *Porn Archives*, edited by Tim Dean, Steven Ruszczycky and David Squires, 356–372. Durham: Duke University Press.

Mazzarella, William. 2006. *Shoveling Smoke: Advertising and Globalization in Contemporary India*. Durham: Duke University.

Mini, Darshana Sreedhar. 2016. 'The Spectral Duration of Malayalam Soft-Porn: Disappearance, Desire, and Haunting.' *BioScope* 7 (2): 127–150.

Mini, Darshana Sreedhar. 2019. 'The Rise of Soft Porn in Malayalam Cinema and the Precarious Stardom of Shakeela.' *Feminist Media Histories* 5 (2): 49–82.

Ministry of Communications and Information Technology (Department of Information Technology). 2011. 'Notification, New Delhi, the 11th April, 2011 [Information Technology (Guidelines for Cyber Café) Rules, 2011].' The Gazette of India: Extraordinary. Accessed May 12 2019. https://www.meity.gov.in/writereaddata/files/GSR315E_10511%281%29_0.pdf.

Murphy, Anne. 2017. 'The Utility of "South Asia".' *South Asian Review* 38 (3): 91–98.

Nabi, Hira. 2017. 'Transient Spaces and Places: Inside an 80s Cinema Hall in Lahore.' *BioScope* 8 (2): 268–279.

Pande, Ishita. 2020. 'Introduction to 'Translating Sex: Locating Sexology in Indian History.' South Asia: *Journal of South Asian Studies* 42 (6): 1093–1104.

Pemberton, Kelly and Michael Nijhawan, eds. 2009. *Shared Idioms, Sacred Symbols, and theArticulation of Identities in South Asia*. New York and London: Routledge.

Popalzai, Shaheryar. 2011. 'Compromised: Official Website of the SC hacked.' The Express Tribune. Accessed 11 May 2019. https://tribune.com.pk/story/261497/hacker-defaces-supreme-court-website/. Savary, Luzia. 2014. 'Vernacular Eugenics? Santati-Śāstra in Popular Hindi Advisory Literature (1900–1940).' South Asia: Journal of South Asian Studies 37 (3): 381–397.

Rao, Pallavi. 2021. 'Caste, Media, and Modernity: Understanding Power and Inequality in India's English-Language News Culture.' Ph.D. diss., Indiana University, 16.

Savary, Luzia. 2014. 'Vernacular Eugenics? Santati-Śāstra in Popular Hindi Advisory Literature (1900–1940).' *South Asia: Journal of South Asian Studies* 37 (3): 381–397.

Shah, Nishant. 2007. 'PlayBlog: Pornography, Performance and Cyberscpace.' In *C'Lick Me: A Netporn Studies Reader*, edited by Katrien Jacobs, 31–44. Amsterdam: Institute of Network Cultures.

Singh, Bhrigupati. 2008. 'Aadamkhor Haseena (The Man-Eating Beauty) and the Anthropology of a Moment.' *Contributions to Indian Sociology* 42 (2): 249–279.

Singh, Kuwar. 2018. 'India Is Trying to Ban Porn Again. Here's Why It Will Fail.' *Quartz*. Accessed May 2 2019. https://qz.com/india/1441110/how-indians-still-visit-pornhub-despite-the-porn-ban/.

Srinivasan, Ragini Tharoor. 2018. 'Introduction: South Asia from Postcolonial to World Anglophone.' *Interventions: International Journal of Postcolonial Studies* 20 (3): 309–316.

Strossen, Nadine. 1999. 'Foreword: In Defense of Pornography.' In *Porn 101: Eroticism, Pornography and the First Amendment*, edited by James Elias, Veronica Diehl Elias, Vern L. Bullough, Gwen Brewer, Jeffrey J. Douglas and Will Jarvis, 13–28. New York: Amherst Books.

Syeda, Farida Batool. 2015. 'New Media, Masculinity and Mujra Dance in Pakistan.' PhD Thesis. SOAS, University of London.

Tarrant, Shira. 2016. *The Pornography Industry: What Everyone Needs to Know*. New York: Oxford University Press.

Thaver, Mohamed. 2021. 'Explained: Why Raj Kundra Was Arrested in Connection with an Adult Film Racket.' *The Indian Express*. Accessed March 21 2022. https://indianexpress.com/article/explained/explained-the-adult-!lm-racket-in-which-businessmanraj-kundra-has-been-arrested-7413305/

Williams, Linda, ed. 2004. *Porn Studies*. Durham and London: Duke University Press.

Part I

Before pornography: sexology and popular sexual discourses

Cast(e)ing and translating sex in the vernacular: the writings of Santram BA in Hindi

Charu Gupta

ABSTRACT

Santram BA (1887–1998), a Shudra caste reformer, wrote several articles and books in Hindi on sex and birth control, including translations of Mary Stopes' writings, in the early twentieth century. This article places Santram's vernacular writings in a larger historical context of the growth of print, which facilitated the widespread production of so-called obscene material as a commodity. Santram's writings not only contribute in creating an archive for the study of sexual sciences, they also help in addressing the vernacular as a significant, if ambivalent, site for the reproduction, transformation and contestation around matters of sex. The article argues that Santram straddled multiple terrains, as on the one hand he drew from classical works on *kamashastra*, referring to them as beneficial sexual sciences, and on the other he relied on western sexologists to underline pleasure and desire as important facets of modern sexual life. Using the medium of vernacular and translation, Santram created spatial-intimate spaces to celebrate sexual relationships, not only conjoining the private–public, but also opening up an ancillary terrain of textures of touch and sexuality and registers of transgressive sexual norms.

Introduction

This article centres on the vernacular writings on sex and birth control, including translations of several books by Marie Stopes into Hindi for the first time in the early twentieth century, by Santram BA[1] (1887–1998), a veteran writer and a radical Shudra caste[2] reformer from Punjab. Santram's claim to fame has largely been as a founder of the Jat-Pat Torak Mandal (JPTM) [Organization to Break Caste] in 1922, under whose aegis he invited B. R. Ambedkar, the pioneering Dalit leader and thinker, to deliver the keynote address at its Annual Conference, which had to be cancelled due to opposition from within. The text of Ambedkar's lecture became the classic *Annihilation of Caste* (Ambedkar 1936). Santram has been largely marginalized from the records of history. The little that exists on him – by some contemporary admirers and Dalit scholars (Dharmvir 2008, 170–189; Bharti 2017) – has focused exclusively on his anti-caste writings, marginalizing other facets of his identity, particularly his huge repertoire of books and articles on matters of sex.

I argue that Santram's pioneering work against caste and in support of inter-caste marriages cannot be separated from his equally copious writings on sex and sexuality, as in different ways both were attempts to question dominant assumptions of power and to undermine hegemonies, patriarchies and ideals of purity. While examining his anti-caste rhetoric, I am interested in how it was intertwined with translation and vernacular in the formation and transmission of sexology, and a sustained theorization of sex. Santram's writings stand at a crossroads, revealing intersections between anti-caste thought, inter-caste marriages, sexology, science, Sanskrit sex classics, translation and the vernacular, in the specific context of an early twentieth-century north Indian milieu. Santram's mediations on these subjects are all the more significant because a Shudra was translating both Sanskrit classics and modern English texts on sexology, which was itself a subversive act.[3] His writings not only contribute in creating an archive for the study of sexual sciences in India, but they also help in addressing the vernacular and translation as a significant, if ambivalent, site for the reproduction, transformation and contestation of matters of sex. Utilizing repertoires of representation and circuits of production, I argue that Santram straddled multiple terrains, as on the one hand he drew from classical works on *kamashastra*, referring to them as beneficial sexual sciences, and on the other he relied on western sexologists to underline pleasure and desire as important facets of modern sexual life. Using the medium of vernacular and translation, Santram created intimate spaces to celebrate sexual relationships, not only conjoining the private–public, but also opening up an ancillary terrain of textures of touch and sexuality and inter-caste registers of love, intimacy and transgressive sexual norms. Sexuality for Santram was a cover story for various kinds of dissonances, as he laid claim to authority by questioning *savarna* [dominant caste] morality, while carving out a space to think about the body beyond the parameters imagined by the burgeoning middle-class and upper-caste world. Through Santram, I thus attempt to speak to different sets of scholarly writings – historical works on caste and Dalits from a gender-sensitive perspective (Chakravarti 2003, 107–111; Rao 2003, 2018; Rege 2006, 2013, 13–56; Chowdhry 2007; Gupta 2016); translation studies that have creatively examined its meanings in the context of gender and sexuality (Bauer 2009, 2015; Larkosh 2011; Santaemilia 2014); the vernacular as a site of contestation (Chatterjee 2008; Shankar 2012; Kumar 2016); and studies on sex and sexual sciences in late colonial India (Ahluwalia 2008; Hodges 2008; Berger 2013; Savary 2014; Botre and Haynes 2017; Pande 2018).

The JPTM, anti-caste thought and inter-caste marriages

Santram was a member of the Arya Samaj, a leading Hindu reformist movement founded in 1875, for a considerable time.[4] He took the middle ground between Gandhi and Ambedkar, bourgeois and subaltern, Arya Samaj and Ad Dharm (a Dalit movement in early twentieth-century Punjab), and love–hate for Hinduism, attempting to create a hybrid liberal domain. It is from this in-between space that he produced his anti-caste rhetoric (Gupta 2017). He folded caste into histories of intimacy and marriage, drawing inextricable connections between caste and gender.

Santram was born on 14 February 1887 in Purani Basi, a village in the Hoshiarpur district of Punjab (Santram 1952, 2; 1963, 5–6). While economically his family had done well, he came from humble social roots, belonging to the Shilpkar *kumhar* [potter] caste, which was low in the caste hierarchy and had a Shudra status in Punjab (*Gazetteer* 1885, 107; Rose 1911, 562). Santram's love for Hindi developed in conjunction with the headway that Arya Samaj was making in Punjab (Santram 1963, 133–134; Manchanda 1971, 1). He went on to write more than 100 books in Hindi, including translations of Alberuni, O. Hashnu Hara and Marie Stopes. Creating a name for himself in the print-public life of the Hindi world, he published largely on two subjects – caste and sex. Santram wrested Hindi from the literate, the casted and the dominant. In his hands, Hindi itself was 'vernacularized' and democratized, becoming a mobile site for the contestation of caste, for celebrating sexual pleasure and for addressing a more heterogeneous audience.

With a group of his friends, Santram formed the JPTM, named so by him (*Jat-Pat Torak Mandal* 1939, 1; Santram 1963, 184–185). Largely an urban-based movement among the literati, Santram was its driving force. He had a tense relationship with Arya Samaj due to some of his radical anti-caste ideas, and was in dialogue with, and an admirer of, both Periyar and Ambedkar (Manchanda 1971, 6; Santram, n.d.).[5] Notably, Santram made a categorical intervention in the arena of inter-caste marriages, making it the central vehicle of his anti-caste articulations. The foremost rule of the JPTM was to break the birth-based caste system and to promote inter-caste marriages (Santram 1929a, 1959; *Jat-Pat Torak Mandal* 1939, 4). Largely due to his efforts, inter-caste marriages became a symbol of progressive urban modernity among a small circle. After the death of his first wife, Santram married a Maharashtrian Brahmin widow. This central focus on inter-caste marriages allowed Santram to underline how caste permeated India's most intimate spaces, and it was here that it had to be challenged the most. He offered multi-pronged arguments to disrupt endogamy, resorting to sacred and scriptural discourses on the one hand and relying on secular and scientific arguments on the other, which together brought different castes into new modes of relationality. He appropriated ideas around national growth, progress, masculinity and eugenics selectively to push for inter-caste marriages, with double-edged implications. Lack of masculine power, lower levels of intelligence, unhealthy progeny, a weak nation – all were depicted as evils of endogamy. Inversely, he stressed, inter-caste marriages ensured stronger, healthier and brighter children, diversified occupational categories, and were central to Hindu progress (Santram 1949, 11–14, 1959; Gupta 2017). Simultaneously, he challenged not only caste hierarchies but also patriarchal hegemonies through his accounts of inter-caste marriages (Santram 1959, 17). Questioning that exclusive endogamous marriage could in any way be regarded as positive, stable or better, he underlined that inter-caste marriages were more robust, rich and meaningful. His anti-caste literature also often reorganized the social and advocated sexual pleasure. For example, Santram (1949, 97–100) attacked the policing of women's desires, whereby women seen laughing loudly or going out at night were viewed with suspicion, and blamed upper-caste scriptures and the *Ramayana*, the ancient Hindu epic, for preaching false notions of women's purity. Once he got into a heated argument with Pandit Hemraj Vaidya of the Arya Samaj on the caste system. Vaidya besieged Santram for not believing in the Hindu *shastras* [scriptures]. At this, Santram asked Vaidya: 'Do you believe in all *shastras*?' Vaidya replied: 'Yes I believe in all of them.' Santram retorted: 'Then you should definitely also believe in *kokashastra* [a classical Indian sex manual].' At this, Vaidya was deeply embarrassed (Santram 1963, 202). The thriving print culture and substantial growth in vernacular publications on sex in early twentieth-century north India provide another compelling socio-historical context for Santram's writings on sexology.

Print cultures and vernacular expressions of sexual sciences

Meanings of the vernacular have crossed disciplines and themes in India. Partha Chatterjee (2008, 21) sees the vernacular as a discursive space which is less alienated from the popular. Shankar (2012, 21) suggests that 'the perspectives of the vernacular and related ideas of the local and the traditional ... are no more worthy of automatic dismissal from theoretical discourse than are the perspectives of the transnational and related ideas of ... the modern'. Udaya Kumar (2016, 182) offers that the vernacular can often be 'marked by innovative transactions with local and cosmopolitan idioms and languages of earlier and newer epochs'.

Significantly, the language of sexual science often needs a corporeal presence and nearness of lived experience that the vernacular can offer. The practice and potential of employing the vernacular, Hindi in my case, as a method for theorizing the conjunction of sex, science and Sanskrit sex classics cannot be underestimated, as it allows us not only to revive new meanings of the sexual sciences, but also to have a dialogue with their pasts and presents. The vernacular has been central to histories and texts of sex and pleasure in modern India. Santram's public-popular writings underscore this, providing a rich social archive of sexology.

From the late nineteenth century, there emerged a vibrant public culture in urban India, which was given a material form through the circulation and consumption of print (Naregal 2001; Ghosh 2006; Stark 2007; Venkatachalapathy 2012). Print aided both the standardization of languages and literatures, and their democratization, stimulating new expressions of vernacular literature (Blackburn 2003, 10–11). By the early twentieth century, Hindi became the dominant print language of a large section of the middle classes, reformers and writers in north India (Gupta 2001; Orsini 2002). This dynamic print-capitalism also facilitated the widespread production of so-called *ashlil* [obscene] material as a commodity, and erotic consumerism became a critical part of this publishing boom, along with a shift in gender relations and conjugal narratives (Gupta 2001). There was a substantial growth in what one scholar has termed 'global/Hindu sexology' literature in Hindi in the early twentieth century (Pande 2018).

Simultaneously, with the British colonial presence, debates around obscenity intensified. There were serious attempts at the moral regulation of society by controlling what were perceived as obscene publications. The first obscenity laws appeared in India in the late nineteenth century. Sections 292, 293 and 294 of the Indian Penal Code were explicitly designed for the prevention of any form of obscenity (National Archives of India 1890). At the international level, British India signed an agreement for the suppression of obscene publications in 1910 (National Archives of India 1913). An international conference in 1923 resulted in the Obscene Publications Act, 1925, in India (National Archives of India 1925). However, in spite of various regulations and agreements, the term 'obscenity' remained vague, encompassing a variety of meanings in common usage. It was often used to attack not only pornography as it is often defined today, but also to outlaw publications on sexual sciences and birth control (Gupta 2001, 30–31).

Most of the catalogues and reports prepared by British officials on vernacular publications in India disliked the sexual vernacular and were repulsed by depictions of sex in many of these books, describing them as 'bazaar trash' and 'grossly indecent' (Danton 2002, 246). It was reported in 1909–1910 that poetical works had grown in quantity and the subjects were largely erotic and immoral (*Report* 1911, 51). It was again recorded that many of these books adopted a semi-pornographic format (*Report* 1926, 112). The inter-war period in particular was a time of great experimentation, when new questions were allowed to proliferate through sexual imaginaries. Erotic sex manuals particularly saw a substantial growth in this period, largely under male authorship. Some of them used a highly Sanskritized language, usually catering to an elite audience. Simultaneously, there were several popular versions and multiple editions, written in colloquial Hindi (Gupta 2001, 49–66). G. A. Grierson, while carrying out his linguistic survey of India, expressed his concern over the widely published erotic works in north India:

> Up to 1900, the existence of such books was known, but they were rare, and impossible to get except through secret channels ... But now these books are openly advertised and published, with full accounts of their contents that leave no doubt as to their nature. (National Archives of India 1925)

There were conjunctural echoes between the colonial powers and a section of the colonized elite, as both overlapped in their attempts to control obscenity, although for different reasons. A section of Hindu reformers and Hindi literati thus also trenchantly critiqued such publications (Gupta 2001). However, people like Santram firmly believed that the intricacies of sex and the erotic life of conjugality needed to be discussed explicitly because sexual pleasure was an important facet of modern married life. It was not easy to make sexual pleasure a focus of the moral panic, as attempts to fashion moral subjects were constantly fractured and re-imagined. The self-governing Indian subject was often able to negotiate the project of colonial modernity on its own behalf and on its own terms (Heath 2010, 177–180). Further, a section of the vernacular print world managed to escape the colonial gaze as it was not dependent on its patronage. Equally, unlike newspapers, reformist commentaries or other political writings, which could be read aloud in tea shops and public spaces, sex literature was often hidden and consumed in private.

Like many other writers, Santram creatively deployed mass print technology, literary diversity and the commercial press to his advantage, bringing sex from the elite to the masses. Embracing the hugely commercial trajectory of the eroticized spectacle, Santram's books included sex manuals and texts offering advice on sexual relationships, often blurring the lines between sexual science, erotic art and obscenity. His books were widely publicized through magazines and advertisements in books, and were available through the post as well as in the newly emerging book markets, local kiosks and railway stations. Vernacular entanglements with colonial knowledge provided disparate understandings of sexual sciences, with various degrees of flexibility and fluidity. Through the vernacularization and translation of Marie Stopes' most important books on the one hand and Sanskrit sex classics on the other, to which I now turn, Santram offered a hybrid sexology that managed to combine classical ideas on sex, sexual notions circulating in the market, western sexologists' viewpoints and emerging notions of conjugality and love.

Translating Marie Stopes and Sanskrit sex classics into Hindi

There have been fascinating debates on translation as original or derivative, primary or secondary, and scholars have also asserted that there is often an inherent transgression and subversion in the act of translation (Venuti 2000). It has also been underlined that translating texts of sex is a political act, with rhetorical and ideological implications, which are also indicative of the translator's attitude towards moral norms, gender identities and sexual behaviours (Santaemilia 2014). Santram's translations from English and Sanskrit into Hindi (along with his own writings) on the subject of sexual sciences are substantial, and here he takes on the role of a cultural translator and a go-between. Supporting translation and the task of the translator, Santram wrote:

> Translation and translator are not respected intellectually in our country. This is a huge mistake. Translators make a valuable service to the civilization. They help in creating a bridge between the past and the present, between a foreign nation and our own people ... Just as honeybees carry pollen from one flower to another, so in the new era, the translator has always had a critical hand. (1963, 160)

Deeply influenced by Dr Marie Stopes, Santram translated her most celebrated books for the first time into Hindi in the 1920s and 1930s, including the following: *Married Love*, which he translated as *Vivahit Prem* (Santram 1925); *Contraception*, which was interestingly translated by Santram as *Santan Sankhya ka Seema-Bahndhan arthat Dampati Mitra* [literally: Limiting the Number of Children; meaning: friend of the couple] (Santram 1926); and *Enduring Passion*, which Santram translated as *Rati Vilas* [Sexual Pleasure] (Santram 1931). Besides these, he wrote his own books on sexology, which were a combination of select translations from Sanskrit sex classics like Vatsyayan's *Kamasutra*, Koka Pandit's (popularly known as Kokkok) *Rati Rahasya* [Secrets of Love],[6] Padmashri's *Naagar Sarvasam*,[7] excerpts from Freud and Stopes, and his own thoughts on the subject. These included *Rati Vigyan* [Sexual Science] (Santram 1950b), a book which was not only instructive but also titillating;[8] *Kam-Kunj* [Garden of Sex] (Santram 1929b), a sex manual for women and men, published by the prestigious Naval Kishore Press of Lucknow;[9] *Adarsh Patni* [Ideal Wife] (Santram 1950a), a book advising women on various matters, including love and sex;[10] and *Adarsh Pati* [Ideal Husband] (Santram 1932), a book on similar lines for men. Mr Rajpal the owner of Rajpal & Sons, a publishing house based in Lahore, published many of his books (Jigyasu 1998). Finally, Santram wrote articles in *Madhuri*, one of the leading women's magazines of the time, in support of 'true' publications of sexual science, which were also publicity material for his sex manuals (Santram 1924). He repeatedly stated that he received hundreds of letters on the subject (Santram 1929b, 168) (Figure 1).

Santram was a firm believer in sexual pleasure. In an interview, he announced that he was an avid reader of books on sex and Sanskrit classics on the subject, and went on to say 'Lala Lajpat Rai's son Amrit Rai was a friend of mine. I found many good books related to sex in the library of Lala Lajpat Rai' (Manchanda 1971, 29). Santram poetically declared:

> Sex is the thing without which the life of a person is monotonous ... Without which the songs of the poets are prosaic, the articles of the writers are dull and the attitude of the world is arid. (1950b, 3)

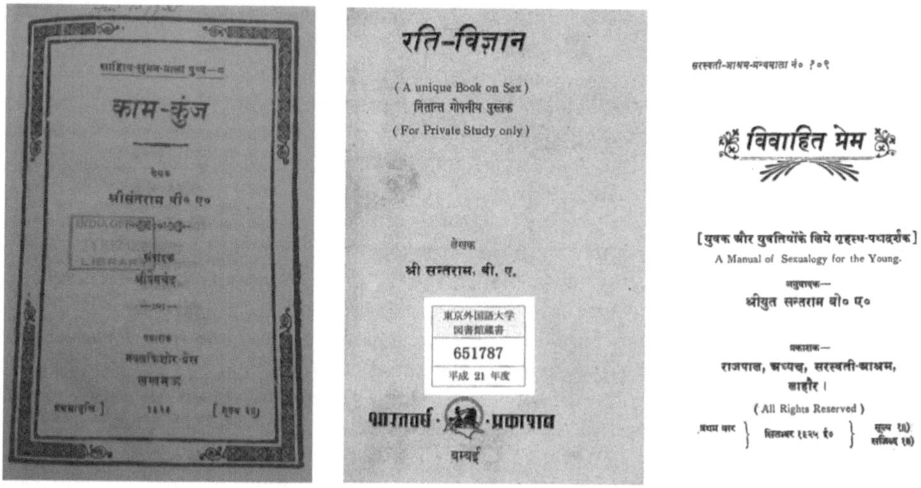

Figure 1. Covers from some of Santram's books: *Kam-Kunj* [Garden of Sex] (Santram 1929b), *Rati Vigyan* [Sexual Science] (Santram 1950b) and *Vivahit Prem* [Married Love] (Santram 1925).

Although Santram was not an established sexologist, his wide-ranging writings on sexual sciences underline that he took up their study and production very seriously, making critical interventions in the field. They offered Santram the opportunity to imagine sexual freedom in the literary domain at a time when it was tenuous in actual practice, as a substantial section of social reformers, nationalists and British officials were looking at it with disdain, and charges of obscenity against such texts were rampant. When reading the translations by Santram, the preface, the translator's note in the beginning and the inserted footnotes become very significant, as it is here that we often get Santram's voice.

Taken as a whole, certain features stand out in these writings of Santram. Like other writers of his time, Santram also repeatedly claimed that his writings were inspired by *shastric* [classical] and scientific literature on *kamashastra* and sexology, quoting extensively from them to reiterate the authenticity of his work, while simultaneously attacking other works on the subject as fake and pseudo. He stated in one article:

> From the letters that I have received, it is clear that there exists a great desire to gain knowledge on the subject of sexual sciences in the public. People are unable to find true texts of such scriptures, so they want to quench their knowledge by purchasing fake texts … They are bad translations of English books, and only contain medical remedies … They contain colorful pictures of naked men and women, and are sold in the name of authentic pictorial *kokashastra* … However, scholars who invented the works of sexual sciences were men of high character … Their texts are very useful for students of human progeny and ethics. For the information of scholars and thinkers, here is a brief introduction to the work of the great Pundit Kokkok on the subject so that the readers can identify the fake from the real. (Santram 1924, 601–602)

Santram claimed that his writings on sexual sciences were prescriptive texts, essential for sexual compatibility and fulfilment. He further underscored their credibility by drawing liberally from key western authors. He often cited Havelock Ellis, Marie Stopes, Sigmund Freud and Richard Schmidt to substantiate his works. It has been argued that western sexual knowledge functioned as a legitimizing source in vernacular texts (Savary 2014). Santram thus wrote:

> Pundit Kokkok's real book is called *Rati Rahasya* ... It has not been translated and printed into Hindi or in any other native language so far ... Mr. [Richard] Schmidt, the teacher of Sanskrit in Germany's Munster University, has translated it into English ... But due to the fear of government reporters, it has not yet been published. In Germany, its translation is available. Many stories are famous about Kokkok. A story, which is mentioned by Professor Schmidt is as follows – Pundit Kokkok was one of the gems of the court. One day a woman from the Hastini tribe came to the court in nude. Out of shame, people hid their faces. But she was not ashamed of anything. The king asked the woman – how dare you come naked in the royal court? The woman replied – I have not seen any real man in this gathering – all are impotent. Then the king ordered his courtiers to calm the woman's sexual fire. But no one succeeded. On seeing the humiliation of the court, Pundit Kokkok, the master of *kamashastra* and its rituals, took the woman to his house and he satisfied her in such a way that she became his mistress and servant ... Then on the request of the king, Pundit Kokkok wrote his book for the benefit of the people ... The book is like a lamp on sexual art. (Santram 1924, 602–603)

The fear of being banned on charges of obscenity was constantly referred to, and, like many other books of this genre, Santram regularly stressed in all his articles, prefaces and introductions that his writings were not *ashlil*. His book *Rati Vigyan* had a chapter exclusively on this subject titled '*Kya Kamashastra ka Vishay Ashlil Hai*' [Is the Subject of Sexual Sciences Obscene] (Santram 1950b, 28–45)? Categorically saying 'no' to the question, he went on to differentiate between *bhava* [sentiment] and *buddhi* [intellect], and *deshachar* [pragmatism] and *vigyan* [science]:

> On hearing just the word *kamashastra*, many people begin to vilify it to uphold their false religiosity and supposed purity ... But even if a miniscule of thought is given to the subject, it will be clear that in branding any book of sexology as obscene, only irrational sentiments are at work, rather than any rationality or intelligence. (Santram 1950b, 28)
>
> A thing that is accepted by reason cannot be obscene. Pragmatism may temporarily declare sexology to be obscene, but in front of science, prudence faces death. A thing that is declared essential by intellect and science cannot be declared as repugnant. (Santram 1950b, 31)

Santram (1950b, 35 and 40–41) went on to quote Sir James Stephen's *Digest of the Criminal Law* and E. H. Starling, a Professor of Physiology at the University of London, to justify the necessity of books on *kamashastra*. In his preface to *Vivahit Prem*, Santram wrote:

> Those who consider *kamashastra* as obscene must read this book. After studying it, they will be convinced that *kamashastra* is a definitive science meant for public benefit. (1925, Preface, gh)

In an article he reiterated:

> If my book on *kamashastra* is published, I have full faith that the readers will get proper knowledge of this art. But how long would it take to print the book, I cannot say ... The government often forfeits such books on charges of obscenity as they do not have learned and liberal officials. (Santram 1924, 605)

Santram thus attempted to craft a sexually liberated Hindi literary counter-public sphere, which could escape charges of obscenity and be beyond the regimentations and censorships of the colonial state.

His mediations of sex through multiple means and diverse texts belonging to different locations and time periods further highlight that he selectively appropriated and conjoined the works of modern sexologists like Stopes on the one hand and Sanskrit sex classics of Kokkok and Vatsyayan on the other, dismissing neither of them. Rather than pointing to contradictions in these diverse sex texts, Santram was more interested in searching for complementarities and harmonies in them. Hindi visions and translations of sexual sciences, which had their origins in western texts, had to not only negotiate local idioms and structures of the vernacular languages, but also a deep and long history of sex classics in the Sanskrit language. Santram tried to provide a bridge between theory and practice by translating and communicating across different domains. While translating Stopes, Santram repeatedly complimented and provided further credence to her views by comparing them with quotes from *Kamasutra* and *Rati Rahasya*. He began his preface of *Vivahit Prem* by entwining Stopes with Kokkok under the heading *Anuvadak ka Nivedan* [Translator's Submission]. He went on to quote liberally from Sanskrit classics in the footnotes of the book (Santram 1925, 27, 32–33 and 97 footnotes). For example, in one place he said:

> In our scriptures on sexual sciences also, it is described as to how should we behave on the first night with our new bride ... Because men and women do not have enough knowledge of each other's nature, they are unable to get full pleasures. (Santram 1925, 27 footnote)

Spatial, linguistic, global, regional, cultural and time differences regarding writings on sexual sciences were mediated through translation, as Santram strategically aligned himself with both platforms. In this 'vernacularization' and 'unruly appropriation' (Fuechtner, Haynes, and Jones 2018) of Stopes and Vatsyayan, sexual sciences became a means that offered a discursive space of thinking and argumentation. It was in this process of selectively weaving together tradition–indigenous–classical–Hindu and modern–western–Christian notions of sex, eroticism and science that new discourses on these subjects were formulated in late colonial India. Santram provided a sexual space that accommodated and intermeshed modern sexual sciences with the Indian classics. It also became a way to make the translations knowable and comprehensible to a larger Hindi reading public at a relatively cheap price. The conjunction of English and Sanskrit by a Shudra anti-caste ideologue could acquire potentially revolutionary meanings in terms of both sex and caste.

Santram (1931, Preface) was a great admirer of Stopes, referring to her as 'the greatest teacher of sexual science', who had 'not only studied sex texts of Sanskrit, but also of many other languages of the world'. Due to her 'vast research, experience and explorations', she had discovered 'precious new truths on sexual sciences'. While translating *Married Love*, Santram (1925) declared on the cover that it was 'A Manual of Sexology for the Young'. He did not consider that ancient Hindu erotica offered all solutions. Rather, he stated in his preface that the eighth chapter of Stopes' book, dealing with 'the correct way of intercourse', went far beyond any classical works on *kamashastra*, as the latter were not always acclimatized to modern sexual yearnings. At the same time, when Stopes' writings travelled far and wide, away from their cultural contexts, they could provide different possibilities. Santram thus reframed Stopes in vernacular idioms and contexts to make his translations viable. Translating global and western sexual norms into local practices and contexts, his writings marked a 'folklorization' of sexual sciences that relied on familiar conceptual categories. He translated Stopes in such a way that it became a sexual narrative of 'us', rather than a mere translation of the 'other'. Stopes' theories on sex combined western ideas of rationalism, science and Christian doctrines. The process of translating western sexual modernity into a Hindi vernacular necessitated that the model used by Stopes be made knowable by referencing the particular social and cultural milieu of colonial north India. For example, while writing the second chapter of *Married Love* titled 'The Broken Joy', which Santram poetically translated as '*Rang mein Bhang*' (meaning something like 'face like a wet weekend'), he mentioned in a footnote:

> The author [Marie Stopes] has written this book keeping in mind the English community. That is why these things are more applicable to them. Here we are married in the manner of a 'lottery.' Here men and women are not given the chance to know and love each other before marriage. (Santram 1925, 23 footnote)

Santram's sexology thus involved a process of cultural filtering by which he made Stopes translatable, comprehensible and accessible to a Hindi reading public. While wishing to remain 'truthful' to the original, Santram was sensitive to local contexts and understandings, carving out a field of creative dialogue and layered imaginaries of sexual sciences.

Santram uses his translations of Marie Stopes' books to constantly publicize his own books in footnotes. For example, when talking of Stopes' views on birth control in *Vivahit Prem*, he wrote in various footnotes that he had translated all of the important aspects of her book *Contraception* in another book (Santram 1925, 11, 140, 158 and 165–166 footnotes). His book *Rati Vigyan* was repeatedly mentioned in the footnotes of *Vivahit Prem* (46, 52, 94, 96, 97, 126 and 207 footnotes). Moreover, his books on other subjects extensively advertised his books on sex. For example, one of his books, *Sukhi Parivar* [Happy Family] (Santram 1950c) had a full-page advertisement for his book *Rati Vigyan* on the back cover, stating that it was a unique book on sex meant for private study, and that it extensively discussed issues of sexual compatibility and sexual adjustment using the works of Vatsyayan, Freud and Stopes. He referred to the book as *kamashastra ka sundar gutka* [beautiful chemistry of sexual sciences].

While translating cultures of sex, Santram added his own voice and views, in his own language, to the texts, often representing the unspeakable from within. He was able to find a tone in vernacular registers that suited that of the translator. All of his translations had creative prefaces that simultaneously reified and destabilized the sexual. In this process, Santram was formulating something new through his own inputs, remoulding a range of writings on sexual sciences to the present times and Indian contexts. These translations by Santram were not just the transferring of texts; they also interrogated dominant and normative assumptions about sex. I now turn to this theme using examples of conjugality, *brahmacharya* [celibacy or sexual self-restraint] and birth control.

Conjugal desires, *brahmacharya* and birth control

Santram was often ahead of his time on questions of sex and gender. He was a firm believer in sexual pleasure for both women and men, was against *brahmacharya* and was in favour of birth control. Scholars like Durba Ghosh (2006), Tanika Sarkar (2001) and Mytheli Sreenivas (2008), among others, have effectively shown how and why gender relations were undergoing significant changes in colonial India, whereby women and men were negotiating complex subjectivities and reformers were reformulating conjugal relations. Substantial work has recently emerged on the intersections between sexual sciences, modern conjugality and vernacular literature in late colonial India (Savary 2014; Botre and Haynes 2017). Santram's writings provide another critical chapter in this tradition of work.

Ideals of modern conjugal sexuality infused Santram's writings as he dealt explicitly with sexual aspects of marriage. He was an ardent advocate of sex education, stressing that the case of human bodies was different from animals, as the former had to be taught the art of sexual pleasure and knowledge, including different sexual positions, passionate intercourse and the importance of arousing the woman (Santram 1950b, 44–45). He further wrote:

> Every heart desires a partner ... The aim of *kamashastra* is to increase pleasure in marriage ... It is indeed ironical that the sexual act is not considered obscene, but its description is branded so! Embraces, kisses and postures are essential for sexual intercourse. Those who are married do all these actions because God has enacted this 'obscene' method for the origin of human beings. Then should we also prosecute God as per Section 292 and 293 of the Indian Penal Code? (Santram 1929b, 166–167)

Even while drawing from both Stopes and Vatsyayan, Santram was attempting to produce a vernacular flavour of conjugality, which could be implemented in the everyday life of the modern Indian couple. Addressing both male anxieties and female desires, he critiqued men for their ignorance on sexual matters, while simultaneously recognizing women as active partners. He subversively deployed sexology to interrogate gender relations, divorcing sex from the reproductive or procreative imperative. His book *Kam-Kunj*, while stressing sexual affinity between the married couple, also reflected on the weakness and incompetence of Indian men in providing erotic fulfilment to women. Santram stated:

> In the name of religion and politics, and due to ignorance regarding sexual sciences, how much crime is spreading in our country is not hidden from the readers. With no true knowledge of women's sexual languages, qualities, desires and gestures, men construct opposite meanings of women's creativity and ethics. (1929b, 1)

In his preface to *Vivahit Prem*, he again wrote:

> A man is often foolish about sexual sciences, and does not understand diverse elements of the art of sex ... Even when he has access to a youthful woman, he is forever deprived of sexual pleasures (Santram 1925, Preface, k)

In the same book, he further observed in a footnote:

> A clever man should excite the woman on the first night by undressing her softly, embracing and kissing her, in order to arouse her. Only when the libido inside her is fully excited and aroused, only then should the intercourse take place. Those men who are totally obsessed with sex and just jump on top of the women are completely stupid. (Santram 1929, 33 footnote)

Recognizing women's bodily desires, Santram felt a need to get his views across to women as well. He expressed:

> *Kamashastra* has been much denigrated nowadays ... Even knowing this, I have dared to pen my thoughts on the subject in a magazine, which is also extensively read by women. The reason for this is that I do not consider sex to be obscene. (Santram 1929b, 160–161)

He often urged husbands to do household work:

> If the husband gives help to the wife in household work – fetches the water, washes the vegetables, burns the fire, lifts the child, then what is there to be insulted? (Santram 1929b, 37)

To give credence to his views, he approvingly quoted Mary Wollstonecraft, the famous advocate of women's rights (Santram 1929b, 171). Also, in the same book, he stated:

> In terms of evolution, it is the woman's body which is the most developed in the world. Female attributes are sharper and her senses much more pronounced in comparison to that of the man ... The final destiny of a man is to become a woman. (Santram 1929b, 152)

Even while working within heteronormative paradigms, his books, including his anti-caste writings, were making marriages more capacious and mobile, renegotiating gender relations and sexual pleasures, crisscrossing gender, caste and religious boundaries, and providing possibilities of living altered gendered lives.

Let me move to Santram's views on *brahmacharya*. It has been underlined that *brahmacharya* was one of the core doctrines of Hindu *dharma* [religion], and the preservation of semen was seen as essential for male empowerment. In the colonial period, *brahmacharya* acquired new contours and was transformed into a modern discourse, intermingling with discussions around masculinity, national upliftment, freedom of movement, eugenics, healthy offspring, body fitness and social service. From Sanatan Dharmists to Arya Samajists, from Dayanand to Vivekanand and Gandhi – all supported it for diverse reasons (Alter 2000, 2011; Mills and Sen 2004; Chakraborty 2011). The market was flooded with prescriptions and books around it (Gupta 2001, 66–83), which in many ways reinstated Brahmanism. Many of the Indian sexologists also supported *brahmacharya*. In this climate, influenced by Dayanand Saraswati, the founder of Arya Samaj, Santram initially became a supporter of *brahmacharya*. However, he soon gave up the idea, and went on to passionately assault it, arguing that it had proved to be greatly damaging for him. Seriously challenging the concept, he stated:

> Due to the influence of Arya Samaj on me, I gave huge importance to *brahmacharya*. Therefore I did not keep my wife with me and even ran away from her shadow. Because of my attitude, my wife remained very sad ... But this supposed *brahmacharya* caused me more harm than benefit. My belief in *brahmacharya* was completely wrong. Later, when I read Mary Stopes' *Enduring Passion*, it greatly helped me ... I decided to keep my wife with me and she was ecstatic because of it. (Santram 1963, 84–85)

After this, whenever he was away from his wife, he wrote passionate letters to her. He even exchanged letters with Stopes, describing intimate details of his life, and seeking her advice:

> Although I am not fortunate enough to have any personal acquaintance with your good self, yet I have read many of your books ... I have been convinced that you are one of the best authorities on venereal diseases ... I am suffering from prostatic discharges after urinating since many years ... After my marriage I tried to observe celibacy under the influence of false religious ideas. Although I and my wife lived together yet we had seldom coitus, after which I had to repent on my inability to keep continence ... This condition went on for

> many years. Then I began to lead married life and got children. This relieved me of seminal ejaculations. (Stopes Papers n.d.)

There were also subterranean resistances to *brahmacharya* as a marker of the modern man, due to factors like the flooding of aphrodisiac advertisements in the market (Gupta 2001, 66–83; Haynes 2012) and the growth of erotic literature and romantic novels in modern India. Santram's opposition to it also revealed that the discourse of *brahmacharya* faced fissures from within.

Lastly, let me come to birth control, which emerged as a prominent issue for debates around sexuality in the early twentieth century, with Gandhi and many others strongly opposing it and anti-caste ideologues like Periyar and sexologists like A. P. Pillay, N. S. Phadke and R. D. Karve firmly supporting it (Anandhi 1998; Ahluwalia 2008; Hodges 2008). Santram, too, was a fervent proponent of birth control, aligning with Stopes on the one hand and influenced by Periyar on the other. His translation of Marie Stopes' *Contraception* was widely publicized as the first book on family planning in Hindi (*Naye Varsh ka Suchipatra* [Catalogue of New Year], n.d., 43). It was a book of 300 pages, vividly describing methods of birth control and how to stop unwanted pregnancies, along with some pictures. While partially influenced by eugenic arguments, it gave the right to birth control to women (Santram 1926). The book created a huge controversy and many people, including members of the Arya Samaj, called it 'immoral' and 'obscene', threatening Santram with a court case. But some thanked him for publishing it (Santram 1963, 161; Jigyasu 1998, 53). Santram stated:

> The publisher of the book and my friend Rajpal told me that those conservative Arya Samajis who criticise you for this book and threaten that they will drag you to the court, their wives too have secretly bought the book and read it with great enthusiasm. (1963, 132)

In the Hindi journal *Yugantar* that he edited, Santram often published articles in support of birth control. For example, in an article titled '*Santiti Nirodh aur Bharat*' [India and Birth Control] (Vanchu 1935) it was stated that *brahmacharya* was totally impractical for the purpose, as it could only be practised by a *mahapurush* [great man] or by someone who was impotent. Thus, birth control was the way forward.

The diverse writings of Santram on sexual sciences, when read in conjunction with his views on inter-caste marriages, provide us with a vocabulary of sexual passion, recalcitrant love and intimacy, along with a rethinking of gender relations. In a sense, he was capitalizing on the scientification of sexuality to theorize the possibilities of social, gender and caste mixing. While the eugenic thrust of sexology was based on racial purity, Santram creatively deployed it for social mobility. He brought to the centre stage desires which were perhaps 'radically unthinkable' (Butler 1993, 59), and had the potential to provide 'new narratives of possibility' (Berlant 2012, 43).

Conclusion

Many other writers and self-proclaimed Hindi–Hindu sexologists were also writing on, and engaging with, sexual sciences at this time. Santram is very much part of this legacy. At the same time, his concerted work to celebrate inter-caste marriages, his friendships with Ambedkar and Periyar, his recognition of women's sexual desires, his location on the margins of caste hierarchies and his creative marrying of both classical sex texts and western sexologists reveal a more complex picture. Unlike many other global/Hindu sexologists, Santram never advocated 'traditional' principles of self-constraint and did not link pleasure with procreation. Instead, by appropriating inter-caste alliances along with sexual sciences, Santram made caste more fluid, enacted a lower caste poetics of sexuality and upheld equality in caste and sex, which contributed to shaping the conflicting desires of the times. His anti-caste and sexology literature flowered in tandem as both were attempts to partially break the limits of marriage and sex by disrupting endogamy and supporting inter-caste unions on the one hand and by upholding pleasure, providing women with a degree of agency and radically questioning *brahmacharya*, on the other. The texts of Santram have thus also to be read as metaphors for the shifts in caste and gender relations in late colonial India. Santram's aim was to introduce readers to a range of literature, whereby medical, scientific and classical explanations about sex were woven through the vernacular to disseminate sexual understandings that would nourish the modern conjugal couple. The attempts at imaginatively crafting a vernacular sexual counter-public sphere and a counter-narrative by a Shudra underline that Santram was simultaneously working in different registers, which were nonetheless complementary to each other. Vernacular idioms, codes and practices became a medium to produce cracks and fissures in dominant caste and sexual embodiments. Offering a hybrid sexology, he brought together the local and the global, the cosmopolitan and the vernacular. Reclaiming messier practices of sexual desire and inter-caste marriages, which constantly interrogate prescriptions, boundaries and hierarchies, was an important site of resistance. Recognizing the deeper links between caste, hierarchy, sexuality and patriarchy, Santram's writings offer a richly textured account of his commitment to inter-caste alliances, along with sexual freedom and equality, which remained the recurrent trope and a ubiquitous subject in his literature.

Notes

1. Santram used his attainment of a bachelor's degree as a kind of honorific.
2. Shudra is the lowest of the four *varnas* or ranks in Hinduism.
3. For some of the debates on the interrelationship between Sanskrit, English and Dalits, see Anand (1999).
4. For details of Santram's life, see his autobiography (Santram 1963).
5. Santram went on to translate Ambedkar's (1936) *Annihilation of Caste* into Hindi, and published it under the banner of the JPTM (Santram 1937).
6. A medieval Indian sex manual, composed in the eleventh or twelfth century CE.
7. An erotic treatise written most probably around 1000 AD by Buddhist scholar Padmashri.
8. Also see Tandon (1951, 307).
9. For details on the press, see Stark (2007).
10. The book went into more than 19 editions (see Santram 1963, 111). I saw the 13th edition of the book.

Acknowledgements

An earlier version of this article was presented at an International Workshop on 'Sex in Translation in Post/Colonial India: Vernacular Archives and Global Itineraries', held at Queen's University, Kingston, ON, Canada, April 19–21 2018. The author is very grateful to all of the participants, especially to Rachel Berger, Ishita Pande, Anjali Arondekar and Douglas Haynes, for their perceptive comments, which have greatly helped in revising the article. The author wishes to further thank the two anonymous reviewers of *Porn Studies* for their insightful suggestions.

Disclosure statement

No potential conflict of interest was reported by the author.

References

Ahluwalia, Sanjam. 2008. *Reproductive Restraints: Birth Control in India, 1877–1947*. Urbana: University of Illinois Press.

Alter, Joseph S. 2000. *Gandhi's Body: Sex, Diet and the Politics of Nationalism*. Philadelphia: University of Pennsylvania Press.

Alter, Joseph S. 2011. *Moral Materialism: Sex and Masculinity in Modern India*. New Delhi: Penguin Books.

Ambedkar, B. R. 1936. *Annihilation of Caste: Speech Prepared for the Annual Conference of JPTM of Lahore but Not Delivered*. Bombay: B. R. Kadrekar.

Anand, S. 1999. 'Sanskrit, English and Dalits.' *Economic and Political Weekly* 34 (30): 2053-6.

Anandhi, S. 1998. 'Reproductive Bodies and Regulated Sexuality: Birth Control Debates in Early Twentieth Century Tamilnadu.' In *A Question of Silence?: The Sexual Economies of Modern India*, edited by Mary E. John and Janaki Nair, 139-66. Delhi: Kali for Women.

Bauer, Heike. 2009. *English Literary Sexology: Translations of Inversion, 1860-1930*. New York: Palgrave Macmillan.

Bauer, Heike. 2015. *Sexology and Translation: Cultural and Scientific Encounters across the Modern World, 1880-1930*. Philadelphia: Temple University Press.

Berger, Rachel. 2013. *Ayurveda made Modern: Political Histories of Indigenous Medicine in North India, 1900-1955*. Basingstoke: Palgrave MacMillan.

Berlant, Lauren. 2012. *Desire/Love*. New York: Punctum Books.

Bharti, Kanwal. 2017. 'Santram BA: A Committed Anti-Caste Warrior.' *Forward Press* July 26. Accessed October 21 2017. https://www.forwardpress.in/2017/07/santram-b-a-a-committed-anti-caste-warrior/

Blackburn, Stuart. 2003. *Print, Folklore, and Nationalism in Colonial South India*. Delhi: Permanent Black.

Botre, Shrikant and Douglas E. Haynes. 2017. 'Sexual Knowledge, Sexual Anxieties: Middle-Class Males in Western Indian and the Correspondence in *Samaj Swasthya*, 1927-53.' *Modern Asian Studies* 51 (4): 991-1034.

Butler, Judith. 1993. *Bodies that Matter: On the Discursive Limits of 'Sex'*. London: Routledge.

Chakraborty, Chandrima. 2011. *Masculinity, Asceticism, Hinduism: Past and Present Imaginings of India*. Ranikhet: Permanent Black.

Chakravarti, Uma. 2003. *Gendering Caste through a Feminist Lens*. Calcutta: Stree.

Chatterjee, Partha. 2008. 'Introduction: History in the Vernacular.' In *History in the Vernacular*, edited by Raziuddin Aquil and Partha Chatterjee, 1-24. Ranikhet: Permanent Black.

Chowdhry, Prem. 2007. *Contentious Marriages, Eloping Couples: Gender, Caste and Patriarchy in Northern India*. Delhi: Oxford University Press.

Danton, Robert. 2002. 'Book Production in British India, 1850-1900.' *Book History* 5: 239-62.

Dharmvir. 2008. *Dalit Chintan ka Vikas* [Development of Dalit Thought]. New Delhi: Vani Prakashan.

Fuechtner, Veronika, Douglas E. Haynes and Ryan M. Jones. 2018. 'Introduction: Toward a Global History of Sexual Science: Movements, Networks, and Deployments.' In *A Global History of Sexual Science, 1880-1960*, edited by Veronika Fuechtner, Douglas E. Haynes and Ryan M. Jones, 1-25. Oakland: University of California Press.

Gazetteer of the Hoshiarpur District, 1883-4. 1885. Lahore: Civil and Military Gazette Press.

Ghosh, Anindita. 2006. *Power in Print: Popular Publishing and Politics of Language and Culture in a Colonial Society*. Delhi: Oxford University Press.

Ghosh, Durba. 2006. *Sex and the Family in Colonial India: The Making of Empire*. Cambridge: Cambridge University Press.

Gupta, Charu. 2001. *Sexuality, Obscenity, Community: Women, Muslims and the Hindu Public in Colonial India*. Delhi: Permanent Black.

Gupta, Charu. 2016. *The Gender of Caste: Representing Dalits in Print*. Seattle: University of Washington Press.

Gupta, Charu. 2017. 'Speaking Self, Writing Caste: Recovering the Life of Santram BA.' *Biography: An Interdisciplinary Quarterly* 40 (1): 16-43.

Haynes, Douglas E. 2012. 'Selling Masculinity: Advertisements for Sex Tonics and the Making of Modern Conjugality in Western India, 1900-1945.' *South Asia* 35 (4): 787-831.

Heath, Deana. 2010. *Purifying Empire: Obscenity and the Politics of Moral Regulation in Britain, India and Australia*. Cambridge: Cambridge University Press.

Hodges, Sarah. 2008. *Contraception, Colonialism and Commerce: Birth Control in South India, 1920-1940*. Aldershot: Ashgate.

Jat-Pat Torak Mandal, Lahore: General Review. 1939.

Jigyasu, Rajendra. 1998. *Dharma ki Balivedi Par: Mahashya Rajpal ji ki Balidan Gatha* [On the Pyre of Religion: The Tale of Mr. Rajpal's Sacrifice]. Delhi: Rajpal & Sons.

Kumar, Udaya. 2016. *Writing the First Person: Literature, History and Autobiography in Modern Kerala*. Ranikhet: Permanent Black.

Larkosh, Christopher, ed. 2011. *Re-Engendering Translation: Transcultural Practice, Gender/Sexuality and the Politics of Alterity*. London: Routledge.

Manchanda, Shyam Lal. 1971. *Interview with Santram BA. May 15*. Oral History Transcript, Accession No. 238. Delhi: Nehru Memorial Museum and Library.

Mills, James H. and Satadru Sen. 2004. *Confronting the Body: The Politics of Physicality in Colonial and Post-Colonial India*. New York: Anthem Press.

Naregal, Veena. 2001. *Language Politics, Elites and the Public Sphere: Western India under Colonialism*. Delhi: Permanent Black.

National Archives of India. 1890. 457-83/October, Public, A, Home Department.

National Archives of India. 1913. 193-204/April, Judicial, A, Home Department.

National Archives of India. 1925. 669, Judicial, Home Department.

Naye Varsh ka Suchipatra [Catalogue of New Year]. nd. Lahore: Rajal & Sons.

Orsini, Francesca. 2002. *The Hindi Public Sphere 1920-1940: Language and Literature in the Age of Nationalism*. Delhi: Oxford University Press.

Pande, Ishita. 2018. 'Time for Sex: The Education of Desire and the Conduct of Childhood in Global/Hindu Sexology.' In *A Global History of Sexual Science*, edited by Fuechtner, Haynes and Jones, 279–301. Oakland: University of California Press.

Rao, Anupama, ed. 2003. *Gender and Caste*. Delhi: Kali for Women.

Rao, Anupama, ed. 2018. *Gender, Caste and the Imagination of Equality*. New Delhi: Women Unlimited.

Rege, Sharmila. 2006. *Writing Caste/Writing Gender: Narrating Dalit Women's Testimonios*. Delhi: Zubaan.

Rege, Sharmila. 2013. *Against the Madness of Manu: B.R. Ambedkar's Writings on Brahmanical Patriarchy*. Delhi: Navayana.

Report on the Administration of UP, 1909-10. 1911. Allahabad: Government Press.

Report on the Administration of UP, 1924-25. 1926. Allahabad: Government Press.

Rose, Horace. A., comp. 1911. *A Glossary of the Tribes and Castes of the Punjab and North-West Frontier Province, Vol. II*. Lahore: Civil and Military Gazette Press.

Santaemilia, Jose, ed. 2014. *Gender, Sex and Translation: The Manipulation of Identities*. London: Routledge.

Santram BA, trans. 1925. *Vivahit Prem*. Of Marie Stopes' *Married Love*. Lahore: Rajpal, Saraswati Ashram.

Santram BA, trans. 1926. *Santan Sankhya ka Seema-Bahndhan arthat Dampati Mitra*. Of Marie Stopes' *Contraception*. Lahore: Rajpal, Saraswati Ashram.

Santram BA, trans. 1931. *Rati Vilas*. Of Marie Stopes' *Enduring Passion*. Lahore: Rajpal, Saraswati Ashram.

Santram BA, trans. 1937. *Jatibhed ka Uchhed*. Of B. R. Ambedkar's *Annilhilation of Caste*. Lahore: Jat-Pat Torak Mandal.

Santram BA. n.d. 'Individual Collections: Papers of Santram BA.' List 430. Delhi: Nehru Memorial Museum and Library.

Santram BA. 1924. 'Rati Rahasya.' *Madhuri* December: 601-5.

Santram BA. 1929a. 'Antarjatiya Vivah' [Inter-Caste Marriage]. *Sudha* July: 596-608.

Santram BA. 1929b. *Kam-Kunj*. Lucknow: Naval Kishore Press.

Santram BA. 1932. *Adarsh Pati*. Lahore: Rajpal & Sons. 2nd ed.

Santram BA. 1949. *Humara Samaj*. Bombay: Nalanda Prakashan.

Santram BA. 1950a. *Adarsh Patni*. Delhi: Rajpal & Sons. 13th ed.

Santram BA. 1950b. *Rati Vigyan* [Sexual Science]. Bombay: Bharatvarsh Prakashan. 2nd ed.

Santram BA. 1950c. *Sukhi Parivar*. Bombay: Bharatvarsh Prakashan.

Santram BA. 1952. 'Taunted and Scoffed by Orthodoxy: Anti-Caste Movement in the Punjab: Experiences Of a Social Reform Leader.' *The Sunday Observer* July 13: 2, 7.

Santram BA. 1959. *Antarjatiya Vivah hi Kyun* [Why Inter-Caste Marriages Only]. Hoshiarpur: Jat-Pat Torak Mandal.

Santram BA. 1963. *Mere Jeevan ke Anubhav* [Experiences of My Life]. Varanasi: Hindi Pracharak Pustakalya.

Sarkar, Tanika. 2001. *Hindu Wife, Hindu Nation: Community, Religion and Cultural Nationalism*. Delhi: Permanent Black.

Savary, Luzia. 2014. 'Vernacular Eugenics? Santati-Sastra in Popular Hindi Advisory Literature (1900-1940).' *South Asia: Journal of South Asian Studies* 37 (3): 381-97.

Shankar, Subramanian. 2012. *Flesh and Fish Blood: Postcolonialism, Translation, and the Vernacular*. Delhi: Orient Blackswan.

Sreenivas, Mytheli. 2008. *Wives, Widows and Concubines: The Conjugal Family Ideal in Colonial India*. Bloomington: Indiana University Press.

Stark, Ulrike. 2007. *An Empire of Books: The Naval Kishore Press and the Diffusion of the Printed Word in Colonial India*. Ranikhet: Permanent Black.

Stopes Papers. n.d. Letter addressed by Santram to Marie Stopes, March 16, 1930, MSS no. ADD 58578. Department of Manuscripts, British Library.

Tandon, Ramnarayan, ed. 1951. *Hindi Sevi Sansar, Vol. 1*. Lucknow: Vidya Mandir.

Vanchu, M. P. 1935. 'Santati Nirodh aur Bharat' [India and Birth Control]. *Yugantar* February: 20-21.

Venkatachalapathy, A. R. 2012. *The Province of the Book: Scholars, Scribes, and Scribblers in Colonial Tamilnadu*. Ranikhet: Permanent Black.

Venuti, Lawrence, ed. 2000. *The Translation Studies Reader*. London: Routledge.

Purging the pornographic, discipling the sexual, and edifying the public: pornography, sex education and class in early to mid-twentieth century colonial Bengal

Arnav Bhattacharya

ABSTRACT
In this article, I study the works of two Bengali sexologists, Abul Hasanat and Nripendra Kumar Basu, in order to unpack the relationship between pornography and sexology in colonial Bengal. I make two arguments. First, I argue that sexologists distinguished themselves from pornography writers by framing sexology as a scientific and educational field. I show how sexology counterposed itself to pornography in order to consolidate its position in the Bengali print market. Second, I argue that this privileging of sexology vis-à-a vis pornography overlapped with the politics of class and respectability in Bengal. Sexology provided elite reformers with a tool that not only policed the sexual but disciplined and 'colonized' it. The middle class, however, did not represent an ideological monolith in terms of their sexual morality. This is revealed through the divergent perspectives of the two sexologists with regard to their differing views on the proliferation of pornography.

Introduction

> For publishing an obscene article, the editor of a Gujerati [*sic*] magazine was sentenced on Tuesday by the Chief Presidency Magistrate, Bombay to one month's rigorous imprisonment and a fine of Rs. 300 or in default three weeks' rigorous imprisonment. In sentencing the accused, Ghulam Hussein Ismailji Nanavaty, a Bohra, the Magistrate, Sir Hormazidar Dastur, remarked that it was time the publication of obscene pamphlets was stopped. Nanavaty pleaded 'not guilty'. It was urged on his behalf that he published the article in question in his journal *Chumban* with the best of intentions, namely, to give the public the most necessary education on sexology. (Anonymous 1936, 15)

Nanavaty's choice of highlighting the educational and sexological nature of the article in his journal before the judicial magistrate during his obscenity trial in 1936 was not an arbitrary or coincidental decision. A classification of the article as intended for the purposes of disseminating sex education would ensure that Nanavaty was absolved of the obscenity charges. From the early years of the twentieth century with the expansive proliferation of pornography, especially in the vernacular, both the colonial state as well elite Indians emphasized the need for the dissemination of sexology and sex education to counter the alleged pernicious influence of cheap and widely available pornographic literature The expansion of printing in the course of the nineteenth and twentieth centuries had resulted in the widespread production of erotic material as a popular commodity and 'erotic consumerism became a part of the publishing boom' (Gupta 2002, 50). The Hindi literary sphere from the early 1900s witnessed the emergence of a wide genre of erotic texts comprising sex manuals, popular romances, and sex advice literature which, as Charu Gupta has shown, 'blurred the lines between sexual science, erotic art, and obscenity' by either presenting themselves as translations of classical Sanskrit erotic treatises or as sexological texts highlighting the 'scientific facts of sexual life' (2002, 53). Even earlier, around 1816, a significant market for Bengali erotica had been established in Calcutta, which grew immensely popular through the nineteenth century. However, by the early twentieth century, the emergence of sexology posed a challenge to Bengali erotica. While Hindi erotica camouflaged itself as sexual science to escape the clutches of obscenity charges, the moral campaign of the colonial state and elite Bengalis led to Bengali pornography being pitted against and competing with Bengali sexology, which cannibalized the diminishing market share of Bengali erotica. This genre of sexology literature in Hindi, Bengali, and other South Asian languages has received substantial scholarly attention in the recent past. The existing scholarship has highlighted the ideas of prominent sexologists such as R. D. Karve (Botre and Haynes 2017, 2018) and Dr A. P. Pillay (Ahluwalia 2018), while also emphasizing the role of subaltern vernacular sexologists[1] through the writings of a female sexologist, Yashoda Devi (Gupta 2020), and an anti-caste crusader, B. A. Santram (Gupta 2019, 2020). Scholars have also shown how sexology was appropriated in historical debates relating to prostitution (Mitra 2020a), child marriage (Pande 2020a), birth control (Ahluwalia 2007; Hodges 2008), and the politics of Gandhian *brahmacharya* [celibacy] and nationalism (Haynes 2020). Although the relationship between pornography and sexology has not been substantially examined in this existing body of sexology scholarship, a few scholars have made brief references to this association.

There have been two divergent approaches to understanding the relationship between sexology and pornography in early to mid twentieth-century India. One approach has been to view pornography and sexology as indistinguishable, as already mentioned with reference to the scholarship of Charu Gupta (2002, 53) on Hindi erotica blurring the lines between erotic art, obscenity, and sexology. In addition to Gupta, Anjali Arondekar, while commenting on Richard Burton's English translation of the *Kama Sutra*, also notes that the:

> assumed cultural and political differences between sexology as a discourse in which matters of 'illegitimate sexualities' are legitimately studied and pornography as a discourse in which the same matter takes shape more furtively, collapse in their shared relationship to empire. (Arondekar 2009, 106)

A more recent approach has been to view pornography and sexology as distinct genres. Projit Mukharji in his recent article on Bengali sexologist Abul Hasanat, who is also an actor in this article, briefly approaches the topic of Hasanat's views on pornography while contextualizing Hasanat's sexology against the commodities mentioned in his work, more specifically pornographic images (Mukharji 2020, 1208). Mukharji argues that Hasanat, 'while not morally against pornography, titillating pictures or "sexy films" was concerned about the extent of the commercialism ... he did not condemn the material *tout court*, but rather expressed anxiety overs its commoditized nature' (2020, 1208). Mukharji's article does not venture into the details of Hasanat's 'thinking on visual erotica' (2020, 1208) but makes it clear that Hasanat's contention extended to the commercialization of pornography and not its content per se.

In this article, I expand on this existing scholarship while simultaneously revising the way in which the relationship between pornography and sexology has been understood in the context of early to mid twentieth-century Bengal. I make two distinct but related arguments. First, I argue that sexologists distinguished themselves from authors of popular erotica by framing sexology as a scientific and educational field. I show how pornography played a significant historical role in the consolidation and legitimization of the field of sexual science in Bengal as sexology came to be framed against the backdrop of a widely proliferating printscape of Bengali erotica. Bengali sexologists were also aware of the commercial popularity of pornography. The positioning of sexology in opposition to pornography was a strategic choice in order to directly intervene in the commercialized erotic print market, make use of the pre-existing networks of print capital, and carve out a distinct space for sexology.

Second, I argue that this privileging of sexology vis-à-vis pornography overlapped with the politics of class and respectability in Bengal. Late nineteenth and early twentieth-century Bengal witnessed a movement of literary reformism championed by Bengali elites who aspired to reform Bengali by expunging the colloquial, racy, and rustic elements from the language. This movement for sanitizing literature was not unique to Bengal but found its earliest expression in the state in the mid nineteenth century, which led to the passage of the first anti-obscenity regulation in India in 1857 (Heath 2010, 165–166). Scholars have shown how elites policed erotic literature by censoring texts and enforcing anti-obscenity regulations (Banerjee 1987; Ghosh 1998; Gupta 2002; Heath 2010). I argue that sexology offered an avenue to the elites to not just police the sexual but also to discipline and colonize it.[2] Sexology wed sexuality with science and medicine, which were markers of middle-class respectability and by the end of the nineteenth century in Bengal had emerged as cultural symbols of an incipient national consciousness (Prakash 1999). Sexology was authoritatively cast as the only field that was scientifically equipped to produce knowledge on sex and suppress the influence of pornography. I therefore argue that sexology offered the middle-class and upper-class Bengalis a means to colonize sex and mobilize sexology in order to perpetuate the middle-class sexual ethic based on conjugality and sexual restraint and further consolidate their class status.

I focus on the writings of two Bengali sexologists, Abul Hasanat and Nripendra Kumar Basu. Both were middle-class public intellectuals in the first half of the twentieth century. Hasanat not only condemned authors of Bengali pornography for unscrupulous profiteering but also branded their writings as 'trash' and 'ephemeral'. He presented sexology and sex education as epitomized in his writings as normative as well as more effective in countering pornography than anti-obscenity regulations and censorship. Basu, like Hasanat, underlined sexology as the most modern and scientific means to produce knowledge on sexuality. Despite his middle-class position, Basu differed significantly from Hasanat in his perspectives on the proliferation of the pornographic and argued that anti-obscenity regulations represented the hypocrisy of the upper classes. Basu's views demonstrate that despite advocating sexology as a specialized and normative field, the sexual politics of the middle class in Bengal was not an ideological monolith and revealed significant cleavages. I begin this article by providing a brief description of the disciplining of the erotic printscape and the rise of sexology in Bengal. I then proceed to analyze the relationship between pornography and sexology by studying the writings of Hasanat and Basu in detail.

The disciplining of the erotic printscape and the emergence of sexology in early to mid twentieth-century Bengal

The earliest instance of a print market in Bengal grew around the Battala region in North Calcutta, in the early nineteenth century. The establishment of Battala was the result of local entrepreneurs who initiated the book trade after the advent of print in Bengal. It was only in the middle of the nineteenth century that the commercial print market boomed with the availability of cheap print technology and a wider number of readers (Ghosh 1998, 177). Battala represented popular literary tastes of the era and the erotic featured prominently among the literature churned out of the Battala press. Some of the most popular genres included satirical prose, farces, scandal, mystery novels, sex periodicals, and erotica. The Battala press churned out erotic fiction in Bengali inspired by Victorian erotica and also produced one of the earliest pornographic works of the era (Biswas 2013, 49). The earliest pornographic periodical with the title *Sambad Rasoraj* [*Amatory Briefs*] was published from Battala in 1849 and ran for two years (2013, 49). The patrons of the periodical were drawn from some of the most well-known families of Calcutta and the stories contained in it portrayed sexual scandals and transgressions involving incest among some of the most well-to-do families of Calcutta (2013, 49). Erotic scandals particularly involving the rich and famous were a staple of the Battla genre (Bhattacharya 2020). Rather than including graphic descriptions of sexual intercourse, nineteenth-century Bengali erotica represented women either as a coy seductress or sexual victims (Biswas 2013, 49). Other aspects of popular Bengali erotic cultures were centred around songs and sayings of prostitutes and their lifestyle in nineteenth-century Calcutta (Banerjee 1987, 1200). The consumers of such erotica were not just men. One particular genre of Bengali print erotica consumed by women were songs and jokes that were customarily enjoyed during wedding nights called *basarghar* songs and jokes (Ghosh 1998, 185). These songs and jokes were strewn with sexual innuendoes and their style was coarse and abusive (1998, 185). Nineteenth-century Bengali folk songs were generally abundant with jokes about the human body, eating, defecation, and fornication (Banerjee 1987, 1201). Such erotica was not just a means of casual jocular or sensuous fun, but was also a weapon in the hands of the lower classes to poke fun at the moral hypocrisy of the elite classes. The Battala genre of writing, as seen from the stated examples, represented an erotic culture that was inclusive, fluid, and diverse. Sexology, which would eventually challenge the dominance of the Battala genre, on the other hand, represented a sexual ethic circumscribed by its principles of norms and pathologies.

The first attempt to survey and catalogue the Bengali print market in Calcutta was made in 1857 by missionary educator Reverend James Long. He published an elaborate report in which he identified that out of 322 books published in Calcutta, 13 of them were classified as 'erotic' with 14,250 copies in circulation (Ghosh 1998, 183). Long's revelation of the widespread circulation of erotic literature in Bengali led to the passage of the earliest legislation against obscenity with the enactment of the Obscene Publications Act of 1857. In the second half of the nineteenth century the campaign against obscenity had acquired a wider imperial and national significance. By the 1880s, the word 'pornography' had become part of the English vocabulary following the public debates about pornography resulting from the Orientalist translations of the *Kamasutra* and the *Arabian Nights* in the 1880s by Richard Burton and F. F. Arbuthnot and the publication of the English translation of Émile Zola's novels (Colligan 2002, 34). While Henry Vizetelly, the publisher of Zola's novels in London, was convicted for obscenity in 1888, Burton and Arbuthnot's translations led to raging debates about pornography but did not invite outright obscenity charges. In India, the impact of such imperial campaigns against the pornographic could be seen during the seizure and global crackdown on English and vernacular translations of Émile Zola's novels, particularly in railway book stalls believed to be stocked with such obscene literature (Heath 2010, 152). By 1925, colonial India already had a panoply of legal provisions against pornography, the most significant of them being the Obscene Publications Act of 1925, which was the revised version of the earlier obscenity act, passed in 1857 (Gupta 2002; Heath 2010). In addition, there were also the Sea Customs and the Post Office Act, which prevented the circulation of any obscene material (Gupta 2002, 31; Heath 2010, 170).

Despite the passage of a series of anti-obscenity legislations, it has been argued by scholars such as Deana Heath that the British state in India did not undertake an all-encompassing biopolitical project to regulate the obscene (Heath 2010, 164). This did not mean, argues Heath, that the state did not act against obscenity as there were multiple obscenity trials held from the closing years of the nineteenth century (Heath 2010, 167). The police also routinely asked publishers to surrenders texts classified as 'obscene' and issued orders for the censoring portions of such texts (2010, 167). However, the strongest impetus for regulating the obscene and the most sustained morality campaigns were conducted not by the British state but by civil society organizations such as missionary and social hygiene groups, reform organizations, and increasingly by elite Indians themselves. Elite Bengali social reformers created the Society for the Suppression of Public Obscenity in 1873 with the hope that that society 'shall aid the executive in the suppression of the most subtle forms of public vice' (Biswas 2013, 50). The society was hailed as an important symbol of 'native progress' and a means of preventing the native languages from running a risk of becoming 'polluted and polluting'.[3] This campaign of sanitization of literature spearheaded by the elites was not unique to Bengal and was visible in print cultures across India.[4] The sensual and the erotic were particularly subjected to the ire of the elite reformers as they were considered to be expressions of debility, femininity, and the rustic coarseness of the lower classes. A standard feature of elite literary reformism was the expunging of the erotic. Sexology, however, provided a means through which the upper and middle classes could not just censor the sexual but also discipline and colonize it.

Bengali sexologists at the turn of the twentieth century had to encounter a print market which was already teeming with books on sex churned out of the Battala press. By the 1920s, however, there had been a shift in the dynamics of the print market as a result of the anti-obscenity campaigns of the colonial state together with the efforts of the literary reformers. This did not lead to a complete disappearance of the Battala literature but a large part of their circulation went underground and had to remain surreptitious (Biswas 2013, 51–52). It was not coincidental that its place was taken by sexology, which now benefited from the same network of print capitalism that had previously allowed the Battala press to flourish. Sexology, in sharp contrast to the unrestrained eroticism of the Battala genre, represented a sexuality that had been disciplined and colonized to reflect elite and middle-class sexual values and sentiments.[5] Sexology represented an association of sexuality with science and medicine. Gyan Prakash (1999), in his seminal work *Another Reason*, argues that by the end of nineteenth century, science and medicine in Bengal had been appropriated by the elite not just as symbols of Western colonial dominance, but as instruments of modernity, social reform, cultural progress, and as the most potent symbol for achieving an autonomous national consciousness. Sexology enabled sexuality to be rescued from the realm of the bawdy, the colloquial, and the racy, represented by the Battala publications. While the unchecked sexual culture of Battala allowed for the production of literature that shed light on the sexual hypocrisy of the elites, sexology endowed scientific legitimacy to the policing of subaltern sexualities.[6] Sexology enabled elite Bengalis to initiate a eugenic discourse on sexual reform as well as imagine a future secured by racial and national fitness. Durba Mitra has extensively studied the writings of Bengali upper-caste and upper-class men of the era who deployed theories of sexual science to brand every expression of non-marital and non-reproductive female sexuality as deviant and classified such women as prostitutes (Mitra 2015, 2020a). Mitra argues that not only did this patriarchal rationale stigmatize female sexuality, but the knowledge of deviant female sexuality centred on the figure of the prostitute also played a critical role in the constitution of diverse fields of modern social thought (Mitra 2020a, 8). It is undeniable that most sexologists viewed female sexual autonomy as severely pathological and disapproved of it to a degree that did not extend to men. But even with respect to advice on sexual health targeted towards men, almost every Bengali sexologist upheld a middle-class sexual ethic that identified marital conjugal bond as the most legitimate site for the expression of sexuality and also propagated the value of restraint and balance in sharp opposition to the world of unbridled sexuality of nineteenth-century Bengali erotica. As sexology counterposed itself as the antithesis to Bengali pornography, a study of the perspectives of Bengali sexologists towards the genre becomes imperative in order to understand the historical process through which sexology supplanted Bengali erotica to represent a vision of the middle-class disciplining of sex. In the subsequent sections of this article, I delve into the sexological writings of two Bengali sexologists – Abul Hasanat and Nripendra Kumar Basu – in order to unpack the relationship between pornography and sexology and also understand the role played by pornography in the constitution of the field of sexology. An exploration of this relationship will also provide a fresh perspective on this history of sex education. Both of the sexologists that I focus on reinforced the edifying and pedagogical nature of sexology to distinguish the field from pornography.

The pornographic and the sexological in Abul Hasanat's writings

> Eighty percent of the books which bear the stamp of sex literature are nothing but pure rhapsodies on lust. These books only serve the purpose of exciting human passions. It is the duty of the state to protect its members from the harmful influence exercised by such books. (Hasanat 1955, 47)

Abul Hasanat's full name was S. Abul Hasanat M. Ismail and he was a police officer in undivided Bengal who, by 1957, had risen to the position of Inspector General of Police in East Pakistan (now Bangladesh), a position by virtue of which he was in charge of the police of the entire province (Hasanat 1957). He was a prolific author and published a number of books on sexology and birth control, the most famous among them being *Sachitra Jouna Bigyan* [*Illustrated Sexual Science*] first published in 1935. He subsequently translated the work into Hindi, Urdu, and English and the book ran several editions in Bengali and was expanded to two volumes. The English version appeared in 1955 and was called *All About Sex, Love and Happy Marriage*. Between 1950 and 1955 he served on the editorial board of the *International Journal on Sexology*, which was a leading international sexual science journal edited by Dr A. P. Pillay and published in Bombay. In addition to sexology, he wrote extensively on crime and criminology and produced a monograph on the subject, *Crime and Criminal Justice* (Hasanat 1939). His articles on criminology were also published in international journals of police, crime, and law. Projit Mukharji mentions that in one of his last published works in 1978, Hasanat was described as a 'Criminologist, Sexologist, Sociologist, Humanist, Rationalist, Psychiatrist – and what not' (Mukharji 2020, 1199). Mukharji demonstrates that despite embodying multiple roles, if there was something that remained constant throughout Hasanat's life, it was his class status. 'He remained roughly upper middle class throughout the period', argues Mukharji as he contextualizes Hasanat's middle-classness through a study of 'commodities and a culture of commodity consumption' manifested in his sexological and literary oeuvre (Mukharji 2020, 1200–1202). As mentioned in the Introduction, Mukharji briefly mentions Hasanat's view on visual erotica but does not elaborate on the theme. In this section, not only do I elaborate on Hasanat's views on pornography, but I also show how his stance of privileging sexology and sex education in order to counter the pornographic further reinforced his class identity as it was reflective of the larger middle-class discourse of disciplining sexuality as well as consolidating the authority of sexology as the normative field of inquiry on sex.

As a police officer and criminologist, Hasanat was familiar with the legal provisions of the obscenity regulations and claimed in his criminological work that 'sex novels and literature depict sexual orgies and exciting situation and in many cases verge on obscenity' (Hasanat 1939, 238). A few nefarious individuals, he argued, had misused the natural sexual curiosity of the young to write obscene books on sex in Bengali (Hasanat 1936a, 70). This was particularly deplorable as he felt that those who used the mother tongue to compose obscene literature and unscrupulously profit from it could never be beneficial to society (1936a, 70). He noted that the police and court were regularly acting against this genre of books and he called upon the state to censor such texts.

Despite advocating for an intensive censorship of obscene texts, Hasanat was cognizant of the misuse of censorship laws. He recollected how works of the prominent British sexologist Havelock Ellis had been at the receiving end of the moral policing of the state:

> Many sexologists on the other hand, have lamented the strict censoring which every civilized country has been compelled to exercise over books written on sex ... The state is often likely to overdo things in respect of censoring. A case in point is the suppression of one of Havelock Ellis' books and the unjust punishment given to its publisher by Sir Charles Hall. (Hasanat 1955, 47)

This instance of the state being 'often likely to overdo things in respect of censoring' did not, however, lead him to entirely negate censorship. Instead, he wanted the state to be more responsible towards what it chose to censor. He wrote:

> The state ought to see to it that along with what is trash and of ephemeral value, that which is priceless and of lasting importance is not destroyed. It should be the duty of the state to encourage scientific discussion of sex, as this will immensely conduce to human welfare. (Hasanat 1955, 48)

As Hasanat tried to evaluate the effectiveness of censorship, he ended up drawing a sharper distinction between the 'scientific discussion of sex' and literature that was 'trash and of ephemeral value'. His appeal to the state to protect and encourage sexology, as it would be conducive to human welfare, shows how pornography was antithetically positioned by Bengali sexologists in order to reinforce the scientific credentials of sexology. Not only did Hasanat demand for the censorship of pornography, he presented sex education offered by sexology texts such as his as the ideal and only permanent solution to the problem of obscenity.

Hasanat contemplated that repressive legislation or an overtly moralistic position alone could never be able to counter the influence obscene literature (Hasanat 1936a, 62). He felt that repressive legislations would only have the adverse effect of driving such literature underground, which would pose a greater menace to the state (1936a, 62). Purists, he declared, falsely assumed that all that was obscene and immoral would disappear with the expurgation of pornography. This was a flawed approach for Hasanat, as the seizure of all sex literature would not do away with the sexual curiosity of men and women. Sex education together with an open and frank attitude to sex represented an ideal solution for him:

> Neither the moral censure of society nor police punishment could extinguish the natural sexual curiosity of men and women. Educating people about the scientific and essential facts of sex would be the only way to ensure an ordered, restrained, knowledgeable and healthy sex life. (Hasanat 1936a, 63)

Historians of sexology in India such as Ishita Pande have argued that the shift in 'reproductive temporality' introduced by the delay in marriage following the passage of the Child Marriage Restraint Act, 1929 created an avenue for the introduction of sex education. She argues that 'global/Hindu' sexologists rendered *brahmacharya* as adolescence, which provided an opportunity for 'the surveillance of infantile sexuality, the management of masturbation, and the pedagogization of sex' (Pande 2020a, 197).[7] However, one cannot also discount the role of the social hygiene movement in India in highlighting the need for sex education and the management of child sexuality. Sexologists like Hasanat were clearly influenced by the social hygiene movement and almost every Bengali sexology manual of the period included a chapter or section on social and sex hygiene. There has been very limited scholarly engagement with the history of social hygiene in India but it assumes immense significance for my argument because not only did the advocates of social hygiene push for the dissemination of sex education, but they did so in order to specifically counter the influence of the pornographic.[8] The social hygiene movement had gained credence in Britain as well as the USA during and after the years of the First World War and aimed to prevent venereal disease, stamp out prostitution, as well as disseminate sex education.[9] Missionary educators and physicians were some of the strongest advocates of social hygiene in India and propagated educational material published by the British Social Hygiene Council (Zimmerman 2015, 29–30). Organizations like the National Christian Council advocated for the introduction of social hygiene-based sex instruction in the biology curriculum at schools and even encouraged parents as well pastors to assist in providing such instruction (Own Correspondent 1930, 15). It was argued that sex education from authoritative sources would prevent children from picking up the wrong ideas from their peers or 'the highly sexed novels of the railway stalls and the loose standards of the cinema'.[10] It was not just missionary educators but also physicians in elite colonial medical institutions who were prominent proponents for the introduction of socially hygiene-based sex education. Lt Colonel Dr Jelal M. Shah, a professor of venereology at Grant Medical College, Bombay, stated that most children even prior to puberty had already acquired some information on sex and many 'fell victim to conduct and action in the sexual sphere' (Anonymous 1938, 5). Arguing that while it was not morbid for children to possess sexual impulses, he underlined the need to equip them with scientific sex instruction from the right sources. He acknowledged the presence of pornographic literature in the market, and felt that 'it was necessary to have some check on such literature' (1938, 5). He regretted that until recently sexology was a neglected field in India and declared sex education by specially trained teachers as vital in dealing with the 'problem of venereal disease' (1938, 5).

Hasanat also bemoaned the lack of sexology education in schools and colleges and envisaged a social hygiene-based discourse on sex education. He justified providing sex education to children based on their 'natural curiosity towards the subject' and argued that children were not 'immune from sexual impulse and excitement' as they witnessed the mating of pets and other domestic animals since childhood (Hasanat 1936a, 63–64). Withholding sex information from children was foolish, argued Hasanat, as they would turn to 'peers and obscene literature to satisfy their sexual curiosity as such sources could be dangerous and unreliable' (1936a, 64–65). The lack of Bengali books on sexology and sex education had caused him great lament, he argued and had compelled him to publish the present work (1936a, 70). He characterized his book as a comprehensive work on sexology that had been produced after consultation with classical Indic sex literature together with Western sexological tracts and based on feedback from his readers (1936a, 71). Rejecting the existing corpus of Bengali sexuality literature as inadequate at best and pernicious at worst, he explicitly presented his work as an alternative to the readers from which they could obtain authentic, comprehensive, and scientific information on sex.

Hasanat's text, as the name suggests, was illustrated. He provided illustrations not just for the anatomical representations of the sexual organs (Figures 1 and 2), but also for practices such as wearing a condom (Figure 3) or douching as a part of menstrual cleanliness (Figure 4). Also included in the books were illustrations of sexual positions (Figures 5 and 6). With reference to the images of the sex positions, Hasanat (1936b, 158) stated that he was including these pictures at the suggestions of his readers. He remarked how ordinarily such images depicting sex positions had been deemed indecent and were generally sold at inflated prices (1936b, 158). He clarified that these particular images, which he had adapted from an American publication, had been included as they were prepared in

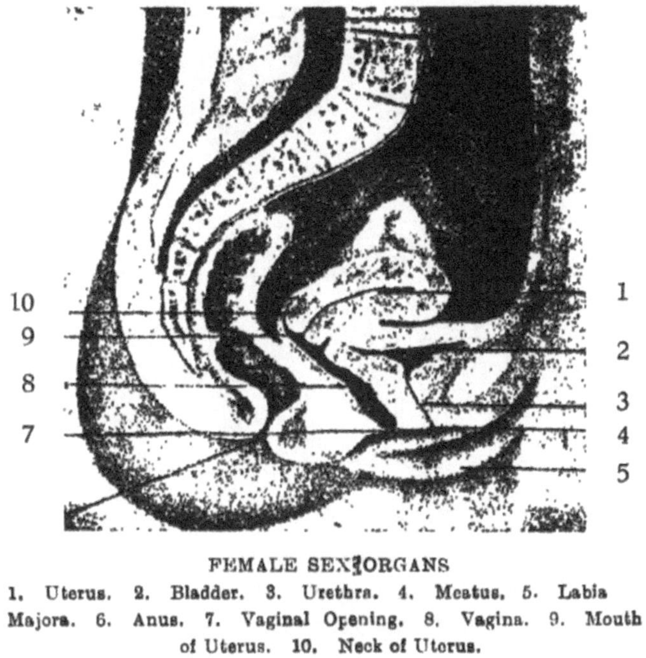

Figure 1. Female sexual organs (Hasanat 1955, 97).

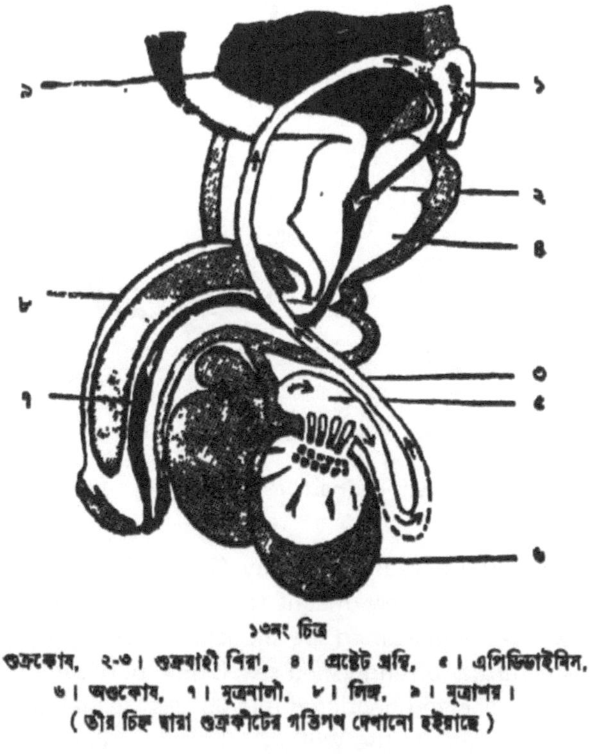

Figure 2. Male sexual organs (Hasanat 1936a, 87).

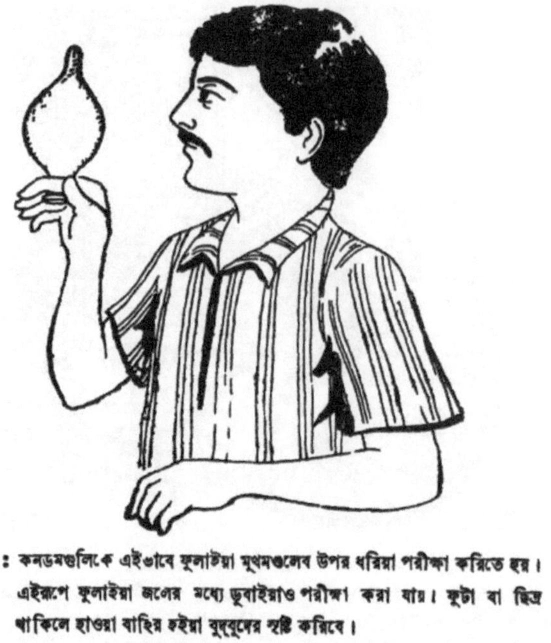

Figure 3. Illustration of checking a condom for perforations (Hasanat 1936b, 52).

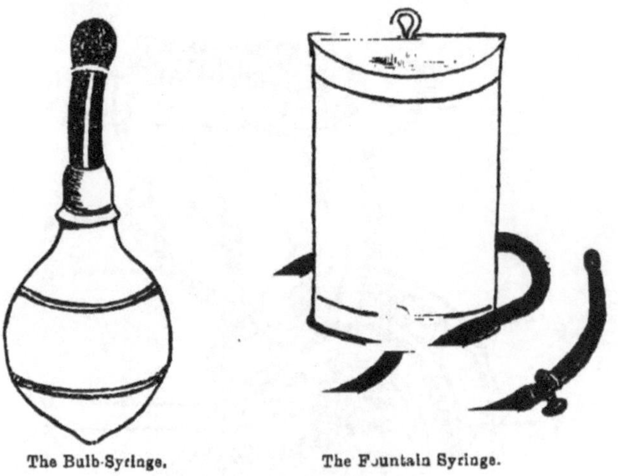

Figure 4. Syringes for menstrual hygiene (Hasanat 1955, 170).

'good taste' and were represented with 'clarity' (1936b, 158). These illustrations, as indicated in the following pages, were meant to entrench the scientific and educational quality of the text. Images demarcating specific sexual positions for men and women produced in 'good taste' further distinguished sexological publication like those of Hasanat from pornography and reflected gendered middle-class sexual moralities.

In the next section, I analyze the writings of another Bengali sexologist, Nripendra Kumar Basu. I show how, despite sharing Hasanat's view on the need for a specialized

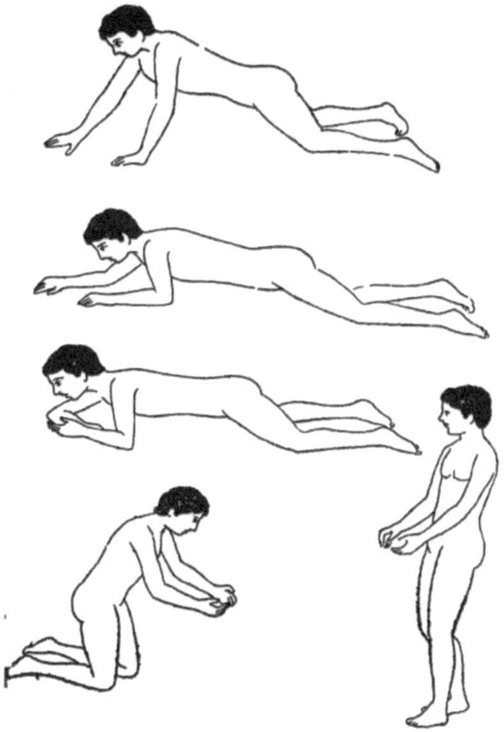

Figure 5. Sex positions for the man (Hasanat 1936b, 159).

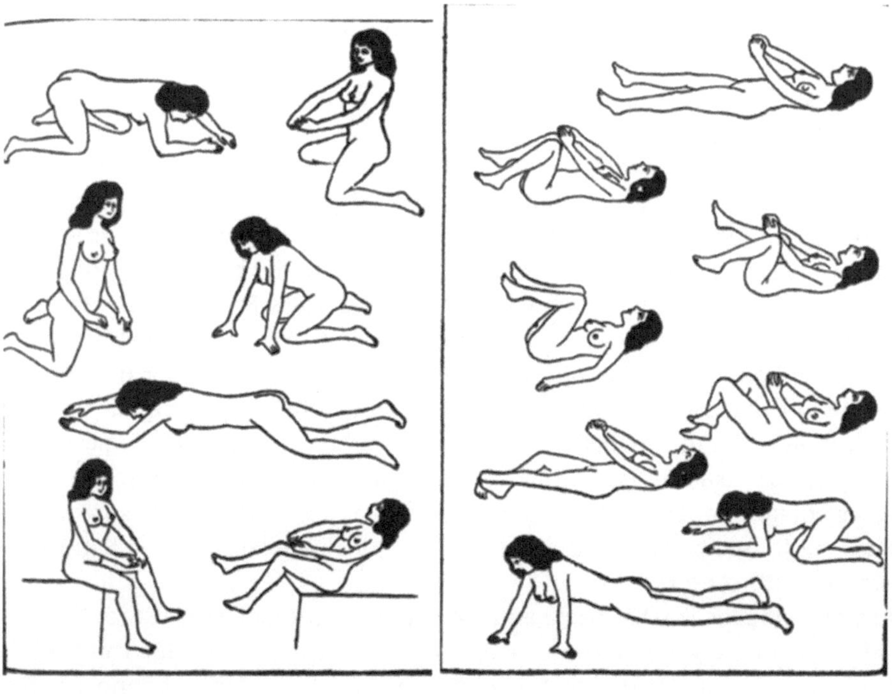

Figure 6. Sex positions for the woman (Hasanat 1936b, 160–161).

field of sexology, Basu had an entirely different perspective on the proliferation of pornography, which revealed cleavages within the sexual morality of the middle class.

Intersection of class, pornography and sexology in Nripendra Kumar Basu's *Encyclopaedia of Sex*

Nripendra Kumar Basu (1898–1979) was a public intellectual who wrote extensively on sexuality between the years 1930 and 1965 (Mitra 2020a, 47). Although not much is known about Basu's life, it can be gleaned from his own work that he studied in Shantiniketan during his formative years (Basu 1938, 51). Durba Mitra, in *Indian Sex Life*, informs us that he was a 'self-made man who migrated to Calcutta from rural Bengal' and eventually became a public intellectual in the 1920s (2020a, 47). He was a prolific author who wrote in Bengali and English and published close to 30 books, which not only included works on sexology, birth control, and marriage but also detective fiction.[11] Some of his works include *History of Prostitution in India* (1933), *Jouboner Jadupuri* [*The Magical City of Youth*] (1936), *Jouno Biswakosh* [*Encyclopaedia of Sex*] (1938) in three volumes, *Cupid Joins the War* (1944), *Koibo Katha Kane* [*I Will Whisper it in Your Ears*] (1946), *Nari Bipathe Jaye Kano* [*Why does the Woman Stray*] (1947), and *Ogo Premik Pita o Mata* [*Advice Manual on Parenting*] (1948). Mitra's scholarship is the first to engage with Basu's work and she mainly focuses on his historical account of prostitution, situating it among other works on the subject which were steeped in philology and used the figure of the prostitute as a symbol of social degradation and all 'deviant female sexuality' (Mitra 2020a, 47–52). There has, however, until now been no engagement with the larger corpus of Basu's work on sexuality and sexual science. Therefore, in addition to analyzing the relationship between class, pornography, and sexology in Basu's *Jouno Biswakosh* [*Encyclopaedia of Sex*], my aim in this section is also draw attention to the importance of Basu as a prolific Bengali sexologist. My analysis is based on the substantial introduction to the first volume of Basu's *Encyclopaedia of Sex*.

Like Hasanat, Basu was critical of the commodification of pornography and repeated Hasanat's charge of unscrupulous authors taking advantage of the sexual impulses of men and women by flooding the markets with pornographic works in order to make quick money (Basu 1938, 57). However, Basu's response to the proliferation of pornography is more nuanced, especially from the perspective of class. Basu is resistant to viewing pornography simply as 'trash' or pernicious literature. His divergence from Hasanat on the subject of pornography can be interpreted as a reflection of the cleavages within elite intellectuals on the issues of obscenity and pornography. In *Purifying Empire*, Deana Heath has shown how the Bengali middle class did not represent an ideological monolith on the matter of sexual morality, but rather comprised 'ideological discursive strands which converged, competed and contradicted each other' (2010, 197). Basu's divergence from Hasanat despite belonging to the same class of elite intellectuals in Bengal can be understood in this context.

Basu argued that unlike the shame and secrecy which shrouded sex in the Middle Ages, the modern youth was eager to know more about sex (Basu 1938, 35–36). This sexual curiosity, however, he argued had upset the elites, who until then had a monopoly over sexuality. He cited the German sexologist Max Hodann in order to strengthen his argument:

> So long as a small inner circle of the governing class amused itself by spicing sex with literature, all was well. The Courts of princes and prelates up to the end of the eighteenth century were not sanctuaries of morality. But when the masses were able to read and to choose their readings – danger threatened! Books priced at round two Guineas are seldom attacked, but six penny pamphlets with equivalent material – are obscene. The Purity Crusades of the various and numerous societies for the suppression of vice are the negative instruments of our special phase of social development, and therefore dearer far [*sic*] to those in authority over us than the efforts of other progressive societies ... [*sic*]. (Basu 1938, 36–37)

Basu's citation of Hodann and his remarks on the hypocrisy of the 'governing class', 'Purity Crusades', and the authorities with respect to erotic literature can be interpreted as a scathing commentary on the politics of sexual morality championed by the elites in Bengal from the end of the nineteenth century onwards. He repeatedly invoked the sexual hypocrisy of the upper classes as the primary reason for censorship and the regulations against obscenity. His arguments against the sexual double-standards of the elite had a transnational basis. He cited the examples of the works of Henrik Ibsen, George Bernard Shaw, and Havelock Ellis which had been considered obscene (Basu 1938, 38). He made specific mention of Radclyffe Hall's queer novel *Well of Loneliness* and D. H. Lawrence's *Lady Chatterley's Lover* as works that had been stigmatized as they gave expression to repressed female sexualities (Basu 1938, 38). He argued that despite restricting the common masses from accessing such literature, several copies of these books were in circulation among the upper classes, amongst whom there was huge demand for them (1938, 38). It is also pertinent to note that Basu, unlike Hasanat, did not take a moral stance on pornography. Basu likened the proliferation of pornography among the masses as an instance of the democratization of erotic writings, made possible due to cheap print and increased access to literature, which he viewed as a symbol of progress (1938, 38). Basu was convinced, nonetheless, that despite the pressure exerted by the morality campaigners, a desire as natural and intrinsic as sexuality could never be suppressed (1938, 40). Contrary to the expectations of the upholders of sexual morality, Basu argued that modernity and the 'age of reason' had stripped the veil of secrecy and ignorance which demanded a clandestine attitude to sex (1938, 35). In such a liberated age, knowledge about sexuality, remarked Basu, whether it be correct, incorrect, or exaggerated, could be found in literature, theatre, correspondences, and most crucially in the literary market (1938, 35). Basu identified the emergence of sexual science and its popularity as a consequence of the robust demand for sexual knowledge and the ubiquitous presence of sexuality in every aspect of society.

Modernity and the enhanced desire for sexual knowledge, remarked Basu (1938, 41), were the reasons why a pre-modern sexual text like *Ratishastra* was insufficient to satiate the sexual curiosity of his contemporary readers. He viewed a text on sexual science as the appropriate response to his audience as they 'desired a more advanced and scientific source on sexuality, something which was more compelling, intellectual and thoughtful' (1938, 41). Basu argued that just as physics or chemistry empowered students with technical knowledge and practical skills, sexual science also represented a specialized and practical field which ensured that adults had fulfilling conjugal lives (1938, 41). Basu, despite his differences with Hasanat, similarly advocated for the introduction of sex education among the youth (1938, 41). He was also a strong proponent of the idea that children possessed sexual impulses, and hence called for the management of their sexuality as well (1938,

42–44). He recounted the countless examples of countries in the West that had introduced some form of sex instruction, whereas 'in the same time during the past fifty years there has not been a single book on sexual science or sex education published in Bengali which would be adequate to prescribe to students' (1938, 55–56). He lamented that while the disciplines of literature, history, and science had flourished in Bengal, a field as vital as sexual science had produced miniscule scholarship (1938, 57). Even among the few existing authors of Bengali works on sexual science and sex education, Basu (1938, 57) felt that the majority them were ignorant and harboured unscientific attitudes. Mirroring Hasanat's perspectives, he argued that many such authors appropriated sexology as a façade to unscrupulously cater to the sexual impulses of young men and women and wanted and profit from such an exercise (1938, 57). Adopting Hasanat's strategy, he positioned his work as an attempt to fill a void within the genre of Bengali sexual science. His encyclopaedia, which he described as an 'exhaustive collection of all the information on love and sex', would serve to provide to Bengali readers a sexological text at par with Havelock Ellis' *Psychology of Sex* and Kraft Ebbing's *Pscyopathia Sexualis* (1938, 57–58). Basu's perspectives represent a complex intersection of the issues of class, pornography, and sexual science. On the one hand, he associated the proliferation of pornography with the democratization of sexuality across class, which he argued enhanced the desire for sexual knowledge. On the other hand, like Hasanat, he also reflected the middle-class preoccupation of delineating a specialized and modern scientific field on sex, managing child sexuality as well as disciplining conjugal sexuality.

Conclusion

Literary moral campaigns championed by the elites came to increasingly target the sexual by the end of the nineteenth century. Existing literature has shown how elite attempts to counter the sexual revolved around censorship and the enforcement of anti-obscenity regulations. In this article, I have focused on early to mid twentieth-century colonial Bengal and argued that the emergence of sexology allowed the elites and middle class to not just counter the sexual, but also discipline and colonize it. In sharp contrast to the diverse and fluid sexual cultures, represented by nineteenth-century erotic Bengali literature churned out by the Battala press, sexology presented its normative perspective on sexuality as the most scientific and authoritative.

I also argue that Bengali sexologists distinguished themselves from pornographic writers as they strove to supplant Bengali erotica and consolidate their own position in the Bengali print market. In this respect, I highlight how sexologists drew inspiration from the social hygiene discourse which was popularized in India by missionary educators as well as physicians. Sexologists following social hygienists reinforced the pedagogic intent of their work in order to counter the pornographic. This was precisely the strategy adopted by one of my actors, Bengali sexologist Abul Hasanat. Citing the obscenity charges levelled against Havelock Ellis, he appealed to the state to strongly distinguish between sexology and that which was 'trash' and of 'ephemeral value'. He further argued that repressive legislations would never be completely sufficient to control the sexual curiosity of men and women. He presented his own sexological work as a scientific and pedagogical tool which would provide authentic information to his readers and satiate their sexual curiosity. However, the Bengali middle class did not represent an ideological monolith in respect to their views on pornography and this is proven by the perspectives of Nripendra Kumar Basu, who is the other actor in this article. Basu viewed the anti-obscenity regulations as an instance of the hypocrisy of the upper classes and a ploy to resist the ever-increasing proliferation of pornographic texts among all classes. He viewed the emergence of sexology as a result of the democratization of sexual print cultures which enhanced the demand for sexual knowledge. Despite his differences with Hasanat, he echoed his views about the need to control the profiteering resulting from unscrupulous sale of pornographic material to unsuspecting men and women. Likewise, Basu also underlined the need for a specialized field to study the sexual and presented his works as filling a void in the Bengali market for sexology books. The works of the two Bengali sexologists in the wider context of the Bengali sexual printscape of the early to mid twentieth century show how pornography came to undergird and counterpose the scientific and pedagogic status of the emerging field of sexology.

Notes

1. The usage of the term 'vernacular sexology' has been debated. Durba Mitra argues that the term 'vernacular' reinforces the colonial power hierarchy and the logic of othering of all Indian languages. On the other hand, scholars such as Charu Gupta, through her work on subaltern sexologists writing in Hindi, have shown how the vernacular could also play a subversive function. Ishita Pande, in her introduction to a recent collection of essays on sexology in South Asia, delves into this debate in detail. For more, see Gupta (2020), Mitra (2020b), and Pande (2020b). In this article, an interest in the 'vernacular' displayed by the British as well elite Indians conveys their preoccupation of wanting to discipline and sanitize Bengali, which also explains why both of my actors underscore the necessity of publishing a Bengali sexological work. The distinguishing of 'popular' Bengali erotica and the 'scientific' credentials of sexology reflects the perspectives of my actors and is tied to my argument about sexology presenting an elite authoritative vision of knowledge production and bringing together science and sexuality as markers of middle-class respectability.
2. Sexology introduced a normative framework which argued that only the specialized field of sexual science had the legitimacy to make any claims on sex. I refer to this process of disciplining sex as a result of the emergence of sexology as the 'colonization' of sex. I have adopted this concept from Sabine Frühstück's work on the history of sexology in Japan, *Colonizing Sex* (Frühstück 2003).
3. This quotation appeared in the missionary-run newspaper in Bengal, *The Friend of India*, approximately in the year 1873 (cited in Banerjee 1987, 1204).
4. In addition to Bengali and Hindi, elite demands for literary reform emerged in several Indian languages during the late nineteenth and early twentieth centuries. For Urdu, see Waheed (2014); for Tamil, see Ramaswamy (1997); and for Telegu, see Mantena (2013).
5. This was true not just of Bengal, but sexology in India generally reflected the values of elites and middle classes. Shrikant Botre (2017) has shown how the emergence of Marathi sexology can be tied to upper-caste impulses to regulate the sexual. Also, Ishita Pande has shown how 'global/Hindu' sexologists represented an 'unruly two-way traffic between Western and Eastern epistemologies' as they projected sexology as an ancient indigenous science (2020a, 171). Pande argues that as the Child Marriage Restraint Act, 1929 raised the marital age for girls to 14 years, it created an age-stratified sexual morality separating the child from the adult. This enabled upper-caste 'global/Hindu' sexologists to further consolidate their caste hierarchy as Brahmacharya, the earliest stage of the Hindu life cycle, applicable to upper-caste Hindus was recast as adolescence and rendered timeless, universal, and resonant with the global and 'secular sciences of the body' (2020a, 169–206). In addition, Haynes and Botre have shown how the festering anxiety among middle-class men resulting from shifts in the age of marriage and the rise of the companionate conjugal model led them to approach and write to sexologists. See Botre and Haynes (2017).

6. Sanjam Ahluwalia has shown how middle-class and upper-class Indian men from the early twentieth century onwards used evidence of increasing population levels from the census as an instance of indiscriminate reproduction among the lower castes and Muslims, and policed their sexual practices by propagating sexual hygiene discourse and birth control techniques. See Ahluwalia (2007, 25).
7. For details on 'global/Hindu sexologists', *brahmacharya*, see note 5.
8. Stephen Legg, in his work on prostitution in inter-war India, has shown how social hygiene influenced colonial policy towards prostitution. For more, see Legg (2013). In addition, Alison Bashford has also shown how social hygiene influenced by sexology, eugenics and contagious disease regulations assumed imperial significance. For more, see Bashford (2004).
9. For more on the social hygiene movement in Britain, see Hall (2004); for the USA, see Luker (1998).
10. This quotation attributed to a missionary school teacher has been cited in Zimmerman's book on the global history of sex education, *Too Hot to Handle* (Zimmerman 2015, 29).
11. Amitranjan Basu has collated the complete bibliography of Nripendra Kumar Basu's work. See https://www.scribd.com/document/47395798/Selected-Bibliography-of-Nripendra-Kumar-Basu.

Acknowledgements

The author would like to thank the two anonymous reviewers for their feedback which helped immensely in strengthening the argument of the article. The author would also like to thank the editors of this special issue, Darshana Sreedhar Mini and Anirban Baishya, for their suggestions and support during the writing of this article. The author would like to thank Projit Bihari Mukharji for introducing him to the works of Abul Hasanat as well as for his support while writing this article.

Disclosure statement

No potential conflict of interest was reported by the author.

References

Ahluwalia, Sanjam. 2007. *Reproductive Restraints: Birth Control in India, 1877–1947*. Urbana: University of Illinois Press.

Ahluwalia, Sanjam. 2018. 'Tyranny of Orgasm: Global Governance of Sexuality from Bombay, 1930s–1950s.' In *A Global History of Sexual Science, 1880–1960*, edited by Veronika Fuechtner, Douglas E. Haynes and Ryan M. Jones, 353–373. Oakland: University of California Press.

Anonymous. 1936. 'Published Obscene Article Editor Jailed.' *The Times of India*. February 5, 1936.

Anonymous. 1938. 'Sex Ed for the Young: Lt. Col. J.M. Shah on its Importance.' *The Times of India*. August 17, 1938.

Arondekar, Anjali R. 2009. *For the Record: On Sexuality and the Colonial Archive in India*. Durham: Duke University Press.

Banerjee, Sumanta. 1987. 'Bogey of the Bawdy: Changing Concept of 'Obscenity' in 19th Century Bengali Culture.' *Economic and Political Weekly* 22 (29): 1197–1206.

Bashford, A. 2004. *Imperial Hygiene: A Critical History of Colonialism, Nationalism and Public Health*. London: Palgrave Macmillan UK.

Basu, Nripendra Kumar. 1938. *Jouno Biswakosh Volume I*. Calcutta: Swasti Sahitya Sadan.

Bhattacharya, Spandan. 2020. 'Reading Anandalok: Obscenity, Cinema and Other 'Prohibitive' Pleasures in 1970s–1990s Bengali Print Culture.' *Porn Studies* 7 (1): 13–18.

Biswas, Hardik Brata. 2013. 'The Obscene, Modern and the Pornographic Family: Adventures in Bangla Pornography.' In *The Sexual History of the Global South*, edited by Saskia Wieringa, and Horacio Sivori, 44–64. London: Zed Books.

Botre, Shrikant. 2017. 'The Body Language of Caste : Marathi Sexual Modernity (1920–1950).' Phd. thesis. University of Warwick.

Botre, Shrikant and Douglas E. Haynes. 2017. 'Sexual Knowledge, Sexual Anxieties: Middle-Class Males in Western India and the Correspondence in Samaj Swasthya, 1927–53*.' *Modern Asian Studies* 51 (4): 991–1034.

Botre, Shrikant and Douglas E. Haynes. 2018. 'Understanding R.D. Karve: Brahmacharya, Modernity, and the Appropriation of Global Sexual Science in Western India.' In *A Global History of Sexual Science, 1880-1960*, edited by Veronika Fuechtner, Douglas E. Haynes and Ryan M. Jones, 163–185. Oakland: University of California Press.

Colligan, Colette. 2002. '"Esoteric Pornography": Sir Richard Burton's Arabian Nights and the Origins of Pornography.' *Victorian Review* 28 (2): 31–64.

Frühstück, Sabine. 2003. *Colonizing Sex: Sexology and Social Control in Modern Japan*. Berkeley, Los Angeles and London: University of California Press.

Ghosh, Anindita. 1998. 'Cheap Books, "Bad" Books: Contesting Print-Cultures in Colonial Bengal.' *South Asia Research* 18 (2): 173–194.

Gupta, Charu. 2002. *Sexuality, Obscenity and Community: Women, Muslims, and the Hindu Public in Colonial India*. New York: Palgrave Macmillan.

Gupta, Charu. 2019. 'Cast(e)Ing and Translating Sex in the Vernacular: The Writings of Santram BA in Hindi.' *Porn Studies* 7 (1): 1–17.

Gupta, Charu. 2020. 'Vernacular Sexology from the Margins: A Woman and a Shudra.' *South Asia: Journal of South Asian Studies* 43 (6): 1105–1127.

Hall, Lesley A. 2004. 'Birds, Bees and General Embarrassment: sex Education in Britain from Social Purity to Section 28.' In *Public or Private Education? Lessons from History*, edited by Richard Aldrich. 93–112. Oregon: Woburn Press.

Hasanat, Abul. 1936a. *Sachitra Jouna Bigyan Vol I*. Dhaka: Standard Library.

Hasanat, Abul. 1936b. *Sachitra Jouna Bigyan Vol II*. Dhaka: Standard Library.

Hasanat, Abul. 1939. *Crime and Criminal Justice*. Dhaka: Standard Library.

Hasanat, Abul. 1955. *All About Sex Love and Happy Marriage*. Calcutta: Sree Kali Press.

Hasanat, Abul. 1957. 'The C. I. D. in East Pakistan.' *The Journal of Criminal Law, Criminology, and Police Science* 48: 447.

Haynes, Douglas E. 2020. 'Gandhi, Brahmacharya and Global Sexual Science, 1919–38.' *South Asia: Journal of South Asian Studies* 43 (6): 1163–1178.

Heath, Deana. 2010. *Purifying Empire: Obscenity and the Politics of Moral Regulation in Britain, India and Australia*. Cambridge: Cambridge University Press.

Hodges, Sarah. 2008. *Contraception, Colonialism and Commerce: Birth Control in South India, 1920–1940*. Hampshire, England: Ashgate.

Legg, Stephen. 2013. 'Planning Social Hygiene: From Contamination to Contagion in Interwar India.' In *Imperial Contagions: Medicine, Hygiene, and Cultures of Planning in Asia*, edited by Robert Peckham and David M. Pomfret, 105–122. Hongkong: Hong Kong University Press.

Luker, Kristin. 1998. 'Sex, Social Hygiene, and the State: The Double-Edged Sword of Social Reform.' *Theory and Society* 27 (5): 601–634.

Mantena, Rama sundari. 2013. 'Vernacular Publics and Political Modernity: Language and Progress in Colonial South India.' *Modern Asian Studies* 47 (5): 1678–1705.

Mitra, Durba. 2020a. *Indian Sex Life: Sexuality and the Colonial Origins of Modern Social Thought*. Princeton: Princeton University Press.

Mitra, Durba. 2020b. 'Sexuality and the History of Disciplinary Transgression.' *South Asia: Journal of South Asian Studies* 43 (6): 1216–1227.

Mitra, Durba. 2015. 'Translation as Techné: Female Sexuality and the Science of Social Progress in Colonial India.' *History and Technology* 31 (4): 350–375.

Mukharji, Projit Bihari. 2020. 'Search for 'Context': Commodities, Consumption and Abul Hasanat's Material Sexscape.' *South Asia: Journal of South Asian Studies* 43 (6): 1196–1215.

Own Correspondent. 1930. 'Social Hygiene Matters in Education of Sex.' *The Times of India*. February 25, 1930.

Pande, Ishita. 2020a. *Sex, Law and the Politics of Age : Child Marriage in India, 1891–1937*. Cambridge, United Kingdom: Cambridge University Press.

Pande, Ishita. 2020b. 'Introduction to 'Translating Sex: Locating Sexology in Indian History.'.' *South Asia: Journal of South Asian Studies* 43 (6): 1093–1104.

Prakash, Gyan. 1999. *Another Reason: Science and the Imagination of Modern India*. Princeton: Princeton University Press.

Ramaswamy, Sumathi. 1997. *Passions of the Tongue: Language Devotion in Tamil India, 1891–1970*. Berkeley, Los Angeles and London: University of California Press.

Waheed, Sarah. 2014. 'Women of 'Ill Repute': Ethics and Urdu Literature in Colonial India.' *Modern Asian Studies* 48 (4): 986–1023.

Zimmerman, Jonathan. 2015. *Too Hot to Handle: A Global History of Sex Education*. Princeton: Princeton University Press.

Part II

Art, print culture and literature at the edges of the pornographic

A short history of the 'Blue-Photo': Bengali sex magazines and the visual empire of printed images (1940–1970)

Bijleeraj Patra

This article explores the mediations of print and photography in an emergent sexual culture in 20th century Bengal. In particular, I examine how Kolkata based Bengali sex magazines such as 'Nara-Nari' and 'Natun Jiban' negotiated between this emergent erotics and the censorial tendencies of the colonial state through a series of discourses around the body, specially those of male bodybuilders and female nude art models. In doing so, I locate the visual form and erotics of what has now come to be called the 'blue-photo'.

Introduction

An important date for rethinking the public life of desire in the context of the eastern-Indian state of West Bengal is 14 March 1966. On this day, Prafulla Chandra Sen, the third chief minister of West Bengal, wrote a letter to a Bengali sex magazine, *Nara-Nari*, congratulating them for their public role in purifying sexuality from the public domain of obscenity.[1] The letter was finally published a month later, in the May 1966 issue of *Nara-Nari* by the editor Mohon Mitra, as a front-page letter. The entire team of *Nara-Nari* went to the office of the Chief Minister to deliver a copy to him, a moment well captured by a *Nara-Nari* photographer. *Nara-Nari* began its journey in 1938 with Sukanta Kumar Haldar, the founder of Nara-Nari Publishing House, as the foundereditor. In 1950, the state government of West Bengal banned the magazine for the publishing of obscene printed images and writings. In a 1948 publication, Nandagopal Sengupta, secretary to Nobel laureate Rabindranath Tagore and a forgotten historian of early Bengali pornography, termed such printed images 'Blue-Photos'.[2] One point about terminology is worth mentioning here: around the 1920s and 1930s, pornographic materials were often referred to by the umbrella term 'naked pictures'. A report published in 1923, in *Nabajug*, a Bengali magazine, cited an incident where the colonial police were searching for such pictures and arrested those associated with its circulation.[3] The term 'blue photo' that Sengupta uses in the 1960s is a later invention, but one that has the more direct connotation of pornography. It is also worth mentioning that such images were part of print vernaculars across the Indian subcontinent in the early twentieth century and represent the vernacularization of desire via print technology in a period where tense cultural negotiations between tradition and modernity were beginning to emerge. The 'Blue-Photo', then, is a manifestation of such relationships in the domain of the printed visual image, and despite the fact that some of these images may not immediately register as 'pornographic' to modern readers, they depict the productive tensions between emerging print and body cultures on the one hand, and questions of tradition and the nation on the other.

The fascinating journey of this sex magazine – *Nara Nari* – from illegality to legalization in the public domain pushes us to rethink the central question of sexuality. In this article, I explore the question of sexuality not only in the domain of repression but also in terms of the history of its circulation. I analyze how through sex magazines, a section of the press, studios, photographers, and models created a printing network for circulating Blue-Photos. One crucial question that arises here is who exactly were the consumers of these Blue-Photos? Nandagopal Sengupta argued that from 1940 onwards, Calcutta, the former colonial capital of India, was the main hub of a bustling porn industry. The new audio-visual industry survived initially with the help of Western porn movies, with incest forming the major backdrop for such storylines. During this period, as Sengupta notes, the most popular Western blue films (as pornographic films are called in India) in Bengal were based on tabooed imaginations of erotic relations between Jesus and Mary.[4] However, there was also a burgeoning production of native pornography, and it is believed that sex workers as well as native aristocratic Bengali men and women were performers in these silent blue films. Since the 1940s, the Bengali blue films also had storylines, and this may well be an effect of a cross-pollination between Western and local forms of erotic imaginaries. Sengupta has shown that despite being illegal, there were multiple private screenings of such movies in Calcutta. Rich, aristocratic, educated, Bengali middle-class *bhadralok* [the middle-class intelligentsia and the cultural elite] brought their female lovers and prostitutes to watch these movies. While some movies were silent, others had soundtracks, and a few were even coloured. The ticket prices were exorbitant for their time, ranging from 100 to 150 Rupees for each show.

With such barriers to accessibility, erotic pleasure was hence a privilege of the rich. The Bengali elites' economic power and Western education gave them the privilege and permission for enjoying such movies. While sex-related motion pictures had restricted circulation, sexual visual content spread more widely among the masses in the form of photographs – what Sengupta has called 'Blue-Photos'. Such logics of class and taste are crucial in determining the consumer base of Blue-Photos. While it would be erroneous to say that the elite class did not consume Blue-Photos, common people had little or no access to motion-picture blue films. Thus, while the erotic moving image catered to a more or less fixed class demographic, the Blue-Photo cut across class boundaries because pornographic magazines were affordable for almost all middle-class people. *Nara-Nari* and *Natun Jiban* (founded 1944), the two earliest Bengali sex magazines, were instrumental in breaking the hierarchal class discourses of sexual pleasure. Available at cheap prices, they circulated Blue-Photos for the common readers, and Bengali sex magazines thus became a strong medium for the circulation of such printed images.

Male bodies, desire, and the discourse of celibacy

It would be prudent to delineate here what exactly constituted the 'Blue-Photo'. Unlike sex magazines of today, the Blue-Photos under discussion here did not usually feature explicit genital exposure. In the popular imagination of the time, 'Blue-Photo' referred to a nude or a semi-nude photograph of a woman. But from a survey of sex magazines published from the 1940s onwards, we can observe that two kinds of Blue-Photos were produced and circulated in the public sphere of Bengal – the male nude photograph and the female nude photograph. Even before sex magazines became popular, a report published in *Amrita Bazar Patrika* in 1924 noted that obscene pictures were sold on Chitpur Road, Calcutta. As a result of the report, the sellers were arrested by the police, fined Rupees 50, and jailed for one week.[5]

During this period, the circulation of Blue-Photos was illegal. Anirban Baishya and Darshana Mini have discussed the role of both social and state prohibition in the history of pornography in India (Baishya and Mini 2020). The colonial government was no exception, as the Obscene Publication Act was passed in 1925. But from the 1940s, through sex magazines, Blue-Photos found a renewed legitimacy in the public sphere. Furthermore, these sex magazines localized sexual desire by selecting native men and women as models for Blue-Photos, bringing into public circulation a vernacular body as the object of the erotic gaze. Especially in the case of the muscular body, as Michiel Baas (2020) argues, it is necessary to understand the confluence of vernacular cultures with the domain of desire. For instance, Bengali male bodybuilders called *Sharircharchakari* [those who used to practice physical exercises] were often featured as models for Blue-Photos, and in one instance, the muscular body of famous Bengali bodybuilder Monohar Aich (later winner at the 1952 NABBA Mr. Universe's Pro-Short Division) was featured on the cover page of *Natun Jiban* in 1950 (Figure 2) (see note 4). Monotosh Roy was another Bengali bodybuilder (and later Mr. Universe in 1951) and was also featured in a similar way in such magazines. In a 1948 shoot for *Nara Nari*, Roy appeared in a semi-nude photograph, apparently battling a snake.[6] Another

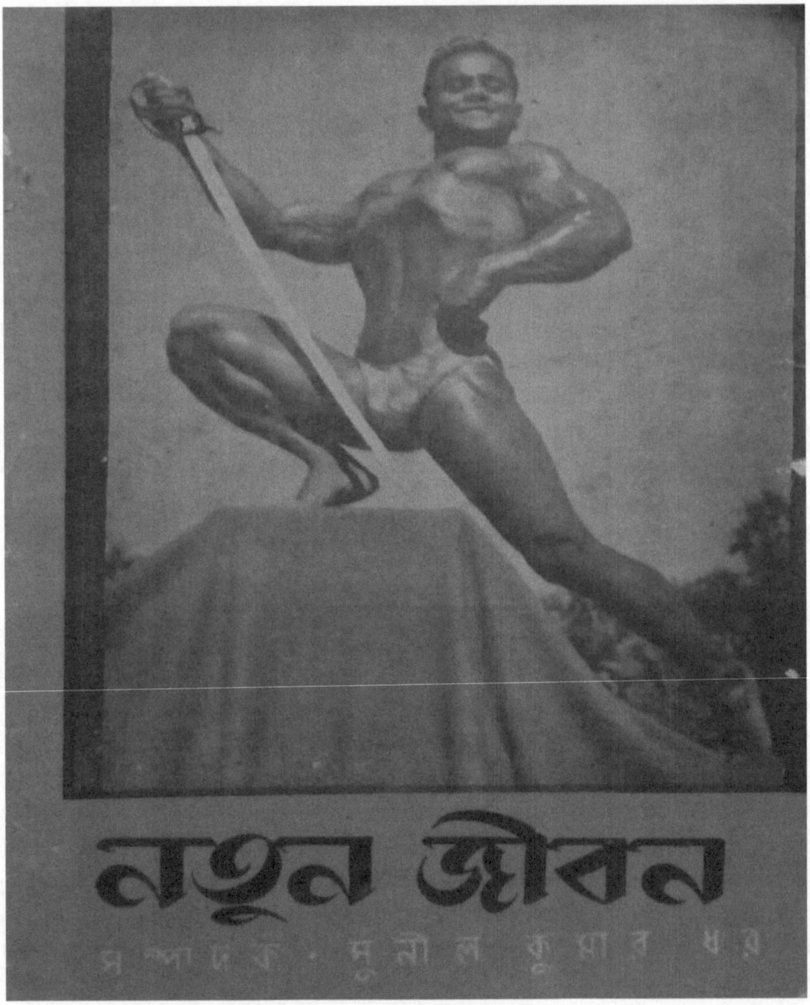

Figure 2. *Natun Jiban*, 1950. Source: Personal collection.

photograph published in *Nara-Nari* in 1949 featured Roy almost fully nude. Lying atop tiger skin, Roy's pelvis is shown perniciously covered with the loose ends of a cloth, giving the photograph its erotic charge. Shot in Sital Studio, Calcutta, the photograph's phantasmagoria is constituted not only by the ambience of thestudio set but also by what Roland Barthes (1981, 41–42) describes (in the context of Mapplethorpe's photographs) as the 'punctum' of the erotic photograph that shifts focus from genital close-ups to the desire evoked by the 'texture of the material' such as clothing and underwear.

One might begin to wonder here about the connection of bodybuilding and the erotic print public. What was the role of male musculature in this new, resplendent pornotopia?[7] In 1867, with the help of Nabagopal Mitra and the Hindu Mela (a cultural festival started by Mitra to foreground home-born art and culture), Bengali bodybuilding transformed into an organized and institutional form. Bodybuilders and their teachers believed that celibacy or *brahmacharya* (a brahminical concept that deems it necessary to retain the sperm and not to waste it) was important to train the body. One example of the impact of *brahmacharya* in Bengal can be found in an anecdote from the end of the nineteenth century, recounted by the famous Bengali literary critic Nirad Chandra Chaudhuri.[8]

Chaudhuri recounts that his brother was obsessed with *brahmacharya* and even kept a log-book where he would record tally marks to note the number of times in the day he would break his celibacy vows. When discovered, their mother was so angered at this transgression of celibacy that she ended up destroying the notebook. Another anecdote, perhaps more pertinent to our discussion of musculature here, can be found in the writings of Sundari Mohon Das, a doctor and a proponent of physical culture. Writing in 1876, Das states that when he lived in a boarding house [*mesbari*] as a student of Calcutta Medical College, he joined Nabagopal Mitra's *akhara* [a training and lodging facility for physical and martial arts] to train in bodybuilding. In accordance with the tenets of *brahmacharya*, Bengali bodybuilders were expected to avoid lust and desire, and in Das' anecdote he states making a blood pledge swearing celibacy by cutting his chest with a sword and declaring that he would protect the country first.[9] Masturbation, marriage, and relationship with a sex worker were considered to be against the practice of celibacy. As Joseph Alter has shown, the celibacy discourse became central not only to the practice

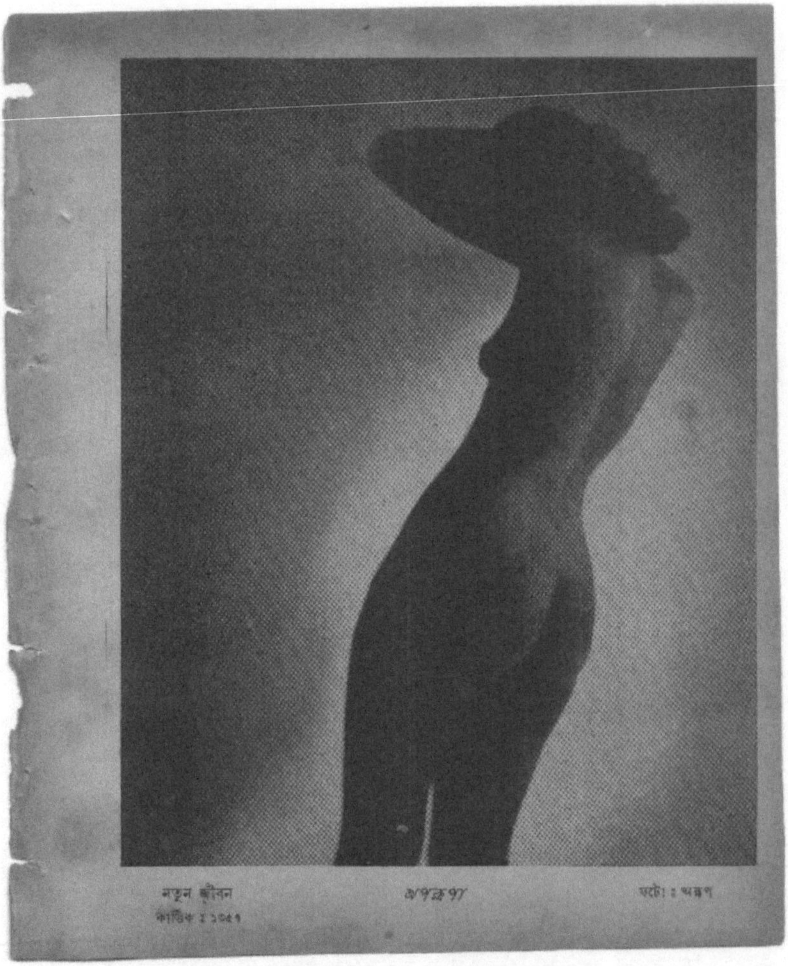

Figure 5. *Natun Jiban*, 1950. Source: Ankan Ghorai.

of bodybuilding in India but also to a concomitant moral discourse in which the preservation of semen and *brahmacharya* were seen to be in the service of the nation itself. As Alter states, the 'so-called "pornographic" novels and magazines' were anathema to this discourse as they were 'said to stimulate desire through fantasy' (1994, 49).

How do we explain the apparent contradiction between the overlapping celibacy and bodybuilding discourses on the one hand, and the explosion of male physical culture in the arena of print erotica on the other? How, if celibacy and *brahmacharya* were the basis of male physical culture at the time, did Monohor Aich and Monotosh Roy end up modelling for magazines that were known to peddle in Blue-Photos? The answer can be found, perhaps, in the related but slightly different discourse of *sangjam* [control over sexual desires]. *Sangjam*, an overused Bengali word in the public sphere of bodybuilding circles since the 1940s, traversed many fields like religion and daily life; in these fields, *sangjam* meant the practice of distancing the body and mind from sexual desire. But in the context of bodybuilding, *sangjam* carried a very different meaning. In 1949, Nandagopal Sengupta wrote in *Natun Jiban* that *brahmacharya* and *sangjam* are two different, even opposing, concepts. He argued that *sangjam* did not prohibit masturbation or

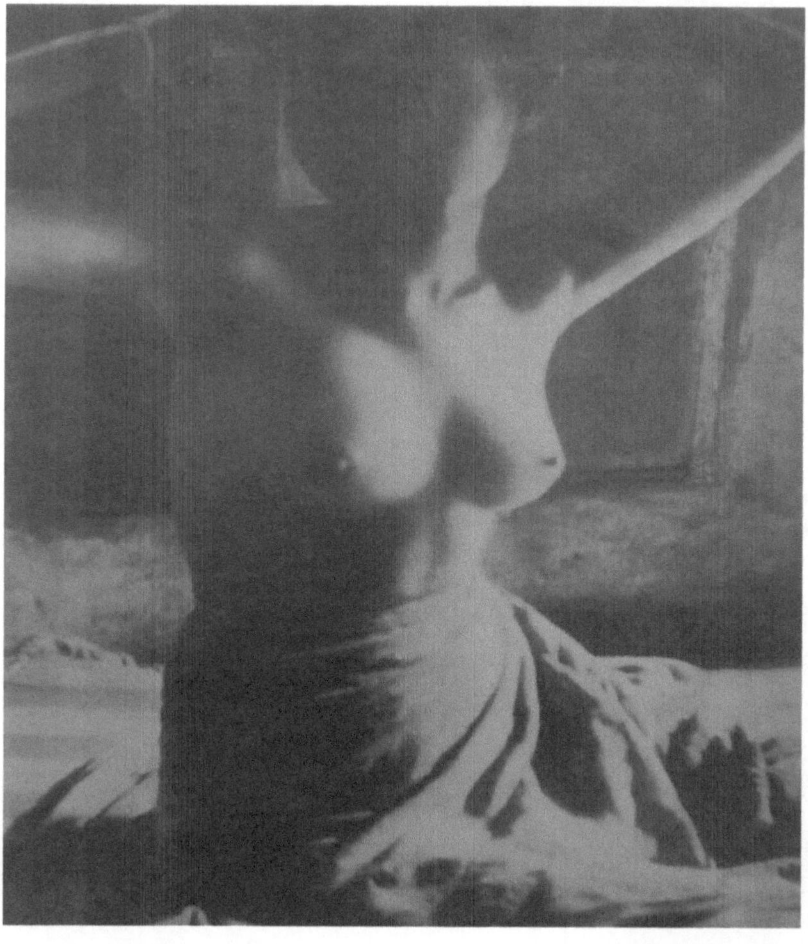

Figure 6. *Natun Jiban*, 1955. Source: Ankan Ghorai.

foreclose any kind of sex life. It just suggested that the balancing of sexual life with other bodily activities could lead to an urge for a good sex life.[10] Monotosh Roy and Monohor Aich followed this training of *sangjam* and going by this logic had no barrier to use their body for a Blue-Photo. In the case of Roy's two photographs mentioned earlier, the juxtaposition of muscular male bodies with animal bodies – snakes and tigers – denotes a kind of sexual prowess that is shown to be in touch with the male body's natural instincts, rather than the kind of repression espoused by *brahmacharya*'s celibate dogma.

Female bodies, nude models, and art practice

This discussion should not, of course, lead us to believe that male bodies were the only ones featured in Blue-Photos and erotic print magazines of the time. In fact, female

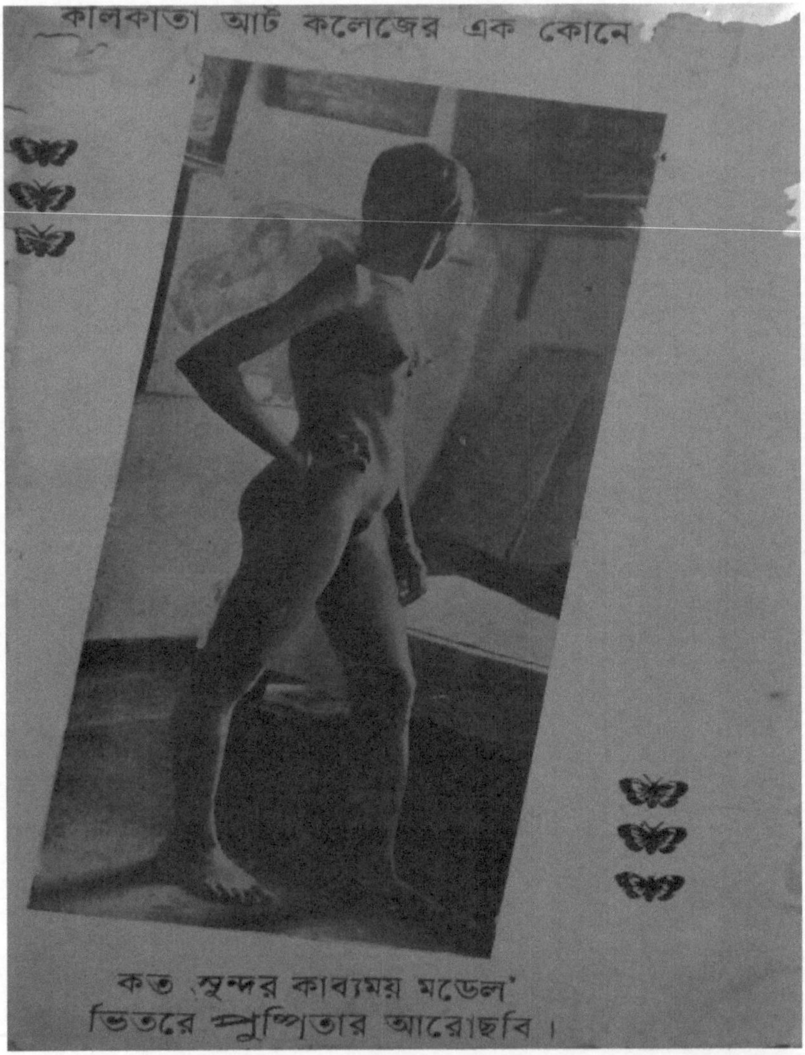

Figure 7. *Urbashi*, 1969. Source: Personal collection.

bodies abound the landscape of Blue-Photos, lending credence to Sibaji Bandyopadhyay's (2018) postulation that repetition is the centre of the porn world.[11] It is with the female bodies of the Blue-Photo that we find a repetitive story in the visual empire of Bengali print pornography. However, unlike the male bodies in Blue-Photos, the faces of female models in such photographs were usually obscured or rendered invisible through framing, lighting, and other aesthetic techniques. Two nude female photographs published in *Natun Jiban* demonstrate some of these practices. In the first (Figure 5), taken by the photographer Arup and published in 1950, the image captures the body from the back. In the second image (Figure 6), taken by the photographer Tasbiran, the face is artistically darkened through a play of light and shade, making the exposed breasts the central subject of the photograph. While these are only two images, tracing the map of published Blue-Photos of women reveals that in the story of these magazines, the name of the

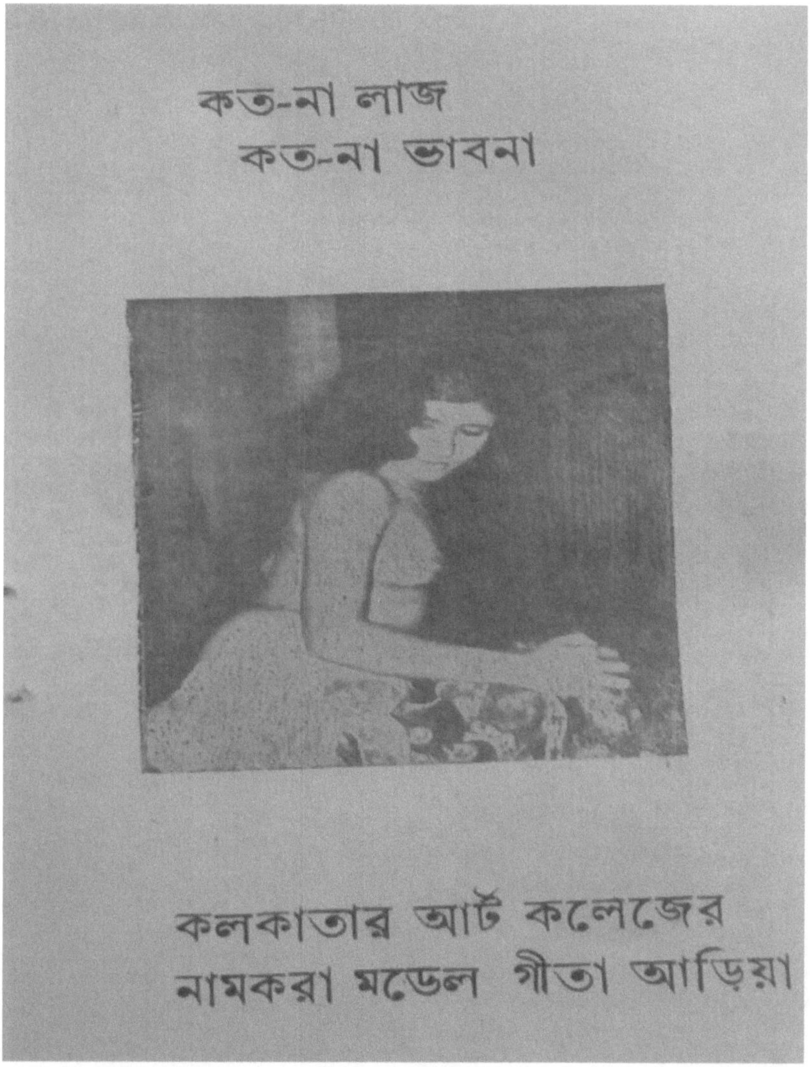

Figure 8. *Urbashi*, 1960–1969. Source: Personal collection.

woman or the face of the woman were not so important. Unlike the muscular male models such as Aich and Roy described in the previous section, the anatomy of the female Blue-Photo is primarily non-facial.

However, there is another narrative that diverges from this tendency. Connected to art practice in Bengal, the name of the woman becomes important in this counter-narrative of the Blue-Photo. In the 1950s and 1960s, nude models of prestigious Government Art Colleges also featured as models of Blue-Photos. One model, Puspita, worked as a nude model at Calcutta Art College in the 1950s for students working on figure studies, and trained herself as a performer to be able to repeatedly perform this task.[12] In one of these sessions, someone photographed her when she unclothed herself. The photograph was published in *Urbashi*, a sex magazine of the 1960s with the tagline *'Koli-kata art colleg'er ek kone'* ['a bride of the Calcutta Art College'] (Figure 7). For the readers,

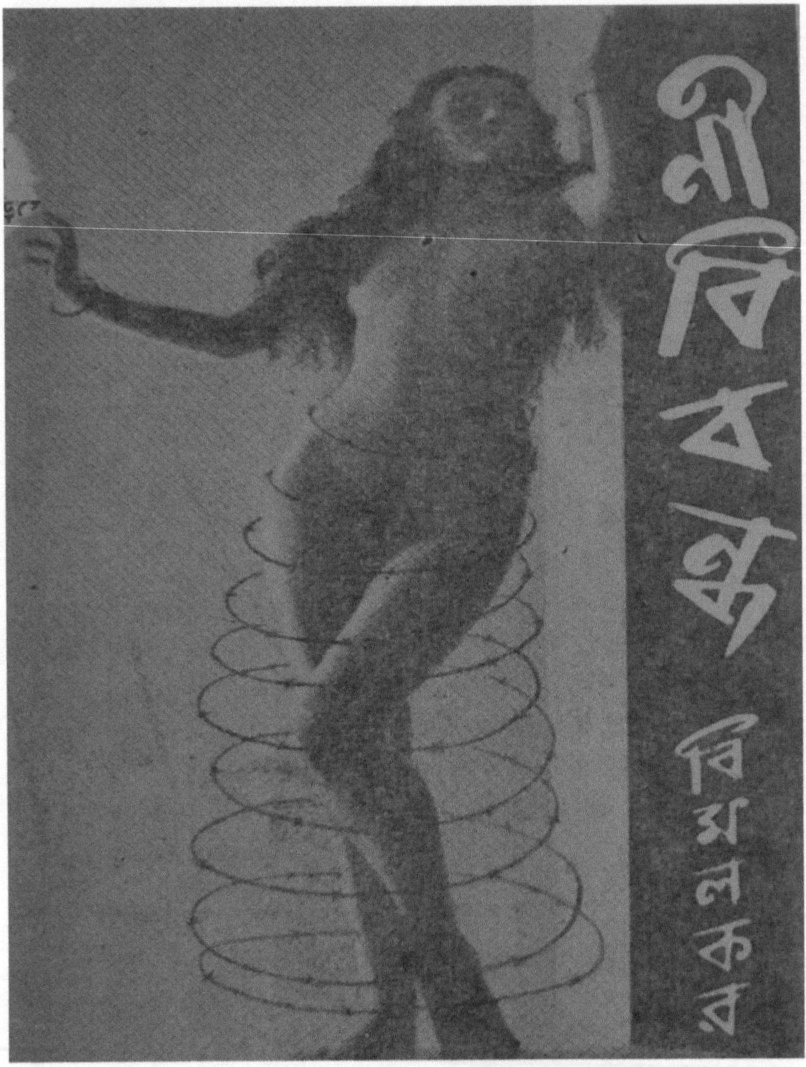

Figure 9. *Natun Jiban*. 1950. Source: Ankan Ghorai.

this was a surprising moment. They knew about nude models in art colleges, but had never seen them. There were other models too – for example, a nude photograph of the model Gita Ariya that was published with the tagline *'Kolikata art colleger name kora model Gita Ariya'* ['the famous model of Kolkata Art College, Gita Ariya'] (Figure 8). This interlink between art colleges, nude models, and printed erotica created a new pleasure practice in the public life of Blue-Photos, with the category of the *'art colleg'er model'* [model in an art college] becoming a staple ingredient in the sexual imaginaries trafficked by erotic print pornography.

Conclusion

What I have presented in this short forum piece is, of course, not an exhaustive history of Blue-Photos in Bengal. In fact, many other layers need to be investigated in much more detail. To end, let me point my readers to the interconnections between the literary sphere and the Blue-Photo. Bimal Kar, a popular novelist in 1950s Bengal, started a serialized novel titled *Nibibandha* in the *Natun Jibon* magazine starting in 1950. The editorial board of *Natun Jiban* used a Blue-Photo as the leading image, suggesting the theme of the novel (Figure 9). Here, it is the visual field of the Blue-Photo rather than the content of the novel itself that suggests a sexual imaginary to the reader. Thus, Blue-Photos played an important role not just as images in themselves but as part of the larger intertextual economy of printed erotica. In fact, it would perhaps not be wrong to suggest that the Blue-Photo was a key signifier in the sexual routes of Bengal's pornotopia.

Notes

1. *Nara-Nari*, Boisakh 1373/1966.
2. For a detailed discussion, see *Jouno Bikriti o Jounaporadh* by Nandagopal Sengupta (1949).
3. *Nabajug*, Shrabon 1331/1923.
4. For a detailed discussion, see *Jouno Bikriti o Jounaporadh*, 1355/1948, 290–291.
5. *Amrita Bazar Patrika*, 3 May 1924.
6. The motif of the snake juxtaposed with the muscular male body also stands as a central theme in the depiction of desire in the context of India. The controversial photographic shoot of Milind Soman in the 1990s for the Tuff Shoes advertisement is a more recent example. For a more detailed discussion, see Shah (2005).
7. Steven Marcus describes the pornotopia as 'the imagination of the entire universe beneath the sign of sexuality' (2017, 242).
8. For a detailed discussion, see *Bangali Jibone Romoni* by Chaudhary (2014).
9. Sundari Mohan Dash, 'Amar Sastha Noitik Jiban', *Jiboner Alo*, Boisakh 1335/1928, 24.
10. Nandagopal Sengupta, 'Jouno Songjom Ki O Keno', *Natun Jiban*, Poush 1356/1949, 508.
11. For a detailed discussion, see Bandyopadhyay (2018).
12. *Urbashi*, Calcutta, 1960–1969.

Acknowledgements

Writing this article was impossible without the help of Tapati Guha-Thakurta, Sibaji Bandyopadhyay and Partha Chatterjee. Darshana Sridhar Mini and Anirban Baishya owes very special thanks for their valuable comments. Thanks goes to Spandan Bhattacharya, Agnivo Ghosh, Barnali Paul, Ujjwala

Sharma, Triparna Sen, Ankan Ghorai and Atmajit Mukherjee for their continuous involvement with my effort.

Disclosure statement

No potential conflict of interest was reported by the author.

References

Alter, Joseph S. 1994. 'Celibacy, Sexuality, and the Transformation of Gender into Nationalism in North India.' *The Journal of Asian Studies* 53 (1): 45–66.

Baas, Michiel. 2020. *Muscular India: Masculinity, Mobility & The New Middle Class*. India: Westland Publications Private Limited.

Baishya, K. Anirban and Darshana S. Mini. 2020. 'Translating Porn Studies: Lessons from The Vernacular.' *Porn Studies* 7 (1): 1.

Bandyopadhyay, Sibaji. 2018. 'Pornoloke Porjoton.' In *Gangchil Patrika*, edited by Bijleeraj Patra, 19–41. Kolkata: Gangchil Publication.

Barthes, Roland. 1981. *Camera Lucida*. New York: Hill & Wang.

Chaudhary, Niradchandra. 2014. *Bangali Jibone Romoni*. Calcutta: Mitra & Ghosh Publishers Pvt.

Marcus, Steven. 2017. *The Other Victorians: A Study of Sexuality in Mid-Nineteenth-Century England*. London and New York: Routledge.

Sengupta, Nandagopal. 1949. *Jouno Bikriti o Jounaporadh*. Calcutta: Standard Publication.

Shah, Nishant. 2005. 'PlayBlog: Pornography, Performance and Cyberspace.' In *C'lick Me: A Netporn Studies Reader*, edited by Katrien Jacobs, Marije Janssen and Matteo Pasquinelli, 31–45. Amsterdam: Institute of Network Cultures.

Reading *Anandalok*: obscenity, cinema and other 'prohibitive' pleasures in 1970s–1990s Bengali print culture

Spandan Bhattacharya

> I always had an interest in film magazines, since I was in sixth or seventh standard in school. I would go to the library and sneak into the film magazine sections. I used to buy *Anandalok* from the book stalls as well and carried them in my school bag. One fine morning I was caught reading *Anandalok* during off period. I was suspended for a few days followed by guardian call, scolding and humiliation. (Shubhojeet Sarkar, employee in the information technology sector, Kolkata)

Introduction: situating *Anandalok* in the porno-spectrum of Bengali print culture

In the 1970s and 1980s, middle-class households in the state of West Bengal were furious consumers of the Bengali film magazine *Anandalok*. Publicized as 'a colourful fortnightly magazine of films' and 'a magazine for readers with modern taste and sensibility',[1] *Anandalok* began operations on 25 January 1975 and received a tremendous response after its first publication. ABP Group (*Anandabazar Patrika*),[2] the media group that published *Anandalok*, claimed that all of the first issues were sold out within a week of its publication. However, *Anandalok* quickly became taboo in the *bhadralok*[3] [the educated and seemingly polished middle and upper middle class] public sphere, soon after its first publication. It created a strong sense of anxiety amongst the Bengali intelligentsia, leaving an impact in their writings, discussions and activities. In this Forum article, I historically contextualize the emergence of *Anandalok* and its tabooed status vis-à-vis the discourse of obscenity and cinema in 1970s–1990s Bengali print culture.

Crucially, *Anandalok* was neither banned nor censored for any of its issues, and neither did the magazine have a non-mainstream or underground circulation. On the contrary, *Anandalok* was very much part of a media network patronized by Bengali middle-class consumers – it was designed for middle-class readers with articles written by middle-class contributors. Contrary to the 'serious' discussion of films in other contemporary film journals published by the film society groups in West Bengal, *Anandalok* set itself apart through its inclusion of images. *Anandalok* claimed that its inclusion of advertising and pin-up images catered to what ABP Group called 'popular demand'.[4] More crucially, *Anandalok* also aligned itself with earlier trajectories of erotic print culture in Bengal and brought the print genres of scandal into mainstream circulation.

Hardik Biswas (2013) points out that the emergence of various print genres classified as 'obscene' was coeval to the arrival of the printing press in Bengal. In 1816, Battala, a publishing district, began to emerge in Calcutta which was very close to Sonagachhi, the largest community of sex workers in the Calcutta region.[5] Along with moral tracts and Hindu mythological texts, Battala published genres like *kechchha* [scandal], *guptokatha* [mysteries] and erotica – print genres that were deemed unsuitable for the taste of the *bhadralok*. Arnab Saha (2009) notes that nineteenth-century magazines like *Sambaad Rasaraaj*[6] and *Pashanda Peeran*[7] popularized *kechchha* or *kechchha sahitya* [scandal literature] – a print genre with the purpose of expressing hatred and anger towards established authors. Stories of the sexual perversion of socially and politically influential persons were the main focus of these *kechchhas*, which narrativized social scandals in print. Biswas (2013) observes that when sexuality became increasingly controlled and sanitized as part of the imagination of a new national self, print genres like *guptokothas*, narratives of incestuous adventures, erotica and sex guides flourished in mid–late twentieth-century Bengal.[8] Many popular magazines from the 1950s, such as *Tomar Jiban* [Your Life], had sections of erotic literature (including translations of D. H. Lawrence) and monochrome or duo-chrome photographs of semi-nude women. By the 1960s and 1970s there was an increase in erotic content, including narratives of incest and photo-essays featuring semi-nude women. While *Anandalok* took pride in its exclusive position by announcing its 'good quality of colored prints', it demonstrated a closeness with the genre of scandal literature from Battala press. *Anandalok*'s focus on celebrity gossip can be seen as a parallel to the *kechchha* texts from the early period. The tabooed status of *Anandalok* can very well be considered a result of publishing scandals and intimate details in its pages.

Anandalok and the discourse of cultural crass-ness

Along with *kechchha* and *guptokatha*, *Anandalok* demonstrated an interesting parallel with another early print genre of the confessions of 'fallen' women in published texts.[9] This could be seen, for instance, in *Anandalok*'s stories about young, successful and controversial female figures like Aparna Sen, a leading Bengali film star of the 1970s and 1980s,[10] or Miss Shephali, a cabaret dancer.[11] In the very first issue of *Anandalok*, the travails of Aparna Sen's divorce were published as the cover story, making reference to her alleged alcoholism and promiscuity.[12] Similarly, *Anandalok* published a story on the popular cabaret dancer Miss Shephali, based on an interview conducted by Bimal Chakraborty.[13] These pieces presented the celebrities as reckless women who freely expressed their desire and independence beyond heteronormative conjugality, and followed an intimate narrative style in detailing the 'private lives' of female performers. For instance, in his story on Miss Shephali, Bimal Chakraborty writes:

> Shephali suddenly becomes restless, throws the cigarette packet away from her, covers her breast with her *saree*, stands out (she was sitting on a sofa) and says 'who does not want a happy conjugal life? But there are some vultures that rip the women's flesh off. They will not allow women like me to settle down, and would rather make me their kept … ' Before completing her sentence Shephali lights up another cigarette … [14]

This narrative style constructs an image of a woman who is successful and famous, but unhappy and lonely in her home. Interestingly, Bengali cinema in the 1970s and 1980s focused intensely on stories of performers or 'fallen' women and provides an interesting parallel to the *Anandalok* stories.[15] Articles on these female performers created imaginaries of public figures who could not be appropriated into the regular *bhadramahila* [respectable, middle-class woman] configuration. Unlike nineteenth-century *kechchha* culture, the stories and reports published in *Anandalok* were not necessarily aimed at shaming influential persons and were part of the celebrity culture in print genres. But they can be considered a new-age extension of the *kechchha* texts discussing scandals and controversies about desiring women targeted at middle-class readers. This is significant as the gendered body and female sexuality became an important issue for the state and the *bhadralok* intelligentsia during the 1970s and 1980s.[16] In this context, *Anandalok*'s excessive focus on female stars, their sexualized presence and their private lives made this magazine taboo in the Bengali public sphere.

Although *Anandalok* drew from scandal literature and enmeshed its cinema journalism with these older forms of the 'obscene', it paradoxically also accommodated the critique of obscenity. Thus, there was a conflicted relationship between *Anandalok*'s debt to *kechchha* literature and its status as a mainstream magazine. For instance, *Anandalok* published a photograph of starlet Padma Khanna taking off her blouse and part of her breasts were shown from a low-angle camera position.[17] This led to serious criticism in the following issues of *Anandalok* (June and July), where many readers stated that they were disappointed to see *Anandalok*'s lack of taste in publishing such obscene images. Although vulgarity is slightly different from the obscene/pornographic, press writings about Bengali cinema often collapsed these categories through the term '*apasanskriti*' – 'crass/bad/decaying culture' (opposite to '*sanskriti*' or culture in Bengali). During the late 1970s–1990s, the term '*apasanskriti*' was widespread in urban Bengali public sphere discourses and connoted the anxiety of losing cultural 'purity' to 'foreign' cultural dominances.[18]

The Bengali intelligentsia targeted different agents or players of *apasanskriti* functioning in the cultural sphere and social lives of Bengal, and popular Hindi cinema was one of the prime suspects. Curiously, *Anandalok* itself contributed to this cultural discourse by publishing articles about the impact of *apasanskriti* (or crass culture) in Bengal. The discourse of *apasanskriti* emerged quite starkly in *Anandalok*, especially in its write-ups of Bombay films. For instance, an article in *Anandalok* derides the sexual overtones of Bombay films, criticizing their adulteration of audience taste. The author writes: 'these films show social disease in the name of reality. They are busy in projecting this "reality" and not artistry and beauty [...] In the name of reality this import of obscenity is wrong'.[19]

Anandalok thus belonged to an interesting moment in Bengali print culture when the binary of the 'serious' (literary) and the 'popular' became stronger than in earlier decades and the new popular was yet to find the appropriate words to defend its position. The tabooed status of *Anandalok* was not solely a product of its focus on sexualized female stars, but also its closeness to the domain of the 'popular'. *Anandalok*'s twin strategy of publishing such material and simultaneously deriding it points towards the complexity of popular culture in Bengal in the 1970s–early1990s.

Conclusion

Towards the late 1990s, *Anandalok* changed along with transformations in Bengali cinema, including the corporatization of the film industry and the incorporation of neoliberal aspirations in films. When the celebrated Bengali film director Rituporno Ghosh took over as editor in 1997, *Anandalok* also began to include news from other public discussions. While the nature of *Anandalok*'s public reception began to change in this period, its initial phase as the antithesis of Bengali middle-class sensibilities in the 1970s–1990s can tell us a lot about the power of print genres as constitutive social artefacts.

I must acknowledge that studying the history of *Anandalok* and the emergence of its tabooed status presents us with certain methodological roadblocks. Most of the libraries and archives in Kolkata did not collect or archive full series of *Anandalok*. Even the tabooed status of *Anandalok* and the charges of obscenity against it remain largely undocumented and unrecorded. This makes it difficult to map the complexity of the issue in texts and records. In many cases, the important source of secondary materials remains in oral narratives, and like the interview excerpt at the beginning of this article, they can sometimes give us insights into the nuances of a poorly documented, but thriving cultural form.

While not strictly pornographic, *Anandalok*'s reception exposed how far the salacious and the obscene became structuring concerns in the Bengali public sphere. While explicit pornographic literature and visual material were available, they remained 'unseeable' and 'unspeakable' – off-limits from the *bhadralok* parlour rooms. On the other hand, as a product of the mainstream press, *Anandalok* dragged the shadows of salacious fantasies out into the open space of the public streets. For instance, the gossip about female performers was very much a part of the oral culture of *bhadralok*[20] and *Anandalok*'s intervention was bringing out those oral narratives in widely circulated mainstream printed forms. Also, while bringing in the idea of the 'pornographic' and the 'obscene' (which were hitherto unavailable in Bengali mainstream print), *Anandalok* narrativized them for the Bengali reading public.

Although it is not within the scope of this Forum piece, a detailed study of the images and stories published in *Anandalok* issues would be useful to understand how they took part in constructing these narratives. However, from the indifference of the libraries and archives in Kolkata in archiving the full series of *Anandalok*, one can read the discomfort and the taboo associated with reading the magazine. In my opinion, this discomfort itself indicates the importance of locating and reading *Anandalok* in the porno-spectrum of Bengali print culture. As is evident from the case of *Anandalok*, its content was not exactly pornographic, yet it evoked the same kind of strong, affective reactions that the middle class had towards pornography. In other words, reactions towards *Anandalok* had more to do with taste, class and respectability. Perhaps it would be worth our time as researchers of cultural objects to look closely at local idioms of taste and respectability – '*apasanskriti*' (or crass culture) in the Bengali case – that can help us expand questions of the pornographic and the obscene beyond that which immediately meets the eye. This further indicates the need to find and formulate methodologies of reading undocumented, unrecorded and sometimes 'absent' accounts while studying the history of the 'pornographic' prints and other media texts in the South Asian context.

Notes

1. As publicized by *Anandabazar Patrika*. See the December 1974 and January 1975 issues of *Anandabazar Patrika*.

2. ABP Group is a media organization based in West Bengal and headquartered in Kolkata. It was established in 1922.
3. *Bhadralok* literally means 'gentle folk' in Bengali and is used to refer to the educated, although not necessarily affluent, middle and upper sections of society. Emerging during the period of British colonization (1757–1947), this was an upwardly mobile group who moved away from physical labour such as agriculture and was marked by a leaning towards western education. Composed of principally Hindu 'upper'-caste groups, they came to exercise social power and cultural dominance over urban centres like Calcutta as well as the rural areas in the late nineteenth century. This category is not only socio-economic but also cultural. For a detailed discussion see *The Sentinels of Culture: Class, Education, and the Colonial Intellectual in Bengal* by Bhattacharya (2005) and *Writing Social History* by Sarkar (1997).
4. See the December 1974 and January 1975 issues of *Anandabazar Patrika*
5. For a detailed discussion on the interrelation between Sonagachhi and Battala, see 'Sonagachhi O Battala: Dui Jamajer Kahini' ['Sonagachhi and Battala: A Tale of a Pair of Twins'] by Bandyopadhyay (2013).
6. *Sambaad Rasaraaj* was first published on 8 June 1849 with Gorishankar Tarkabaagish as editor.
7. *Pashanda Peeran* was first published on 20 June 1846 with Ishwar Gupta as editor.
8. For instance, titles like *Maharane Duronto Madan* [God of Love in the Battlefield] were quite popular. There were series published around the 1940s in Kolkata that fictionalized the sexual exploits of nurses and wives of soldiers at the World War II front, and depicted military brothels and sex crimes during war. Also see 'Mulato Parno, Tatsahao Gnyancharcha' by Patra (2018).
9. For a detailed discussion of this print genre, see Bhattacharya (2013).
10. Aparna Sen is also a successful filmmaker and screenwriter.
11. Miss Shephali faced opposition from the state government for her performances and she was criticized for promoting 'obscenity' in Bengali theatre, as she has documented in her autobiography (Miss Shefali 2014).
12. See *Anandalok*, 25 January 1975.
13. See 'Ora Amake Ghar Bnadhte Debena' ['They Will Not Allow Me to Marry'] in *Anandalok*, 26 July 1975, 24–25.
14. Ibid., 25. Author's translation.
15. For a general idea about the transformation of Bengali film culture during 1970s and 1980s please see 'Bangla Cinemar Palabadal/ The Changing Phase of Bengali Cinema' by Ghosh (1990); 'Bengali Cinema' by Raha (1991); 'Bangla Chalachchitra Kathakata O Anyanyo Prabandho' by Raha (2004) and 'Banglar Chalachitra Sanskriti' by Roy (2001).
16. During the 1980s, public halls in Calcutta, including some state-owned ones like Rabindra Sadan, did not allow famous singer Usha Uthup to perform, alleging that her songs and performances of disco music were examples of perverted/bad culture. Mrs Uthup filed a petition and the case went to the P. C. Borooah bench in the Calcutta High Court. P. C. Borooah's bench ruled that the constitution had been violated by blacklisting a performer without giving her any opportunity of showing cause, leading to a denial of natural justice. See Borooah, Bench and Borooah (1983). Also see 'Sandhya Raater Shephali' by Miss Shefali (2014).
17. *Anandalok*, 17 May 1975 issue, accessed at Bangeeyo Sahitya Parishat Library, Kolkata.
18. For a detailed discussion of this please see 'Janasangjoger Mukti: Chalachchitra, Betar, Television'. *Proma* (1) October by Bandyopadyay (1978); *Apo-sanskriti?* by Bhattacharjee (2003); 'Sattar Dashaker Bangla Chhabi' in *Sattar Dashak (The Decade of 1970s)* by Bhowmick (1981) and 'Janapriyo Chalachchitrer Manastattwa: Utsa Theke Bikaar Ebong Niramoyer Ingit' in *Anushtup* 21 (4) by Gangopadhyay (1987).
19. See Subrata Mukherjee, 'Rape O Bastra Unmochon' ['Rape and Removing Clothes'] in *Anandalok*, 14 June 1986, 37, accessed at Bangeeyo Sahitya Parishat Library, Kolkata. Also see 'Darshak Ruchi Ke Namiye Anar Protijogita Shuru Hoyechhe' by Kumar (1991).
20. My interviews with people who were young during 1970s and 1980s confirmed the gossip about Miss Shephali and Aparna Sen in *bhadralok* gatherings.

Disclosure statement

No potential conflict of interest was reported by the author.

References

Bandyopadhyay, Samik. 1978. 'Janasangjoger Mukti: Chalachchitra, Betar, Television.' *Proma* 1 (1), October: 168–177.

Bandyopadhyay, Sumanta. 2013. 'Sonagachhi O Battala: Dui Jamajer Kahini.' In *Unish Shataker Kolkata O Sarswatir Itar Santan*, 228–246. Kolkata: Anustup.

Bhattacharji, Sukumari. 2003. *Apo-sanskriti?* Calcutta: Camp.

Bhattacharya, Tithi. 2005. *The Sentinels of Culture: Class, Education, and the Colonial Intellectual in Bengal*. New Delhi: Oxford University Press.

Bhattacharya, Sanchari. 2013. '"No Hungry Generation Tread Thee Down?"- Exploring the Poetics of Alterity.' *Margin: A Journal of Literature and Culture* 3: 128–155.

Bhowmick, Someshwar. 1981. 'Sattar Dashaker Bangla Chhabi.' In *Sattar Dashak (The Decade of 1970s)*, edited by Anil Acharya, 28–43. Kolkata: Anushtup Publication.

Biswas, Hardik. 2013. 'The Obscene Modern and the Pornographic Family: Adventures in Bangla Pornography.' In *The Sexual History of the Global South: Sexual Politics in Africa, Asia and Latin America*, edited by Saskia Wieringa and Horacio Sívori, 43–63. London: Zed Books.

Borooah, P., P. Bench, and P. C. Borooah. 1983. *Calcutta High Court: Mrs. Usha Uthup vs State of West Bengal And Others*. September 1.

Gangopdhyay, Shrikumar. 1987. 'JanapriyoChalachchitrerManastattwa: UtsaThekeBikaarEbong NiramoyerIngit.' *Anushtup* 21 (4): 26–38.

Ghosh, Somen. 1990. *Bangla CinemarPalabadal*. The Changing Phase of Bengali Cinema. Calcutta: Shyamali.

Kumar, Anup. 1991. 'Darshak Ruchi Ke Namiye Anar Protijogita Shuru Hoyechhe.' *Anandalok*. August 17.

Miss Shefali. 2014. *Sandhya Raater Shephali*. Kolkata: Ananda Publishers.

Mukherjee, Subrata. 1986. 'Rape O BastraUnmochon.' *Anandalok*. June 14.

Patra, Bijoliraaj. 2018. 'Mulato Parno, Tatsahao Gnyancharcha.' Rabibaroyari, Sunday supplement of *Ei Samay*. June 10.

Raha, Kiranmoy. 1991. *Bengali Cinema*. Kolkata: Nandan, West Bengal Film Centre.

Raha, Partha. 2004. *Bangla Chalachchitra Kathakata O Anyanyo Prabandho*. Kolkata: Ratna Publication.

Roy, Rajat. 2001. *Banglar Chalachitra Sanskriti*. Calcutta: Sristi publication.

Sarkar, Sumit. 1997. *Writing Social History*. New Delhi: Oxford University Press.

Saha, Arnab. 2009. 'Bhagnangsher Jounotopia.' In *Jounota O Bangali* (Sexualities and Bengali Culture), edited by Anil Acharya and Arnab Saha, 93–130. Kolkata: Anustup.

Pornography and Indian miniature painting: the case of Avadh, India

Natalia Di Pietrantonio

ABSTRACT

This article investigates miniature paintings produced in Avadh, India, during the reign of the nawabs of Avadh (r. 1722–1856) that have been consequently labelled as pornography. My case studies include Avadhi miniature paintings that have been installed and categorized as pornography and/or as obscenity starting in the nineteenth century and into the present day. British colonial administrators first applied the label of obscenity to these paintings when they began to taxonomize and donate their collections to museums in the 1800s. In the British Library, for example, painting albums such as Richard Johnson's *Album J.42* were sequestered alongside other material that might provoke sexual arousal. Curators later marked this album for destruction in 1830. When the word pornography started gaining wider currency in the nineteenth and twentieth centuries, these paintings moved from the parameters of obscenity into pornography. Rather than focusing entirely on the censorship practices undertaken in museums and archival libraries with regard to these paintings, this article builds on recent scholarship that interrogates the use of the languages of colonialism and race in the formation of the category of pornography.

Introduction

In northern India and particularly Avadh (present-day Uttar Pradesh) throughout the eighteenth century, European colonial officers patronized and collected Rāgamālā paintings. Rāgamālā paintings are an indigenous art form of South Asia that contain anthropomorphized musical notes along with erotic imagery and representations of Hindu deities. The paintings were usually bound in series of 36–42 folios (Ebeling 1973, 13). Each rāga (musical mode) contains standard iconography that aids the viewer to identify each musical note. For instance, the standard iconography of the dīpak rāga is two lovers embracing next to a set of candles. Because the rāgamālā series was ever evolving, some deviations and permutations arose from this base iconography. In the case of Figure, the imagery for this dīpak rāga explicitly shows a scene of copulation next to the standard candles. Scenes of penetration were not always represented in the dīpak rāga; here, however, the artisan was given license to further the genre's conventional iconography.

With these slight variations in composition, rāgamālā paintings including dīpak rāga folios were popular throughout the sixteenth to nineteenth centuries in northern India. Once these images entered European institutions in the nineteenth and twentieth centuries, however, colonial officers and museum personnel began to call for their destruction and erasure. These institutional figures regulated rāgamālā albums by breaking apart manuscripts and separating out individual folios that contained explicit images of sexual acts. By isolating these folios, museum personnel inadvertently brought maximum visibility to moments of sexual climax. Whereas these erotic folios had once been part of a poetic sequence of the rāgamālā genre, representations with sexual acts now became the entire compositional focus for the viewer. In tandem with the dismantling of albums, curators also began to label paintings as obscenity, erotica, and pornography, vacillating among these categories without regard to whether these terms conveyed any distinctions or intellectual subtleties. Although European officers collected erotic rāgamālā albums and paintings during the early colonial period, museum personnel quickly thereafter sequestered these images in private storage rooms in the name of public decency throughout the twentieth century. Proclamations of pornography come late towards the end of the twentieth century and into the present day in Indian museum catalogues and in western academic scholarship.[1]

This article charts how the history of colonialism and the collecting practices of eighteenth-century Europeans remapped the construction of rāgamālā as erotic. I present a micro-history of European collecting practices of rāgamālā albums by homing in on the collector Richard Johnson (1753–1807), who was active in eighteenth-century Avadh. Next I turn to how Johnson's collection of rāgamālā albums was catalogued and installed in museums in England in the nineteenth century. Following this I examine how museum personnel in India dealt with rāgamālā images after the images attained the status of fine art in the twentieth century, when, now attached to the notion of art, erotic miniature paintings operated with greater visual legitimacy than they had when they were merely craft. I track when the signifier of art is dropped from usage for rāgamālā images and when the term domesticates its sexual imagery in order to permit depictions of sex in public spaces. I conclude this article making no attempt to resolve the tension between erotica and pornography. Instead, by straddling these two categories, rāgamālā images reflect how the history of colonialism animated the emergence of the category of obscenity and pornography.

Colonialism and collecting history

High-ranking and low-ranking colonial officers such as Richard Johnson collected rāgamālā painting throughout northern India in the mid-eighteenth century. Most of these early collectors were bibliophiles, and these rāgamālā painting albums were one part of their comprehensive collections devoted to 'oriental' literature.[2] The collectors, including but not limited to Richard Johnson and Sir William Jones (1746–1794), also traded and circulated among each other folios from their painting albums (Gude 2009, 4). Art historians have found a number of shared compositions among Europeans' rāgamālā albums; artists copied images from Johnson's rāgamālā album into albums sponsored by other Europeans.[3] Many of these collectors bought both whole albums and individual folios, and they also instructed their artist workshops to create new rāgamālā albums according to the collectors' specifications. While these collecting practices were closely aligned with how local elites such as the nawabs of Avadh (r. 1722–1856) collected rāgamālā albums, figures such as Johnson enacted new meaning-making practices for these paintings by imposing a Hindu religious framework on them. In this early stage, European collectors readily accepted sexualized imagery in painting albums, in part because they considered such images to be authentic representations of a perceived Hindu visual canon. This impulse to collect authentic representations was also aligned with the East India Company state's project to better 'know the people' they governed (Alam and Alavi 2001, 43).[4]

Rāgamālā paintings pictorialize rāgas, Indian melodies comprising five to seven notes. As such, these paintings are also considered sound forms. A rāga's visual and musical structures express moods or a set of emotions such as melancholy, passion, or serenity. Each melodic composition also features various subsets of seasons, landscapes, deities, and humans. Courtship, lovers' quarrels and reconciliation, scenes of prayer, and entertainment by jugglers are common motifs.[5] Rāgamālā paintings evoke Hindustani music, a musical genre that contains Indic along with Indo-Persianate and Islamicate features.[6] Both Muslim and Hindu courtiers, including the nawabs of Avadh who were a Shi'a ruling elite, patronized the rāgamālā genre in the miniature format and bound them in albums. The miniature paintings in these albums reject verisimilitude. Although the artisans' fine, delicate brushstrokes could have been used in the service of naturalism, the miniature paintings' compositions always call attention to the materiality of paper, jarring the viewer away from the pictorial composition to the medium itself.

British civil servant Richard Johnson collected both treatises on rāga theory along with rāgamālā painting albums (Randle 1941; Falk and Archer 1981, 14–29; Schofield 2018). For instance, Johnson collected the musical treatise *Risāla-i Rāgamālā* on May 13 1779, and later, in around 1780, juxtaposed it with a painting album, *Album J.42* (see Figure 3).[7] Thakur Das wrote the *Risāla-i Rāgamālā* in 1744, most likely in Delhi.[8] Lal Thakri recopied it for Johnson in 1779, utilizing both the Hijri calendar and the Bengali calendar to mark the occasion. Johnson collected the *Risāla-i Rāgamālā* from Lal Thakri either in Lucknow (a city in Avadh) or in Calcutta.[9] The text contains references to Islamic prophets and Sufi mystics along with explanations of Hindu deities, attempting to translate the rāgamālā system into an Indo-Islamic idiom. Richard Johnson understood a basic level of Persian, but it is unclear how much he could glean from the text or whether he could understand the multiple religious symbols that Thakur Das employed. Even though Johnson may not have fully comprehended the text, he found the *Risāla-i Rāgamālā* important enough to commission artists to paint sections of the treatise into a rāgamālā album in 1780 while he was in Lucknow.[10]

Johnson had one of the largest collections of rāgamālā albums created by Murshidabad, Hyderabad, and Lucknow artists. In one of his sponsored manuscripts, the *Divan* of Qamar-ud-din Minnat, completed in 1781–1782, Johnson's portrait survives.[11] In it, Johnson sits in a European chair on a terrace that recalls many Indo-Persianate portrait scenes (Figure 2), noteworthy examples of which include 'Portrait of William Fullarton Receives a Visitor' (c. 1760–1764), 'Colonel Polier Watching a Nautch' (c. 1774), 'John Wombwell' (c. 1785), and 'Sir David Ochterlony Watching a Nautch' (c. 1820).[12] In Figure 2, a native servant, who carries a fly whisk and a parasol, both of which were local symbols of rank, attends to him. In this miniature painting, Johnson is represented as one of the many intermediary colonial figures in eighteenth-century India who attempted to balance European and Indo-Persianate aesthetics. Johnson seems to emulate Indian aesthetics of rank and aligns himself with local practices, yet he retains his British red coat as a mark of difference.

Johnson was involved in British and European intellectual circles in India. One of his most prominent friends was William Jones, another British civil servant who had a penchant for Hindustani music and who wrote in 1784 a treatise titled *On the Musical Modes of the Hindus*. Jones and Johnson first met when Jones arrived in India in 1783. Later, after Johnson moved to Calcutta in 1785, they exchanged manuscripts and musings on

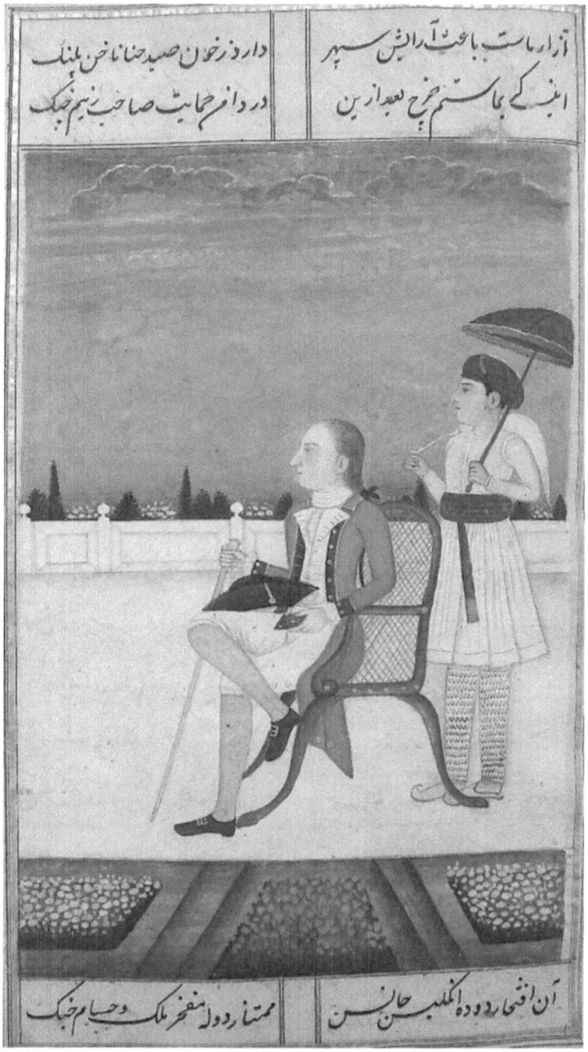

Figure 2. Richard Johnson portrait. BL Or.6633, f. 68r. © The British Library Board.

Persian texts (Falk and Archer 1981, 22). Jones wrote that Johnson was a 'great enthusiast for Hafiz'[13] and would borrow copies of manuscripts from his collection.[14] When writing *On the Musical Modes of the Hindus*, Jones thanked Richard Johnson and another British civil servant, Mr Hay, for introducing him to the rāgamālā painting albums, stating that 'the most beautiful are in the possession of Mr. R. Johnson and Mr. Hay' (Jones 1799, 431). William Jones, more so than Johnson, sanskritized Hindustani music and dismissed the Indo-Persian markers in the rāgamālā genre (Bakhle 2005, 10; Bor 2006, 6). Sanskritization, also called Hinduization, is a search for authenticity through texts, envisioning India as 'static' with a true Hindu past (Cohn 1996). Jones believed that Muslims had tainted and ruined the musical arts of South Asia (Jones and Cannon 1970, 759).[15] In his letters, Johnson never explicitly clarifies whether he agrees with this belief. A short time later, Johnson did somewhat conform to Jones' sentiments and consider his rāgamālā albums to be a 'Hindu' product.

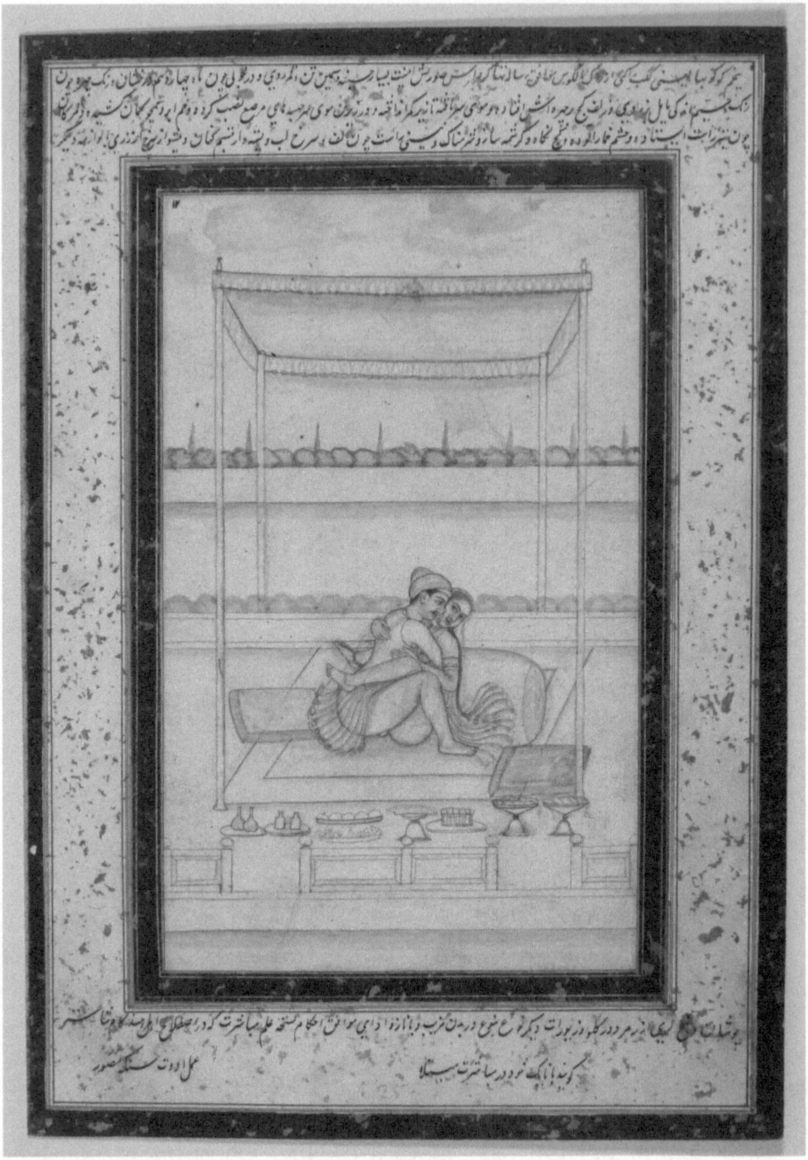

Figure 3. *Album J.42*, folio 12. © The British Library Board.

Johnson, unlike other British and European collectors, was invested not in the artistic style of the miniature paintings but in their thematic relationship to musical literature. When he was posted to Calcutta in 1783, Indian scholars such as Mir Muhammad Husain accompanied him on his journey (Jones 1799, 212 and 553).[16] Through the intercession of native aides, Johnson was able to collect both textual manuscripts and painting albums. Falk and Archer state that 'it was the relationship between Indian music, poetry and painting as illustrated by rāgamālā paintings that aroused Johnson's curiosity' (1981, 307). To satiate his appetite for Indian music, Johnson commissioned artists such as Ghulam Reza, Udwat Singh, Mohan Singh, and Gobind Singh to undertake new rāgamālā folios along with collecting textual manuscripts. Johnson did not merely buy completed folios from dealers. While he was first based in Lucknow as assistant resident to Nathaniel Middleton in October 1780, he commissioned a number of albums. Johnson also used the *charbas* [tracings] from his albums to create new paintings (Falk and Archer 1981, 232–234; Gude 2009, 144–314).[17]

Johnson turned to musical treatises in an effort to understand rāgamālā painting more fully. In the process, he did more than translate the language; he also translated the meaning of the paintings. Besides the *Risāla-i Rāgamālā*, Johnson also collected the following musical treatises: *Usal al-Naghmat*, *Saṅgīta Ratnākara* (thirteenth-century treatise), *Saṅgīta Darpana* (seventeenth-century treatise), and *Tuhfat al-Hind* (Persian text by Mirza Muhammad ibn Fakhr al-Din Muhammad during Aurangzeb's reign) (Falk and Archer 1981, 23).[18] He used these texts to create new painting albums. For instance, his painting albums *Album J.35*, *Album J.36*, and *Album J.39* include excerpts from the Sanskrit text *Saṅgīta Darpana*.[19] The text of *Tuhfat al-Hind* is illustrated in his *Album J.34*. Consequently, his paintings rely more on textual treatises than did earlier rāgamālā painting. In essence, Johnson introduces the idea that musical texts held more evidentiary truth about India than did the visual iconography of the rāgamālā album.

After falling into financial difficulty, Richard Johnson sold his paintings along with his manuscript collection to the India Office in 1807. The paintings were not highly regarded. On February 9 1807, Charles Wilkins, the first director of the India House Library, assessed Johnson's collection. He wrote: 'Their value can only be estimated by taste, fancy and fashion.'[20] For Johnson, however, they were so valuable that in his reply to Wilkins he had difficulty pricing his collection because he had carefully curated their production.[21]

Johnson never provides an explicit rationale for why he sponsored his rāgamālā albums. The only clue comes when Johnson decides to sell his collections. For the first time, he positions them as part of the Hindu mythological canon. On January 30 1807, Johnson writes:

> The pictures contain portraits of kings, and most eminent nobles, warriors and men of learning while others are explanatory of the hindoo mythology, with their singular personification of the musical modes.[22]

Although the rāgamālā genre does contain Hindu iconography, the texts that Johnson collected also included an Islamicate chain of transmission. Furthermore, Johnson adds that these rāga pictures are of value because they offer a 'clearer understanding of the history and religion of that important country of which a larger proportion is now under the sovereignty of the Company than ever was held by their most successful Emperors'.[23] Johnson's collecting practices, including his love for rāgamālā painting, thus line up with a larger colonial politics in which British civil servants extracted knowledge of their colonial subjects in order to more effectively govern (Cohn 1996, 98–105).

Johnson's sponsorship of albums such as rāgamālā *Album J.42* was a didactic move intended to render the rāga theoretical texts in a visceral, immediate visual form and provide a textual rationale for the rāgamālā's multilayered iconography. Although Johnson may not have comprehended the *Risāla-i Rāgamālā* or any other musical texts, through his native informants and his European colleagues he was able to direct his artisans to paint albums based on these manuscripts. In turn, these artisans matched each description of a rāga with a corresponding image. Thus, the more Indo-Persianate features of the *Risāla-i Rāgamālā*, such as its references to Sufi and Persianate figures such as Nizamuddin Aliya, Gayumars, and the prophet David, were not visualized.[24] As a result, by excising the more explicitly Islamicate imagery, Johnson did slightly alter the rāga's meaning. Moreover, by imposing elaborate textual captions, Johnson seemed to be suggesting that his rāgamālā paintings served a narrative purpose and were not just decorative representations of the body.

Johnson's arrangement of rāgamālā painting albums does follow the visual genre's long history of manipulation. From its inception, the rāgamālā genre was continually reworked to fit into courtly protocols and visual agendas. Johnson, too, had his biases. By inserting textual explanations for each rāga, Johnson rendered the visuals more accessible for other colonial agents who were attempting to learn Sanskrit and Persian, and who favoured text over image. Johnson's views on *Album J.42* and other rāgamālā albums were also slightly less rigid than those of his peers such as William Jones. While Johnson never imposed his morality on the nude compositions in his album collection, he did end up sublimating the Islamic elements of the textual and visual genre to advance the narrative of a native Hindu painting tradition, an idea that would be taken up by future cataloguers and scholars. Later British colonial officers utilized this narrative of a pure native Hindu culture to bypass Muslim elites and to create greater frictions between these two communities. Erasing Muslim contributions to rāgamālā paintings, in particular, echoed the colonial practice of 'compartmentalizing indigenous learning into linguistically defined Hindu and Islamic categories' (Alam and Alavi 2001, 43). In doing so, these early colonial collectors and officers, to varying degrees, elevated the Hindu elements of the rāgamālā system as its authentic aesthetic expression.

Museums

Once Johnson's albums entered the India Office in 1807, various staff members catalogued his collection and forced the paintings into the archival parameters of their institution. Figures such as Charles J. Mickle and anonymous personnel perceived visible sexual organs to be obscene. As this museological history of Johnson's rāgamālā albums is traced, there is an arbitrariness in the identification and isolation of obscenity and erotica that complicates our knowledge of the boundaries of erotica, obscenity, and pornography. As a working definition, pornography consists of visual representations and speech that cause sexual arousal, which displaces the definition onto the viewer, who must decide based on their personal experiences what is or is not pornography. As Linda Williams has stated, '[O]ne person's pornography is another person's erotica' (1999, 6). Likewise, as rāgamālā was institutionalized, there was no consensus as to what qualified as obscene, subversive, or erotic. While the history of rāgamālā albums aligns with recent scholarship on obscenity that positions it as a non-monolithic category (Nead 1992; Williams 1999, 2008, 323–313; Guha-Thakurta 2004, 247), researchers have not yet discussed how museums and libraries in the nineteenth century acted as purveyors of colonialism and imperialism by allowing certain images from the colonies to come to be deemed obscene.

Like other obscene materials in the nineteenth century, many rāgamālā images were marked for destruction. Unlike erotic objects of European providence, however, rāgamālā paintings were kept for posterity because they stood as testaments to the necessity of colonial policies. The logic follows that if the art of the colonized was obscene, then a more rational approach of governance from the British was needed to properly moralize them and their visual culture (Mitter 1994a, 387–394). Erotica from South Asia was then translated into a Victorian system of morality in order to further the colonial project of civilizing the colonized. For the British, foreignness was also a way to import erotica into their culture and blame it on outsider groups. In a sense, rāgamālā paintings were deemed most acceptable early on, when colonial figures collected them, the paintings' acceptability coming from their association with music. They were literary and 'philosophical' artefacts at first, and then became visual objects in their own right (Jones 1799, 413). While the rāgamālā paintings became more institutionally acceptable as time went on and once they were reclassified as art, the pornography designation actually arrives late. Rāgamālā paintings, thus, complicate an easy narrative of increasing acceptability over time.

Charles Wilkins, the director of the India House Library, was deeply invested in literature from India. Nonetheless, he never undertook a comprehensive evaluation of Johnson's collection, noting only that the collection was organized in loose portfolios. He states:

> [T]he Books having been recently taken from chests, and of course entirely deranged as to classification, or any kind of order, I was under the necessity or passing every vol. through my hands to get at the title. And assort them according to their subjects. This proved a very tedious operation.[25]

Because of the haphazard way the albums were arranged, staff decided to create a more coherent catalogue. During this time, they also handled the day-to-day management of the albums. In 1813, the library sent one of Johnson's albums to be bound.[26] Other albums were rebound in 1824.

In around 1830, Charles J. Mickle, who was a clerk at the India Office library from 1808 to 1832, undertook a formal valuation of Johnson's picture albums in a catalogue titled *List of the Oriental Drawings Belonging Chiefly to Mr. Johnson's Collection*, in which he introduced a moral code for the albums.[27] Charles J. Mickle asked that some of Johnson's albums be censored, writing that *Album J.42* should be 'destroyed' because it was 'excessively obscene'.[28] He also called for other rāgamālā albums, such as *Album J.44*, to be 'obliterated'. *Album J.66* was described as 'containing several mythological and other obscene pictures'.[29] Sometime between 1807 and 1830, another librarian attendant wrote on a flyleaf of *Album J.42*: '36 drawings some of which are very obscene'.[30] In the process of building a library of colonial subjects, Mickle enforced his Victorian sensibilities of public decency. Beyond his own person, Mickle did not explain who or what constituted the invisible public he was attempting to protect. It seems Mickle set his own limits of morality. For instance, one image from *Album J.42* was presumably marked for 'destruction' because the couple is in the midst of copulation and the man's testicles are peeking out beneath his buttocks (Figure 3). Today such an image would be considered benign, since the depiction does not appear to be as graphic or lifelike as it might be in a different medium such as oil painting, photography, or cinema. But, even in the context of strict Victorian sensibilities, to destroy rather than censor such an image seems harsh. For comparison, consider the case of Michelangelo's *David*. In 1857, the staff of the South Kensington Museum infamously censored a cast of *David* by covering the statue's genital with a fig leaf. Ostensibly, *David* offended Victorian sensibilities because of its hyper-realism and large scale.[31] Figure 3 is quite tame in comparison. The male figure's genitals are rendered more miniscule in scale when compared to *David*. Perhaps it was the fear of a racial other that propelled Wilkins to impose harsher moral pronouncements on these images than he otherwise would have done had such images been produced in London or in Europe.

The instability of the obscenity premise is discernible in the case of two folios of the same rāga, lalīta rāginī, which usually shows a lover arriving back to his beloved after a period of separation. In *Album J.30*, the lalīta rāginī portrays two women in an amorous embrace (Figure 4).[32] One of them fondles the other's breast. Besides the sexual tension between these two lovers, one of the women is committing an act of transgression by cross-dressing in a turban designed for a man. Both female figures are covered with diaphanous robes and jewellery. In the scene, the curtain, cushion, and symmetrical

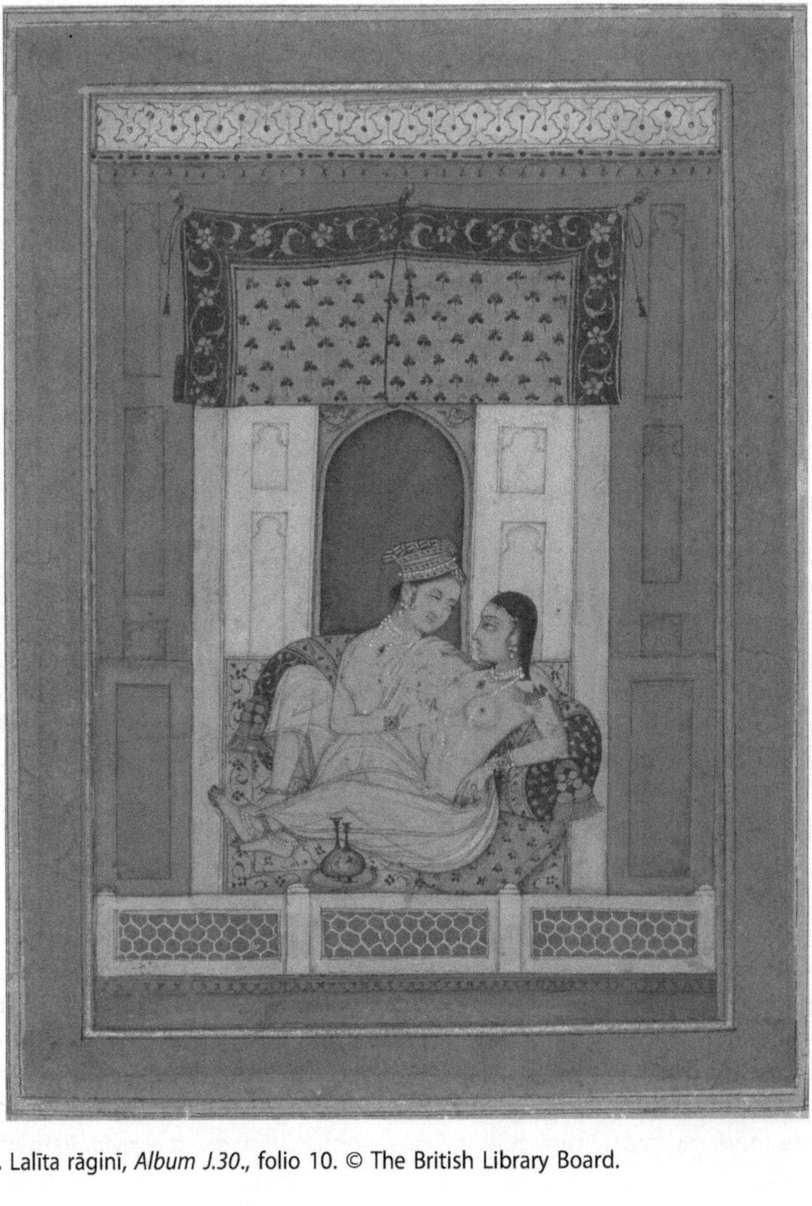

Figure 4. Lalīta rāginī, *Album J.30.*, folio 10. © The British Library Board.

architectural features of the doors all visually highlight the amorous state of the couple. This is one of 34 folios in *Album J.30*. Neither this lalīta rāginī nor its album has ever been labelled as obscene or as erotic. Evidently, therefore, pictorial depictions showing female lovers in various degrees of nudity and displaying transgressive gender codes of cross-dressing did not necessarily warrant censoring.[33] What, then, has driven Avadhi folios to be labelled as erotic, obscene, or pornographic? It is clearly not merely the subject matter: the lalīta rāginī of *Album J.30* escaped censorship while similar compositions did not. At first, I assumed that a folio would not be considered obscene if surrounded by enough innocuous material. In the British Library, however, the whole of *Album J.44*, which contains 42 miniatures, was deemed 'obscene' and marked out for 'obliteration' in 1830 because of one painting: folio 23 (Figure 5).[34] Folio 23 is another

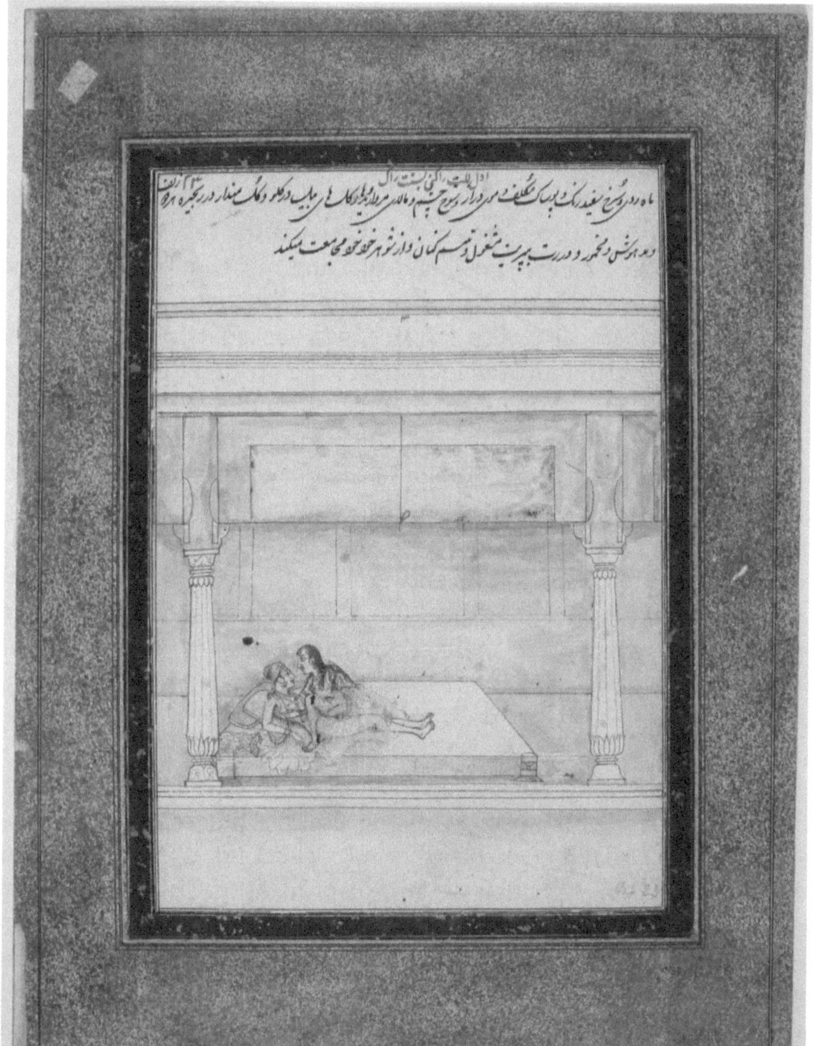

Figure 5. Lalīta rāginī, *Album J.44*, folio 23. © The British Library Board.

depiction of lalīta rāginī. In this iteration, according to Falk and Archer, the couple 'on a bed are engaged in sexual intercourse' (1981, 175). The Persian inscription of Figure 5 echoes Falk and Archer's brief statement, but goes further. It first attributes lalīta rāginī's beauty to her specific features, including her eyes and her hair, and then describes how at night, while intoxicated [*madhūsh*, *maḵẖmūr*], lalīta rāginī copulates [*mujāma'at*] with her husband. The image corresponds with the Persian text.[35] The main female figure straddles her supine male companion. The artisan seems not to have finished depicting their sexual organs, as the male figure's erect penis is painted in a faint line in comparison to the coarse, dark line of the female's countenance. Another possibility is that Mickle decided to physically erase their sexual organs during his cataloguing process.[36] The presence of a graphic phallus is also not the defining factor, as other miniature paintings with male genitalia were not censured. Both Figures 4 and 5 represent lalīta rāginī as moments of intrusion, but only one of these was marked for censorship, revealing an ambivalence around what constitutes an obscene form of sexual expression.

Mickle's charges of obscenity coincided with two important events in the history of porn studies: Ashbee and Pompeii. Recent scholarship has shown that pornography is not an essential category since the term is a recent innovation and came to be deployed more frequently at the end of the nineteenth century as a result of the formation of archives and museums (Kendrick 1987, 12–32; Sigel 2005, 7; Dean, Ruszczycky and Squires 2014). In 1900, Henry Spencer Ashbee donated his vast collection of literature to the British Museum, the terms stipulating that the museum also had to accept his erotica. The British Museum decided to guard those elements of Ashbee's collection that contained sexual material in the Private Case, locked bookcases housed in the keeper's office (Gibson 2001). Prospective readers were obliged to submit an application in order to read these books, which meant that only a handful of scholars actually gained access. The question of the value of images that have sexual content erupted once more during the excavation of Pompeii at the end of the nineteenth century. Kendrick argues that these Greek libidinal relics needed to be preserved as 'source knowledge' of the Roman Empire and to be remembered for European history. The Pompeiian artefacts were stored in a 'secret museum' to prevent a volatile public from negative effects (Kendrick 1987, 11). To be sure, both the Ashbee case and the Pompeii case certainly have their own complex histories, but they do share certain similarities with the case of Mickle and Indian miniature painting. In all of these cases, once these purportedly sexual objects entered institutions and became part of archives, their meanings began to shift to the realm of obscenity.

The rāgamālā albums were not placed in the Private Case like Ashbee's collection. Instead, they were placed in dark racks of the British Library's iron room away from the public from 1867 until 1954, dates that correspond to the life span of the Private Case. As a result, more scholars had access to Ashbee's collection than to the iron room, a remote, dusty storage facility that held miscellaneous, unwanted objects. Moreover, the creation of the category of obscenity arose partly as a result of the rise of print culture and the mass circulation of texts about sex in Europe. Rāgamālā images could barely be circulated. They are fragile and need to be handled carefully. Few people in Europe could read their Persian, Sanskrit, or Hindi textual captions. Thus, print did not have a strong effect on the reception of rāgamālā albums. In addition, unlike the Pompeiian artefacts, the rāgamālā images were not preserved in order for Europeans to create bonds of affiliation with a distant past. The rāgamālā albums were preserved because they played into colonial fantasies about India that Indians needed to be civilized, providing a rationale for the British colonial apparatus (Mitter 1977, 239; 1994a, 393).[37] The cataloguing practices of these early librarians were, in a way, reminiscent of colonial policies of divide and rule. Museum personnel compartmentalized India and its objects into consumable parts and dissoluble, knowable bits. These were separated into stylistic categories to help future viewers understand a racial and political other.

Because of their sequestering, the rāgamālā albums barely surface in the library's official record throughout the twentieth century. On February 1 1912, librarian Dr F. W. Thomas, who worked there from 1903 to 1917, removed some rāgamālā folios from their albums so he could take them to the 'S and S room' for preservation, which was most likely the conservation wing.[38] S. C. Sutton, who was librarian from 1949 to 1972, reorganized the entire collection in the 1950s because of the increased public demand to see parts of the Indian Office's collection of images. To prevent the public from ruining the delicate folios, the paintings were mounted separately and disbound from their albums (Falk and Archer 1981, 308). At around the same time, in 1954, Mildred Archer was employed to catalogue the Johnson collection and discovered that many of the albums were in the 'iron room where the rent books were stored' (Archer and Archer 1994, 139). She states:

> They were shelved on iron mobile racking which ran on rails suspended from the ceiling—an invention which when it was installed in 1867 was the acme of modernity. Armed with a torch, I crept between the dark racks, peering for any volumes, which might possibly contain drawings. Sure enough, a number came to light. ... There was also the splendid collection of miniature collection in India by Richard Johnson (1753–1807). These paintings were either loose in portfolios or guarded in old albums.

Over the course of the library's cataloguing history, some of Johnson's albums, especially *Album J.42*, were labelled obscene. Retracing how rāgamālā were stored suggests that library staff continued to preserve rather than destroy these images because few people had access to them and could not protest against their visual elements. The rāgamālā albums were presumably stored in the dark racks of the iron room from 1867 until Archer found them in 1954. Or, given that they are absent from the library's official textual record, it is possible that some of the albums could also have been placed in the library's famous Private Case and secretum, sections of the library reserved for obscene materials (Gaimster 2000).

In our own times, these albums are both meticulously preserved and carefully concealed. Although they are not as directly proscribed as they were in the nineteenth and twentieth centuries, their access continues to be restricted in different ways. Indeed, few people have access to them today. To gain access, you first need to present identity documentation and credentials to obtain a library card and be admitted into the British Library as a researcher. Second, all of the rāgamālā albums are stored today in the Library's Prints Room, which is open only for a few hours every weekday. When you are in the room, a librarian continues to monitor you. In these ways, these images continue to be restricted from public view, even if they are not actively censored. One might even say that the bureaucratic processes and academic credentials required to access these images today function as contemporary forms of 'censorship'.

In the twentieth century, museum and library personnel in England considered erotica as an extension of colonial subjects' degenerate cultures, which further pathologized native religions and aesthetics. This line of argumentation ignores the contributions of figures such as Richard Johnson who shaped the aesthetic output of these albums as much as any local native elite. In 1914, Vincent A. Smith, an art historian and British civil servant, denounced Mughal pictures, particularly those in Johnson's collection, for 'indecency'. Because of museum and library policies, Smith claimed he had not seen many of these 'lascivious' images, stating he only had access to four such images (1911, 336; 1914). He further asserted that 'decent' Europeans 'seldom bought' the indecent paintings that circulated in the art market. Smith contended he had only heard of the existence of these lascivious miniature paintings through rumours that circulated underground since Europeans had rare contact with such works.[39] Since rāgamālā images and other miniature paintings were inaccessible, British art historians mythologized Muslims and Hindu rulers as the ones who promoted and sponsored indecent aesthetics. In the process, the role of colonial officials in the configuration of power for patronizing these images is ignored. Around the same time that Smith made his obscenity assertion, the British Museum in 1913 decreed three types of books indecent. One of these categories was 'subversi[on] of religion' (Fryer 1966, 52). As Smith's statement attests, miniature paintings including rāgamālā images were associated with distant religions such as Islam and Hinduism, which presented an affront to Christian values.[40] Erotic rāgamālā images and other sexual representations, with their religious connotations, started to stand for a narrative about colonial subjects as aberrant.

Having a vacillating barometer for what constituted erotica and obscenity meant that librarians and, later, British civil servants exercised their own judgement in defining obscenity. When rāgamālā images were still encased in albums and placed in depositories, there was no consistent pattern for when the individual folios would be considered obscene. The process of declaring objects obscene became even more fraught when the albums were dismantled and individual erotic folios were sold and circulated as singular paintings, which removed them from their historical and eighteenth-century textual context. Most librarians and viewers could not read the text that Johnson juxtaposed with the images; they could only see the figural bodies. Thus, the charge of obscenity was created over time and was not a separate enterprise from British colonial politics. In the end, British imperial politics benefited from the obscenity category by degrading the visual culture of the colonized.

The emergence of pornography and art

In the usual procedures of high art, explicit iconography within images is controlled by the boundaries of the category of art. The sexual, 'unruly body' is elevated to one that embodies truth and beauty (Nead 1992, 2). During the second half of the twentieth century, Indian miniature paintings were transformed from craft into art thanks to the rise of exhibitions and art historical scholarship on the paintings. While some styles were praised more highly than others, Indian miniature painting overall acquired the status of art. So identified, many works depicting naked figures were thus neutered with the term 'nude', which was meant to regulate dangerous visual knowledge of the body (Nead 1992, 2). In the case of Avadhi rāgamālā albums, despite being newly designated as art, some, such as *Album 30* and *Album 32* from the Raza Library in Rampur, were also identified as pornography. The new shift of rāgamālā miniatures from craft to art did little to ease the potential danger of the erotic.

Interrogating the binary between art and pornography allows us to see how these two different concepts were applied to the same material in different contexts of Britain and India in the second half of the twentieth century. A forked path followed here for rāgamālā painting: high art in England and pornography in India. However, while this is true to an extent institutionally, rāgamālā paintings that contain various degrees of nudity are not regularly displayed in England to this day. It is also hard to track whether audiences in England and India continue to perceive these paintings as art. Therefore, this section of the article continues to focus on museums because they provide documents that show how personnel and perhaps a wider public viewed these objects. I show how museums in India utilize the label of pornography for these paintings to satisfy a national narrative. In particular, by purposely labelling these objects as pornography, Indian museum personnel distanced themselves from a tradition they perceived to be degenerate and debauched (a perception that was itself produced through colonial collecting practices) and instead began to privilege spiritual interpretations of Indian art. As a result, the artistic tradition of rāgamālā, with its dense network of Islamicate, Indic, and corporeal symbols, was reconceived as being grounded purely in spirituality.

Through the scholarship of a handful of art historians, most schools of miniature painting underwent a categorical transformation from craft to art. The work of Ernest Binfield Havell (1861–1934) and Ananda Kentish Coomaraswamy (1877–1947) further moved on the discussion of Indian painting as art objects by identifying separate artistic schools of painting and imbuing these objects with spiritual significance. Both scholars had a vast impact on the field. In their wake, 'Indian arts and antiquities were now recast as Indian art and aesthetics' (Guha-Thakurta 2004, 156).[41] Havell and Coomaraswamy both advocated for an 'authentic' Indian art, reviving aesthetic objects produced under royal 'Hindu' rule. A seminal book that helped collectors and museum staff to compartmentalize miniatures into stylistic schools was Percy Brown's *Indian Painting under the Mughals*, completed in 1924. Another was N. C. Mehta's *Studies in Indian Painting* in 1926. In these two works, objects and paintings were granted greater historical, artistic, and social weight, which had the effect of increasing their financial worth. This, in turn, encouraged local collectors to establish museums, exhibitions, and journals to meet the growing demand for viewing and possessing these paintings. The Bharat Kala Bhavan museum, for instance, was founded by Rai Krishnadasa who claimed to be 'spurred by Coomaraswamy's exhibition of paintings (Kumar 2015, 161)'.[42] Another aesthete inspired by Coomaraswamy was O. C. Gangoly who started the art journal, *Rupam*, in 1920 (Guha-Thakurta 1992, 198 and 225). In 1935, O. C. Gangoly began to write scholarly articles on the rāga system, which culminated in his book *Rāgas & Rāginīs* (1948).[43]

With the country's independence in 1947, many more collectors and scholars in India were driven to collect, inspired by a new wave of scholarship and exhibitions. An exhibition of Indian and Pakistani art was held in 1947–1948 at the Royal Academy of Arts and Burlington House in London. In this exhibition, organizers laid out objects according to their geographic site of production in India (Guha-Thakurta 2004, 188). Basil Gray, keeper of the Department of Oriental Antiquities at the British Museum from 1946 to 1969, wrote the catalogue for this exhibition, which was used by scholars and elite buyers. In India, from 1947 to

1975, there was an upsurge in museums and other institutions acquiring painting collections from many Indian royal families and princely states who were liquidating their estates' art objects and shedding their collections of 'old surplus or unwanted paintings', which consisted largely of Rajput rāgamālā paintings (McInerney 2001, 6). The National Museum of India was founded in 1949 and purchased the miniatures that flooded the Indian art market. They also amassed a large amount of art from private donations (Guha-Thakurta 2004, 188). In 1948, V. S. Agrawala held a rival exhibition to the Burlington House exhibition in order to create a 'grander, more representative show' (Guha-Thakurta 2004, 188). The movement of the Bengal School of Art, led by artist Abanindranath Tagore (1871–1951), also affected how local Indian aesthetics were appraised. Artists who participated in this movement revived indigenous Asian genres such as miniature paintings and transported the format into the modernist movement, which allowed Indian painting to be utilized as an aesthetic tool of *swadeshi* [Indian nationalism].

Legal and institutional proclamations of pornography were issued in India coinciding with the rise of museums such as the Raza Library, which was established in Rampur in 1957, and the founding of the Indian nation-state in 1947. Obscenity and pornography were legal categories imported to India from British imperial policies. Simultaneously, with the rise of Indian nationalism, the borders of art needed to be policed to accommodate the needs of the nation-state. When India and East and West Pakistan were founded in 1947, many museums were created, including the Raza Library.

In 1957, the nawab of Rampur, Raza Ali Khan (r. 1930–1966), merged his collection of art with the rest of his ancestral collections such as paintings from the first nawab of Rampur, Faizullah Khan (r. 1774–1794). Nawab Raza Ali Khan also collected many miniatures from the burgeoning art market in India in the twentieth century. To house these collections, Nawab Raza Ali Khan and his trustees acquired a large estate called Hamid Manzil, which became the permanent home of these objects. From this diverse collection, staff in the Raza Library began to catalogue objects, pronouncing some obscene under the influence of old British policies and the demands of Indian nationalism. Tapati Guha-Thakurta, for instance, has shown how the temple sculptures of Khajuraho, which feature lovers in the throes of copulation, were permissible for the Indian nation-state because it made allowances for a Hindu spirituality; on the other hand, Indian nationalists protested modern artist M. F. Husain's work for transgressing the erotic boundaries of a Hindu goddess (Guha-Thakurta 2004, 237–267). In this sense, the rāgamālā paintings do not present a coherent story of an erotic Hinduism that could be marshalled in the name of the Indian nation like the Khajuraho sculptures.

In the Raza Library, there are four painting albums labelled as 'pornography' (Schmitz and Desai 2006, vii, 64, and 65). Two of these are from Lucknow: *Album 30* and *Album 32. Album 30* is composed of nine folios, and the numbering indicates that the album once had 30 folios. Figure is from *Album 30* and shows two women engaging in sexual intercourse. Figure is an image from *Album 32*, which contains only three miniatures. Another painting from *Album 32* opened this article. The flyleaf of *Album 32* states: '[O]bscene (foḥ. sḥ) muraqqa' rāgamālā. Three on paper (was. .lī).'[44] The folios of *Album 30* clearly were once part of a larger rāgamālā album, and *Album 32* was also most likely part of a larger *muraqqa'* album, a scrapbook of alternating calligraphies and paintings. Either Nawab Raza Ali Khan or an anonymous librarian curated albums deemed 'obscene' by removing any imagery that did not contain obvious sexual activity.

Whereas Mildred Archer brought rāgamālā images out of the shadows of the iron room in London in the 1950s, at the Raza Library in Rampur the opposite occurred. There, the label of pornography served as a barrier for art historians and scholars to study these objects as part of the South Asian art canon.

With all these factors in mind, it is hard to determine why certain Avadhi miniatures are considered perverse and others normative. With miniatures containing corporeal representations, it is not merely the showcasing of sexual organs that shifts them into the categories of obscenity and pornography. For instance, Avadhi amorous images in the Victoria and Albert Museum were never saddled with the terms obscenity or pornography. One might assume that the Victoria and Albert Museum images escaped censorship because they entered institutions already legitimized as housing art, whereas others such as *Album J.42* entered the India House Library at an earlier stage, before these images had been normalized. However, the history of Raza Library at Rampur proves otherwise. The legitimacy of the art category did not dispel the potential perversity of the erotic rāgamālā folios and their ability to provoke desire.

Based on the different accounts of when rāgamālā albums came to be seen as licentious, it is clear that such designations are socially and historically contingent on the audience that catalogues the material. In England, museum personnel such as Mickle and art historians such as Smith envisioned rāgamālā images as being derived from a racial and political alterity to European politics. Rāgamālā paintings disrupted the morality of an imagined white, British audience. Later, once rāgamālā paintings were considered art, the charges of obscenity appear less frequently in museological records. In India, by contrast, the images were conceived of as pornography when they were already elevated as an art form because they were not reproducible for the nation-state as an iconic image of a past, revered visual culture. The charges of obscenity are thus managed and based on the demands of the archival process, which is circumscribed by institutions' locations and their historical needs. Each location – England and India – had its own hierarchy of political relationships, and these paintings were moments of transgression of this perceived order.

Conclusion

When trying to study an early modern South Asian form of erotica and pornography, we cannot isolate it from the regimes of power that pronounced objects respectable or disrespectable. Previous scholars have taken a 'detour of colonialism' in their historical scholarship on sex and pornography (Arondekar 2009, 104). In *Governing Pleasures*, Sigel qualifies some Victorian pornography as part of the mechanics of imperialism, naming this genre 'imperial pornography' (2002, 23). Through a broad sweep of history, McClintock (1995) discusses how imperial forces sexualized foreign geographies. Building on these works, I have provided a specific case study of Johnson and rāgamālā albums. In the course of cataloguing rāgamālā albums, museum personnel, librarians, and art historians deemed them pornography or obscenity because these personnel did not take into account the musical components of the text, the role of European collectors, or the archival demands of museums that constrain translation.

This article has, thus, explored the question of how Avadh's eroticism and erotic visuality were produced and reproduced by the very nature of archive formation and colonial institutions. Anjali Arondekar's work on archives and sexuality has, in many ways, laid the foundation for such an inquiry. In her book *For the Record: On Sexuality and the Colonial Archive in India*, Arondekar traced 'how sexuality is made visible in the colonial archive and … how this process paradoxically discloses the very limits of that visibility' (2009, 3). My study of Indian miniature painting similarly finds that sexual material is not absent from canonical archives, such as the British Library, but is inescapably present. Although archives like the British Library enacted exclusionary practices, such as calling for the eradication of certain rāgamālā paintings, they needed excised or censored objects in order to conform to a normative ideal of what an archive should be and what its collections ought to contain. In this way, the archival treatment of sexual material was central to the formation and self-definition of those archives. Indeed, as Arondekar proposes, sexuality is at the 'center of the colonial archive rather than at its margins' (2009, 4).

During the eighteenth century, Johnson initiated the transformation of the rāgamālā folio as a symbol of India's Hindu and Sanskritic past. Different colonial agents had different takes on the matter. Even so, neither Richard Johnson nor William Jones, both heavy proponents of rāga music and rāgamālā painting, consistently sought to invoke the acts and beliefs of Muslim patrons like the nawabs of Avadh. By collecting and establishing a Hindu framework for the paintings, Johnson and Jones were the first to provide an intellectual paradigm for how these images should be defined and viewed.

In institutions and depositories, these images once again garnered a new wave of interpretation. Museum personnel in England worried over the erotic nature of the imagery and chose to separate folios from their albums and sequester them in storage rooms. In catalogues, items were reconceived as obscenity and as erotica. Museum personnel in England in the nineteenth century and in India in the twentieth century, unlike previous patrons and owners in Avadh, had to address and negotiate the fact that the images could become a public spectacle. In Avadh in the eighteenth century, on the other hand, rāgamālā albums were shared within a close circuit of courtiers. Moreover, viewers in these museological institutions no longer had a Sanskritic or Persianate knowledge base on which to judge and understand the albums and folios. Thus, museum staff acted to shield and protect an anonymous, nebulous public through the concealment of improper paintings. Rāgamālā paintings became obscenity, like many objects before them, through acts of censorship and regulation on the part of staff and as a result of exposure to a larger audience that frequented exhibitions. Collecting practices and the art market also had a hand in this matter since erotic folios were separated from their book formats, which left so-called illicit scenes without any visual or textual context.

The definitional parameters of pornography, obscenity, erotica, and art are fuzzy; Avadhi rāgamālā albums such as *Album J.42* have at one time or another been considered most of these. They are not mutually exclusive categories. When an object is granted the status of fine art, erotica is usually the descriptive attachment rather than pornography. To wrestle with why and how Avadhi rāgamālā paintings became obscene, it is presumably also necessary to tell the story of how and when miniature paintings became 'art'. Pornography carries with it a stigma of low art that is supposed to disassociate it from high art. Even though the form of miniature painting attained the status of art during the twentieth century, rāgamālā albums came to be considered pornography in museological institutions in India. These two categories were not so separate in the reception of rāgamālā albums in India at the end of the twentieth century.

I take a pause here at this impasse. I do not advocate that any of these categories – art, pornography, erotica – be called misreadings of rāgamālā paintings and musical texts. That would require staking my own claims for what constitutes an authentic rāgamālā formation and to make one for what distinguishes these categories. For such a discussion, there are multiple histories available that explore the visual evidence of *Album J.42* and similar rāgamālā albums. It is more interesting to see what arises when incorporating this multifaceted history into academic disciplines. To add these rāgamālā albums into art history is to tackle what constitutes normative South Asian art. To add them into South Asian studies is to reignite the discussion of colonialism and its role in creating pornography.

Notes

1. This article does not have sufficient space to track instances in which scholars trained in western institutions retain the term pornography for rāgamālā paintings and for miniature paintings more generally. For the most recent study, see Boone (2014, 396–408). He positions miniature paintings along a historical trajectory with pornography. For the rest of this article, instead of zoning in on individual academics, I focus on how museums in both India and England create the category of pornography and obscenity.
2. For more information on these early collectors, see Archer and Archer (1955), Welch (1978), Archer (1987), and Eaton (2013).

3. Specifically, there are visual congruencies with Johnson *Album J.31* and *Polier Album I-5062*. Polier was a Swiss entrepreneur based in Lucknow who, like Johnson, had an affinity for miniature painting.
4. Richard Johnson's father argued, for instance, that his son's collection provided a 'public utility' for the Company. See British Library (BL) IOL E/1/85, f. 75a. In his letters, Johnson also explained that his collection of manuscripts could aid the Company's governance of India. Likewise, historians have suggested that Warren Hastings, who was part of the same small network of collectors as Johnson, collected in order to solidify 'the future of British rule in India' as well as out of pleasure (Marshall 1973, 252–254). Presumably, Johnson, like Hastings, must also have gained pleasure from his albums.
5. For more information on the genre markers for rāgamālā paintings, see Mal (1931), Gangoly (1948), Waldschmidt (1967), Ebeling (1973), Gude (2009), and Glynn (2011).
6. For more information on Muslim patronage of the rāga and rāgamālā system, see Sarmadee (1978), Losty (1983), Zebrowski (1983, 63), Delvoye (1994, 1997, 2000), Michell and Zebrowski (1999, 153–162), Trivedi (2008), Schofield (2014), and Haidar and Sardar (2015, 60).
7. BL OMS/I.O. Islamic 1739, Risāla-i Rāgamālā, f. 14r. Following a Bengali calendar system, Lal Thakri states the 'month of Baisak on the 30th of 1186', which is equivalent to May 13. With the Hijri calendar, he states '1193 25th rabia'th thani (rabi' II)', which is May 12, not May 13.
8. BL OMS/I.O. Islamic 1739, Risāla-i Rāgamālā, f. 14r. Hijri: Muharram 1188. Bengali 1181.
9. Richard Johnson was appointed assistant resident of Lucknow from 1780 to 1782. Before this, he was mainly in Calcutta. Because Lal Thakri recopied the text in 1799, Johnson could have been residing in Calcutta or Lucknow at the time of transcription. See Falk and Archer (1981, 323). They suggest that the *Risāla-i Rāgamālā* was commissioned in Calcutta.
10. Other copies of Thakur Das and Lal Thakri's text have not surfaced. It most likely circulated throughout Delhi, Lucknow, and Calcutta in the latter half of the eighteenth century. Lal Thakri copied Thakur Das' text in the naskh script, a type of calligraphy that expedites the writing process. The text is more legible in Richard Johnson's 1780 rāgamālā album.
11. BL Or.6633, f. 68r.
12. Many of these miniatures are reproduced in various catalogues. For ease of reference, see Welch (1978, 26, 84, 91, and 108).
13. Yale Library, Beinecke dl 14462274, f. 115.
14. Yale Library, Beinecke dl 14462274, f. 7.
15. Letter to the second Earl Spencer dated August 4–30 1787.
16. Jones (1799) states Johnson was in either Hyderabad or Calcutta.
17. *Charbas* of *Album J.31* were used for rāgamālā *Album J.66* (no. 4v–9v). *Album J.45* also has similar compositions to folios in *Album J.31* and *Album J.32*.
18. For *Usal al-Naghmat*, see IOL Persian Ms. Ethe 2023: I.O.2083. For *Sangīta Ratnākara*, see IOL Sanskrit Ms. Eggeling 1118: I.O.2383. For *Sangīta Darpana*, see IOL Sanskrit Ms. Eggeling 1120: I.O. 2231. For *Tuhfat al-Hind*, see IOR Pers. Ms. 1861.
19. *Album J.35*, 1–30, inscribed with verses from Harivallabha's Hindi version of the *Sangīta Darpana* and with Sanskrit verses. *Album J.36*, 1–36, each picture inscribed on the reverse with verses from Harivallabha's Hindi translation of the *Sangīta Darpana*. *Album J.39*, 1–36, inscribed with Sanskrit verses from Damodara's *Sangīta Darpana*.
20. BL IOL E/1/115/, f. 75v. Reproduced in Falk and Archer (1981, 28).
21. BL IOL E/1/115/, f. 76. The library ended up paying Johnson a fraction of the cost of his original asking price and gave him scant compensation.
22. BL IOL E/1/115/, f. 78; Falk and Archer (1981, 26–27).
23. BL IOL E/1/115/, f. 78.
24. Two mentions of the prophet David are still retained textually in the descriptive header of *Album J.42* for the kernātēk rāginī, found on folio 21, and for the rāmakalī rāginī, found on folio 15.
25. BL IOL E/1/115/, f. 75.
26. BL IOL Mss. Eur.239, f. 142v (Falk and Archer 1981, 307). Falk and Archer also mentioned that museum personnel sent *Album J.30* to be bound.

27. Catalogue Eur. D486 is dated to 1820 in the British Library. In one of its folios, there is a watermark of 1826. A flyleaf of the catalogue reads 1830. Hence, Falk and Archer have dated the catalogue to 1830. I have followed accordingly.
28. BL IOR Eur. d486, f. 19v.
29. BL IOR Eur. d486, ff. 19v, 28r.
30. British Library, 'India Office Library'. Accessed December 1 2016. http://searcharchives.bl.uk/primo_library/libweb/action/display.do?tabs=detailsTab&ct=display&fn=search&doc=IAMS040-003287275&indx=1&recIds=IAMS040-003287275&recIdxs=0&elementId=0&renderMode=poppedOut&displayMode=full&frbrVersion=&dscnt=0&frbg=&scp.scps=scope%3A%28BL%29&tab=local&dstmp=1481565557465&srt=rank&mode=Basic&&dum=true&vl(freeText0)=J.42&vid=IAMS_VU2
31. Victoria and Albert Museum, 'David's fig leaf, perhaps by D. Brucciani & Co., about 1857'. Accessed June 1 2018. http://www.vam.ac.uk/content/articles/d/davids-fig-leaf/. For more on Victorian attitudes towards classical and antique statues from Europe, see Gaimster (2000).
32. The composition is repeated in Victoria and Albert Museum IS.272-1952.
33. While the image does clearly represent two figures in amorous embrace, it is not clear whether the archival staff comprehended that the miniature represented two women rather than a man and a woman. My interest in the archival treatment of such images relates to the question of precisely when the nude slips into the category of obscenity and when bodies in the nude transform into bodies in the midst of copulation. Is this an image depicting intercourse, or is it an image depicting two figures embracing without a sexual charge? With such questions, I interrogate how decisions are made to categorize and censor images when they fall across this very fuzzy boundary, especially when there is a comparable visual programme across miniatures. Such questions also point to the blurriness of the art historical debate of naked versus nude.
34. BL IOR Eur d486, f. 19v.
35. I do not have the space here to discuss fully the vernacular meanings of the Persian inscriptions located on *Album J.42* and *Album J.44*. In short, many of the Persian inscriptions found within Johnson's rāgamālā albums explicitly mention sexual activity, which explains the curators' decisions to regulate these images as representations of sex. However, it is crucial to note that the inscriptions also contain a myriad of vernacular meanings and associations that are not easily contained in the category of sex. These include the lover/beloved category ['ashiq/ma'shūq] and the erotic sentiment [sringara rasa]. For a full translation of the Persian inscriptions of *Album J.42* and for a more detailed analysis, see Di Pietrantonio (2018, 105–149).
36. The erasure marks are mostly restricted to the figure's genitals. This would suggest that whoever erased their sexual organs, whether it was Mickle, the artist, or other museum personnel, did so intentionally as the rest of their bodies including their faces and their feet are not disfigured.
37. While Mitter does not mention the rāgamālā canon specifically, he argues that Victorian art critics in general evaluated Indian aesthetics informed, in part, by evangelism. Moreover, in the 1850s, the British established art schools so that new Indian artists could undergo 'morality training', which would allow the nation to be lifted from its artistic and economic decline. For further information, see Mitter (1994b, 29–32).
38. BL IOR Eur. d486: ff. 3r, 10v, and 28r–28v for *Album J.4*, *Album J.15*, *Album J.66*, and *Album J.67*.
39. Smith arrives at this conclusion by reading the travel writings of Monsieur Jean de Thevenot, which were published in 1687.
40. For contemporaneous art historians who classified rāgamālā as a Hindu art form and imbued it with spirituality, see the writings of Ananda Commaraswamy. For a complete bibliography of Coomaraswamy, see Crouch (2002). In one particular instance, Coomaraswamy (1916, 66) states that rāgamālā 'art is essentially religious'.
41. I do not have the space to do these two aesthetes justice. For more information, see Raja Singam (1974), Davis (1997, 176–179), Mittter (1994b 223, 351–354), Guha-Thakurta (2004, 156), and Kumar (2015, 20 and 39–144).
42. Within South Asia, British intellectuals also helped to establish museums such as the Indian Museum of Calcutta in 1814.

43. Besides Coomaraswamy, Gangoly was also influenced by European art theory. Tapati Guha-Thakurta has argued that 'European romantic theories of art' were a pivotal conceptual base for Gangoly, as they helped to develop his concern with 'sublimity emotion and idealism' in his art criticism of rāgas and Indian aesthetics (1992, 190). For Gangoly (1948, 161), the rāgas produced a 'spiritual emotion' for the viewer and listener, especially through a focus on the sensual. According to Prajnanananda (1986, 201), Gangoly's emphasis on the emotional value of the rāgas represented his focus on the 'psychic'. A contemporary of Gangoly was Lala Kannoo Mal who, like Gangoly, argued that the theme of love was a hallmark of the rāga aesthetic, and of Indian aesthetics more broadly.
44. Raza Library in Rampur, *Album 32* cover.

Disclosure statement

No potential conflict of interest was reported by the author.

Funding

This work was supported by the American Institute of Indian Studies [Junior Research Fellowship]; Andrew W. Mellon Foundation [Institute of Historical Research Mellon Pre-dissertation Fellowship]; Metropolitan Museum of Art [Jane and Morgan Whitney Fellowship].

References

Alam, Muzaffar, and Seema Alavi. 2001. 'Introduction.' In *A European Experience of the Mughal Orient: the I'jāz-i arsalānī (Persian Letters 1773–1779) of Antoine-Louis Henri Polier*, 1–91. New Delhi: Oxford University Press.

Archer, Mildred. 1987. 'The British as Collectors and Patrons in India 1760–1830.' In *Treasures from India; The Clive Collection at Powis Castle*, edited by Jonathon Marsden, and Julia MacKenzie, 9–16. London: Herbert.

Archer, Mildred, and William G. Archer. 1955. *Indian Painting for the British, 1770–1880*. London: Oxford University Press.

Archer, William G, and Mildred Archer. 1994. *India Served and Observed*. London: BACSA.

Arondekar, Anjali R. 2009. *For the Record: On Sexuality and the Colonial Archive in India*. Durham: Duke University Press.

Bakhle, Janaki. 2005. *Two Men and Music: Nationalism in the Making of an Indian Classical Tradition*. Oxford: Oxford University Press.

Boone, Joseph Allen. 2014. *The Homoerotics of Orientalism*. New York: Columbia University.

Bor, Joep. 2006. 'Three Important Essays on Hindustani Music.' *Journal of Indian Musicological Society* 36 (7): 5–16.

Cohn, Bernard S. 1996. *Colonialism and Its Forms of Knowledge: The British in India*. Princeton: Princeton University Press.

Coomaraswamy, Ananda K. 1916. *Rajput Painting: Being an Account of the Hindu Paintings of Rajasthan and the Panjab Himalayas from the Sixteenth to the Nineteenth Century Described in Their Relation to Contemporary Thought*. London: H. Milford, Oxford University Press.

Crouch, James S., and Ananda K. Coomaraswamy. 2002. *A Bibliography of Ananda Kentish Coomaraswamy*. New Delhi: Indira Gandhi National Centre for the Arts.

Davis, Richard H. 1997. *Lives of Indian Images*. Princeton: Princeton University Press.

Dean, Tim, Steven Ruszczycky, and David D. Squires. 2014. *Porn Archives*. Durham: Duke University Press.

Delvoye, Françoise 'Nalini'. 1994. 'Indo-Persian Literature on Art-Music: Some Historical and Technical Aspects.' In *Confluence of Cultures: French Contributions to Indo-Persian Studies*, edited by Françoise Nalini Delvoye, 93–130. New Delhi: Manohar.

Delvoye, Françoise 'Nalini'. 2000. 1997. 'The Image of Akbar as a Patron of Music in Indo-Persian and Vernacular Sources.' In *Akbar and His India*, edited by Irfan Habib, 188–214. New Delhi: Oxford University Press.

Delvoye, Françoise 'Nalini'. 2000. 'Indo-Persian Accounts on Music Patronage in the Sultanate of Gujarat.' In *The Making of Indo-Persian Culture: Indian and French Studies*, edited by Muzaffar Alam, Françoise Nalini Delvoye, and Marc Gaborieau, 253–280. New Delhi: Manohar Publishers & Distributors.

Di Pietrantonio, Natalia. 2018. 'Erotic Visions: Poetry, Literature, and Book of Arts of Avadh, 1754–1857.' Cornell University.

Eaton, Natasha. 2013. *Mimesis Across Empires: Artworks and Networks in India, 1765–1860*. Durham: Duke University Press.

Ebeling, Klaus. 1973. *Ragamala Painting*. Ravi Kumar: Basel.

Falk, Toby, and Mildred Archer. 1981. *Indian Miniatures in the India Office Library*. London: Sotheby Parke Bernet.

Fryer, Peter. 1966. *Private Case—Public Scandal*. London: Secker & Warburg.

Gaimster, David. 2000. 'Sex and Sensibility at the British Museum.' *History Today* 50 (9): 10–15.

Gangoly, Ordhendra Coomar. 1948. *Rāgas & Rāginīs: A Pictorial & Iconographic Study of Indian Musical Modes Based on Original Sources. Vol.1*. Bombay: Nalanda Publications.

Gibson, Ian. 2001. *The Erotomaniac: The Secret Life of Henry Spencer Ashbee*. Cambridge: Da Capo.

Glynn, Catherine Ann, Robert Skelton, and Anna L. Dallapiccola. 2011. *Ragamala Paintings from India: from the Claudio Moscatelli Collection*. London: Philip Wilson.

Gude, Tushara Bindu. 2009. 'Between Music and History: Rāgamāla Paintings and European Collectors in Late Eighteenth-Century Northern India.' UCLA.

Guha-Thakurta, Tapati. 1992. *The Making of A New 'Indian' Art: Artists, Aesthetics, and Nationalism in Bengal, c. 1850-1920*. Cambridge: Cambridge University Press.

Guha-Thakurta, Tapati. 2004. *Monuments, Objects, Histories: Institutions of Art in Colonial and Postcolonial India*. New York: Columbia University Press.

Haidar, Navina Najat, and Marika Sardar. 2015. *Sultans of Deccan India, 1500–1700: Opulence and Fantasy*. New York: Yale University Press.

Jones, William. 1799. *The Works of Sir William Jones: In Six Volumes*. London: printed for G. G. and J. Robinson; and R. H. Evans.

Jones, William, and Garland Hampton Cannon. 1970. *The Letters of Sir William Jones*. Oxford: Clarendon Press.

Kendrick, Walter. 1987. *The Secret Museum: Pornography in Modern Culture*. New York: Viking.

Kumar, Brinda. 2015. 'Of Networks and Narratives: Collecting Indian Art in America, 1907–1972.' Cornell University.

Losty, Jeremiah P. 1983. 'Early Bijapuri Musical Paintings.' In *An Age of Splendour, Islamic Art in India*, edited by Karl J. Khandalavala, and Saryu Doshi, 128–131. Bombay: Marg Publications.

Mal, Lala Kannoo. 1931. *Kāma-kalā: A Comprehensive Survey of Erotics, Rhetorics, and Science of Music with Special Reference to Sex Psychology*. Lahore: Punjab Sanskrit Book Depot.

Marshall, P. J. 1973. 'Warren Hastings as Scholar and Patron.' In *Statesmen, Scholars and Merchants: Essays in Eighteenth-Century History Presented to Dame Lucy Sutherland*, edited by Anne Whiteman, J. S. Bromley, and P. G. M. Dickson, 242–262. Oxford: Clarendon Press.

McClintock, Anne. 1995. *Imperial Leather: Race, Gender, and Sexuality in the Colonial Conquest*. New York: Routledge.

McInerney, Terence. 2001. 'On Collecting Indian Miniature Paintings: Twentieth-Century Issues and Personalities.' In *Intimate Worlds: Indian Paintings from the Alvin O. Bellak Collection*, edited by Darielle Mason, and B. N. Goswamy, 1–11. Philadelphia: Philadelphia Museum of Art.

Michell, George, and Mark Zebrowski. 1999. *Architecture and Art of the Deccan Sultanates*. Cambridge: Cambridge University Press.

Mitter, Partha. 1977. *Much Maligned Monsters: History of European Reactions to Indian Art*. Oxford: Clarendon Press.

Mitter, Partha. 1994a. '"Decadence in India": Reflections on a Much-Used Word in Studies of Indian Art.' In *Sight and Insight; Essays in Honour of E. H. Gombrich at 85*, edited by E. H. Gombrich, and John Onians, 379–397. London: Phaidon Press.

Mitter, Partha. 1994b. *Art and Nationalism in Colonial India, 1850–1922: Occidental Orientations*. Cambridge: Cambridge University Press.

Nead, Lynda. 1992. *The Female Nude: Art, Obscenity, and Sexuality*. London: Routledge.

Prajnanananda, Swami. 1986. 'O.C Gangoly's Findings on the Origin and Psychic Value of the Ragas and Raginis of Indian Music.' In *Rupanjali, in Memory of O.C. Gangoly*, edited by Kalyan Kumar Ganguli, S. S. Biswas, and O. C. Gangoly, 195–202. Calcutta: O.C. Gangoly Memorial Society.

Raja Singam, and S. Durai. 1974. *Ananda Coomaraswamy: Remembering and Remembering Again and Again*. Petaling Jaya: Raja Singam.

Randle, H. N. 1941. 'A Note on the India Office Ragamala Collection.' *New Indian Antiquary* 4 (5): 162–173.

Sarmadee, Shahab. 1978. *Ghunyat-ul-Munya: The Earliest Known Persian Work on Indian Music*. Bombay: Asia Publishing House.

Schmitz, Barbara, and Ziyaud-Din A. Desai. 2006. *Mughal and Persian Paintings and Illustrated Manuscripts in the Raza Library, Rampur*. New Delhi: Indira Gandhi National Centre for the Arts.

Schofield, Katherine Butler. 2014. 'Indian Music in the Persian Collections: The Javahir al-Musiqat-i Muhammadi (Or.12857),' 2 parts, *British Library Asian and African Studies Blog*. https://blogs.bl.uk/asian-and-african/2014/10/indian-music-in-the-persian-collections-the-javahir-al-musiqat-i-muhammadi-or12857-part-2.html.

Schofield, Katherine Butler. 2018. 'Words Without Songs": The Social History of Hindustani Song Collections in India's Muslim Courts, c. 1770–1830.' In *Theory and Practice in the Music of the Islamic World: Essays in Honour of Owen Wright*, edited by Owen Wright, Rachel Harris, and Martin Stokes, 173–198. New York: Routledge.

Sigel, Lisa Z. 2002. *Governing Pleasures: Pornography and Social Change in England, 1815–1914*. New Brunswick: Rutgers University Press.

Sigel, Lisa Z. 2005. *International Exposure: Perspectives on Modern European Pornography, 1800–2000*. New Brunswick: Rutgers University Press.

Smith, Vincent A. 1911. *A History of Fine Art in India and Ceylon: From the Earliest Times to the Present Day*. Oxford: Clarendon Press.

Smith, Vincent A. 1914. 'Painting and Engraving in Agra and Delhi in 1666.' *Indian Antiquary* 43: 124.

Trivedi, Madhu. 2008. *'A Congenial Space: The Cultural Context of Indo-Persian Synthesis in Medieval North Indian Music.'* In *Indo-Iran Relations: Papers Presented at the Seminar Held in February 2001*, edited by Shah Mohammad Waseem, 129–167. New Delhi: Iran Culture House.

Waldschmidt, Ernst, and Rose L. Waldschmidt. 1967. *Miniatures of Musical Inspiration in the Collection of the Berlin Museum of Indian Art*. Bombay: Popular Prakashan.

Welch, Stuart Cary. 1978. *Room for Wonder: Indian Painting During the British Period, 1760–1880*. New York: American Federation of Arts.

Williams, Linda. 1999. *Hard Core: Power, Pleasure, and the 'Frenzy of the Visible.'* Berkeley: University of California Press.

Williams, Linda. 2008. *Screening Sex: Linda Williams*. Durham: Duke University Press.

Zebrowski, Mark. 1983. *Deccani Painting*. London: Sotheby Publications.

'Raped, outraged, ravaged': race, desire, and sex in the Indian empire

Anubhav Pradhan

ABSTRACT

Venus in India is unique amongst pornographic literature of the long nineteenth century for being located almost exclusively in the Indian subcontinent. As men, goods, and services streamed across trade routes and expanded the frontiers of British dominion, there was a concomitant layering to the fluid, trans-cultural economy of British desire. This article evaluates this consuming anxiety generated by protracted and direct contact with the racialized other. The infrastructural and institutional paraphernalia of the British Raj act as active determinants in the nexus of desire and intercourse in this text. The narrator, a military man happily and faithfully married by his own estimation, laughs 'at the idea that there existed, or could exist, a woman in India, who could raise even a ghost of desire in me'. However, desire is generated and finds recurrent realization within the carefully racialized confines of British India. Accordingly, in considering the various gradations of desire as they operate and frame the action and logic of *Venus in India*, this article will not just consider how the forbidden and the taboo work closely to inform each other, but also how the spectre of interracial desire serves as an agent of both political and libidinal titillation.

The emergence of the pornographic through the long nineteenth century has been persuasively linked to the tenuous consolidation of bourgeois selfhoods along racial and sexed axes on one hand (Stoler 1995; Arondekar 2009a) and to the steady surge of a mass culture premised on the erotic, the sensational, and the obscene on the other (Gamer 1999; Marcus 2009). There is also an ample body of scholarship on desire (Burton 1998), gender (Sinha 1995; Levine 2004), and hybridity (Randall 2000; Caplan 2001) in and during the Raj, even of the Raj – the space of empire – itself as desire (Burton 1995). Work on dissident sexual practices and sexualities (Holden and Ruppel 2003) emergent from imperial as well as hybrid alterities of the self (Krishnaswamy 1998) has brought to the fore the fragmentations and fusions which occurred in tandem with each other as consequences of direct and indirect British rule in South Asia. Much of the work on British writings on India concerns itself with these tensions (Franklin 2006b; Malhotra 2012): from Philip Meadows Taylor to Maud Diver, a few recurring themes may well be discerned in the unfolding narrative of literary imaginations of the Indian subcontinent (Nayar 2008).

The nature, space, and effect of Victorian pornography, then, are necessarily products of these intersections of race, desire, and sex. Even as the fear of growing miscegenation propelled the East India Company to finally allow entry to British women in its dominions, the gradual domestication of the British in South Asia made the memsahib one of the mainstays of imperial hagiographies of the age. The pervasive presence of British women within the sphere of a predominantly masculine imperial polity brought attendant anxieties relating to not just rape but also miscegenation, not simply the violation of imperial white bodies but also the spoliation of imperial selfhood through the spectre of mixed-blood offspring. Working with these ubiquitous anxieties prevalent as much in the socio-cultural determination of British selfhoods as in the spatialities of imperial policy, this article will seek to loop together lust and anxiety as they become apparent upon a close reading of *Venus in India, or Love Adventures in Hindustan* (1889). Published by the notorious Auguste Brancart in 1889, *Venus in India* may well be considered a watershed in South Asian pornography: narrating the sexual exploits of an English army officer stationed in British India, this memoir dramatizes race and class as corollaries of the networked imperial apparatus of British India. Unlike earlier pornographic texts set in South Asia, such as Edward Sellon's *The Ups and Downs of Life: A Fragment, Venus in India* (1867) seems to be the first true pornographic text in English on India. It displays heightened awareness of the racial and geopolitical realities of the Indian subcontinent, making these active determinants in the nexus of desire and intercourse operating in this text. In other words, the text's action is premised crucially on its location in British India, enmeshed as it is in an intricate network of imperial infrastructure and racially inflected processes of selfhood. Accordingly, this article will read various gradations of desire as they frame the action and logic of *Venus in India* against its spatial configurations to better understand not just the localization of desire as a geo-racial anomaly but also the spectre of interracial desire serving as an agent of both political and libidinal titillation. In other words, it is only through the outrage of ravishment and subsequent retribution that the fragile peace of empire and its libidinal economy can be maintained in *Venus in India.*

Contextualizing Victorian pornography

Most histories of pornography agree in coupling its emergence with industrialization and the concomitant structural changes in British society from the early nineteenth century. Industrialization had a closely symbiotic relationship with overseas trade and expansionism. These were responsible in equal measure for not only professionalizing the rapidly expanding urban bourgeois class but also giving cogent shape to a distinct working-class identity (Abrams and Greenblatt 2000). The regimentation of class and gender identities in close synergy with the demands of manufacturing, trade, conquest, and governance brought a surge in socio-economic unrest, which manifested itself routinely as crises of and in religion, remittance, and respectability. Even as successive phases of reform saw suffrage become available to greater sections of the adult male population, the position of Victorian women became increasingly restricted in terms of the avenues of self-expression available to them. Exponential urbanization and the emergence of medical sciences made this expedient: the growth of a masculine, industrialized urbanity welded to overseas imperial interests made it necessary to enforce the divorce of sexuality from the quotidian through segregation and suppression of biological needs and processes. As Steven Marcus postulates:

> By a variety of social means which correspond to the psychological processes of isolation, distancing, denial, and even repression, a separate and insulated sphere in which sexuality was to be confined was brought into existence ... the growth of pornography was one of the results of these processes. ([1964] 2009, 283)

A prime agent of these processes, as Marcus and many others assert, was the written word. Indeed, one of the more significant revolutions in nineteenth-century England was in letters, marked by a steady rise in literacy levels accompanied by a phenomenal growth in publishing. As the variety and quantity of books, journals, magazines, periodicals, broadsheets, and penny dreadfuls increased steadily through the course of the century, so did the volume and tenor of complaints that much of this disparate literature was risqué and obscene (Randall 2000, 56).[1]

Yet the popularity of such literature seems directly related to the discordant anxieties which informed the constitution of British bourgeois identity at this stage in history. The world's first industrialized culture, Victorian England experienced considerable stress on the markers which framed its identity: the Mutiny of 1857, for example, brought realignments in racial notions of Britishness (Attridge 2003, 134), just as the crystallization of public school culture gave shape to gendered notions of duty and valour (McDermott 2008, 375). Class hierarchies could no longer be upheld by the immanent fact of birth or inheritance, and gender roles and norms were constantly unsettled by the racialization of sexuality. In colonies such as India, the manifold risks to the cultivation of bourgeois selfhood arose as much from within the ranks of titular Britishness as from the proximity to colonized subjects and the geospatial conditions – climate, foodstuffs, even housing design – of colonial governance. Therefore, a wide and influential range of conduct literature, household manuals, and medical treatises prescribed specific rules of bodily behaviour and moral hygiene only because it had it become apparent that:

> ... what sustained racial membership [to the hegemonic class] was a middle-class morality, nationalist sentiments, bourgeois sensibilities, normalized sexuality, and a carefully circumscribed 'milieu' in school and home. (Stoler 1995, 105)

In this context of tenuous self-fashioning involving minute and constant negotiation, the sensational and titillating framed in racial and economic terms enabled both the creation of this milieu as well as the displacement of anxieties attendant on what it meant to be British. Hence, although the pornographic as impulse is trans-historical and its origins seem allied to the fortunes of the novel (Marcus [1964] 2009, 282), its genesis as a distinct genre of cultural production is rooted to heated contestations over obscenity which guided considerable civil and legal energy through the long nineteenth century. The Obscene Publications Act of 1857, Hicklin's Test of 1868, and campaigns by the Society for the Suppression of Vice through the mid-nineteenth century all allowed the obscene to be tenaciously identified as a category of writing which depraved and corrupted the minds of readers. These attempts to curtail the effect and impact of the obscene acted as an originary moment for pornography as well. They created space and scope for pornography to be identified as a specific kind of writing, lending it a 'specific cultural status producing specific social and legal conflicts' (Gamer 1999, 1045).

Imagined in this sense, less as a formulaic set of practices and more as a bundle of 'perceived readerly effects' (Gamer 1999, 1046), the pornographic seems much more open to localized, contextual analyses. Much of this has been undertaken in recent years, with Linda Williams' *Porn Studies* (2004a) having set the trend for detailed study of both effect and affect of the pornographic in our times. Unsurprisingly, this volume and many others in its wake are devoted almost wholly to the cinematic and the virtual, with just one essay on the comic.[2] Nonetheless, an important set of tools and hypotheses emerge from these studies: for one, Williams' notion of on/scenity as a feature of the 'tension between the speakable and the unspeakable' (2004b, 4) may helpfully facilitate critique of the graphically visual in the written. It is also useful to situate on/scenity as a defining characteristic of cinematic pornography along with Williams' proposition in *Hard Core* to treat pornography 'as the visual (and sometimes aural) representation of living, moving bodies engaged in explicit, usually unfaked, sexual acts with a primary intent of arousing viewers' (1989, 30).

Taking into account the palpable synergy between this intent and its readerly effects, it is possible to think of pornography as a genre of cultural production which graphically visualizes hitherto hidden sexual desires and practices for mass consumption. Hence, even as pornography is the 'coincidence of sexual phantasy, genre, and culture in an erotic organization of visibility' (Brown 1981, quoted in Williams 1989, 269), the meanings it generates can variously explode and implode overlapping regimes of sexual, racial, and class relationships which constitute the dynamic basis of individual and social selfhood.

Thus, in the context of Victorian society, 'pornography became the prescribed discourse of transgression' even as 'the imagined space of the colony ... [became] an imagined breeding ground for a spectrum of imagined sexual vices' (Arondekar 2009b, 105). The racialized other – individuals and civilizations – in Victorian pornography acts as the site of a phobic fetishization which facilitates in contemporary pornography the cultivation of 'desire across racial borders' (Williams 2004c, 277). Read alongside theorizations on the racialization of bourgeois sexuality (Stoler 1995) and on the materiality of pornography within colonial modes of production (Arondekar 2009), the recurrence of the interracial in Victorian pornography as both desire and disgust allows for a critical layering of JanMohamed's proposition that 'the preservation of white patriarchy and the preservation of its self-image require that it deny a "scientific-discursive" knowledge of its sexual violation of the racial border' (1995, 102). In other words, the proliferation of racialized colonial others in Victorian pornography as both tangible bodies and materials and as discursive knowledge domains contingent for bourgeois selfhood graphically vocalized the 'peculiar silence' (1995, 104) which distinguished racialized sexuality from bourgeois sexuality.

Desire and sexuality in Victorian South Asia

Significantly, it is important to remember that the master/slave – white/black – dynamic which constitutes this silence in much contemporary interracial pornography does not fully hold in the South Asian context. The networks of patronage, alliance, and coercion which constituted British rule in India were far from simple slavery. The governance paradigm of the East India Company has been persuasively described as a military fiscalism, its sovereignty the form of a garrison state (Bayly 1998). The military infrastructure created by the Company throughout its dominions – cantonments, arsenals, roads, communications networks – was strengthened further by the Crown. The transfer to direct governance by the British Crown after the Mutiny of 1857 also saw a bolstering of the civic machinery, drastically increasing the quantum of British soldiers and administrators in India. The spread of railways and the creation of military and civil stations outside Indian towns contributed to the appearance of a networked infrastructure which formed the bedrock of British rule in the subcontinent.

However, even though the velvet glove of British legitimacy in India cloaked an iron fist of a beleaguered militarism, to think of Company and Crown rule as simply military fiscalism is to ignore the civilizational current of moral and racial superiority which informed British perceptions of their mandate to rule. The British believed they alone were fit to rule India, divinely ordained to bring to it the fruits of civilization, order, and culture (Cohn 1987). Their military apparatus served to safeguard their interests, commercial and territorial, but the rationale for rule lay in notions of an inherent, racial pre-eminence. Unlike, say, the British in the Caribbean, or the British – and later their descendants – in America, the British in India had to repeatedly justify to themselves and to their subjects the necessity of their rule. The moral and ethical code which thus emerged was framed by acute concerns about opinion, 'that an image of British moral and racial superiority always be preserved in their Indian subjects' eyes' (Sramek 2011, 2) so that the high opinion of the justice of British rule be publicly maintained.

Combining these two related interpretations of British rule through the long nineteenth century provides a helpful framework to locate the fraught question of desire in and of the subcontinent. British women, it is well known, were not allowed within Company dominions in India until the 1830s, when the consolidation of the Company's administrative reach and the growing embarrassment of mixed-blood, Anglo-Indian progeny forced relaxation in these restrictions. By this time, however, an elaborate, networked infrastructure of desire and its fulfilment was in place throughout the Company's dominions. Gravely concerned about the rising incidence of venereal diseases amongst its rank and file and the economic, political, and moral consequences of the spread of such diseases, the Company instituted a medico-military apparatus to regulate sex work in and around its cantonments (Wald 2014). This resulted, on the one hand, in the creation of regularized lal bazaars within the jurisdictional limits of each major cantonment for soldiers to satisfy their sexual needs with women certified healthy by army surgeons. On the other hand, it led to a conceptual narrowing of hegemonic views on Indian womanhood – women were either respectable or prostitutes. The clubbing of different groups of women – courtesans, temple dancing girls, and nautch girls – practising different occupations under the homogenized label of prostitute inevitably led to the sexualization of not just Indian women but also of India, the space of their operation.

Crucially, while this sexualization of race and space reinforced emergent notions of an aggressive, adventurous British masculinity, it effeminized Indian men as deviant, devious, and prone to sexual excess. From medicine to history, this discourse of effeminacy found expression across various registers of colonial governance: it became increasingly prevalent through the nineteenth century and may well be considered an ideologeme enabling 'the racialized construction of "femininity-in-masculinity" as a pathological condition' (Krishnaswamy 1998, 19). As first the Company and then the Crown imposed greater control on their vast dominions, empire took a more tangibly cohesive form in the shape of networked infrastructure and spatial reorganization on racial lines. This made the hybrid alterity of Indians' sexuality a moot point of colonial discourse: Indian women became either hapless victims in need of the benevolent paternalism of British rule or hypersexed prostitutes preying on the virile masculinity of British men in the line of duty. Similarly, Indian men became either untrustworthy and – especially after the Mutiny – dangerously predatory or obsequiously passive and regressive (Krishnaswamy 1998). Consequently, India, as the site of these hybrid alterities, became crystallized in nineteenth-century British thinking as the site of deviance, a diseased land generative of debauchery and disease as a miasmic force debilitating to the moral and physical sinew of British rule (Wald 2014).

That these beliefs complemented the enduring Orientalist notion of India as an ancient civilization with a rich legacy of past achievements is apparent in the manner in which India's romanticized antiquity was also seen as a mark of its essential weakness, of Indians' inability to exercise restraint in matters public and private (Krishnaswamy 1998). This pathological sexualization of Indians and India bolstered these popularly held beliefs. From history to fiction, from science to commerce, the means whereby the British gained familiarity with the subcontinent bolstered layered and inter-connected perceptions of it as passive yet dangerous, in a state of historical stasis yet fallen from the grace of moral and sexual discipline. These perceptions, as they found articulation in a diverse body of literature, have been commented upon by a considerable body of scholarship: as have the contours of desire, romantic and sexual, which foundationally informed British conceptions of their position in and relation to the subcontinent. However, even as Victorian England was all of this, it was also a deeply hybrid and anxious culture wherein hegemonic ideas of propriety and conduct were relentlessly undermined by a vibrant counter-culture of the hedonistic pursuit of pleasure. The dangers of India, tangibly and otherwise, lay in its pleasures: in the suspension of the normative, in reversals of the codes and hierarchies which bound British society. If India was an unpredictable source of profound anxiety in colonial governance, it was also the seed of unadulterated pleasure in colonial writing and fiction.

Orientalist pornographies in the nineteenth century

The convergence of these tropes and anxieties in pornographic fiction is what I am interested in here. *The Lustful Turk*, published anonymously in 1828, seems to be one of the earliest instances of the racialized sexualization of the Orient in English fiction. Following the well-established epistolary convention of novels of the age, it narrates through the course of 18 letters over a period of two years the machinations of the Dey of Algiers in acquiring white, Christian, European women as slaves for his harem (Anonymous 1828). Along with the neighbouring Barbary states Tripoli and Tunisia, Algiers had been an active centre of maritime piracy affecting English, European, and American trade interests in the Mediterranean and the eastern Atlantic. Its economy was largely dependent on the fruits of this privateering, trade in slaves and goods, and protection extracted as tribute from shipping and national interests.[3] The Dey of Algiers was known for his large slaveholdings as well as considerable harem by the conclusion of the Napoleonic Wars.

These were composed, in part, of Christians who were routinely enslaved and ransomed for exorbitant sums, much to the outrage of the English, the French, and the Americans.[4]

The action of *The Lustful Turk* plays out against this tense backdrop of enslavement of white European Christians by black Turkic Muslims. However, it plays to fears of rape and miscegenation by performing a reversal of anxiety: the horror of desire for and intercourse with the racial and religious other is replaced by an eager anxiety to partake and please. Emily Barlow and Sylvia Carey, English maidens journeying out to India, are captured and enslaved by the Dey. Initially, both express revulsion at the prospect of being the Dey's slaves; but they succumb almost immediately to the delights of the flesh which he initiates them in as a man much experienced with women. Tears, supplications, and shrieks are supplanted by joy, sighs, and blushes: the Dey schools his white slaves into absolute, outright enjoyment of the body, enslaving them fully to his virile, unrestrained sexuality. What emerges, therefore, is a pornotopia of sorts: the Dey arranges his pleasures as a devious, predatory animal, procuring women with great care and effort; his English slaves respond to his attentions with an animal-like regression into 'nature', their trappings of race, class, and religion falling away. Lust, effectively, is the preserve of 'the Turk' as much as the English women, who are changed for life into seekers of priapic delights.

These reversals in the moral and racial order of British society are significant: they give insights into the sublimation of anxiety effected as an inevitable consequence of the transculturation following overseas expansion of British trade and territorialism. These encounters modified 'both the center and the periphery, in some ways reversing their roles and polarities' (Franklin 2006a, 18). *The Lustful Turk* is a quaint if typical eruption in the incipient annals of early pornography: it is rare in performing a total implosion of the polarities which constituted the bedrock of nascent medico-moral discourses on race, religion, and sexuality. As British involvement in India deepened and as the metropole became more familiar with its Indian dominions, these discourses ossified into the basic tenets of imperial governance and selfhood even as they simultaneously became targets for defiance and subversion. That, significantly, much of this is apparent as subterranean currents of cross-cultural desire in a wide gamut of nineteenth-century English writing on India indicates not just the strength of this ressentiment but also the capacity of writing to safely articulate and contain these longings.

English writing on India more often than not took the form of romance, for the conventions of travel writing and the expectations of the reading public made it expedient to present it as such. This literature has been the attention of recent scholarship for the erotic hybridity which informs its plots through interracial desire and sex, rape, and homosexuality (Krishnaswamy 1998; Franklin 2006). Until at least the Mutiny, general public and political interest in India seems to have been low (Marshall 2006). After the Mutiny, a broad base of anecdotal, historical, and fictional writing emerged on Indian depredations and British sacrifices during the tumult of 1857–58: these turned the vexed question of interracial relationship from being an acceptable containment device for desire to an abomination accommodated only by death. The anxiety of miscegenation and rape raised itself with shrill regularity throughout the Victorian period, and necessitated not so much a peculiar silencing (JanMohamed 1995) as a kind of literary on/scenity which graphically articulated the possibility of interracial sex but maintained it as an unbreakable taboo.

Therefore, even as the obscenely erotic – eminently pornographic – flourished in England through the nineteenth century, its themes and locations remained more or less English. A prime indicator of the trend of the pornographic through much of the century is Henry Spencer Ashbee's *Index Librorum Prohibitorum: Being Notes Bio-Biblio-Icono-graphical and Critical, on Curious and Uncommon Books*. Published under the pseudonym of Pisanus Fraxi in 1877, it is the first authoritative catalogue 'devoted to writings of a pornographic or sexual character' (Marcus [1964] 2009, 35) in the English language. True to its title, it lists not just bibliographical and biographical details of books and authors but also provides extracts to substantiate its critical assessment of them. Amongst these many hundreds of entries organized alphabetically, only four pertain to India. These are *Annotations on the Sacred Writings of the Hindus* (1865) by Edward Sellon; *History of the Sect of Maharajas* (1865) by Karsandas Mulji; *Kama-Shashtra, or The Hindu Art of Love*; and *The Ups and Downs of Life: A Fragment* (1867) by Edward Sellon (as quoted in Fraxi 1877). Notably, none of these purport to be fictional texts, and except for Sellon's autobiography the others are presented as treatises and answer more to the charge of obscene in the Victorian sense of the term than the pornographic. The publication in 1889 of *Venus in India*, hence, is a landmark in these terms: it seems to be the first fictional pornographic text in English located entirely in India, with a plot and characterization emergent almost exclusively from this spatial alignment.

Libidinal imperialism in *Venus in India*

If the narrative form of *The Lustful Turk* followed the epistolary conventions of its time, then *Venus in India* is written in the form of an adventure travelogue, the preferred choice of Victorian travellers, traders, and administrators (Korte 2000). Its subtitle, *Love Adventures in Hindustan*, is indicative of the reorientation of this familiar form to unfamiliar content: the text dramatizes love-as-adventure as a quest in its own right. Through its title the text aligns itself to the set of readerly effects which framed the pornographic as a distinct set of writing within the much larger literary market in Victorian England: a considerable number of obscene and forbidden books devoted themselves to the worship of Venus. Venus and love act as metaphors for the unrestrained pursuit of sex, the reification of an entire range of relationships, emotions, and experiences into the seamless, feckless consumption of bodies. Even as these texts mirror the literary conventions of their more respectable counterparts – romance, adventure, and travel – they modify their moral, sexual, and racial underpinnings to generate a wholly different set of readerly effects.

Venus in India does precisely this. It purports to be an experiential, autobiographical account of Captain Charles Devereaux,[5] an officer in the British Indian Army, and his years in India, and as such is presented as many memoirs of the time were. The narration begins just as 'war in Afghanistan appeared to be coming to a close', which makes it likely to be 1880, and continues across the length and breadth of what Devereaux refers to as northern India for another two years. The experiences which it recounts, however, are devoted wholly to his pursuit of women and sexual gratification during the time he spends serving his regiment in India. The narrative is divided into two volumes, although the second hints towards a third and concludes with an abruptness which lends the text the appearance of a fragment rather than a rounded plot. Nonetheless, this fragmentariness seems significant in informing the action and affect of the text: pornography works often as a sexualized fragment overturning the established, familiar mores and codes of daily life. The subversions it enacts threaten the social order by presenting themselves as hidden truths, but these remain localized and contextual: it is ultimately the order of things which frames the functioning of the pornographic, making it an aberrant taboo by virtue of implicit comparison.

In *Venus in India* the narrative takes the form of an anecdotal revelation, the intensely personal musings of a man on incidents and entanglements long past. Its effect is to sexualize not only relationships amongst the British in India but also their engagement with and understanding of the natives subject to them: that is, the prudent, rational, civilizing self-image of the Raj appears supplanted with a libidinal empire which thrives on constant and continuous sexual gratification. Immediately upon his arrival in Bombay, Devereaux obtains some French novels to occupy himself on the long journey to Cherat, his destination at the North-West Frontier. Amongst these is a copy of Theophile Gautier's *Mademoiselle de Maupin*, which is described as a 'masterpiece of drawing-room erotic literature' (Devereaux [1889] 2010).[6] Reading it ardently through the long and tiresome rail journey to Jhelum excites all those passions which Devereaux believed he faithfully left behind in England with his wife[7] – narrating these as recollection enacts a crucial function of the pornographic: it differentiates aesthetically veiled depictions of sex from graphically visible portrayals as an aggregate of heaving, moving, panting organs. Furthermore, when Devereaux assures the reader that he will not fail in executing that 'minute painting [which] was what was wanted to complete the rapturous sensations raised by that marvelous romance' ([1889] 2010), he not only bridges the distance between Gautier's text and his own as a matter only of convention, of the degree to which passion is voiced and not of passion itself, but also appropriates for himself the position of a tenuous normality.

That the truth of Devereaux's narration may well be general and not just specific to him is suggested all through the text. His lapse from the moral high ground of a faithful husband occurs as soon as he arrives in India: he purchases the corrupting French novels on Indian soil, to pass the tedium of an Indian rail journey. In Allahabad, en route to Jhelum, he is 'tempted' by an Indian with the offer of a 'very pretty little half-caste'. Upon his arrival at the cantonment town of Nowshera, he is told by J. C., an officer returning from the Afghan frontier, that 'the entire British Army was just simply raging for women!'. His servant Soubratie has no qualms in using Mrs Soubratie to satisfy officers' and soldiers' sexual needs – although at a premium. A similar premium, albeit a princely one of £500, is also demanded by Mrs Searles, the estranged wife of Major Searles of the Nowshera cantonment, for her services to a select coterie in the forests off Ranikhet.[8] In the hill sanatorium of Cherat, too, wives of soldiers still to return from the front are 'only too glad to be fucked' as they chaff at being sequestered from the rest of the cantonment, and pine 'for the longed-for prick, and the accompanying rupees'.

It is India, therefore, and the peculiar circumstances of the Indian empire which produce such pervasive moral and sexual latitude: 'the elsewhere of empire', as Arondekar (2009b, 120) suggests, 'is meant to generate and sanction untrammeled libidinal responses'. India had been consistently considered debilitating to European constitutions, by the British as well as their colonial rivals, the French and the Portuguese. The subcontinent's climate and foods were known to effect 'long-term transformation of firangi bodies' (Harris 2015, 24), to necessitate an Indianization of their morals and habits as a key prerequisite of survival. For the British, deeper involvement in India and a higher stake in its governance brought similar fears of acclimatization, of going native. An identitarian, reformist code of conduct emerged by the turn of the eighteenth century to ensure Britishness remained as untouched as possible from the contexts of rule. Hence, for example, even though European soldiers[9] were considered necessary for the maintenance of British supremacy in India, they were often viewed by their superior officers as low class and therefore necessarily degraded and infantile (Wald 2014): it was important to keep them sexually satisfied and also regulate the avenues of sex so as to control the incidence of venereal diseases. Since 'regulated drink and sex were the only things consistently on offer for the men's leisure activities' (Wald 2014, 58), the prevalent medico-moral order found it expedient to institutionalize regulated prostitution through the establishment of lal bazaars. India, Hindustan, became not just the trope of erotic, Oriental fantasies: it was an actively sexualized space reinforcing the potent myth of an aggressively masculine imperialism.

This is apparent throughout *Venus in India*. The action of the text is framed consistently by the networked infrastructure of the Raj, detailed description of which also 'turns the pornographic narrative into a proximate anthropology' (Arondekar 2009b, 120). Devereaux has to obtain warrants to proceed upcountry on arrival in Bombay: he travels by train, ferry, and dak gharry, and stays in a public bungalow in Nowshera. A host of Indians manage day-to-day operations under the supervision of khansamahs, native major-domos. Ekkhas and ponies[10] needed for the climb up to Cherat have been requisitioned by the returning troops, and it is due to this disruption of ordinary lines of military transport that Devereaux is able to have a week of almost uninterrupted sex with Lizzie Wilson – a memsahib of means. Similarly, his impending arrival to Cherat is signalled by the Station Staff Officer by heliograph, a vital link in military communication in mountainous areas. Cherat itself is a military sanatorium, emerging in the wake of the Afghan wars to allow European soldiers of the British Indian Army to recuperate from their exertions in the field. The eventual march back to the plains is again through various halting stages until Rawalpindi, whence the regiment takes a train to Fackabad, their final destination in Bengal. In each of these stages, his acquaintance, Colonel Selwyn, employs Mrs Soubratie for his pleasure – in Fackabad, Devereaux's bungalow in the cantonment is arranged to be close by for whenever he feels 'cunt hungry'.

Significantly, Indians more than India are considered responsible for the relentless licentiousness of the British in the subcontinent. Their polluting influence seems to emerge from a civilizational depravity, the very essence of what it means to be India. The men appear to be effeminate and unscrupulous, as evidenced in Soubratie prostituting his wife/female companion[11] for extra income. The women come across as predatory nymphs, beautiful but cavernously libidinal: with ayahs (nannies) like Sugdaya at hand 'children [the Selwyn girls – Fanny, Amy, and Mabel] learn about things which girls sixteen and seventeen know nothing of at home', making them dissolute women as they move to adulthood.[12] This insidious abandonment to sexual profligacy emerges as a hallmark of Indians: Sugdaya, as Devereaux recalls towards the closure of Volume 2, not only corrupts the Selwyn girls but also acts as a 'born procuress ... in finding me sweet cunts, besides her own, during the next three or four years'.[13] Unsurprisingly, as hyper-sexualized beings Indians often appear reified, represented only as the sum total of their sexual organs. Mrs Soubratie, for instance, is described repeatedly in terms of the consumptive commodity value of her insatiable sexuality: 'brown skin and somewhat mellow charms ... bubbies otherwise fine and plump', 'active and diligent grotto', 'succulent and very active cunt', and 'fine, fat, brown cunt'.[14]

Crucially, the plot hinges on this pathological sexualization of the so-called natives of the subcontinent. As Colonel Selwyn departs for Peshawar to take his pleasure among the twelve young women selected to be the regiment's prostitutes, Afghan tribesmen in the locality of Cherat conspire to rape Fanny, Amy, and Mabel, 'the only fuckable girls in Cherat' (Devereaux 1889), as revenge for some of the English soldiers collectively taking the virginity of two Afghan girls in the neighboring countryside'). They are aided in this by the girls' ayah, a local woman with Afghan blood contracted by Mrs Selwyn in Peshawar: apart from her racial enmity, this woman also has a personal axe to grind because 'Mrs. Selwyn made a mortal enemy of her by boxing her ears for either some impertinence or slackness of duty'. With her active connivance, two Afghans secretly enter the Selwyn's quarters, kill most of the servants, drug Mrs Selwyn and the younger children, and proceed to rape Fanny and Amy. Providentially, however, the narrator arrives in time to prevent their ravishment, and manages to kill one of the Afghans at considerable danger to himself. Although both girls are penetrated, Fanny's virginity is saved by her menses and Amy's by the Afghan's sodomizing her: 'buggered she had been, but not ravished'.

This distinction is significant, for even in an avowedly aberrant text like *Venus in India* some societal strictures of natural and obscene operate: 'Victorian pornography', in this case, 'solidifies and struggles with already established prohibitions and prejudices concerning race and gender' (Arondekar 2009b, 102). English men using, raping, native women for sexual satisfaction is acceptable and even necessary, but the acute fear of English women being raped and the horror of miscegenation threaten to unhinge the libidinal order of the text. Even as the narrative gives vivid expression to the forbidden in terms of adultery and paedophilia, a tension still remains in racial terms of what can and cannot be said: its on/scenity, so to say, rests on a polar duality between the wholesome virility of English men and women on one hand and the perverse sexuality of natives on the other. That the Afghans are guided by a primitive sense of honour is suggested in their mutilating and burning alive the two girls who had sex with the English soldiers for money. That they are not man enough to extract their revenge openly but conspire to do so covertly is apparent in their being guided by the ayah in executing their plan. That their sexuality is either aggressively unnatural or not masculine enough is apparent in one of them preferring anal over vaginal sex in Amy's case and the other not being able to break through Fanny's hymen.

Therefore, the readerly effect of this central sequence is to obsessively reinforce the sexual hierarchies and fears which constituted not only the gendering but also the functioning of the Raj. The attempted rape shocks the narrator for 'the incredible insolence which could have animated a native, in time of peace and in our own borders, to commit such a crime'. The possibility that Fanny may have been impregnated appears to be a 'terrible catastrophe', made unbearable by the thought that 'within those so lately virgin portals were lodged the accursed spawn of a loathsome Afghan!'. Although the narrator manages to kill the Afghan who penetrated Amy, the entire cantonment is 'ready to kill every Afghan that comes in'. Traumatized by this incident, Colonel Selwyn is unable to come to terms with it: racked on one hand by the 'lust' which brought his departure to Peshawar, he is also unable 'to think a daughter of his could be buggered, therefore [believes] she had not been buggered' on the other. The truly obscene, the forbidden at the cusp of imagination, lies in the reversal of the penetrative schema: not white men on brown women, but brown men on white women.

Empire and pornography: an anxious coupling

In other words, *Venus in India* articulates the ongoing negotiation between the obscene and the permissible framing of Victorian imaginations of India: it parleys across this border even as it remains bound by the stereotypes which create it (Williams 2004a). These borders segregated the sexualized spaces of the Indian empire: they sought to police the aggressive, unnatural effeminacy of Indian sexuality, to contain an acute anxiety for the honour and chastity of English women. Exacerbated by the Mutiny, the spectre of this historical taboo of interracial sex presented itself in fiction and manifested itself publicly in the pathologically sexual sequestering of the British from their native subjects in India. By actualizing it, by articulating it graphically, *Venus in India* provides an affective challenge which threatens to catapult it from the obscenely erotic to the luridly horrific.

Thus, in contrast to its Orientalist predecessor *The Lustful Turk* or many of its latter-day successors in the twentieth and the twenty-first centuries, desire in *Venus in India* is complexly graded. It emerges due to the peculiar conditions of British rule in India, due to the corrupting influence of India and Indians on British health and morality. It is in direct consequence of the racialized constitution of British bourgeois selves (Arondekar 2009), and is hierarchically arranged in racially sexed terms of speakable and unspeakable, permissible and taboo. Although the text titillates with a vision of English womanhood being sacrificed at the altar of native excess, it nonetheless reinforces its racially sexualized order by not allowing its violation: the offending Afghan is killed, and Devereaux gains the vital opportunity for realizing his own desire for the Selwyn sisters. While this may well appear a pornotopia, *Venus in India* is far from being indifferent to place (Marcus [1964] 2009, 268). It is keenly conscious of its cultural and racial contexts, and reaffirms many of the race, class, and gender hierarchies of Victorian England, of the Britain's empire in India. What emerges, hence, is a curious calibration of the pornographic itself, of the subservience of desire constituted as uncontrollable and transgressive to racial and sexual anxiety: the boundaries it frankly subverts are also the borders it strives to uphold.

Notes

1. Such tirades have a long history in the annals of English literature and criticism, but by the middle of the nineteenth century they seem to have acquired an urgency and vehemence akin to zeal.
2. Indeed, although this is far from the case, this pervasive scholarly trend seems to unwittingly imply that pornographic writing seems to have completely died out.
3. See Treaty of Peace and Friendship between the United States of America and the Bey and Subjects of Tripoli of Barbary, ratified 1796.
4. This widespread sense of national – even civilizational – outrage seems to have informed the rhetoric behind such incidents as the Bombardment of Algiers in 1816 and the Second Barbary War in 1815.
5. The authorial question in *Venus in India* is necessarily vexed: Charles Devereaux appears to be a pseudonym, and what is known satisfactorily is only the publisher's identity.

6. Having used an open source edition of *Venus in India* from Wikisource, I am unable to provide page numbers for quotations from the text in this article.
7. 'But for the burning pictures of love and passion, drawn in the wonderful prose poem, perhaps I might have escaped from the nets in which love entangled me'.
8. Victim as much of her husband's violence as well as his inclination for anal sex, a habit inculcated amongst boys during service in Persia, Mrs Searles presents a liminal example of the fallen memsahib. Sodomized by her husband, she is the object of pity; a beautiful woman herself, her establishment at Ranikhet is supported by the crème de la crème of colonial society, including the Viceroy; yet, as a woman who can be bought, she is, as Mrs Selwyn angrily exclaims, 'a disgrace to sex' and to the reputation, amongst natives, of the British as a people. Mrs Selwyn's keen concern for conduct and example, particularly amongst the so-called gentle classes, neatly allows for the extension of Sramek's (2011) thesis in *Gender, Morality, and Race in Company India* to the latter half of British rule as well.
9. Often the literature itself – primary and secondary – seems to enact this racial implosion of disparate identities of English, British, Scottish, and Irish as simply 'European'.
10. Devereaux's detailed description of the ekkha in Volume 2 is yet another indication of the text's deep involvement with the networks of imperial and racial power in British India. He refers to it as 'a two-wheeled conveyance much used in Northern India', goes on to describe its structure and design, and declares that although 'it can go almost anywhere' it is nonetheless 'not a kind of carriage which I can recommend as forming one of the comforts of Indian travel'.
11. Devereaux doubts whether they are actually married: 'a capable man he was, and one who had an eye to business, for whether he was married or not I do not know, but he brought a very fine young native woman with him'.
12. 'Mabel was a lascivious little girl, a grand poke. Like Lizzie Wilson her mission in life is to fuck. The dear reader will not be surprised to hear that she joined that select number of fair women, who, nominally "kept" by wealthy lovers take delight in relieving the pains of numerous adorers … To her was the glory of having the first to give palpable proof of the ecstasies of fucking to no less a personage than one of the Royal Princes'.
13. But for this small aside, Arondekar's thesis that the pornographic in *Venus in India* is 'at once transgressive and deeply self-regulatory' (2009b, 106) would hold: Devereaux does have a racially determined moral code which guides his sexual entanglements, but this does not preclude sex with native women. Therefore, *Venus in India* is only selectively self-regulatory of the limitations of bourgeois sexuality in the racialized domain of British India: its transgressions rather than its self-regulations make it uniquely pornographic for its context.
14. This is, of course, one of the central distinguishing marks of pornography, but in *Venus in India* it is a mark reserved specially for Indians. The Selwyn sisters are also often referred to in terms of their 'delicious cunts', and Devereaux does not shy away from referring to himself as just a prick, but as a rule characterization of the British endows them a range of emotions and motives beyond sexual organs and sex as well.

Disclosure statement

No potential conflict of interest was reported by the author.

ORCID

Anubhav Pradhan http://orcid.org/0000-0002-7099-3621

References

Abrams, M. H., and Stephen Greenblatt. 2000. 'Introduction.' In *The Norton Anthology of English Literature: The Victorian Age*. 7th ed, edited by M. H. Abrams, and Stephen Greenblatt, 3–27. New York: W.W. Norton & Company.

Anonymous. 1828. *The Lustful Turk*. Web. Accessed October 29 2017. Wikisource, https://en.wikisource.org/wiki/The_Lustful_Turk

Arondekar, Anjali. 2009a. 'Introduction: Without a Trace.' In *For the Record: On Sexuality and the Colonial Archive in India*, 1–26. Durham: Duke University Press.

Arondekar, Anjali. 2009b. 'Archival Attachments: The Story of an India-Rubber Dildo.' In *For the Record: On Sexuality and the Colonial Archive in India*, 97–130. Durham: Duke University Press.

Attridge, Steve. 2003. 'Disoriented Fictions: Indian Mutiny Novels.' In *Nationalism, Imperialism, and Identity in Late Victorian Culture: Civil and Military Worlds*, 107–139. Basingstoke: Palgrave Macmillan.

Bayly, C. A. 1998. 'The British Military-Fiscal State and Indigenous Resistance: India 1750–1820.' In *Origins of Nationality in South Asia: Patriotism and Ethical Government in the Making of Modern India*, 238–275. Delhi: Oxford University Press.

Burton, Anoinette. 1995. 'Fearful Bodies Into Disciplined Subjects: Pleasure, Romance, and the Family Drama of Colonial Reform in Mary Carpenter's "Six Months in India".' *Signs: Journal of Women in Culture and Society* 20 (3): 545–574.

Burton, Anoinette. 1998. 'Mapping a Critical Geography of Late-Nineteenth-Century Imperial Britain.' In *At the Heart of the Empire: Indians and the Colonial Encounter in Late-Victorian Britain*, 1–25. California: University of California Press.

Caplan, Lionel. 2001. 'Introduction.' In *Children of Colonialism: Anglo-Indians in a Postcolonial World*, 1–20. Oxford: Berg.

Cohn, Bernard. 1987. 'Representing Authority in Victorian India.' In *An Anthropologist Among the Historians and Other Essays*, 632–682. Delhi: Oxford University Press.

Devereaux, Charles. (1889) 2010. *Venus in India*. 2 vols. Brussels: Auguste Brancart. Accessed June 14 2016. Wikisource, https://en.wikisource.org/wiki/Venus_in_India

Franklin, Michael J. 2006a. 'General Introduction and [Meta]Historical Background [Re]Presenting "The Palanquins of State; Or, Broken Leaves in a Mughal Garden".' In *Romantic Representations of British India*, edited by Michael J. Franklin, 1–45. Abingdon: Routledge.

Franklin, Michael J. 2006b. 'Radically Feminizing India: Phebe Gibbes's *Hartly House, Calcutta* (1789) and Sydney Owenson's *The Missionary: An Indian Tale* (1811).' In *Romantic Representations of British India*, edited by Michael J. Franklin, 154–179. Abingdon: Routledge.

Fraxi, Pisanus. 1877. *Index Librorum Prohibitorum: Being Notes Bio-Biblio-Icono-Graphical and Critical, on Curious and Uncommon Books*. London: N.P. Web, Accessed October 29 2017. Hathi Trust. https://babel.hathitrust.org/cgi/pt?id=osu.32435074909615;view=1up;seq=9

Gamer, Michael. 1999. 'Genres for the Prosecution: Pornography and the Gothic.' *PMLA* 114 (5): 1043–1054.

Harris, Jonathan Gil. 2015. 'Garcia da Orta, the Hakeem of Bombay and Ahmadnagar.' In *The First Firangis: Remarkable Stories of Heroes, Healers, Charlatans, Courtesans & Other Foreigners who Became Indian*, 22–46. Delhi: Aleph Book Company.

Holden, Philip and Richard J. Ruppel. 2003. 'Introduction.' In *Imperial Desire: Dissident Sexualities and Colonial Literature*, edited by Philip Holden and Richard J. Ruppel, ix–xxvi. Minneapolis: University of Minnesota Press.

JanMohamed, Abdul R. 1995. 'Sexuality On/Of the Racial Border: Foucault, Wright, and the Articulation of "Racialized Sexuality".' In *Discourses of Sexuality: From Aristotle to AIDS*, edited by Domna C. Stanton, 94–116. Ann Arbor: University of Michigan Press.

Korte, Barbara. 2000. 'Travel Writing in the Nineteenth Century.' In *English Travel Writing From Pilgrimages to Postcolonial Explorations*, translated by Catherine Matthias, 82–105. Basingstoke: Macmillan Press Ltd.

Krishnaswamy, Revathi. 1998. *Effeminism: The Economy of Colonial Desire*. Ann Arbor: The University of Michigan Press.

Levine, Philippa. 2004. 'Introduction: Why Gender and Empire?' In *Gender and Empire*, edited by Philippa Levine, 1–13. New York: Oxford University Press.

Malhotra, Ashok. 2012. 'Romantic Representations of the Subcontinent: "Subliming India" and Configuring Its Geopolitical Significance.' In *Making British Indian Fictions, 1772–1823*, 57–90. New York: Palgrave Macmillan.

Marcus, Steven. (1964) 2009. *The Other Victorians: A Study of Sexuality and Pornography in Mid-Nineteenth Century England*. New Jersey: Transaction Publishers.

Marshall, P. J. 2006. 'British–Indian Connections *c.* 1780 to *c.*1830: the Empire of the Officials.' In *Romantic Representations of British India*, edited by Michael J. Franklin, 45–64. Abingdon: Routledge.

McDermott, Emily A. 2008. 'Playing for His Side: Kipling's "Regulus," Corporal Punishment, and Classical Education.' *International Journal of the Classical Tradition* 15 (3): 369–392.

Nayar, Pramod K. 2008. 'Introduction: Aesthetic Negotiations.' In *English Writing and India, 1600–1920*, 1–7. Abingdon: Routledge.

Randall, Don. 2000. 'The Genealogy of the Imperial Boy.' In *Kipling's Imperial Boy: Adolescence and Cultural Hybridity*, 24–61. Basingstoke: Palgrave Macmillan.

Sinha, Mrinalini. 1995. 'Reconfiguring Hierarchies: The Ilbert Bill Controversy, 1883–84.' In *Colonial Masculinity: The 'Manly Englishman' and the 'Effeminate Bengali' in the Late Nineteenth Century*, 33–68. Manchester: Manchester University Press.

Stoler, Ann Laura. 1995. 'Cultivating Bourgeois Bodies and Racial Selves.' In *Race and the Education of Desire: Foucault's History of Sexuality and the Colonial Order of Things*, 95–136. Durham: Duke University Press.

Sramek, Joseph. 2011. 'Introduction.' In *Gender, Morality, and Race in Company India, 1765–1858*, 1–16. New York: Palgrave Macmillan.

Wald, Erica. 2014. *Vice in the Barracks: Medicine, the Military and the Making of Colonial India, 1780–1868*. Basingstoke: Palgrave Macmillan.

Williams, Linda. 1989. 'Speaking Sex: "The Indiscreet Jewels".' In *Hard Core: Power, Pleasure, and the 'Frenzy of the Visible*, 1–33. Berkeley: University of California Press.

Williams, Linda. ed. 2004a. *Porn Studies*, Durham: Duke University Press.

Williams, Linda. 2004b. "Porn Studies: Proliferating Pornographies On/Scene: An Introduction.' In *Porn Studies*, edited by Linda Williams, 1–26. Durham: Duke University Press.

Williams, Linda. 2004c. 'Skin Flicks on the Racial Border: Pornography, Exploitation, and Interracial Lust.' In *Porn Studies*, edited by Linda Williams, 271–308. Durham: Duke University Press.

Between aunties: sexual futures and queer South Asian aunty porn

Kareem Khubchandani

ABSTRACT
The aunty appears as a common vernacular figure in South Asian film, television, memes, novels, and porn. 'Aunty porn' names a large body of pornography that features fat, older, South Asian women; this genre is unique in that it features aunties as protagonists. In other media, aunties are only afforded minor roles as difficult, stubborn, and traditional, and this archetype positions them as an antagonist to queer sexual futures. This article scavenges a selection of queer aunty porn from South Asian diasporic novels to demonstrate aunties' capacity to cultivate sexual futures, showing how sex between aunties exists in continuum with archetypal aunty attributes like cooking and gossip. While aunty sexualities are usually interpreted in relation to younger generations, this article points to the many ways that ageing South Asian women rehearse queer sexual futures for and between themselves.

'Aunty' is used vernacularly in South Asian public cultures, in the subcontinent and diaspora, to name women of an older generation. While many South Asian languages have specific titles that differentiate fathers' and mothers' sisters, 'aunty' can refer to women relatives more broadly and to people who are not related by blood or marriage. Aunties can be neighbours, shopkeepers, relatives, or even frenemies. While aunty generally refers to older women, it is also a 'role' that is done, not necessarily something that one is (Cobham-Sander 2021); one can thus have an aunty aesthetic or be read as aunty without necessarily identifying as one. For example, in Toronto-based visual artist Meera Sethi's series 'Upping the Aunty', aunties are characterized through their eclectic style – prints, garments, and accessories mixed and matched across regional origin, colour, and pattern. However, when aunties are staged in relation to younger generations, this role concretizes around scripts, aesthetics, and affects that render aunties unflattering and unmodern. Young content creators on TikTok and Instagram churn out memes about loud, gossipy, ostentatious, fat, stubborn, accented, religious, unfashionable, and nosey aunties – hence the repeated refrain, 'Don't call me aunty!'

The term 'aunty' bursts with meanings that exceed its naming of a social relation, offering more and messier ways to interpret gender and kinship. Aunty works differently from friend, sister, mother, woman, lady, or person, and disorganizes normative social relations: aunty 'return[s] names to women who [have] been lost to marriage and children … Instead of "wife to" or "mother of," women could be Auntie Jane or Auntie Mary' (Macharia 2021). Thinking with aunties can disrupt South Asian cultural tendencies to hold wife and mother in a sanctimonious light; to think of mothers and wives as aunties reconfigures how we might relate to them, desire them, (dis)like them. Across this project, aunty is a capacious term that encompasses older South Asian women (Tincknell 2020), women of one's parents' generation (Sethi 2016), familiar femme authority figures (Lewis 2017), recurring characters in 'aunty porn' such as the desirable sister-in-law (Menon 2018), and people (like myself) who embody the excessive and outdated aesthetics and affects associated with aunties (Sandhu 2019). While popular South Asian representations iteratively represent aunties as narrowly invested in heteronorms, I think about aunties queerly by exploring their potential to expand gender and sexual possibilities rather than diminish them.

Across literature, film, and television, aunties surveil young people's gender and sexual lives, snitching on youths' transgressions to their parents (Bradby 2007). In Shyam Selvadurai's *Funny Boy* (1996), a queer coming-of-age novel set in Colombo, Sri Lanka, London-returned Kanthi Aunty catches the pre-teen protagonist Arjie wearing a sari and lipstick and ridicules his gender transgression in front of the entire family. Sushmita Mukherjee plays a stubborn, short, fat, leopard-print-clad aunty in the gay-themed Hindi film '*Dostana*' [Friendship] (Mansukhani, dir. 2008), who refuses to let her ward (Priyanka Chopra) have a single man as a roommate. The film doubles down on her aunty-ness with an extra-diegetic echo of 'Aunty, Aunty' when she is on screen. Netflix's coming-of-age series 'Never Have I Ever' depicts in Episode Four two different cohorts of bitchy aunties at a Hindu festival in California. One trio disapprovingly whispers about someone's divorce, and the other intimidates youngsters with their fixations on wealth, religion, and status. Each of these short-lived encounters with aunties and their conservative notions of gender, marriage, and propriety shape the narrative's moral universe.

Surveilling the family from outside, aunties can police gender and sexual freedoms, but their liminal location also allows them to sneak sex, gossip, and scandal into the home. In Aditi Brennan Kapil's 2013 play 'Brahman/i', Auntie filters pornography, sex education, and anti-colonial history into her sibling's home, offering an intersex kid illicit knowledge with which to think and make their gender. Even *Funny Boy* offers an important complement to Kanthi aunty; in the Chelvaratnam joint-family household, Arjie's headstrong Radha aunty makes room for him to dabble in the feminine tendencies that cause his parents to cringe. But as aunties commonly do, Radha disappears from the narrative midway.

While aunties are desexualized by feminist and queer youngsters who decry their sexual conservativism (Wong 2006, 458), their age and advanced experience can also make them erotically appealing. This sexualization of the aunty is reflected in an extensive body of softcore and hardcore pornography referred to as 'aunty porn', in which aunty-ness is fetishized. In this abundance of film, photograph, cartoon, and written erotica, women are staged as aunties through their association with domestic spaces, age, clothing (sari, nightie, caftan, salwar khameez), and full-figured bodies. This genre of commercial and amateur Indian erotica features fat, 'dark-skinned, middle-aged, married women' and encompasses a wide range of social positions; she can be 'bhabhi [sister-in-law], aunty, didi [older sister], maid, wife, housewife, or even mother' (Mukhopadhyay 2012, 147). For the young sexual initiate, she embodies the wealth of experience that comes with age, that might graduate them into adulthood. For example, porn cartoon character Velamma, a South Indian aunty, 'is sexually available for initiating young men into the pleasures of lovemaking' (Sreedhar Mini and Baishya 2020, 125). Lesbian narratives of teenage desire also cite the aunty; 'Filthy Sumana' writes in a 1995 letter to the Delhi-based lesbian organization Sakhi, 'my aunt had a highly erotic scent in armpits, pussy (just in the morning)' (Dave 2012, 47). Aunties are positioned as the conduit towards young people's sexual futures; they mentor, initiate, and inspire their sexual awakenings. But what of their own sexual futures?

Despite their ubiquity in South Asian public cultures, aunties are afforded minor importance in South Asian narratives; they appear as interstitial characters landing a joke or criticism before disappearing from the story. The discursive disposability of the aunty, Anmol Nayak (2020; original emphasis) argues, is especially associated with her age, having 'basically served her purpose of marriage and child bearing, and is hence rendered *useless*'.[1] Aunty porn is exciting in that it teaches us to centre aunties as protagonists, celebrating their sexuality and style. However, this porn largely caters to straight men, and in these narratives aunties commonly facilitate heteronormative futures by initiating younger men into adulthood. In other media, especially feminist and queer narratives and imagery, aunties are often the judgemental villains who orbit young people's lives. When they do offer queer and feminist possibilities or mentorship to younger people, their own erotic desires are rendered inconsequential. Aunties both manage and incite the sexual futures of young people through gossip, advice, surveillance, style, and even sex, but their own sexual futures rarely occupy centre stage, and are even more rarely imagined as queer. This article tracks depictions of aunties that invest in their own sexual futures, that show their gender and sexuality as ongoing, creative, and self-serving.

In imagining 'sexual futures' for aunties, I adopt Juana María Rodríguez's terminology to name people's capacity to fantasize and manifest versions of desire, kinship, and erotics that are not prescribed by social norms, state, law, and racial capitalism (Rodríguez 2014). 'Futurity' in queer theory has often been theorized through the figure of the child, and scholars have, on the one hand, critiqued the obsessive investment in childhood innocence as an impulse to secure heteronormative futures (Edelman 2004) and, on the other, troubled abandoning the child as a subject of queer study (Allen 2009; Muñoz 2009), theorizing how to bring your kids up gay and to protect trans kids from hateful legislation and epistemic erasure (Sedgwick 2004; Gill-Peterson 2018). For queer and trans kids of colour, or what Chris Eng (2018) refers to as the 'minor minor', whose gender, sexuality, and morality are often overdetermined by colonial histories and diasporic journeys, (sexual) innocence becomes an untenable performance (Bernstein 2011). The diasporic child is under greater pressure to conform to heteronorms, to reproduce, given the perpetual precarity that colonized and migrant communities feel about their racial and national futures (Eng 2001; Gopinath 2005). However, as a burgeoning body of scholarship develops to valorize the queer agency of minor minors, other minor figures – aunties – are suspended in heteronormativity, or even villainized in public culture as the antagonists of queer diasporic futurity.

Rodríguez's scholarship is especially useful to think about queer aunty porn in her insistence on sex – particularly sex between women and femmes – as well as her consideration of ageing. For Rodríguez, the debate around queer futurity elides the potential of sex as a venue for sociality and creativity. In response, she develops 'sexual futures' as a gesture towards inventive and playful social–sexual lives that are not limited by, and even play with, scripts of patriarchy, family, and coloniality. She brings care to thinking futurity, always naming children and elders as she argues for 'the right to our erotic lives' (Rodríguez 2014, 67). Rodríguez (2015, 2017) has gone on to think sexuality, pornography, and gender transition alongside ageing, theorizing emotional, aesthetic, and sexual becomings across the experience of queer and trans lifespans. The breadth of her work on futurity, ageing, and sex enables me to think about aunties not only through the futures they promise or deny young people, but the sexual futures they build 'between aunties' as they age.

This article argues for a consideration of aunties' queerness that is not always or solely measured through their relationship to younger generations, offering 'between aunties' as an alternative episteme to witness queer aunty erotics. I examine four South Asian diasporic novels in which queerness manifests through aunty figures. These stories feature young people who regard these characters as aunties; however, the aunties' quotidian performances are not solely directed towards intergenerational care, desire, or discipline. Rather, the aunty actions and affections that matter most are between aunties. I begin with Indian American writer Rakesh Satyal's *Blue Boy* (2009) to show how aunties, as minor figures tucked into the interstices of the narrative, offer the pre-teen protagonist resources towards a queer future. I argue that there are limits to understanding the queerness of aunties only through their relationship to younger generations, and look to Satyal's second novel, *No One Can Pronounce My Name* (2017), for queerness between aunties. Drawing on minor characters and their brief sex scene in *No One*, I discuss the obstructions that impede imagining the queerness of aunties. I follow with longer readings of Punjabi diasporic writer Balli Kaur Jaswal's *Erotic Stories for Punjabi Widows* (2017) and Sri Lankan American writer Mary Ann Mohanraj's *Bodies in Motion* (2005) to think about aunty porn in continuum with practices commonly associated with aunties: cooking and gossip.

To position queer sex, gossip, and cooking in the same mundane universe that I describe as 'between aunties' echoes Juana María Rodríguez's fantasy for:

> another kind of sexual future, where intercourse engages all manner of touching, where interdependence and mutual recognition constitute the daily labor of making lives livable for ourselves and each other, where articulating our most cherished desires is seen not as naïve, but as wholly necessary. (Rodríguez 2014, 27)

By placing sex and sensation in continuum with other practices that aunties are known for, such as cooking and gossip, I am insisting that the older women I discuss here are not exceptional to the infamous and unlikeable aunty archetype. The difficult, rigid, and impossible nature of the aunty potentially occludes us from seeing the creativity, sexuality, and play that she reserves for her time with other aunties. I hope this article provokes a conversation about what South Asian culture and criticism could be like if we afforded aunties queerness instead of pinning them to heteronormativity.

Aunty is also this article's method, allowing me to make big deals out of small scenes in true aunty fashion. K'eguro Macharia (2021) offers that aunties 'scavenge dead and dying stories' (see also Halberstam 1998, 13), and I too pick between the bones of cultural texts to find sex between aunties. Attending to 'minor' scenes, gestures, or figures does not elide a study of macro-structures, but rather observes how the 'major' is sutured into the mundane and incidental, and can thus be disorganized through re-combinatory performances of the everyday (Shankar 2019). My aunty-like penchant for sensational news, eager to wring the smallest fruit for a fraction of juicy scandal, sets a low bar for titillation that allows me to read scenes in these novels as pornographic rather than softcore. Where the aunty is commonly understood through an intergenerational framework, I broaden aunty discourse to include interactions 'between aunties' that reveal the ongoing collective creativity aunties engage in to invent pleasure, play, and autonomy beyond the sexual scripts prescribed to them.

The queer aunty porn I scavenge from diasporic narratives certainly looks different from the images, stories, and cartoons that comprise the more well-studied category of 'aunty porn' (Srivastava 2007; Mukhopadhyay 2012; Menon 2018; Sreedhar Mini and Baishya 2020). However, my selection of texts remains in line with the migratory, diasporic, and transnational routes of other South Asian pornographies.[2] I examine pornography alongside cooking and gossip, important place-making practices for people whose lives are epistemically and physically set into motion by global disjuncture and displacement. In doing so, I uplift sex as a valuable practice of diasporic and migrant worldmaking. Lesbian sex is far from new to Indian pornography (Chatterjee 2017), but representations of Indian lesbians have largely leaned towards light-skinned, thin, feminine, young women (Nair 2008). What might queer sex look like between those accented, older, unassimilated, un-cosmopolitan, backward, stuck-in-their-ways, frankly impossible women, who we just cannot seem to place in the present, let alone afford a future?

Interstitial aunties

Across South Asian texts, aunty encounters are brief, fleeting, or even entirely off-screen (for example, see Mannur 2021); however, aunties accrue relevance in their recurring appearances. In Rakesh Satyal's novel *Blue Boy* (2009), a queer coming-of-age story set in 1990s Cincinnati, Ohio, aunties orbit the heteronormative home, always working in concert with the mother, while also positioning her as an exceptional figure. The novel offers a useful example of how aunties acquire importance in queer storytelling despite their interstitial appearances. Where aunties are considered enforcers of normative gender and sexuality, *Blue Boy* affords an opportunity to think queerly with aunties.

Satyal's preteen protagonist Kiran Sharma measures his aunties by their distance from his mother:

> There are five core aunties in our circle of friends ... My mother occupies a very interesting place in this bevy. She is, by far, the most Americanized of these mothers ... My mother is a plump woman, but she falls in the middle of the spectrum, somewhere between Anita Gupta's rail of a frame and Rashmi Govind's centripetal force. (Satyal 2009, 32)

Kiran's mother is the most Americanized, his aunties being then the most foreign, the furthest from 'here'. His mother's fatness is the median by which aunties are measured in their bodily and affective difference. Aunties, whether or not they are mothers themselves, are narrated in relation to the protagonist's mother, turning her into the exception of her generation or cohort. Despite the collective labour that goes into raising younger generations, aunties become women we have permission to dispose of, dislike, or perhaps even desire because they are not the protagonist's mother. They function as a foil to the mother, allowing us to critique her generation, without demonizing her individually. Thinking 'between aunties' turns the mother into an aunty too, and potentially destabilizes the unattainable sanctity mothers are beholden to.

The excessive styles associated with aunties, 'gaudy and over the top', brings them into the aesthetic realm of drag queens (Sandhu 2019, 56). Similarly, in *Blue Boy*, aunties fuel Kiran's burgeoning queer theatricality:

> The aunties always greet me enthusiastically because I know how to observe decorum. Anita Gupta screeches larangytically when I ask if she has brought her spicy *channa* again. Ratika auntie dryly offers some murky Hindi as I say hello, and Kavita Auntie expounds on it with more Hindi. Here, in the crucial opening moments of this get-together, my eye for ostentation serves me well. (Satyal 2009, 127)

In these passing moments, aunties affirm Kiran's penchant for elaborate aesthetics and comportment. Later that evening, he finds himself enchanted by the grandeur of Nisha Auntie's expansive bathroom, and locks himself in to indulge in 'the cool plastic of Nisha Auntie's makeup compacts, lipsticks, and mascaras', transforming gender in the mirror. Kiran's performance at his school's talent show, 'part-ballet, part-*khatak* [*sic*], part-bananas', borrows from the kathak lessons Hema Auntie offered in his living room. His mother would invite Hema over for tea, and slyly transition these tea dates into dance lessons. Although Kiran eventually catches on to the ruse and Hema Auntie's visits cease, he repurposes her choreography for the talent show, indulging in 'a sense of freedom he has not experienced offstage' (Eng 2018, 49).

In *Blue Boy*, aunties' ostentation, make-up, and dance become tools for Kiran's practice of effeminacy, fabulousness, gayness, creativity, and racialization. Even though he has to steal time in Nisha Auntie's loo or disidentify (Muñoz 1999) with Hema Auntie's kathak, performing it in such a way that would leave her 'mortified', this extended world of aunties expands the gendered resources of the home space and family that make possible Kiran's queer creativity. In contrast to the mediated sounds and images of Whitney Houston and Lynda Carter that inform Kiran's queer worldmaking, aunties are intimate, fleshy, similarly racialized femme figures that orbit and govern his everyday style. These aunties are not queer, in fact they are squarely positioned as unmodern figures invested in gender conformity and heteronormativity. But if we pay attention to the many minor encounters that Kiran has with them, we see that even in their most heteronormative incarnation they cultivate resources with which to craft queerness.

Through *Blue Boy*, I have rehearsed a way of queering aunties, affording them the grace of inspiring queerness, helping Kiran grow 'sideways' even as they are trapped in/by heteronormativity. Fixed as unmodern or backward, aunties appeal to '[t]he "gay" child's fascinating asynchronicities', offering other directions to grow into in addition to growing up (Stockton 2009, 11). Other queer South Asian artists also draw on the images and sounds associated with their parent's generation to imagine queer futures for themselves. In *Ode to Lata* (Dhalla 2002), Ali's fondness for Lata Mangeshkar, which he listened to with his mother and aunties, becomes his soundtrack to wandering the thickly erotic bathhouse. LaWhore Vagistan, my own drag persona, attributes her drag aesthetics to my aunties (Khubchandani 2017). But in these and many other reparative projects that repurpose the music, dress, and dance of South Asian aunties and mothers, queerness draws from the past but leaves those women in it. Nostalgia for our mother's generation can facilitate queer futures, can inspire the imagination of alternative worlds such as the one Kiran builds on stage. However, the aunties from whom we borrow queer aesthetics are not the protagonists or even residents of these alternate worlds.

Representations of queer sex between aunties are opportunities to imagine the world-making practices of older women, practised over a lifetime, that locate their queer pleasures in the present. Porn allows us to watch them in the act of becoming such that they too have sexual futures; it offers tools to make explicit aunties' queerness. It may seem old-fashioned or unsophisticated to align queerness with sex, but without it, aunties are rendered only resources – mentors and inspiration – towards queer futurity and not its inhabitants. Sex offers a fleshy, embodied, sensuous lens to think about aunties. Also, thinking 'between aunties' potentially returns queerness to the perpetually straightened South Asian mother, placing her in the company of other women rather than only in relation to husband or child.

Impossible aunties

I tripped into thinking about sex between aunties reading Satyal's second novel, *No One Can Pronounce My Name* (2017), where the impossible nature of aunties – difficult, backward, stuck, set in their ways – occluded their erotic subjectivity and made their desires impossible – unthinkable, unimaginable. One of the book's protagonists is Indian immigrant Harit, who is coming into his gay identity as an adult. *No One* begins with Harit's mourning ritual for his recently dead sister Swati. He returns home from work, dons Swati's sari and lipstick, and descends the stairs to greet his mother Parvati, who spends entire days listless on a chair in the living room, paralyzed by grief. When Harit is at work, Gital Didi ('didi' is an honorific meaning older sister, as well as a common figure in aunty porn) visits Parvati to bathe her, cook, and chat, even though Parvati says almost nothing. Like any good aunty, she makes Parvati's home hers, cooking in her kitchen despite Harit's protests; aunties never listen! In fact, Satyal variously describes the two widows, Gital and Parvati, as wilful, obsessive, unflagging, inhuman, and unapproachable – such aunty traits.

Parvati gets little character development in the novel, except for an 11-page chapter that efficiently narrates her journey from a 'willful youth' raised on a farm in an unnamed village outside Delhi to her emotionally paralyzed present in Cleveland. Despite several clues about Parvati's queerness – mentions of her short hair, her jealousy over her husband's girlfriend – the chapter's final paragraph took me by surprise:

> Meanwhile, Gital had insinuated herself into their home, and Parvati was well aware that Gital had become obsessed with her. One quiet night, Gital lowered herself before Parvati's chair and kissed her cheeks, then her mouth, and a few days later, Parvati lay with her on the couch, Gital touching Parvati's lips with her own soft, lightly wrinkled lips. Gital twisted herself along Parvati's length until she gave a tough but meaningful cry. Parvati then did the same with Gital. (Satyal 2017, 115–116)

When I first read this paragraph, let me tell you I screamed out loud, that scandalized 'Ooooooh biiiiiitch!!!' faggot scream.

Somehow, I had not fathomed a writhing, moaning sex scene between 60-year-old aunties on the living room couch, however discretely wrapped in the opaque language of mutual twists and cries. I was taken by how the texture of their lovemaking is tied to their ageing bodies: 'lightly wrinkled lips' and 'tough [...] cry'. Attuned to Harit's coming out journey, I assumed his immobile mother to be stuck in place and emotion. Harit was the one supposed to have a sexual future, and I had not made room to imagine the aunties' sexual experimentation. Moreover, the aunty-ness of these two women – squarely confirmed by terms like unflagging, obsessive, unapproachable, performed through afternoon gossip and meals transported between households – occluded their queerness. In this way, I fell into the pattern of rendering desire 'impossible': 'the unthinkability of a queer female subject position within various mappings of nation and diaspora' (Gopinath 2005, 15; see also Dave 2012, 44). Like a good 'paranoid reader', my gaydar is always on, perhaps in overdrive (Sedgwick and Frank 2003). But I did not see Parvati and Gital's queer sex coming because of the characteristic impossibility of aunties – impossible this time taken to mean recalcitrant, unreasonable, difficult, old-fashioned – which rendered their queerness unthinkable.

Queer theorist Gayatri Gopinath (2005) offers us the field-defining formation of 'impossible desires' that names the unthinkability of South Asian queer women's desires. South Asian women and girls, carrying the burden of nation, culture, authenticity, and diasporic futurity, are rarely imagined to have the gender and sexual malleability afforded by queerness. Gopinath challenges this burden, pointing to the epistemic obfuscation of femme desires in South Asian public cultures, and using queerness to make pliable the rigid embodiments of diaspora required by various forms of nationalism. Her book leans on a promiscuous archive that skews towards youthful, thin, light-skinned bodies: Archie Punjabi in *East is East*, Madhuri Dixit in *Hum Aapke Hain Kaun?*, Rekha in *Utsav*. A particular kind of South Asian gender performance, aunty-ness, seems tougher and more recalcitrant to Gopinath's 'queer diasporic reading'. There are exceptions in her study, such as Shabana Azmi as the older sister-in-law in *Fire* (Mehta, dir. 1996). She also discusses homosociality between mothers-in-law singing suggestively sexual lyrics to each other in the all-women's space of Giddha in *Monsoon Wedding* (Nair, dir. 2001). However, she explains how these aunties' homoeroticism is foreclosed by the film's containment of queerness in the figure of the effeminate boy Varun (Gopinath 2005, 120–123) – the younger queer person again occludes aunties' queer erotics.

Perhaps the most aunty-like figure in Gopinath's book comes in its final pages, a 2003 photograph titled 'Southall Market' by artist Parminder Sekhon standing naked beside her mother, who sports salwar khameez, sweater, scarf, and grocery trolley – a full aunty look that remarkably resembles the aunties in Meera Sethis photographs. Gopinath writes, 'Sekhon's queerness is formed in and through her relation to home space, even as it radically disrupts and reterritorializes this space. Her nude body ... places queer female subjectivity at the center of diasporic public cultural space' (2005, 194). While Sekhon does not need to leave home to be queer, femme, or artist, the accented and ageing South Asian woman that stands in for home or mother is seemingly desexualized; although she does not antagonize queerness, she herself is certainly not queer. The mother's aunty aesthetic, that she can be read as aunty, stiffens her heteronormativity, makes her gender and sexuality less pliable. Similar to Kiran's aunties in *Blue Boy*, she is the rigid formation through and against which youthful queer, sexual, femininity can be performed. Placing the mother amongst other aunties, thinking 'between aunties', can offer sexuality, multiplicity, and queerness to the mother, to the women around her, to her generation. This project leans into Gopinath's assertion that queerness need not leave the South Asian home to find its futures; thinking with aunties and their capacity to blur the borders of home allows us to expand its spatial and temporal limits, and affords more opportunities to find queerness there.

Aunties can assist, facilitate, and inspire queerness but are rarely, if ever, imagined to be queer themselves. Their queer desires are rendered impossible (unimaginable, untenable) because they themselves are impossible (unpleasant, stubborn, backward). This article pursues impossible desires between impossible aunties – the characters I encounter in the following are simultaneously difficult and desirous. I continue to develop 'between aunties' as a framework that evidences the erotic and social relations that aunties build with each other – in addition to the intergenerational care and discipline they perform – to sustain and grow their pleasures.

Gossip at the gurdwara

Balli Kaur Jaswal's *Erotic Stories for Punjabi Widows* intertwines the lives of Nikki and Kulwinder. Nikki is a Punjabi British 22-year-old university drop-out, hired by the surly Kulwinder to teach a writing workshop at a Southall gurdwara. The job does not live up to expectations when Nikki realizes that most of the women, migrants from Punjab who are mostly widowed or deserted by their husbands, do not know how to write at all, let alone read and write in English. Although Kulwinder and Nikki are in conflict with each other for much of the narrative, particularly because Nikki allows her students to write erotic fiction, Kulwinder comes to Nikki's rescue at its climax, dragging her from a burning apartment. Kulwinder and Nikki are at the centre of *Erotic Stories*, but I am interested in the novel's minor figures, Nikki's students, the gaggle of women named in the title who litter the novel with comic relief and sexy stories. The erotica they collectively script is also cast into a minor mode, printed in italics, set apart from the narrative, interstitial.

While one might think of erotic writing as the exposition of individualist fantasies, in *Erotic Stories* the aunties' pornography is cooperatively constituted through gossip. Aunty gossip is often presumed to report on and dissuade younger generations' gender and sexual freedoms and experimentation, but in *Erotic Stories* it incites sexual pleasures. I understand gossip as collective informal exchanges of information and ideation, scripted and rescripted through oral delivery, surreptitious circulation, and inaccurate repetition. The heteroglossic style of gossip, its implicitly illicit nature, its unpredictable itineraries, and its theatrical delivery all shape the pornographic writing in *Erotic Stories* and the pleasures it nurtures between aunties.

Gossip, in *Erotic Stories* and elsewhere, is bound to the figure of the aunty, but it is a trope that fixes aunties to the past, it is a bad habit, an old-fashioned way of managing information. In her book-length 'guide' to aunties titled *Trust No Aunty*, illustrator and writer Maria Qamar begins with 'Aunties aren't born aunties. First they are molded by their predecessors and trained rigorously in the arts of plotting, black magic, and neighbourhood gossip' (2017, 6). Qamar introduces us to 'The online stalker aunty [who] can be a risk to befriend online. Especially if you plan to upload pics in your teeny-weeny Hello

Kitty bikini this summer' (2017, 147). The reader is recommended to 'trust no aunty' because her intimate information networks, infused with moral judgement, will find your sexual transgressions and publicly deride you for them. *Erotic Stories* offers valuable alternatives to the notion that aunty gossip only polices younger generations' fun.

Generational difference, the novel suggests, is predicated on radically different gender and sexual mores. Preetam reprimands Nikki for using only her first name, '"That's Bibi Preetam to you, young lady", she said stiffly. "Or Aunty. Or Preetam-ji"'. Meanwhile, Sheena has no desire to be called aunty: 'if you call me Bibi or Aunty, I'll just die because I must only be ten or fifteen years older than you'. Sheena, closer in age to Nikki than the other women, is also less aunty-like because she can read and write in English; she takes on the intermediary role of transcribing the orally composited erotic stories. Generational difference is also entrenched by differing attitudes to pornography. When Nikki was not present in the classroom, the women huddled over her copy of *Red Velvet: Pleasurable Stories for Women*, a prank gift she had purchased for her sister. Their titillation over this book is what incites the aunties to write their own pleasurable stories. Nikki is shocked at the first story they write, leaving the women confused: 'You read stories like this yourself'. Nikki explains that she bought the smut for her sister as a prank, and a confused Preetam says: 'I don't get the joke. Were you supposed to buy her a different book?' The widows do not have the ironic distance Nikki does from this discarded pornographic object fished out of a thrift store; it is genuinely titillating to them. Their whispers and titters over the book replicate the hushed excitement that characterizes gossip.

Aunty gossip operates throughout *Erotic Stories*, but it is not mere information. Rather, it is characterized by melodramatic narrations that imbue an excess of meaning. Jaswal introduces us to Auntie Geeta:

> She was a friend of [Nikki's mum] who lived up the road and often dropped in unannounced, her eyebrows wiggling with all the secrets she struggled to contain. 'Not gossiping, just sharing,' she always claimed before unpacking the ruins of other people's private lives. (Jaswal 2017, 28)

Aunties like Geeta penetrate the family home with unseemly or private information that should not have crossed its sacred threshold. Gossip is not neutral information; the embodied theatrics that it comes with – hushed voices, wiggling eyebrows, scandalized reactions such as Preetam's '*Hai*, Nikki I might faint' – suggest that there is always moral value and excess meaning inside these 'facts'. Such animated modes of delivery reveal that gossip surpasses objectivity. In Preetam's dramatic exclamation, gossip appears as a distinctly racialized and gendered performance of knowledge that cites the hyperbolic emotions of Indian television serials that she incessantly watches.

For communities displaced by migration and borders, gossip is a valuable mode of entertainment, information, and social influence, and in *Erotic Stories* Jaswal shows the many ways it operates. Where migrations strain systems of value and morality, as well as traditional family roles, gossip circulates narratives and expectations that discipline people back into gendered norms (Dreby 2009, 35). Aunty gossip is especially notorious for surveilling young peoples' 'vices' (Bradby 2007), but it is also used to police other aunties. Sheena explains of a high-end beauty parlour called Chandani's: 'It's a cesspool of gossip. Worse than the langar hall. Those women can't be trusted'. *Erotic Stories* importantly teaches us that gossip is not just the purview of women, and the widows warn Nikki of a network of men referred to as the Brothers who operate as the neighbourhood's moral police. The Brothers too work through gossip: 'A girl runs away from home with her Muslim boyfriend and the Brothers send the word out through their network of taxi drivers and shop owners to spot her and bring her home'. Per the novel's big reveal, the fear of 'what people will say' about an intergenerational relationship even costs one person their life. Gossip's diffuse pathways and unmeasured power has the potential to be a matter of life and death, and for this reason gossip is often cast as reckless and immoral – one more reason aunties are stigmatized. However, the novel tempers this bias by also staging the danger of the written document, the supposedly respectable form of information; the climactic scandal that almost kills Nikki revolves around an incriminating signature on a piece of paper.

Where aunty gossip supposedly entrenches patriarchy, in *Erotic Stories* it distributes sexual pleasure amongst women. One day, Geeta Auntie visits Nikki's mum's home with something especially tantalizing:

> 'Now tell me,' Geeta said after taking a sip of tea, 'have you heard about these stories?'
>
> 'What stories?'
>
> 'The *stories*' Geeta said. (Jaswal 2017, 206; original emphasis)

The erotic stories circulated through intimate networks, attracting more and more women to Nikki's classes: 'Emails. Somebody scanned a story and all of a sudden they were being sent to mailing lists everywhere'. Gossip is a site of contestations over power and knowledge (Rodríguez Navas 2018, 24), and the aunties protected themselves by circulating stories only through surreptitious networks, given both the surveillance of the Brothers and panopticaunt Kulwinder. Indeed, when Kulwinder finds out about the secretly written stories, she angrily seizes the pages from Nikki. Yet when she reads them at home: 'Her face, her hands and feet felt very warm, almost hot. She could feel the pulsing of her heart and another pulsing in a very private place'. Erotic stories by aunties get other aunties hot and bothered as they circulate, igniting their libidinal desires. Gossip facilitates the circulation of illicit forms of knowledge that do not serve patriarchal interest, but rather privilege women's engagement with their own bodies and fantasies. This is one mode of 'between aunties', where aunties gift each other hot sex through the distribution of stories. These stories travel not as advice from an older aunty to a younger person on how to please her husband, nor through anonymous channels such as sex advice columns, published erotica, or internet searches. This lateral network of peers, people who know each others' names, homes, partners, and children, people who practice their faith together, offer each other sexual pleasure.

'Between aunties' names how erotic stories are circulated through gossip, but it also captures how gossip facilitates writing. The stories are aunty-like in their collectivity, in the plurivocality characteristic of gossip: 'individual voices trade riffs, and melodies, and a voice of the group emerges over any single speaker' (Adkins 2017, 8). This is clear when Sheena reads her first transcription: 'I've written a story. It's a combined effort from all of us': '*His throbbing organ was the colour and size of an aubergine, and as she gripped it with her hands and guided it towards her mouth, he became so excited that his knees began to shake*'. When Arvinder is stuck on how to continue her story, Sheena suggests 'Describe his organ [...] Big or small?' The women, bantering in Punjabi, respond by talking about skinny carrots being disappointing, sweet potato being too painful, and bananas being of a nice size and shape. English words like cock, balls, pussy, tits, and arse send the women into giggle-fits, but vegetables and fruits are familiar. As daily objects they encounter in the kitchen and grocery store, objects whose name they regularly speak, produce items make sense to the women, to their everyday life and mundane touch.

Sexuality in India has long been articulated through English language, particularly because of 'the purging of sexual terminology from Indian languages that began with British colonialism and gained momentum in national formations of Indian identity' (Hall 2019, 491). But for these diasporic women, English is also not an ideal language for speaking sex; as Tarampal say about her lack of facility with English, '[The English] haven't made their country or customs friendly to me. Now their language is just as unfriendly'. Using Punjabi words for fruits and vegetables, the widows circumvent the loss of sexual language under colonialism and migration, without having to resort to the unfriendly sounds of English. Gossip's orality, its spoken quality, engenders intimacy (Adkins 2017, 9), and for this group of widows who do not know how to read and write, orality is that intimate mode of making erotica. As they parse through scandalous and familiar terminologies, they cooperatively develop an accessible vocabulary for speaking sex.

Gossip is an illicit mode of communication, with its own erotic embodiment. The collective work of scripting erotic stories is done in hushed tones, attempting to avoid Kulwinder's paranoid ear; this is certainly not the writing class she had advertised! Whispering cultivates a titillating atmosphere:

> we whisper not only to avoid being heard by others but also because of the pleasure we draw from performing their exclusion, from performing our own membership in the gossiping in-group, and from highlighting our mutual participation in a restricted and unsanctioned act. (Rodríguez Navas 2018, 13–14)

Because gossip covers up its sources and elides rigorous citation, this mode of hearsay protects the aunties from having to take individual ownership over the risqué content of their writing.[3] Also, the erotic stories, assembled through gossip, incite even more chatter as speakers are interrupted with mentions of the Brothers, affairs, abductions, mysterious suicides, children's academic and career success, and whose son is gay. These gossipy punctuations of the women's erotic storytelling bind sex to other matters in the community and situate sexual fantasy in continuum with numerous aspects of migrant life.

As news of the class spreads by word of mouth, new aunties bring fresh stories too. Newcomer Tanveer offers a story with a 'twist': Meera's home life is disrupted when a new sister-in-law Rita moves in; Meera likes her house just so. Moreover, she can hear the newlyweds loudly fucking in the adjoining room. But her annoyance one day takes a turn:

> All she could see when she shut her eyes was Rita's smooth flat tummy. Her mind's eye roved higher and she could picture the girl's firm, round breasts, her nipples flushed pink and alert. She pictured a pair of lips closing around those nipples and was horrified to realize that those lips belong to her. (Jaswal 2017, 140)

Tanveer's story innovates on the everyday by sexualizing the predicaments of Indian joint-family households. But she pauses when Meera finds Rita's dildos: '*"You teach me?" Meera retorted. "I'm your elder". But as she spoke, Rita had leaned forward and kissed her on the neck. Lightly, with her tongue'*. Tanveer's creativity stalls there, but the other women jump in with advice and gossip: 'They help each other out'; 'Two girls in my village were rumored to serve each other as well, but I believe they just used their hands'; 'We don't have to have men in all the stories'. The fictional Meera is granted sexual futures here, new bodily pleasures such as a tongue on the neck and dildos, despite her being the 'elder' bhabhi, and she wonders *'if she would ever be able to go to bed with her husband after experiencing Rita'*. Additionally, gossip invites memories of queerness, the two girls in the village, signalling that queerness is not completely new to the widows. In Tanveer's brief appearance in *Erotic Stories*, various modes of 'between aunties' nurture their sexual futures. Gossip leads new aunties to the gurdwara, facilitates story-writing, incites discussion about sexual pleasure, and makes room to both recall and dream queerness. Queer porn between bhabhis, scripted between aunties, operates in domestic and religious life, is constituted by gossip, and also incites it.

Erotic Stories stages pornography in continuum with aunty gossip, and erotica is inscribed through vernacular practices of collective oral creativity in homes, kitchens, langar halls, and Nikki's classroom. Although aunty gossip is often imagined to police and stigmatize sexual dissidence, here it becomes the means of making naughty stories, inciting aunty sexualities widely, and rousing queer desire between aunties. Tanveer's story is especially exciting in its queering of the pornographic bhabhi trope. In the category of 'aunty porn', the sister-in-law-as-aunty has been especially popularized by infamous porn-toon Savita Bhabhi. Here, I transition to more sex between sisters-in-law to think about how the kitchen becomes a site for intimacies between aunties.

Bhabhis in the kitchen

The buxom bhabhi or sister-in-law is a central trope in aunty porn that capitalizes on the possibilities of transgressive sex in domestic spaces (Sreedhar Mini and Baishya 2020, 117). Madhavi Menon (2018) describes Deepa Mehta's film *Fire* (1996) as an innovative queering of the well-worn seduction-of-the-sister-in-law trope; the film tracks the developing emotional and sexual affair between sisters-in-law Radha and Sita. Food is central to queer seduction in *Fire* (Mannur 2010); however, the opaque sex scenes between Radha and Sita are confined to the bedroom, separated from food, while more titillating flirtations happen in plain sight of the husbands – massaging each other's feet, cooking together, observing religious rituals (Gairola 2002; Gopinath 2005; Donnell 2007). In the spirit of Rodríguez's sexual futures, I am interested in how queer aunty porn can entwine sex acts and everyday life. Mary Ann Mohanraj's *Bodies in Motion* brings sex between bhabhis to the kitchen, 'always already a homosocial space that allows for articulations of same-sex intimacy to emerge through and against the strictures of a regimented heteronormativity' (Mannur 2013, 393).

Bodies in Motion stages bhabhi porn in continuum with various forms of aunty knowledge about sexuality and food. In her collection of essays, Mohanraj links the intersecting kinships of two Sri Lankan families as they traverse cities, continents, and oceans over five decades. Two chapters dwell on Mangai, a character who is already aunty-like in her youth, and who we meet at the book's end in her old age, a veritable aunty being stared at by young children. Food studies scholar and literary critic Anita Mannur (2013) has offered a loving analysis of these two chapters to demonstrate how culinary practice cultivates queer intimacy. In retelling Mangai's story, I focus on ageing and aunty-ness by offering two additions to Mannur's study: first, I name how Mangai's relationship to food and sex is routed through aunties – older relatives, sister-in-law, maid – and second, I detail how her solo cooking and eating is not only a scene of solitude, but delicately recalls sister-in-law-sex. Aunty knowledge rehearsed collectively in the kitchen is meant to promise and secure heterosexual futures, to teach girls how to be wives; indeed, Mangai's aunties advise her how to cook, and gently chastise her failures. But as we meet Mangai at either end of the book, we see that this very knowledge also teaches characters to fuck and to enjoy their bodies. Over the two short stories that bookend *Bodies in Motion*, the impossible character of Mangai – stubborn, competitive, intense – ages into auntyhood, sustaining queer pleasures through the knowledges of her aunties, rather than by rejecting them, further using them to make love to and life with other aunty figures.

We learn early on that aunties are responsible for the transmission of sexual knowledge. In the book's second chapter 'Seven Cups of Water', teenage Mangai finds newlywed Sushila crying in the kitchen after her wedding night, she is bleeding after her first time having penetrative sex. Similar in age to Sushila, Mangai questions Sushila's naivety: 'But didn't she have any aunts?' (Mohanraj 2005, 27). The transmission of sexual knowledge is the purview of aunties, and even at age 16 years Mangai is, in comparison to Sushila, already aunty-like. In typical aunty porn, the youngster is presented as innocent of sexual knowledge, and aunty is available to initiate them into adulthood. But here, Mangai is no naïve subject; and in fact the older, recently married sister-in-law is presented as the youthful subject. Mangai never gets to fully occupy the aesthetic form of girlhood; instead she observes these characteristics in Sushila – 'too-short, too-plump Mangai with her coarse hair and flat chest [Sushila] was slender and fair [...] Her legs were so smooth and fragile; for a moment, I felt like a hairy cow'. The sisters-in-law continue to meet in the kitchen every night. Sushila, thirsty, licks a spilled cup of water off her own hand, and then Mangai's. Mangai kisses water from her mouth into Sushila's. Sushila sucks the water off Mangai's wet sari blouse. Unlike in *Fire*, where the kitchen is a site of subtle flirtation, in *Bodies in Motion* it becomes the habitual site for inventive and explicit sexual practice.

It is curious that the kitchen is where Mangai practices her queer sexuality, because it is also where she finds herself repeatedly disciplined for her improper feminine comportment. Young Mangai was not a good cook:

> Her mother would come and pinch the extra flesh on her arm, hard. When she did not slice thinly enough. Punishing her for two sins at once – for being too clumsy, too fat. Probably for being too dark as well. (Mohanraj 2005, 269)

Mangai had to prepare afternoon meals for the full house of wedding guests:

> After every meal, one of the aunts would point out, kindly, that Mangai really had to be careful not to put too much tamarind into the fish curry, or too little salt in the sambar. After all, with her looks, it was important that she be a good cook. None of those meals came out perfectly – somehow, she always managed to ruin them. Secretly, she was glad. (Mohanraj 2005, 270)

Implied here is that being fat, dark, clumsy, and altogether impossible, she needs to be a good cook to attract a husband.

But if her aunties' instructions, offered in service of heteronormativity and to compensate for her undesirable embodiment, lead Mangai to ruin the meals, queer sex is where she learns that precise culinary skills might actually be efficacious. One night, clumsy Mangai brings her best focus to finely chopping chili peppers, rubbing them over Sushila's bare torso and breasts, creating unbearable heat as the capsaicin leaches into her skin, and then licking the peppery paste off Sushila's body like a sexual martyr when she runs out of water to wipe it with. Where she has been reluctantly cooking all week, purposefully messing up dishes, in sex she finds value in precise knife skills, the alchemy of spices, and the texture of ingredients. By the book's end, she is renowned for her cooking: 'Mangai aunty is cooking. Go. Watch.' Mothers tell their children to follow the 70-year-old lady home, and girls in a gaggle observe through the window while she prepares a meal for herself. Now occupying the public role of aunty, her finely honed skills were coveted by the young girls who watched in preparation of their own heteronormative futures, witnessing instead that cooking does not have to be in service of a husband or kids. The opportunity for the reader to witness elderly Mangai still cooking, even after she purposefully messed up recipes as a teen, suggests that sister-in-law sex offered its own lesson in the value of culinary techniques that exceed rehearsal towards heteronormative futures.

The community's interest in Mangai is not limited to her culinary skills; she is mired in stigma and suspicion because of her ethnicity (she is Tamil in a conflict-riven Colombo), and because she lived for decades in a single-bed home with her recently passed servant Daya. Maids too are figured into the vernacular category of 'aunty' (Mukhopadhyay 2012, 147), foreign figures in the home that can participate in sexual transgressions in domestic spaces. Daya's presence in the text is merely spectral, in the way that aunties often are. Mannur's reading of Mangai's solitary cooking in the book's final scene convincingly names her 'a queer single figure' (2013, 404). However, flagging the importance of Daya, I wonder whether we might linger on the ghosts she leaves in Mangai's home. Although we never meet Daya, we know that Mangai grieves her absence. If cooking, as I demonstrate in the following paragraph, has the capacity to recall queer sex with Sushila, might this slow and sensual practice also drag into the lonely present the sex and meals Mangai and Daya shared too?

As Mohanraj meticulously describes the meal Mangai cooks for herself in the final chapter, she returns us to the vividly described sexual exchanges in Chapter Two. In this way, elderly Mangai's performance of preparing a meal multiplies pleasure: her own gastronomic indulgence, the time spent preparing meals with and for Daya, and the ecstasy of sex with Sushila. In plain sight of the girls watching her cook, Mangai progressively undresses out of her sari. First, the drape is pulled off her back and tucked into her waistband. Then her blouse is undone. Later, she rotates the wrapped sari off her waist. Finally, she takes off the petticoat and eats the decadent meal, alone and naked. In Chapter Two, as the sisters-in-law make love, Mangai narrates the many ways they navigate their saris to access each other's bodies: pulling the drape down so that the blouse is exposed; lifting the pleats to reveal thighs; taking off Sushila's blouse, 'I peeled back the fabric, baring her breasts. They were ripe, dark mangoes bursting with juice'. This image is mirrored in the Epilogue. Halfway through her meal preparation, the older Mangai takes off her blouse: 'Her breasts had always been small; now they are further shrunken. The cold still makes her nipples harden.' Mohanraj allows Mangai's ageing aunty body to remain sexual, harkening back to teenage trysts as well as naming her continued sensuousness. When Mangai sits down to eat, she cuts her lip on the sharp edge of the steel cup – another evocation of Chapter Two, when the two girls sharpen a cup's edge to cut their thighs, letting blood as both a ritual parting and sexual pain play. By echoing the nighttime kitchen rendezvous between Sushila and Mangai, in the home that Daya and Mangai inhabited together, Mangai's solo cooking is filled with queer sex. Much like gossip between aunties is inextricable from sexual possibility in *Erotic Stories*, Mohanraj allows cooking to live in the same erotic universe as sex. This is central to the author's literary approach; although her early writing focused on erotica, she eventually became interested in the continuums between sexuality and the everyday, 'in the way peoples sexual choices influence their lives' (Hong 2005, 14).

In Mangai's kitchen, food porn and aunty porn are intertwined. Mannur describes Mohanraj's sensuous description of meal preparation as 'gastro-pornography' (2013, 402), a hyper-sensorial experience in which readers experience leeks soften under heat, cough with the rising smoke, and feel the spoon's resistance when stirring potatoes into curry mix. Danielle Seid (2018), writing of Asian American aunties' web-based cooking shows, explains how they refuse the 'food porn' aesthetics of hipster cooking shows, which emphasize gastronomical innovation and stylized visuals. Rather, these aunties 'showcase well-honed food preparation skills based on years of repetition and refinement' and the cameras turn 'to the Asian aunties themselves, who exude joie de vivre and an infectious passion for cooking' (2018, 781). Mohanraj replicates this tactic, focusing us on Mangai's well-rehearsed skills, panning our vision to her sensate body as she cooks. Mohanraj's writing mimics the aesthetics of Asian aunties' cooking shows, as she stages the rustic, processual, and fleshy aesthetic of the aunty's erotic; eschewing the flash and fusion associated with food porn, Mohanraj's gastro-pornography exhibits a distinctly aunty ethos.

In contrast to Parminder Sekhon's photograph in which she stands naked next to her modestly dressed mother, at the end of *Bodies in Motion* it is aunty who is naked, shrivelled, and indulgently queer. Aunty need not only gesture to queer futures for young femmes like Kiran in *Blue Boy* or the young women watching Mangai cook, she herself may also be queer. Clumsy, fat, hairy, horny, teenage Mangai tells herself of her encounters with Sushila, 'This was impossible, so impossible it wasn't even forbidden'. Developing Mangai's pleasure through the aunties that taught her to cook, sex with her sister-in-law, and a long-term relationship with Daya, Mohanraj allows us to see aunties on the other side of impossibility.

Enduring impossibility

'Between aunties' is a framework that honours the erotic and life-giving labours aunties do for each other as they age out of youthful promise, aesthetic, and affect, as they become difficult, disappointed, rigid, and bitter, simply impossible. Each of these stories describes a mode of 'between aunties'; even as aunties offer younger generations knowledge, care, and discipline, they also do each of these things for each other. In *No One Can Pronounce My Name*, 'between aunties' describes the food, company, and home care that accompanies sex between two older Indian women. In *Erotic Stories for Punjabi Widows*, it refers to bhabhi porn written by aunties, collective inventive orality, and the dissemination of erotica through intimate routes of friendship. In *Bodies in Motion*, 'between aunties' names nourishment and creative sex between sisters-in-law and between an elderly woman and her 'maid'. To think between aunties is to take stock of the work that queer people do to raise each other over a lifetime, to recognize each other's impossible desires and make room for them to grow, change, and become, regardless of how set in our ways we supposedly are. To think about the collective work of aunties is to bear witness to a lifetime of innovation under heteropatriarchal nationalisms that cannot fathom their existence, joy, queerness, or future. If we must marvel at the creativity of queer and trans children of colour to survive (Muñoz 1999, 37), can we also express wonder for aunties who collectively innovate and perform pleasure across a lifetime of impossibility?

Notes

1. This is not necessarily the case for the relatively young Radha aunty, although her ephemerality mimics the common tendency for aunties to appear only briefly in South Asian narratives.
2. Iconic porn-toons Savita Bhabhi and Velamma were created by US-based South Asian artists, Bollywood crossover star Sunny Leone began her career as a porn star in Canada before moving to India, and 'footpath erotica' sold to working-class people in India is meant to appeal to migrants, travellers, and other people in motion.
3. On gossip as a form of protection and care, see Lee (2016).

Acknowledgements

The author's deepest gratitude goes to the three anonymous reviewers whose encouraging and detailed feedback on this project have greatly improved the shape, argument, and voice of this article. Central to the development of this article were the Tufts 2019–2020 Mellon Sawyer Seminar 'Defamiliarizing the Family: Genealogy and Kinship as Critical Method' as well as the New England Humanities Council 2020 Seed Grant for 'Undisciplining Performance'. The author's gratitude also goes to Darshana Sreedhar Mini and Anirban Baishya for the opportunity to think in community about aunties, to Christine Mok for her brilliant advice, and to Tufts colleague Manjari Mukherjee for the foundational work she did in the earliest stages of researching this article.

Disclosure statement

No potential conflict of interest was reported by the author.

References

Adkins, Karen. 2017. *Gossip, Epistemology, and Power: Knowledge Underground*. Cham: Springer International Publishing AG.

Allen, Jafari. 2009. 'For "the Children", Dancing the Beloved Community.' *Souls* 11 (3): 311–326.

Bernstein, Robin. 2011. *Racial Innocence: Performing American Childhood from Slavery to Civil Rights*. New York: New York University Press.

Bradby, Hannah. 2007. 'Watch out for the Aunties! Young British Asians' Accounts of Identity and Substance use.' *Sociology of Health & Illness* 29 (5): 656–672.

Chatterjee, Tupur. 2017. "I am a Porn Star!' Sex and Sunny Leone Unlimited in Bollywood.' *Porn Studies* 4 (1): 50–66.

Cobham-Sander, Rhonda. 2021. 'Amital Queer: Towards a Definiton of the Aunty in Caribbean Literature.' Critical Aunty Studies. Accessed March 30. https://www.criticalauntystudies.com/03-keynote.
Dave, Naisargi N. 2012. *Queer Activism in India: A Story in the Anthropology of Ethics*. Durham: Duke University Press.
Dhalla, Ghalib Shiraz. 2002. *Ode to Lata*. Los Angeles: Really Great Books.
Donnell, Alison. 2007. 'Feeling Good? Look Again!.' *Journal of Creative Communications* 2 (1-2): 43–55.
Dreby, Joanna. 2009. 'Gender and Transnational Gossip.' *Qualitative Sociology* 32 (1): 33–52.
Edelman, Lee. 2004. *No Future: Queer Theory and the Death Drive*. Durham: Duke University Press.
Eng, Chris A. 2018. 'Toward the "Uncommonly Beautiful": Queer-of-Color Youth and "Delectable Deformity" in Rakesh Satyal'sBlue Boy.' *Melus* 43 (4): 33–56.
Eng, David L. 2001. *Racial Castration: Managing Masculinity in Asian America*. Durham: Duke University Press.
Gairola, Rahul. 2002. 'Burning with Shame: Desire and South Asian Patriarchy, from Gayatri Spivak's "Can the Subaltern Speak?" to Deepa Mehta's Fire.' *Comparative Literature* 54 (4): 307–324.
Gill-Peterson, Jules. 2018. *Histories of the Transgender Child*. Minneapolis: University of Minnesota Press.
Gopinath, Gayatri. 2005. *Impossible Desires: Queer Diasporas and South Asian Public Cultures*. Durham: Duke University Press.
Halberstam, J. 1998. *Female Masculinity*. Durham: Duke University Press.
Hall, Kira. 2019. 'Middle Class Timelines: Ethnic Humor and Sexual Modernity in Delhi.' *Language in Society* 48 (4): 491–517.
Hong, Terry. 2005. 'From X to PG-13-"Sexuality Activist" Mohanraj Goes Mainstream.' *Asianweek* 27 (8): 14.
Jaswal, Balli Kaur. 2017. *Erotic Stories for Punjabi Widows*. First edition. New York: William Morrow.
Khubchandani, Kareem. 2017. 'Aunty Fever: A Queer Impression.' In *Queer Dance: Meanings and Makings*, edited by Clare Croft, 199–204. New York: Oxford University Press.
Lee, Erica Violet. 2016. 'I'm Concerned for your Academic Career if you Talk about this Publicity.' *Moontime Warrior*. February 5. Accessed March 7. https://moontimewarrior.com/2016/02/05/im-concerned-about-your-academic-career-if-you-talk-about-this-publicly/.
Lewis, Mel Michelle. 2017. 'A Genuine Article: Intersectionality, Black Lesbian Gender Expression, and the Feminist Pedagogical Project.' *Journal of Lesbian Studies* 21 (4): 420–431.
Macharia, K'eguro. 2021. '7 Scenes with Aunties—(and a note on method).' *Critical Aunty Studies*. Accessed March 30. https://www.criticalauntystudies.com/02-enumerations.
Mannur, Anita. 2010. *Culinary Fictions: Food in South Asian Diasporic Culture*. Philadelphia: Temple University Press.
Mannur, Anita. 2013. 'Perfection on a Plate: Readings in the South Asian Transnational Queer Kitchen.' In *Eating Asian America*, edited by Robert Ji-Song Ku, Martin Manalansan and Anita Mannur, 393–408. New York: NYU Press.
Mannur, Anita. 2021. 'Upstairs, Downstairs: The Unseen Labor of Aunties in Ritesh Batra's *The Lunchbox*.' Critical Aunty Studies. Accessed March 30. https://www.criticalauntystudies.com/04-work.
Mansukhani, Tarun, dir. 2008. *Dostana* [Friendship]. India.
Mehta, Deepa, dir. 1996. *Fire*. Canada.
Menon, Madhavi. 2018. *Infinite Variety: A History of Desire in India*. New Delhi: Speaking Tiger.
Mohanraj, Mary Anne. 2005. *Bodies in Motion: Stories*. 1st ed. New York: HarperCollins Publishers.
Mukhopadhyay, Bhaskar. 2012. *The Rumor of Globalization: Desecrating the Global from Vernacular Margins*. London: Hurst and Company.
Muñoz, José Esteban. 1999. *Disidentifications: Queers of Color and the Performance of Politics*. Minneapolis: University of Minnesota Press.
Muñoz, José Esteban. 2009. *Cruising Utopia: The Then and There of Queer Futurity*. New York: New York University Press.
Nair, Meera, dir. 2001. *Monsoon Wedding*. United States.

Nair, Sridevi. 2008. 'Hey Good Lookin'!: Popular Culture, Femininity, and Lesbian Representation in Transnational Regimes.' *Journal of Lesbian Studies* 12 (4): 407–422.

Nayak, Anmol. 2020. 'The "Aunty" Body and All That Follows.' Feminism India. Accessed December 21. https://feminisminindia.com/2020/07/13/aunty-body-all-that-follows/.

Qamar, Maria. 2017. *Trust no Aunty*. First Touchstone hardcover edition. New York: Touchstone.

Rodríguez, Juana María. 2014. *Sexual Futures, Queer Gestures, and Other Latina Longings*. New York: New York University Press.

Rodríguez, Juana María. 2017. 'Diasporic Divas: Working Sex, Transing Biography.' Queer of Color Criticism and Performance, Medford MA, October 13.

Rodríguez, Juana María. 2015. 'Pornographic Encounters and Interpretative Interventions: *Vanessa del Rio: Fifty Years of Slightly Slutty Behavior*.' *Women & Performance: a Journal of Feminist Theory* 25 (3): 315–335.

Rodríguez Navas, Ana Belén. 2018. *Idle Talk, Deadly Talk: the Uses of Gossip in Caribbean Literature*. Charlottesville: University of Virginia Press.

Sandhu, Arti. 2019. 'India's Digital Drag Aunties: Breaking New Ground Wearing Familiar Fashions.' *Dress* 45 (1): 55–73.

Satyal, Rakesh. 2009. *Blue Boy*. New York: Kensington Books.

Satyal, Rakesh. 2017. *No One Can Pronounce My Name: A Novel*. First edition. New York: Picador.

Sedgwick, Eve Kosofsky. 2004. 'How to Bring Your Kids Up Gay: The War on Effeminate Boys.' In *Curiouser: On the Queerness of Children*, edited by Steven Bruhm and Natasha Hurley, 139–150. Minneapolis: University of Minnesota Press.

Sedgwick, Eve Kosofsky, and Adam Frank. 2003. *Touching Feeling: Affect, Pedagogy, Performativity*. Durham: Duke University Press.

Seid, Danielle. 2018. 'The "Anti-Hipster" Feminism of Asian Auntie Cooking Web Series.' *Feminist Media Studies* 18 (4): 779–782.

Selvadurai, Shyam. 1996. *Funny Boy: A Novel*. 1st U.S. ed. New York: W. Morrow and Co.

Sethi, Meera. 2016. 'Upping the Aunty.' Accessed July 2. https://meerasethi.com/upping-the-aunty.

Shankar, Karin. 2019. 'Tracing Minor Gesture in Maya Krishna Rao's Kathakali-Influenced Performance.' *Women & Performance: a Journal of Feminist Theory* 29 (2): 125–145.

Sreedhar Mini, Darshana and Anirban K. Baishya. 2020. 'Transgressions in Toonland: *Savita Bhabhi, Velamma* and the Indian Adult Comic.' *Porn Studies* 7 (1): 115–131.

Srivastava, Sanjay. 2007. *Passionate Modernity: Sexuality, Class, and Consumption in India*. New Delhi: Abingdon: Routledge.

Stockton, Kathryn Bond. 2009. *The Queer Child, or Growing Sideways in the Twentieth Century*. Durham: Duke University Press.

Tincknell, Estella. 2020. 'Monstrous Aunties: The Rabelaisian Older Asian Woman in British Cinema and Television Comedy.' *Feminist Media Studies* 20 (1): 135–150.

Wong, Jock. 2006. 'Contextualizing Aunty in Singaporean English.' *World Englishes* 25 (3-4): 451–466.

Part III

South Asian porn and the digital turn

The X factors of sex: hijras, Victorian law, and digital porn in postcolonial India

Rahul K. Gairola

ABSTRACT

This essay expands and transposes Kimberlé Crenshaw Williams' notion of 'intersectionality' in the geographical and historical context of contemporary India. The article offers the theoretical heuristic of 'intersex/tional' identity to re-think the erotic lives of hijras in India following the Supreme Court of India's legal recognition of the so-called third gender. I begin by establishing a rationale for doing so, and then briefly move into a history of the pathologization of hijras as non-confirming genders from British colonial times to now. Following this introduction, I examine the limited representation of hijras in digital pornography, expanding my scope to the queer purview of Digital India. The questions that I ask and propose to answer are as follows: in what ways are digital articulations of hijras as erotic figures complicated through technology; and are these new modes of subjectivity that challenge hegemonic pathology of non-gender-conforming subjects?

Gender trouble with third genders

In April 2014, the Supreme Court of India legally codified the 'third gender', a category that largely comprises those citizen-subjects assigned as male at birth (according to medicalized male anatomy) who undergo surgical and socialization procedures. LGBTQI+ activists in and beyond the subcontinent heralded this legislation as inaugurating a new era of national liberalness with respect to gender and sexuality. Citing the recognition of transgender peoples in Pakistan since 2009 and that country's 2017 decision to issue passports for them under the categorical designation 'X' (see Maizland 2017), Indian LGBTQI+ activists applauded India's initiative to 'catch up', so to speak, with its Raj-fashioned arch rival. Such legal codifications by the Indian and Pakistani states suggest that 'transgender' describes anatomical sex and gender identity at odds sans sexual orientation, whereas hijras are males, and sometimes intersex people, who sometimes – but not all of the time – undergo ritualistic castration and adopt the female gender identity.[1] This supports the contention of theorists and activists including Kat Callahan (2014) and Living Smile Vidya (Semmalar 2014, 287) that male privilege is a prerequisite for those who transition from male to female, which posits the body politics of gender squarely in the crosshairs of jurisprudence.

Despite claims of democratic equity regardless of gender identity, there are contradictions and biases that are, conversely, enabled and propagated by this legal recognition – namely with the ongoing, institutionalized stigmas related to Section 377 of the Indian Penal Code. In this article, I understand 'transgender' to socially signify non-binary gender expressions, including movements between gender categories and gender identities that oscillate between 'male' and 'female' polarities, rather than a fixed sexual orientation. I meditate on these and other problems of third gender identity politics as they relate to erotic representations because those are arguably omniscient – even in absence and prohibition. Indeed, we might ask how hijras (also called 'Aravani' and 'Kinnara') are, in Geeta Patel's words, 'inside the most pedestrian fantasies of what tends to be understood as central, normal, or home' (2016, 65). As social subjects who are simultaneously nowhere and everywhere, they occupy the margins of the powerful nexus of gender and sexuality, namely as legally codified subjects whose third gender-ness is sanctioned by the government in the face of social stigma and nationalist masculinity in Narendra Modi's India.

The British Raj instituted Section 377 to criminalize gender-based sexual acts between consenting adults. In Zaid Al Baset's (2012) formulation, 'Section 377 was born out of a desire to sexually discipline the colonial subject imagined as erotically perverse in 1860. It criminalizes "unnatural offences" which include voluntary "carnal intercourse" against the "order of nature" with any man, woman or animal. Section 377 further explicates that penetration is sufficient to cause "carnal intercourse". "Carnal intercourse" in this instance, has been interpreted as "anal sex, oral sex and other forms of non-procreative although penetrative sexual acts"' (2012, 95). Much of this colonial-era law was largely repealed by the Supreme Court of India on 8 September 2018, wherein prohibition was deemed 'irrational, indefensible, and manifestly arbitrary' (McGoldrick 2019) excepting bestiality, rape, and underage sex. However, the social mindset justified by the law still lingers. Despite decriminalization, in Alok Sarin's words, 'The discourse of the legal system, which criminalises homosexuality, and that of scientific thought, which pathologises it ... have informed each other and that both are, in a sense, a reflection of how society views homosexuality' (2014, 5).

Sarin's observation compels us to see how ostensibly objective science can buttress the totalizing rationality of legal discourse. As a means for understanding the linked sexualization and classification of hijra communities in Indian jurisprudence, I engage in close readings of select transgender pornographic videos on digital websites. I conclude with a reformulation of Kimberlé Crenshaw Williams' (1989) notion of 'intersectionality' and transpose it onto the geographical and historical context of contemporary India. I reformulate Crenshaw's heuristic in the context of hijra pornography to critically read how these 'legally liberated' subjects are yet trapped in the gender binary. In my reading, the concept of 'intersex/tionality' embodies, beyond semantics, a heuristic through which we may critically re-read the erotic lives of hijras in India following the Supreme Court of India's legal recognition of the third gender and decriminalization of consensual queer sex. To arrive at the lens of 'intersex/tionality', I begin with a history of the pathologization of third gender peoples as non-conforming since British colonial times. I then offer a juridical background on Section 377 to render a history of today in the digital representations of transgender sex.

Following this, I examine the kind (and lack) of representation of hijras in digital pornography, thus expanding my scope to the sexual purview of Digital India,[2] wherein both prohibition of pornography and its repeal occurred in the same week of August 2015 (Cain 2015). While sexual media in India are admittedly limited while all pornography constructs fantasies around fetishized body parts, this nonetheless enables us to critically read the third gender subject of Indian law and that of pornography as surprisingly similar. That is, in both cases, the third gender figure is a stand-out subject that, despite its democratic inclusion, is nonetheless fetishized. The questions that I ask and attempt to answer are: how does the third gender/ hijra, as a juridico-historical figure in contemporary India, complicate the binaristic ways in which we view gender roles; how does this figure texturize available models of erotic representation of hijras in and through digital pornography; are such representations innovative modes of subjectivity that challenge former and current prejudices against non-gender-conforming subjects; and, finally, how might our divergent answers complicate the semiotics of marginalized queers today beyond an intersex/tional class of Indian citizens who inhabit the thresholds of erotic agency in and beyond postcolonial India?

In attempting to answer these questions, I return to questions of criminality in India and legal recognition of the so-called third gender. I engage this query in a bid to map out and forecast further juridical developments for third genders that will re-shape, and perhaps even revolutionize, the erotic landscapes of the digital milieu. As all gendered and sexualized subjects cannot socially exist beyond law and are instead defined and bestowed agency by it, I operate from the premise that law is a profound site of representation that we must examine along with digital pornography. That is, the Indian Penal Code marshals the boundaries of gender and what constitutes 'obscene' materials – what constitutes 'unnatural' sex and what must be punished by law. Gayatri Chakravorty Spivak (2014, 26) speaks to these fault lines in social equity of the world's largest democracy and the ongoing problems that haunt the nation with respect to women's safety and human rights when observing that 'all bodies are, in fact, borderlines', and that the female body in particular must be consciously reckoned with.

Spivak moreover notes that 'the short-term work is law: changing and implementing … [This is a place where attending to] borders is very important. That is where I would go: law, training, attending to borders' (2014, 26). If Section 377 materializes gender, as in 'the female body', into intelligible borderlines which govern waking life, I would argue that the preoccupation of femaleness as it appears on men's bodies and how it is absent from women's bodies is an ongoing anxiety crystallized in India by Section 377 despite the September 2018 ruling. This is arguably due to a massive colonial hangover over the mixing of blood and anxieties about reproduction (Stoler 2002, 42) in the post colony (although India was not a settler colony like Australia, South Africa, and/or Canada), and in other independent nations with Victorian-era laws still on the books. Borderlines and laws: the same kind of drawings of boundaries yet at different sites that inculcate imaginary meanings (Rushdie 1991, 16) onto terrestrial and corporeal masses. In this frame, borderlines of gender and law condense, and become braided together, in the digital pornography that depicts hijras. Hence, it is impossible, from the outset of this particular argument, to disaggregate from law the voyeuristic allure of transgender pornography and whether or not viewing it constitutes a crime.

Imperialistic prohibitions of queerness

As we have seen in the era before Section 377's partial repeal in September 2018, archaic notions of 'criminality' based on incongruences between gendered anatomies and sex acts saturate both legal discourse and erotic voyeurism. They link the notion of 'unnatural' erotics to offence of law, thus delineating legally constructed borderlines that sculpt into sharp relief the prototype of the sexually transgressive figure in contemporary India. India's sexual prohibitions to date harken back to the hegemonic imperium that finally departed in August 1947, partly due to the British Raj's dour view that India was no longer profitable (see Tharoor 2016; Singh, Iyer and Gairola 2016). The institutionalization of racist Victorian dictums was greatly influenced by the many forms of 'mimicry' (Bhabha 1984) in language and culture that resulted from the implementation of Thomas Babington Macaulay's infamous 'Minute on Indian Education' of 1835. As a Legal Member of Council who favoured the Anglicist perspective over the Orientalists, Macaulay proclaimed, with the flourish of his officiating pen, that English would be the language of schooling and government in colonized India (Carter and Harlow 2003, 227).

This policing of the ways that Indian subjects would write themselves into existence in the image of their colonizers foreshadowed how Macaulay would later enshrine sexual propriety onto colonized bodies in India. Indeed, Macaulay is less notorious for another drastic policy that he imposed on the Raj's indigenous subjects: he was the architect of the 1860 implementation of Section 377, the 'unnatural offences' statute, of the Indian Penal Code. Section 377 was a particularly insidious act because it sutured the very notion of 'nature' (that justifies the violence of colonialism, slavery, and indentured servitude) through scientific rationality. This statute deployed 'nature' as a means of criminalizing queer gender and sex acts that did not conform to heteronormative ideals propagated by Victorian gender propriety:

> **377. Unnatural offences**: Whoever voluntarily has carnal intercourse against the order of nature with any man, woman or animal, shall be punished with imprisonment for life, or with imprisonment of either description for term which may extend to ten years, and shall also be liable to fine.
>
> **Explanation**: Penetration is sufficient to constitute the carnal intercourse necessary to the offense described in this section. (Misra 2009, 21)

The statutory meaning ostensibly pivots around carnal intercourse and (un)natural offences, but the addition of an 'explanation' strategically denies individual interpretation since the interpretation of law is unwarranted. This overdetermined predicate reflects the ways in which gender, like 'unnatural' sex acts realized by penetration, was also militantly situated by the Raj. As Jessica Hinchy notes, colonial officials referred to hijras as men because:

> the use of the masculine pronoun was, in fact, a linguistic strategy to erase *hijras* as a distinct gender category and restore the binary division of gender that *hijras* challenged [original emphasis] ... Masculinity was also fundamental to British ideologies of rule in India, in which British men were represented as the masculine ideal. (2017, 112)

Such pre-conditions of gender and sexuality which would influence pornography laws wrested away from sexual agents what M. Jacqui Alexander (1996, 64) aptly dubs 'erotic autonomy' in the context of the postcolonial Caribbean.

As Alexander suggests in formulating her landmark concept, psychological borders of empire established by the British and inherited by a patriarchal elite in independent nations like The Bahamas and India – places in which her majesty's 'subjects' were viewed as other, criminal, for having brown and black skin – operated as disciplinary sites. In these disciplinary topographies of mind and land, interested forces transposed production and labour extraction from bodies of territory to human bodies. In this transposition, the woman of colour's body arguably morphed into a locus of social anxiety because it was the vessel for 'tainted' citizenry reproduction (see Weinbaum 2004). Since such women symbolize the reproductive potential of coloured bodies, we may surmise how hijras challenge British biopolitical order (Foucault 1976) in the domain of 'proper gender'. The hijra was non-reproductive, and thus viewed as 'really' a man although her social life was clearly that of a non-heteronormative subject. Thus, the 'crime' at stake here was evinced by the right body parts matched to the wrong gender identity which itself was non-productive in the purview of both the British Raj and the postcolonial elite.

The colonial officials imposed this misrecognition into a constellation of legal codifications that inaugurated a historical precedent for pathologizing transgender folks today. Some scholars note that this legally commenced with the 1871 Criminal Tribes Act. According to Meena Radhakrishna, the Criminal Tribes Act:

> came into force throughout the [Madras] Presidency in 1911, [and] had replaced an earlier Act of 1871 which was restricted in its application and extended only to certain provinces in Northern India. The new Act of 1911, which applied to the whole of India, drew substantially from the earlier Act with some important modifications. (2001, 27)

This act sought to legally codify the notion that:

> crime was a genetic trait transmitted over generations in a family through parents and ancestors. The concept of a 'hereditary criminal class,' was an important and attractive one, and a consequence was the deflection of serious enquiries into the causes of crime. Notions of criminality were located and developed sometimes in the social, sometimes in the scientific context, the two not necessarily excluding each other. (Radhakrishna 2001, 2)

British officials deemed such designated groups to be fatally deceitful like the Thuggee cult, which was popularized in Steven Spielberg's film *Indiana Jones and the Temple of Doom* (1984), which operated like highway robbers who gained the trust of travellers and then strangled them. Hijras, or 'eunuchs' in colonialist language, were registered and policed under Part II of the Criminal Tribes Act. In addition to linking transgressive gender identifications to criminality, that Act also forced class and ethnicity into the legal parameters of juridical 'perversions'.

However, there is debate about the veracity of these ubiquitous cults, and some have argued that tribal chiefs were in fact criminalized as a precaution after the 1857 Sepoy Rebellion (see Radhakrishna 2001, 2). Susan Abraham writes:

> The British colonialists thus ensured that sections of the Indian population were permanently linked to the world of crime, thereby actually forcing many to engage in criminal activities. Aboriginal tribes, backward castes and nomadic communities were arbitrarily brought under the purview of the CTA (Criminal Tribes Act). (1999, 1753)

In addition, it is crucial to recognize how class intervened in the stigmatization of hijras in indigenous Indian communities in the second half of the nineteenth century. Indeed, Charu Gupta notes that the dominant view was that 'monogamous, heterosexual, and companionable marriage' linked to female reproduction and male virility constituted 'a modern, civilized, Hindu nation' (2011, 14). Gupta (2011, 15) moreover notes that the rise of print culture and urbanization creates 'colonial publics' that crystallized a discriminating middle class in colonial India.[3] According to Ruth Vanita and Saleem Kidwai, becoming a hijra was often viewed as the only option for working-class gay men, although 'the conflation of hijras with homosexual men' imbibes 'an homophobic refusal to acknowledge homosexual men as full-fledged "men" living in mainstream society' (2000, 202).

As we can see, 'caste' and 'tribe' both operate as class markers during (and after) Britain's colonial project in India. The rise of an Indian middle class steeped in colonial mimicry[4] exacerbated the pathologization of poor people and sexual minorities. In contrast to the colonial policing of gender and sex, it would seem that contemporary Indian statutes that recognized the 'third sex' and repealed the ban on pornography are relatively progressive. However, closer scrutiny of the history of hijras and the contradictions that arise from the Supreme Court of India's legal recognition of the third gender while upholding the constitutionality of Section 377 in December 2013 suggests otherwise. Legal codification of the third gender exacerbated the grounds for criminalizing queer sexuality that are anchored to intelligible gender roles – hijra and/or female/male – and some historical framing is needed to better understand why. Curiously (and in contrast to this tendency towards criminalization), popular belief in South Asia holds that the appearance of hijras at births, weddings, and other auspicious occasions bestows blessings (or curses if the visitors are ill-treated or not paid properly for their merry-making) on the spot (Gairola 2018).

This particular colonial-era statute breaks the ancient tradition of venerating members of the third sex. The British colonial administration instituted the Criminal Tribes Act of 1871 that criminalized indigenous subjects who transgressed normative gender roles. According to Nancy A. Naples and Barbara Gurr:

> By specifically regulating gender/ sex identities, the colonial project in India legally imposed a heteronormative binary which marginalized those who stepped outside of the legal bounds of gendered sexuality ... The British colonial powers incorporated hijra into a grander, criminalized category which included all non-heterosexual identities without distinction. (2012, 314–315)

As Indrani Sen Gupta notes, the Criminal Tribes Act of 1871 includes 'An Act for the Registration of Criminal Tribes and Eunuchs' in Part II to make more explicit, and enforceable, 'the link between criminality and sexual non-conformity' (2005, 188). This brief reflection on the historical roots of criminalization of those whose gender identities do not match Occidental social norms suggests why social activism for third gender rights are timely in the wake of India's legal recognition of 'third gender' with Section 377's legacy of bigotry still intact.

Indeed, the legal reservations accorded to hijras by the new law deliver paltry remedies in contrast to the dominant mentality of patriarchal male privilege that looks down on femininity as an abject ontology. This comes into sharp focus in an issue brief titled 'Hijras/Third Gender Women in India: HIV, Human Rights, and Social Exclusion', submitted to the United Nations Development Programme, India, by Dr Venkatesan Chakrapani (2010). The report is of importance to this discussion of hijra porn and mobile digital media[5] because it details the many forms of 'social exclusion' experienced by third gender peoples. Such social exclusion includes familial, social, and cultural participation, discrimination in healthcare settings, exclusion from economic participation and lack of social security, which includes lack of livelihood options and health and life insurance schemes, and exclusion from political participation (2010, 8–9). Chakrapani's report elucidates that one's gender identity has ramifications that stretch far beyond the sexual, impacting the most vital aspects of communal belonging that materialize in diverse trajectories of the quality of life. In the context of digital media, this report is of particular relevance as the dynamics of exclusion can be magnified or reduced at an exponential rate in the public sphere of mobile culture.

Regional transgender communities are of course not monolithic, and subsequently have different experiences in India from region to region. In her study of hijras in southern India titled *With Respect to Sex: Negotiating Hijra Identity in South India*, Gayatri Reddy conducts a timely ethnographic study of a community in South Asia whose complex reception include celebratory welcomes and violent rejections. She writes:

> For the most part, hijras are phenotypic men who wear female clothing and, ideally, renounce sexual desire and practice by undergoing a sacrificial emasculation – that is, an excision of the penis and testicles ... In recent years, hijras have emerged as perhaps the most frequently encountered figures in the narrative linking of India with sexual difference. As the quintessential 'third sex' of India, they have captured the Western scholarly imagination as an ideal case in the transnational system of 'alternative' gender/sexuality. (Reddy 2010, 2)

Reddy's observation of the hijra as a dual symbol of India's 'alternative' gender and sexuality in the western imagination speaks to the complex ways in which we can view the hijra as a legal subject from different perspectives. On the one hand, the legally sexed-subject is enshrined as universal, while on the other it circulates as an essentialist stereotype in the mainstream. Legal recognition carries with it other pitfalls. It has the potential to be more damaging to overall social justice for non-binary folks. This is because state projects of equity across genders are questionable given the statistics of third gender-identified folks in India. I note this because the majority of subjects are male-assigned based on gendered anatomies. Because they are 'born with male sex organs' and thus identified as 'men' by a heteronormative society in the first instance, becoming third gender may be viewed as derivative of male privilege.

While this is certainly true in some cases, male privilege is often provisional and conditional rather than being automatically linked to biology (Callahan 2013; Vidya 2013). This is a nuance that legal codifications gloss over. Aniruddha Dutta recognizes the fraught reasoning of the Supreme Court ruling, observing that axiomatic externalities, including psychological tests and surgery, nourish the ideology of 'biological essentialism, that is, the reliance on biological and physical attributes (such as genitalia and hormones) that are positioned as "essences" of gender and used to verify or certify someone's gender identity' (2014, 227). They go on to note that such essentialist formulations of gender are further complicated by state-sanctioned reservations and other such social services (2014, 227). Dutta's observation behoves us to further meditate on the conditions around which legal codification of the third gender has been celebrated in India. In another formulation of thinking the hijra, Ratna Kapur also gives us a way to know the male-born, third gender subject as a 'sexual subaltern' (2000, 16).[6] Both Dutta's and Kapur's framings are key points of orientation in this article because they invoke biological essentialism, on the one hand, and class status on the other. As such, both lenses are intimately braided with the pornographic representations of hijras on digital platforms.

Getting off on the third gender

A recent *GQ: Gentlemen's Quarterly* article reports that the four top pornography websites by numbers of users are: (1) Pornhub, with 8.624 million viewers; (2) Porn555, with 7.170 million users; (3) BongaCams, with 5.711 million users; and (4) XVideos, with 1.979 million users (Sharma 2017). Each website deploys various strategies of marketing, or rendering in/visible, third sex performers, and these range across different levels. However, delimiting the search category with the keyword 'hijra' is telling: while XVideos returned the most hits of digital clips organized by a range of categories cross-listed by the key term 'hijra', BongaCams yielded zero hits under 'hijra', 'kinnara', and/ or 'aravani'. For this reason, I removed BongaCams from the list of digital porn sites that I have herein examined. On further examination, the website Porn555 had zero hits when conducting a search with the keyword 'hijra', 419 hits with the words 'shemale', and 24 hits with the keyword 'third gender' (zero hits with the keywords 'kinnara' and/or 'aravani'). In contrast to the thousands of videos on these websites featuring white bodies, these numbers underscore the reductive novelty of third gender bodies across national boundaries. Further, Porn555 ostensibly centres the white phallus as the privileged appendage of third gender experience, even to the point of skewed visibility and invisibility. In contrast, BongaCams completely erases third gender erotica.

These two distinctions in the marketing of the porn videos featured on the Porn555 and BongaCams websites, despite their relatively large viewerships in India, suggest that the target market for both sites are global viewers whose erotic desires privilege heterosexual sex even beneath the rubric of queer sex. That is, these websites propagate what Judith Butler calls 'Compulsory heterosexuality… [as] the true, the authentic; the norm that determines the real' (1997, 312), even in the homogeneous fantasy worlds produced by porn. In plain terms, the sex featured on these two websites reifies a hegemony of heteronormative desires – whiteness, patriarchy, and standard ideals of beauty and lust – that exclude hijras, transgenders, and other queers. I thus focused on two of the most widely used digital porn websites in India: XVideos, which had a variety of categories for hijra; and Pornhub, which had a very limited number, but which nonetheless had them. Under the keyword 'hijra' the latter features six videos, while the keywords 'Indian hijra' yielded a whopping 1209 videos.

This suggests that these digital clips are, like feature films, categorized along national lines where the abstract form of the nation-state crystallizes into a particular form of transgressive sexual fetish corresponding to particular stereotypes. When we compare these numbers to searches in Indian porn sites including the Free Sexy Indians blog, Antarvasana, and Indian Sex Videos, the keyword 'hijra' yields single-digit hits. The discrepancy between semantics is telling, despite theorizing transgender digital porn in relation to national fetishes, as it invokes the familiar allure of the exotic, oriental, fetishized East. The difference in hits when conducting a video search with the same keyword but from a different country or in the Hindi language versus in English also suggests this fetishization.

For example, in contrast to the 339,728 hits on XVideos under 'hijra sex' in the United Kingdom, XVideos in India features 340,109 hits for the same keyword search – a difference of 381 hits. This difference has many implications, ranging from the languages that a diverse constituency of viewers use online to signifying the British Empire's global institutionalization of the English language. As I have just observed, the use of Hindi seems to 'authenticate' the exotic and sexualized subject that merges two genders into a category, the third gender, which does not exist as a legally legible subject for western viewers. That is, the 'hijra' as both a search keyword and a national sexual fetish is a function of localizing pornographic imagery in cyberspace to make it more titillating and 'real'. The orientalization of the sexual fetish seems to verify its supposed authenticity.

In this context, the ongoing bias institutionalized by Section 377 in India feeds the 'perverse' imaginations of western voyeurs who desire queer, brown bodies online. Given the psychological and cultural legacy of Section 377 and the taboo around pornography in India (despite lasciviously suggestive dance numbers in a whole range of Bollywood films), we can make three general observations about the XVideos retrieved by the keyword 'hijra': many of the videos do not feature sex acts, and rather feature hijras clapping in a campy manner or dancing in a manner that parodies the nautch girls in popular Bollywood films like *Mughal-e-Azam* (Asif 1960) and *Pakeezah* (Amrohi 1972); most sex acts are oral and penetrative sex wherein the hijra is submissive and the face of the penetrator is concealed (presumably to mask his identity) – despite his concealed face, his body signifies as male (arms, hairy flat chest, gut, etc.); and in a number of these videos, the recipient of the oral sex and/ or the penetrator is slapping or cursing at his third gender partner.

We might here critically meditate on how XVideos presents these contradictory subjects[7] who are culturally valued as performers yet illicit as sexualized fetishes, notably since most are amateur videos which performers have uploaded themselves. Since the hijra is playing the submissive role, such films echo concerns over domestic violence and 'the rape culture of India' (Wirth 2018) that is rampant throughout some parts of the subcontinent, expressly towards hijras (Narrain 2004; Reddy 2005). In one video thumbnail, the caption reads 'thapad mar ke hijaryse lond chousya', which roughly translates to 'slapped a hijra until she sucked my dick'. In most cases, the penetrator masks his face, suggesting his shame, fear of being identified, and/or need to conceal his identity due to being in a heteronormative family (married with kids in a joint family household, etc.)

With only six hits under the keyword 'hijra' and zero with the keywords 'aravani' and 'kinnara', Pornhub returns many video hits when 'Indian hijra' is used in the keyword search. Yet, on further investigation, the search keywords return all results linked to 'Indian' rather than 'hijra', and include many unrelated videos. As such, Pornhub's search algorithm defaults to what appears a taxonomy based on nationality (Indian) that invokes the broad characteristics of orientalism described by Edward Said (1978) which are encoded in 'classical' and mainstream art, culture, film, and media. Indeed, a survey of the 1209 videos retrieved by the keywords 'Indian hijra' feature popular heterosexual fantasies, namely Indian American women pornstars Angela Devi and Priya Rai – the latter playing roles including a MILF (mother I'd like to fuck), a maid, and a 'Busty Asian Wonder Slut'. In the purview of Pornhub's search algorithm, hijras and straight Indian women are the same, and hijras are pooled into categories including 'mother', 'maid', and 'slut'.

While I do not here want to wrest Rai's and Devi's sexual agency from their profession, I do want to critique the ways in which these videos are taxonomized and made accessible on Pornhub since erotic data are arguably just as important to critique as sexual representation. These sexual representations moreover imbibe what Said calls 'impressive ideological formations that include notions that certain territories and people require and beseech domination, as well as forms of knowledge affiliated with domination' (1994, 9). In concluding my analysis of Pornhub, I want to draw readers' attention to two screenshots that merge agents of law and order into queer fantasy. As is commonly known, many strands of porn feature uniform fetishes and a variety of sexual scenarios in which police, authority, military, and powerful figures catalyze the erotic scenario. One particular short film titled *Bollywood Kinnar ki Leela* [Bollywood Hijra's Song] depicts police coercion and sexual exploitation of hijras, which complicates the sexualized signifiers of pornography. This film gestures, I would propose, towards what Tara Atluri calls 'a sexual citizenship after, beyond, and outside orientalism' (2012, 721) for the extended ways in which it combines police violence with what is deemed to be sexual. In this clip, a sexually frustrated driver is making rounds at night while a passenger and his partner are making out in the backseat. Scenes of a police officer apprehending two hijras on a remote road are cross-cut with a sequence of the frustrated driver encountering a hijra prostitute and hav ing sexual fantasies about her.

Pornhub's presentation of this particular video stands out from the others in relation to Atluri's formulation. To start, none of the thumbnails that appear when one's mouse arrow hovers over the video selection sexually depict hijras. Conversely, most thumbnails depict hijras moving in groups as a community. *Bollywood Kinnar ki Leela* devotes more time to the narrative of police harassment of, violence against, and sexual exploitation of hijras than the sexual fantasy typically expected from a pornographic film with no social message. Here, the police officers who are usually fetishized are hardly depicted as sexually virile subjects. Rather, the officer in charge is a bumbling oaf before the catty and elegant hijras, whose witty answers to his coarse questioning prompts him to detain the elder one and force the younger one behind a remote building. This sequence is cross-cut with another sequence of the driver speaking to a hijra through the half-opened window on the car's passenger side.

As he is urging the sex worker to get into the car, he imagines her performing a solo sex show for him with the medicalized anatomy of both genders. The club music on the soundtrack of this video mixes aspects of Bollywood music with the social commentary of Indian Parallel Cinema[8] and amateur pornography. Here, the hijra as a contradictory figure seems to embody sexual citizenship beyond orientalism that is both liberatory and also dangerous. The subject's ability to seduce the imaginations of all of those involved, including viewers, certainly displaces our erotic imaginations beyond routine colonialist stereotypes that orientalism has propagated in queer representations.[9] These figures seem to oscillate between the space of subjects and agents, at times manacled to sexual acts intended to exact hegemonic order and domination while at the same time inhabiting queer imaginings that disrupt all semblance of police order and masculine desire. These digital sequences disrupt the power that viewers associate with the police and disrupt the libidinal eroticism of more mainstream pornography.

The residual hermeneutical violence of Section 377 towards the ostensibly liberated third gender comes into sharp focus in one sequence in which the officer in charge forces the younger hijra behind the structure. He imagines a heterosexual fantasy in which a strapping soldier is having sex with a young woman in the fields and seems to unzip his pants while the frightened hijra drops to her knees. Here, the obscuring camera angle and the expression on the officer's face suggest that he is expropriating queer sex work from the hijra. But when this fantasy dissolves and viewers are returned to the present moment with the young hijra, the reality reflects the violence of colonialist law that continues to oppress non-heteronormative subjects. He mocks her for dropping to her knees and assuming he wants a blowjob, instead shoving the barrel of his gun into her mouth. After later taking her back to his place, he expresses shock that his friend was 'like that' (presumably 'funny'/queer/third gender) and asks her if she is too. She responds that she has had surgery in Thailand, and the following sequence ends with them fornicating in themissionary position (which was never regarded as 'unnatural' in Section 377). This transgender pornographic narrative is far more complex than a specious foray because it invokes transnational movement, access to surgical procedures, body modification, and police violence. Its immersion of viewers into the social world of hijras is one way of humanizing them while working against the grain of national fetishes for and stereotypes of exotic South Asian sexualities.

I conclude with this brief analysis of *Bollywood Kinnar ki Leela* because I believe that it aptly uncovers social issues facing hijras in the visual realm of digital pornography, the gendered realm of heteronormative erotica, and the legal realm of valid citizenry in contemporary India. In the final section, I propose a heuristic for re-thinking how all three of these realms converge in a manner that offers hijras, and other 'third gender' community members, shelter from colonialist bigotry in contemporary India. In *An Era of Darkness*, for example, Shashi Tharoor writes:

> In India there has always been place for people of different gender identities and sexual orientations ... the British-drafted Indian Penal Code criminalized aspects of human behavior and human reality that in India had not previously been regarded as criminal or requiring legal sanction. (2016, 116–117)

When we carefully examine the persistence of colonialist laws in India and the diverse ways in which they continue to militate sexual behaviour today (Gairola 2002), there should be little wonder why even porn websites reproduce biases against non-white queer subjects.[10] Indeed, perhaps the most magical property of all porn is to make us feel as if our sexual urges are primal, as if they are unfettered and unshaped by the mental manacles that surround us beyond the intimacies of the bedroom and the sexual fantasies that linger there and in the depths of the closet.

From black feminism to transgender castes: intersectionality to intersex/tionality

Tharoor's survey of the Raj in colonial India squarely recognizes the insidious impact of Victorian-era jurisprudence on indigenous genders and sexualities. He writes:

> Section 377 of the Indian Penal Code and the Criminal Tribes Act of 1871 target the transgender community as well as the homosexual community. They violate the Indian ethos and the traditions of perhaps at least 2,000 years of Indian cultural practice, mythology, history, the Puranas, and Indian ways of living. Instead of India's traditional tolerance and 'live and let live', the British saddled the country with a colonial-era interpretation of what was good and right for Indians. (Tharoor 2016, 116–117)

I would like to meditate on Tharoor's crisp observation of the history of British law as it disciplined Indians through normative taxonomies of gender and sexuality (Gairola 2012) along with Atluri's notion of 'a sexual citizenship after, beyond, and outside orientalism' for hijras (2012, 721). For Atluri's call braids together two identities that are often at odds with one another: being a sexual agent and being a legal subject. Being a sexual agent, in the existing frameworks of gender, can be oppressive even beneath the signifier 'queer' – unto the point of violent bullying and chauvinistic murder. In an interview with Sara Ahmed, Judith Butler intimates that:

> Many trans people, or trans advocates, have argued that queer is exclusionary, that it does not include or describe trans experience ... If 'queer' means that we are generally people whose gender and sexuality is 'unfixed' then what room is there in a queer movement for those who understand themselves as requiring – and wanting – a clear category within a binary frame? Or what room is there for people who require a gender designation that is more of less unequivocal in order to function well and to be relieved of certain forms of social ostracism? (Ahmed 2016, 490)

Butler's revision of her largely influential theory of gender as performative is problematic for hijra communities in contemporary India, especially with legal recognition of the 'third gender' or 'transgender'. Aniruddha Dutta and Raina Roy sharply contextualize my concerns here, writing:

> while there are certain ways in which transgender has emerged as a South Asian category of identity and community formation, the same ease of adoption, translation, and negotiation vis-a-vis the transnational circulation of 'transgender' and 'transsexual' categories may not be available to everyone. (2014, 323)

Indeed, the reductive scope that attends the taxonomization of gender and sexuality may ultimately result in, in Gayatri Reddy's reading, 'a disservice to the complexity of their lives and their embeddedness within the social fabric of India' (2010, 4). Through legal codification, the hijra as a citizen in Atluri's sense is slowly being realized, but to what extent that citizenship emerges free from bigotry based on sexuality, class, caste, colour, religion, and/or orientalism, versus (third) gender recognition, is highly dubious.

We are thus left asking: if hijras are born 'men' who are Indian citizens who identify as women of colour, as Butler describes transgenders as requiring or wanting to embody the female gender, how can we learn from the juridical lessons of the past for securing erotic agency? What lenses can we adopt/update/develop to realize the hijra as that legal citizen-subject of the twenty-first century for which Atluri argues? I propose that we reconsider theories of third world feminism[11] along with queer South Asian studies to formulate such a hermeneutical model. To this end, I want to contribute to ongoing dialogues concerned with rigorously interrogating the relationships between transgender identity, caste/class, and skin colour in which some scholars are already engaged (Bey 2017; Ellison et al. 2017; Durban-Albrecht 2017; Warren 2017). To do so, I want to return to one particular entry point: Kimberlé Williams Crenshaw's notion of 'intersectionality'. Crenshaw, a legal scholar and professor, coined the term intersectionality in 1989 to articulate the stakes involved in examining race and gender as constitutive, rather than separate or parallel, categories of legally codified subjects.

In her foundational essay 'Demarginalizing the Intersection of Race and Sex: A Black Feminist Critique of Antidiscrimination Doctrine, Feminist Theory and Antiracist Politics', Crenshaw writes:

> I argue that Black women are sometimes excluded from feminist theory and antiracist policy discourse because both are predicated on a discrete set of experiences that often does not accurately reflect the interaction of race and gender. These problems of exclusion cannot be solved simply by including Black women within an already established analytical structure. Because the intersectional experience is greater than the sum of racism and sexism, any analysis that does not take intersectionality into account cannot sufficiently address the particular manner in which Black women are subordinated. (1989, 140)

Intersectionality's turn to multiple registers of identity, rather than a single register of social transgression, is both useful and necessary, even for those who have critiqued it as a reductive or overdetermined methodology (Puar 2007; Nash 2008; Wiegman 2012). In fleshing out the concept a couple of years later, Crenshaw writes:

> The problem with identity politics is not that it fails to transcend difference, as some critics charge, but rather the opposite – that it frequently conflates or ignores intragroup differences. In the context of violence against women, this elision of difference in identity politics is problematic, fundamentally because the violence that many women experience is often shaped by other dimensions of their identities, such as race and class. (1991, 1242)

To put this another way, identity politics over the last three decades has unwittingly reified essentialist categories of personhood while often turning a blind eye to race and gender. Surely, today it is elementary to repeat that black women are exposed to both race and gender-based bigotry – perhaps so elementary that we have normalized such behaviour in the right-wing, fascistic rituals of Trumpism and Hindutva.

Despite the critiques of intersectionality from the last few decades, I propose that Crenshaw's concept promises a timely intervention in transgender studies by challenging language formations that consign others to limited taxonomies in languages of law. A re-thinking of intersectionality in the current moment in India's sexual politics moreover allows us to critically appraise the judicial power relations involved while simultaneously resisting the exacting notion that various 'isms' intersect only at given points. By doing so, re-thinking intersectionality illuminates the ways in which US jurisprudence systemically obscures overlapping terrains of gender and race oppression that configure the daily existence of black women in the United States (Gairola 2016, 33). While I do not want to suggest that black women in the 1980s are the same as hijras in contemporary India, I think we can learn from legal history at a very important juncture in Indian jurisprudence, especially with the Supreme Court's August 2017 declaration that privacy is a fundamental right of all citizens.

Indeed, the Supreme Court of India's recent ruling juridically gestures towards something that intersectionality would later anticipate. To be sure, some years later Crenshaw and co-authors Sumy Cho and Leslie McCall began 'interrogating the ways that states constitute regulatory regimes of identity, reproduction, and family' (Cho, Crenshaw and McCall 2013, 785). What is not mentioned in this elegant formulation is the 'regulatory regime' of language, and how such regimes are complicated by the identity politics of social inclusion and the after-effects of the production of identity between empires and nations. This elision limits the gamut for interrogating the hegemony of meaning-production and its 'social articulations', to draw on Stuart Hall's (1996, 43) terminology. Intersectionality makes important contributions by black feminism to trans studies by invoking race and gender, and it could be further expanded in the gamut of transgender class and caste studies as it is in myriad other fields of study. Since race is always already at issue due to India's colonial history and the Raj's policing of non-heteronormative genders and sexualities during its time on the subcontinent, a heuristic borrowed and developed from black women's feminism seems a formidable place to look towards.

To this end, I want to linguistically mark the intersectional relationship between race, gender, sexuality, and class as 'intersex/tionality'. This 'x' is not the same, capitalized 'X' that marks the legalized, sexed subject in Pakistani passports. Rather, in replacing the 'c' with an 'x' in 'intersex/tionality', I mean to emphasize the contexts in which sexuality always attends race, gender, and class in intersectional analyses.[12] In this frame, the lowercase 'x' embeds 'intersex' into Crenshaw's original formulation, but at the same time it avoids gender assignment, as in the 'x' in 'Latinx' (Reichard 2015). It is the shared 'x' in the chromosomal genotype and phenotype XX–female and XY–male. As in algebraic equations or the *X-Files*, I also deploy this 'x' to signify the unknown variables of gender and sexuality which cannot be designated with a capital 'X', as such would signify a proper subject who is completely known and bestowed its own agency. Like the untranslatable meaning between languages, or the incommensurable value between words in different languages on either side of the hermeneutical equal sign, the 'x' in 'intersex/uality' represents knowledge of the unknowable.

This 'x' can mark, for some queer subjects, the G-spot as a locus of erotic pleasure in and through social alienation (since the realization of prohibited erotic zones often carries transnational consequences in language). In doing so, it privileges the tenuous hermeneutical and erotic zones between sex, the in-between spaces that are neither/nor. That is to say, 'intersex/uality' gives us a heuristic which posits 'intersex' as a bona-fide destination rather than a transitory gap anchored on either side by gender and sexuality, male and female. An intersex/tional heuristic illuminates the fraught history of queer sexuality through the racialized and gendered experiences of black women as its point of access. As the glyph for multiplication, 'x' also stands for the multiplicity of subjective possibilities even as it reduces and limits them to a single glyph formed by two diagonal lines stretching into infinity beyond their junction. Intersex/tional thinking, in other words, simultaneously addresses the exponential, overdetermined indeterminacy of the queer of colour subject even as it must other it only by claiming to have full and perverse knowledge of it.

I would consequently argue that intersex/tional thinking, developed from Crenshaw's original field of application (legal studies), is especially compelling when deployed to reconsider juridical discourses in the frame of contemporary India and historical power relations between the entire subcontinent and the West. An intersex/tional model for examining these and other junctions of meaning beyond traditional queer studies and legal studies allows us to push forward complex interrogations of how and why power operates through history and law. The socio-political stakes for intersex/tionality are particularly urgent in our current historical moment of perpetual war, profitable incarceration, and a global refugee migrant crisis in the frame of gender and sexuality on a global scale beyond India. Indeed, as Adnan Hossain (2018) has crucially noted, studies of 'the hijra' tend to be Indo-centric. In proposing intersex/tionality as a strategy for securing sexual citizenship beyond orientalism, I would forward that it holds the potential to compel the Indian juridical machine to view language, race, class, caste, sexuality, and nationality as inextricably linked while also providing a multi-pronged strategy of allied conceptualizations rather than a blanket concept intended to act as a pan-hermeneutical fix-all.

I would thus argue that an intersex/tional heuristic is not, and cannot be, the privileged hermeneutic in according hijras agency in law or pornographic representation. If it was, it would simply default back to a hegemonic binary like the primary/'top' and secondary/'bottom' binary position that gender roles attempt to normalize and from which it is escaping. That is, intersex/tionality, like intersectionality, risks transforming into a (neo)liberal mantra that simply reformulates the power axis of dominant and subordinate rather than ultimately displacing the polarizing structure. When we think about intersex/tionality in the digital milieu, the work of Moya Bailey, who also, like Crenshaw, theorizes black women's subjectivity, is instructive here. In critically meditating on the ways in which 'Black [*sic*] trans women negotiate unique threats to life and health as those multiply marginalized by gender, race, sexuality, and the disproportionate amounts of violence their communities face', Bailey (2018, 229) offers another lens that we may transpose to trans communities in India which likewise face caste discrimination.

Bailey examines the hashtag #girlslikeus to advocate what she calls 'digital alchemy as health praxis designed to create better representations for those most marginalized in the Western biomedical industrial complex' (2018, 229) to render digital agency to who have been silenced by the 'medical gaze' (Foucault 1973). While I would again not conflate Black trans women with transgender women in India, I would conclude by reiterating that the latter can learn much from the critical paradigms that the former have struggled to put into place in the interest of dignified recognition and social justice in the digital milieu. Indeed, if we re-orient ourselves to think intersex/tionally about marginalized subjects online, we may come closer to empowering both voices and representations in law and cyberspace. The work of Crenshaw, Bailey, and many other scholars of colour working in these fields contributes to the myriad ways in which new genealogies and heuristics can dramatically augment the fields of knowledge that limit us as human beings in realms of gender, sexuality, and online identities.

As the colonialist legacies of Section 377 of the Indian Penal Code continue to haunt the erotic imaginations of Indians in and beyond the world's biggest democracy (Bose and Bhattacharya 2007) during India's 2019 general elections, my hope is that a turn to intersex/ional thinking will dramatically catalyze indigenous social justice movements in and beyond the digital milieu. I would moreover hope for a large block of Indian voters who are united by caste, gender identity, and skin colour to challenge the exclusionary populism of Modi. Against the terrifying backdrop of lynchings and horrific sexual assaults against women, intersex/tional politics can be a formidable force of social change in the material world that will cast a ripple effect across and beyond contemporary India. For even in the wake of assemblage models that challenge Crenshaw's intersectionality, such movements, even those born from a re-naming and re-thinking of a heuristic that has travelled from the US context to South Asia, traumatically compel us to re-negotiate race, class, gender, and sexuality in the fraught and violent resurrections of the British Empire and its inheritors.

Notes

1. Nalini Iyer writes that 'hijras are often referred to as India's "third sex", and they have become the subjects of numerous scholarly works in recent times. Hijras are born males (sometimes hermaphrodite or intersexed) who perform their sexual identity as female. Many adult hijras have undergone *nirvan* surgery (castration operation) as adults. Hijras wear female clothing such as saris, grow their hair long, pluck facial hair, wear lots of jewelry and makeup, and adopt exaggerated female body language' (2009).
2. 'Digital India' is a Government of India initiative of the Modi administration launched on 1 July 2015 that seeks to deploy technology to the service, and of course surveillance, of Indian citizens. The Digital India programme claims to consist of three core components: the development of secure and stable digital infrastructure; delivery of government services digitally; and digital literacy for all Indian citizens.
3. See also Benedict Anderson, *Imagined Communities* (1998).
4. I am here using the term 'colonial mimicry' to invoke Homi K. Bhabha's claim that 'colonial mimicry is the desire for a reformed, recognizable Other, as a subject of a difference that is almost the same, but not quite. Which is to say, that the discourse of mimicry is constructed around an ambivalence; in order to be effective, mimicry must continually produce its slippage, its excess, its difference' (1984).
5. Mobile digital media are also referred to as 'the Fourth Screen'.
6. Kapur is drawing on the work of the Subaltern Studies Collective, in general, and more specifically referring to the celebrated essay 'Can the Subaltern Speak?' by Gayatri Chakravorty Spivak (1988). We must here note that, for Spivak, the 'subaltern' is not a concrete class location. Rather, it involves a 'social silence' that is based on exclusion from political legibility, social mobility, and/or access to circuits of capital.
7. For more on this contradiction, see Reddy (2005, 263).
8. Here, I refer to the Bengali cinema movement that started in the 1950s which favoured naturalism, realism, symbolism, and serious plot lines over popular song-and-dance films (Bollywood). These films also seemed to be deeply invested in taking the pulse of India's socio-political climate at the time.

9. For more on this, see Boone (2015).
10. For more on the ways in which digital content is mediated by biased algorithms, see Noble (2018).
11. I am using 'third world' here in Chela Sandoval's sense of 'U.S. Third World Feminism', which she defines as 'a location wherein the praxis of U.S. third world feminism links with the aims of white feminism, studies of race, ethnicity, and marginality, and with postmodern theories of culture as they crosscut and join together in new relationships through a shared comprehension of an emerging theory and method of oppositional consciousness' (1991, 17).
12. For more on the limitations of language, see Jameson (1972), Voloshinov (1973) and Bakhtin (1981).

Acknowledgments

This article is in memory of Meena Alexander (1951–2018). The author thanks Anirban Kapil Baishya and Darshana Sreedhar Mini for their saintly patience and meticulous commentary and the anonymous reviewers who gave rigorous feedback. He also thanks Clarissa Smith and Anna Thompson at Routledge. Since coming to Perth, the author has availed the kind support of Paul Arthur, Tully Barnett, Ethan Blue, Tim Flanagan, Rikki Kersten, Timothy Laurie, Simone Lazaroo, Melissa Merchant, Vijay Mishra, Lauren O'Mahony, Grant O'Neill, Michael Prince, Nadia Rhook, Anne Schwenkenbecher, Leonie Stickland, Anne Surma, Arjun Subrahmanyan, Heather Tinsman, Carol and Jim Warren, Robert Wood and the inspiring students at Murdoch University. The author also thanks far-away colleagues who nourished this research: Barbara Bordalejo, Elisabeth Burr, Ana Mari Cauce, Adrian Chitralla, Megan Cytron, Rohit Dasgupta, Radhika Gajjala, Nalini Iyer, Dorothy Kim, Shabnam Rathee, Nishant Shah, Gayatri Chakravorty Spivak, Bonnie Zare, and my Digital Humanities Alliance of India (DHAI) and Global Outlook Digital Humanities (GO::DH) colleagues.

Disclosure statement

No potential conflict of interest was reported by the author.

References

Abraham, Susan. 1999. 'Steal or I'll Call You a Thief: "Criminal" Tribes of India.' *Economic and Political Weekly* 34 (7) (July 3–9): 1751–1753.

Ahmed, Sara. 2016. 'Interview with Judith Butler.' *Sexualities* 19 (4): 482-492.

Al Baset, Zaid. 2012. 'Section 377 and the Myth of Heterosexuality.' *Jindal Global Law Review* 4 (1): 89–109.

Alexander, M. Jacqui. 1996. 'Erotic Autonomy as a Politics of Decolonization: An Anatomy of Feminist and State Practice in the Bahamas Tourist Economy.' In *Feminist Genealogies, Colonial Legacies, Democratic Futures*, edited by M. Jacqui Alexander, and Chandra Talpade Mohanty, 63–100. New York: Routledge.

Amrohi, Kamal, dir. 1972. *Pakeezah*. India.

Anderson, Benedict. 1998. *Imagined Communities: Reflections on the Origin and Spread of Nationalism*. London: Verso.

Asif, K., dir. 1960. *Mughal-e-Azam*. India.

Atluri, Tara. 2012. 'The Prerogative of the Brave: Hijras and Sexual Citizenship After Orientalism.' *Journal of Citizenship Studies* 16 (5-6): 721–736.

Bailey, Moya. 2018. '#Transform(ing) DH Writing and Research: An Autoethnography of Digital Humanities and Feminist Ethics.' In *Disrupting the Digital Humanities*, edited by Dorothy Kim and Jesse Stommel, 227–248. Goleta: Punctum Books.

Bakhtin, M. M. 1981. *The Dialogic Imagination: Four Essays*, edited by Michael Holquist, translated by Caryl Emerson and Michael Holquist. Austin: University of Texas Press.

Bey, Marquis. 2017. 'The Trans*-Ness of Blackness, the Blackness of Trans*-Ness.' *TSQ: Transgender Studies Quarterly* 4 (2): 275–295.

Bhabha, Homi K. 1984. 'Of Mimicry and Man: The Ambivalence of Colonial Discourse.' October 28 (Spring): 125–133.

Boone, Joseph. 2015. *The Homoerotics of Orientalism*. New York: Columbia University Press.

Bose, Brinda and Subhabrata Bhattacharya. 2007. *The Phobic and the Erotic: The Politics of Sexualities in Contemporary India*. Kolkata: Seagull Books.

Butler, Judith. 1997. 'Imitation and Gender Subordination.' In *The Second Wave: A Reader in Feminist Theory*, edited by Linda Nicholson, 300–315. New York: Routledge.

Cain, Rob. 2015. 'India Comes Together to Overturn Internet Porn Ban.' *Forbes*. August 5. Accessed March 4 2019. www.forbes.com/sites/robcain/2015/08/05/india-comes-together-to-overturn-internet-porn-ban/#5a805ea8160a.

Callahan, Kat. 2013. 'Cis Feminists Need to Understand 'Provisional' Male Privilege.' Accessed June 24 2018. https://roygbiv.jezebel.com/[object%20Object.

Callahan, Kat. 2014. 'I Don't Care About MichFest's Trans Exclusion, You Shouldn't Either.' *Jezebel*. August 14. Accessed June 19 2018. http://roygbiv.jezebel.com/i-dont-care-about-michfests-trans-exclusionyou-should-1621468728.

Carter, Mia and Barbara Harlow, eds. 2003. *Archives of Empire: Volume I*. Durham: Duke University Press.

Chakrapani, Venkatesan. 2010. 'Hijras/ Third gender Women in India: HIV, Human Rights, and Social Exclusion.' In *United Nations Development Programme*(UNDP), India. Accessed January 11. http://www.undp.org/content/dam/india/docs/hijras_third gender_in_india_hiv_human_rights_and_social_exclusion.pdf.

Cho, Sumi, Kimberlé Williams Crenshaw and Leslie McCall. 2013. 'Toward a Field of Intersectionality Studies: Theory, Applications, and Praxis.' *Signs* 38 (4) (Summer): 785–810.

Crenshaw, Kimberlé Williams. 1989. 'Demarginalizing the Intersection of Race and Sex: A Black Feminist Critique of Antidiscrimination Doctrine, Feminist Theory and Antiracist Politics.' *The University of Chicago Legal Forum* 140: 139–167.

Crenshaw, Kimberlé Williams. 1991. 'Mapping the Margins: Intersectionality, Identity Politics, and Violence Against Women of Color.' *Stanford Law Review* 43 (6) (July): 1241–1299.

Durban-Albrecht, Erin. 2017. 'Postcolonial Disablement and/ as Transition: Trans* Haitian Narratives of Breaking Open and Stitching Together.' *TSQ: Transgender Studies Quarterly* 4 (2): 195–207.

Dutta, Anniruddha. 2014. 'Contradictory Tendencies: The Supreme Court's NALSA Judgment on Third Gender Recognition and Rights.' *Journal of Indian Law and Society* 5 (Monsoon): 225–236.

Dutta, Aniruddha and Raina Roy. 2014. 'Decolonizing Transgender in India: Some Reflections.' *TSQ: Transgender Studies Quarterly* 1 (3): 320–337.

Ellison, Treva, Kai M. Green, Matt Richardson and C. Riley Snorton. 2017. 'We Got Issues: Towards a Black Trans*/ Studies.' *TSQ: Transgender Studies Quarterly* 4 (2): 162–169.

Foucault, Michel. 1973. *The Birth of the Clinic*. New York: Pantheon Books.

Foucault, Michel. 1976. *The History of Sexuality: Volume One*. New York: Pantheon Books.

Foucault, Michel. 1977. *Discipline and Punish*. New York: Pantheon Books.

Gairola, Rahul K. 2002. 'Burning With Shame: Desire and South Asian Patriarchy, From Gayatri Spivak's "Can the Subaltern Speak?" to Deepa Mehta's *Fire*.' *Comparative Literature: Journal of the American Comparative Literature Association* 54 (5): 307–324.

Gairola, Rahul K. 2012. 'Occupy Education: An Interview with Gayatri Chakravorty Spivak.' *Power & Culture*. September 25. Accessed December 3. https://politicsandculture.org/2012/09/25/occupy-education-an-interview-with-gayatri-chakravorty-spivak/.

Gairola, Rahul K. 2016. *Homelandings: Postcolonial Diasporas and Transatlantic Belonging*. London and New York: Rowman and Littlefield International.

Gairola, Rahul K. 2018. 'From Bombay Dost to Global Host: Mobile Imaginings of Cybergaysians in Contemporary, Queer India.' In *Disrupting the Discourse: New Feminisms in South Asian Film, Literature, and Social Media*, edited by Alka Kurian and Sonora Jha, 85–104. New York: Routledge.

Gupta, Indrani Sen. 2005. *Human Rights of Minorities and Women: Third Gender Human Rights, Volume 2*. New Delhi: Isha Publishers.

Gupta, Charu. 2011. 'Writing Sex and Sexuality: Archives of Colonial North India.' *Journal of Women's History* 23 (4): 12–35.

Hall, Stuart. 1996. 'Race, Articulation, and Societies Structured in Dominance.' In *Black British Cultural Studies: A Reader*, edited by Houston A. Baker Jr., Manthia Diawara and Ruth H. Lindeborg, 16–60. Chicago: University of Chicago Press.

Hinchy, Jessica. 2017. 'Obscenity, Moral Contagion and Masculinity: Hijras in Public Space in Colonial North India.' In *Contestations Over Gender in Asia*, edited by Lyn Parker, Laura Dales and Chie Ikeya, 274–294. London: Routledge.

Hossain, Adnan. 2018. 'De-Indianizing Hijra: Intraregional Effacements and Inequalities in South Asian Queer Space.' *TSQ: Transgender Studies Quarterly* 5 (3): 321–331.

Iyer, Nalini. 2009. 'Hijra/ Hejira.' In *Encyclopedia of Gender and Society*, edited by Jodi O'Brien, 420–422. London: Sage Publications.

Jameson, Frederic. 1972. *The Prison-House of Language: A Critical Account of Structuralism and Russian Formalism*. Princeton: Princeton University Press.

Kapur, Ratna. 2000. 'Law and the Sexual Subaltern: A Comparative Perspective.' *Cleveland State Law Review* 48 (15): 15–23.

Macaulay, Thomas Babington. 1835. 'Minute on Indian Education.' Accessed April 19 2016. http://www.columbia.edu/itc/mealac/pritchett/00generallinks/macaulay/txt_minute_education_1835.html.

Maizland, Lindsay. 2017. 'Pakistan just issued its first passport with a transgender category.' *Vox*. June 23 2017. Accessed August 18 2018. https://www.vox.com/world/2017/6/23/15861620/pakistan-transgender-passport-human-rights.

McGoldrick, Dominic. 2019. 'Challenging the Constitutionality of Restrictions on Same-Sex Sexual Relations: Lessons from India.' Human Rights Law Review online. Accessed February 29. https://doi-org.libproxy.murdoch.edu.au/10.1093/hrlr/ngy041.

Misra, Geetanjali. 2009. 'Decriminalising Homosexuality in India.' *Reproductive Health Matters* 17 (34) (November): 20–28.

Naples, Nancy A. and Barbara Gurr. 2012. 'Genders and Sexualities in Global Context: An Intersectional Assessment of Contemporary Scholarship.' In *The Wiley-Blackwell Companion to Sociology*, edited by George Ritzer, 304–332. Oxford: Wiley-Blackwell.

Narrain, Arvind. 2004. *Queer: Despised Sexuality, Law and Social Change*. Bangalore: Books for Change.

Nash, Jennifer. 2008. 'Re-Thinking Intersectionality.' *Feminist Review* 89: 1–15.

Noble, Safiya Umoja. 2018. *Algorithms of Oppression: How Search Engines Reinforce Racism*. New York: New York University Press.

Patel, Geeta. 2016. *Risky Bodies & Techno Intimacy: Reflections on Sexuality, Media, Science, Finances*. New Delhi: Women Unlimited Press.

Puar, Jasbir. 2007. *Terrorist Assemblages: Homonationalism in Queer Times*. Durham and London: Duke University Press.

Quraishi, Muzammil. 2005. *Muslims and Crime: A Comparative Study*. Aldershot: Ashgate.

Radhakrishna, Meena. 2001. *Dishonoured by History: 'Criminal Tribes' and British Colonial Policy*. Hyderabad: Orient Blackswan.

Reddy, Gayatri. 2005. 'Geographies of Contagion: Hijras, Kothis, and the Politics of Sexual Marginality in Hyderabad.' *Anthropology and Medicine* 12 (3): 255–270.

Reddy, Gayatri. 2010. *With Respect to Sex: Negotiating Hijra Identity in South Asia*. Chicago: University of Chicago Press.

Reichard, Raquel. 2015. 'Why We Say Latinx: Trans and Gender Non-Conforming People Explain.' Accessed July 14 2016. www.latina.com/lifestyle/our-issues/why-we-say-latinx-trans-gender-non-conforming-people-explain.

Rushdie, Salman. 1991. *Imaginary Homelands: Essays and Criticism 1981–1991*. London: Granta/Penguin Books.

Said, Edward. 1978. *Orientalism*. New York: Pantheon Books.

Said, Edward. 1994. *Culture and Imperialism*. New York: Vintage Books.

Sandoval, Chela. 1991. 'U.S. Third World Feminism: The Theory and the Method of Oppositional Consciousness in the Postmodern World.' *Genders* 10: 1–24.

Sarin, Alok. 2014. 'On Criminalisation and Pathology: A Commentary on the Supreme Court Judgment on Section 377.' *Indian Journal of Medical Ethics* 11 (1): 5–7.

Semmalar, Gee Imaan. 2014. 'Unpacking Solidarities of the Oppressed: Notes on Trans Struggles in India.' *WSQ: Women's Studies Quarterly* 42 (3-4) (Fall/ Winter): 286–291.

Sharma, Paloma. 2017. 'These Are the Most Popular Porn Sites in India.' GQ. Accessed December 30. https://www.gqindia.com/content/these-are-the-most-popular-porn-sites-in-india-and-pornhub-isnt-even-among-the-top-3/#xvideos.

Singh, Amritjit, Nalini Iyer and Rahul K. Gairola. 2016. 'Introduction: The Long Partition and Beyond.' In *Revisiting India's Partition: New Essays on Memory, Culture, and Politics*, edited by Amritjit Singh, Nalini Iyer and Rahul K. Gairola, xiii–xxxv. Lanham: Lexington Books.

Spielberg, Steven, dir. 1984. *Indiana Jones and the Temple of Doom*. USA.

Spivak, Gayatri Chakravorty. 1988. 'Can the Subaltern Speak?' In *Marxism and the Interpretation of Culture*, edited by Cary Nelson and Lawrence Grossberg, 271–313. Chicago: University of Illinois Press.

Spivak, Gayatri Chakravorty. 2014. *Readings*. Kolkata: Seagull Books.

Stoler, Laura Ann. 2002. *Carnal Knowledge and Imperial Power: Race and the Intimate in Colonial Rule*. Berkeley: University of California Press.

Tharoor, Shashi. 2016. *An Era of Darkness: The British Empire in India*. New Delhi: Aleph Book Company.

Vanita, Ruth and Saleem Kidwai. 2000. 'Introduction: Modern Indian Materials.' In *Same Sex Love in India*, edited by Ruth Vanita and Saleem Kidwai, 191–217. New York: Palgrave.

Vidya, Living Smile. 2013. '(Trans)gender and caste lived experience – Transphobia as a form of Brahminism: An Interview of Living Smile Vidya.' Accessed June 24 2018. http://sanhati.com/excerpted/6051/.

Voloshinov, Valentin. 1973. *Marxism and the Philosophy of Language*. Cambridge: Harvard University Press.

Warren, Calvin. 2017. 'Calling into Being: Tranifestation, Black Trans, and the Problem of Ontology.' *TSQ: Transgender Studies Quarterly* 4 (2): 266–274.

Weinbaum, Alys Eve. 2004. *Wayward Reproductions: Genealogies of Race and Nation in Transatlantic Modern Thought*. Durham: Duke University Press.

Wiegman, Robin. 2012. *Object Lessons*. Durham and London: Duke University Press.

Wirth, Maria. 2018. 'Why This Focus on 'Rapes in India' by World Media?' Accessed March 2 2019. https://www.organiser.org/Encyc/2018/5/3/Why-This-Focus-on-Rapes-in-India-by-World-Media.html.

Pleasure, bodies and risk: women's viewership of pornography in urban India

Ketaki Chowkhani

ABSTRACT
The intention of this article is to examine women's experiences of consuming pornography and to discuss what these tell us about female sexuality. The article attempts to open up a debate about young women's viewership of pornography in urban India, asking what are the dangers and risks for them in viewing pornography online; what are the possibilities for pleasure; and how are sexual subjectivities and bodies constructed through their consumption?

Introduction

Scholarship on pornography has moved into what Feona Attwood (2002) marks as a 'paradigm shift' in research and a concern with pornography as a cultural product and text, with sexual cultures and practices, and with the reception of pornographic texts. As Alan McKee (2005) notes, there is a need to bring the voice of consumers into debates about porn (in Attwood 2007, 1). There is also a need to recover 'counter-discourses [which] focus on the potential therapeutic, recreational or oppositional usages of pornography' (Smith 2012, 156). Clarissa Smith has stressed the importance of understanding what it means to women to watch porn and what importance it holds in their lives. She argues that analysis of women's viewership of porn 'complicates the claims that porn viewing is entirely tied up in the structural inequalities of heternormative, patriarchal society. It is important to recognize the very individual personal histories that are intertwined with the sense-making and pleasures of pornography' (2012, 160–161).

There has been little research on how women view pornographic film, although women's porn magazines have received more attention in studies of *Playgirl*, *Viva*, *Cleo*, and *For Women* (Smith 2007; Beggan and Allison 2009; Le Masurier 2011; Owens 2014; Beggan, Vencill, and Garos 2013). Beggan and Allison (2009) examine *Viva* and the viewership of male nudes, arguing that the magazine imagines women's sexuality to be homologous to men's. Beggan, Vencill, and Garos (2013) argue that the averted gaze of the male nudes is a way to avoid being too threatening and direct with their female spectators. Le Masurier (2011) examines the nude male centrefold and ordinary women reader's responses to it as a practice of popular feminism and 'one of the early representations of popular feminist desire in mainstream women's magazines' (215). Smith's (2007) work suggests that women do look at and do get turned on by the naked male body.

Unlike this research which looks at how women view pornography that is addressed to them, my project is to examine how women view porn online 'in general' and how this relates to ongoing debates about sexual violence and the construction of female sexuality. This is especially important in the present climate in India when discussions about pornography continue to focus on the 'ill effects' of porn. The recent Public Interest Litigation[1] filed by an Indore-based lawyer in 2013, proposing to ban pornography and make its viewing a non-bailable offence, has been questioned and ridiculed in the media,[2] but it has also opened up the old debate about links between porn and rape. The focus of this debate is on men and rests on an assumption that pornography is viewed only by men. It ignores the fact that women consume pornography too and renders women marginal to the debate. How do women view pornography online? What are the dangers and risks for young urban women viewing online pornography? What are the possibilities of pleasure for women viewing pornography? How are meanings, sexual subjectivities, and bodies constructed through this consumption, and what does this consumption suggest about the location of the erotic? What does women's viewership of pornography online tell us about pornography and sexual violence and the move to ban pornography?

In the Indian context, scholarship on pornography has examined pornography, law and technology (Malhotra 2011), 'footpath' pornography[3] (Srivastava 2004), pornography and modernity (Srivastava 2013b), and the relationship between erotics and the internet (Bhattacharjya and Ganesh 2011). Manjima Bhattacharjya and Maya Ganesh have explored how the internet 'facilitate[s] the exercise of sexual rights and the expression of sexualities, particularly of women living in different socio-political, economic and cultural contexts' (in Kee 2011, 8). They briefly examine viewership of pornography online and how pornography has different meanings for women. On the one hand, pornography is rendered 'naturalized' since many women view it. At the same time, women view porn as something which is produced for men and believe that they might be called a 'bad girl' or get a bad reputation for watching it. Many married women watch porn with their husbands while some question the very definition of what is pornographic (Bhattacharjya and Ganesh 2011). In the absence of sex education, pornography appears to become a means of self-education, but viewing pornography for the first time can be a shocking experience, both for women and men.

Clarissa Smith, Martin Barker, and Feona Attwood's (2011)[4] recent preliminary findings of online viewership of porn indicate that it may be women in the age group 26–35 who are most likely to view pornography. My discussion focuses on in-depth interviews carried out in 2013 with six women between the ages of 25 and 30, located in the metropolitan city of Mumbai in India. Their backgrounds are similar: educated, English speaking, middle class, and urban.[5] They are all in so-called 'respectable professions'. Out of the six, one woman identifies as bisexual while the rest identify as heterosexual. Three women are research students, one is a consultant, one is a media professional, and one is a psychologist. None of them are married and they all live away from their natal homes. Only one identifies as currently being in a heterosexual relationship.

The group of interviewees is purposefully small because the attempt is not to provide a comprehensive analysis of women's viewership of porn, but to open up the debate on how women view porn. A qualitative approach is taken to uncover how women experience viewing pornography and how they negotiate sexually explicit material, drawing on the idea that 'sexually explicit media texts are experienced and understood in a variety of ways and evoke strong and often contradictory reactions, not all of which are represented in public debates about pornography' (Attwood 2005, 65). Smith also notes that:

> female consumers of pornography are constantly dogged by questions of harm, subordination, objectification and authenticity and the need to consider women's well being before their own pleasures in watching or reading pornography – but this may be as much to do with the questions and approaches researchers take. (2012, 167)

While many of the women I interview were concerned about authenticity and the well-being of women on screen, as a researcher I purposefully concentrated more on women's own pleasures in viewing pornography.

The context of porn consumption in India

The consumption of porn by middle-class women in Mumbai is circumscribed by what Phadke (2005) has described as the impossible demand for women to be 'sexually desirable' as well as 'sexually virtuous' in a context where 'urban modernity' appears to both provide new possibilities of self-expression as well as articulating older concerns about 'morality' and 'Indianness' (Srivastava 2013a, 19). The internet is configured as a 'new public space' which raises the tensions of risk and danger. The consumption of porn by women can be seen as a tension and entanglement between pleasure and risk where 'the search for pleasure is shadowed by the spectre of virtue' (2013a, 20).

It is also important to look at what porn is being consumed by women. Some of the women I interviewed refused to say what they watched, or even give the name of any website. Others mentioned that they accessed sites like youporn.com, redtube.com, soft porn on YouTube, Savita Bhabhi (kirtu.com),[6] metacafe.com, and dailymotion.com.[7] Most of the porn that the women accessed was not produced in India or 'Indian porn'. Although some of the respondents did watch 'Indian porn',[8] they did not take much pleasure in watching it; instead they seemed to prefer watching white bodies on screen.[9]

Risks and dangers of accessing pornography

Most of the women I spoke to were aware of the risks of accessing pornography. Nisha[10] reported she was scared that if her parents found out they would judge her. In her late twenties and under pressure to get married, Nisha's concerns about watching pornography were tied to the idea of respectability. She locked her room where she felt safest when alone. She was careful not to make any noise and to masturbate quietly, but all this was difficult because she had a roommate and she had to wait for her to leave. She was also careful to delete her internet history.

Consuming pornography in the public space of internet cafes was also difficult. Nita started watching pornography here because she did not have a personal laptop. Her boyfriend taught her some safety measures, such as deleting internet history, using headphones at all times, and being alert not to 'scandalize' those around her. She got used to the place first: frequenting a café in a shopping complex far from her house. After eight to 10 months, she dared to access pornography, but she still did not browse for pornography too often. Since the café had systems of tracking the sites visited by the users, she was scared she might be discovered:

> ... That kind of public space was a big threat for me being a female. You know it would be a kind of crime or it would be a very unacceptable thing which you are doing. That kind of constant fear was always there, what if I'm caught, what if someone caught me viewing these kinds of things ... I always used to be very careful. I used to keep parallel windows open, I will open that window and hide the porn site if I think someone is coming near ... Because of this I couldn't concentrate properly, because all the time I was wondering: who is coming, who is seeing, what is the time; these kinds of common threats were always there. I was never caught – but I had to cope with all the fears – it was the worst part I guess. And it always kept me under a stupid burden that: am I doing some crime or something or committing a ... .

Having a personal laptop also carried its own risks:

> I never had a personal internet access. So it was always either through my educational institution where I studied, or where I worked. I always used to access my hostel internet. They used to track down your IP address. I remember one incident when I was studying for a particular degree. Once I was trying to access these sites and I was showed the message that these sites are banned, blocked – but somehow I managed to open it. And suddenly I got a message that you are being tracked and your IP address is under surveillance – then I was like shit – I might be expelled from the institution – and what if people would get to know that I was expelled because I was, you know, consuming pornography on my personal laptop from the internet access of the institution! So this kind of fear was there. So at a point I stopped doing that and I took a resolution that now I will never do that, but how long? Two months, four months, five months? I couldn't resist. Then I talked to my friends; they told me that I should visit a proxy server ... Then I started browsing again. But again I was afraid that I am in an institution which is religiously dominated and I'm a girl and of course they won't understand it. ... there were no consequences. But I kept thinking – there could be a letter against me any day ... Because the sites always asked me my age and my institutional log in.

Nita also described the problems of accessing pornography in different spaces, in particular at home, the need to delete her computer browsing history since her family members also use her laptop, 'moral and social pressures', and feeling guilty about watching pornography. For Shila, living in a hostel and using a personal laptop made it possible for her to 'plug in and the world doesn't really know what you are watching'. But since she shared the room with another girl, she only watched when her roommate was not there. Rati also watched pornography on her laptop when she was alone in her room. But once she started living with her boyfriend she was not as comfortable as when she had her own space. She felt uncomfortable that:

> People know that I watch porn. I would prefer if people didn't know. I feel uncomfortable that my boyfriend also knows that I watch porn, because he won't get it. He would say – am I not satisfying you? [Laughter]

For the women, watching pornography was deeply tied to space: to having a room to themselves or time alone in a room. As Smith (2012, 159) notes, the 'setting aside of time is a symptom of our cultural shame around viewing pornography but is also a requisite of engaging properly with the material'. Consuming pornography demands a safe space, and very often that is provided outside the house, in a hostel, an internet café, or a room of one's own in a city away from one's family. They were aware that as women they were transgressing by watching pornography and that if people knew they watch pornography they would attribute this to them being single, unmarried, frustrated, and unsatisfied. They felt a sense of guilt and shame stemming not just from the fact that they might be discovered, but from a deep-seated sense of the 'immorality' of watching pornography. As Nita put it, she felt a kind of moral guilt, and asked herself: 'am I turning into a prostitute or slut?' For Nita the real fears lay in the form of a partner who might not understand, and of friends who might be shocked and change their attitudes towards her. The fears were those of being ostracized and not belonging. At the same time there was also the fear of being seen as too knowing and consequently sexually available. Similarly, Smith (2012, 158) discusses how her interviewees demonstrated 'a constant "self-surveillance" in relation to the arguments about harm'.

Shila voiced guilt in a different manner. She watched pornography on the sly because there was a judgement attached to it. But she recognized that this was not enough to stop her from watching it because her 'need for pleasure from the consumption of it is more' than the guilt. Discussing what kind of pornography she might want to watch, she said that she did not feel that there is really a choice:

> There is so much guilt attached to it. Then to saucily tell [others that] I don't get this variety ... you might as well consume what is available ... There would be many individuals who tell me: this is just a passing fad, till you get married or whatever, till the first good sex of your life ... when you get more of the real thing you'll be cured of that ... It is basically an affliction, a passing fad, a pathology. As a woman it is definitely pathological, you are the nurturing woman. I'm expected to be the nurturing woman, what the hell am I doing thinking about sex as outside of motherhood and stuff like that ... I take what is given to me ... I can't ask a friend: give me the name of another porn site. It is not something you'll have a discussion about in the canteen over samosa and tea. So I guess the choices are limited, but the true explorer will explore and find out online.

Shila's descriptions point to the ways in which pornography upsets normative notions of womanhood and motherhood. When she watched a man being suckled[11] she said that she was not comfortable, because it:

> Rubs my guilt right in my face. And it's a porn site and what is a mother and a grown man doing as a child there? Take the woman as a woman.

Thinking about women's viewership of pornography allows us to think differently about what violence means in relation to pornography and women. Shilpa Phadke (2010, 85) argues that what constitutes 'normal' violence in the context of women's access to public spaces are the 'everyday negotiations: how when, and with whom to commute, when not be out at all, what to wear, where to walk, how to modify one's gaze, and other strategies that women employ in public spaces'. She argues that violence is only visible when women are physically or verbally attacked/harassed, but that women 'have to deal with the possibility of attack and/or harassment every day, even when it does not happen. This effectively circumscribes their access to public space, yet unless women are actually attacked, no violence is seen to have been committed' (2010, 86). Violence can be understood as the negotiations and strategies women employ to stay out of danger. The act of consuming pornography is one of being 'at risk'. I argue that violence lies in the risks and dangers of watching pornography and in the fears of losing respectability. At the same time, the fear of being constructed as sexually available leaves women vulnerable to sexual violence.

Bodies, pleasure and locations of the erotic

One question which I had to repeatedly ask and which often stumped my respondents was: what are the pleasures of watching pornography, what do you enjoy the most, which visuals do you find most erotic? The location of the women's desires lay in the body of the women that they saw on screen. When asked about the images they found most appealing and erotic, most described the body of a woman in pleasure. Nisha enjoyed watching a woman as she reaches an orgasm, when she is moaning in pleasure. She wished she could be the woman on screen. Sima also enjoyed watching a woman at the 'height of her excitement', how she lets a man inside her, which she views as a process of trust. Rati spoke about how the sound of people orgasming is more erotic for her than the visuals. Rati and Nita said that they enjoyed the woman being on top, and taking control. For Rati, 'the focus [should be] on what [the woman] is going through, how she is feeling, how her body is moving, how her body is looking'.

Most of them also spoke of touch, not of penetrative sex, but of the man caressing the woman's body, of two people touching each other and of trust and warm and softness. They spoke of erogenous zones which were clearly non-genital: wrists, the neckline, the nape of the neck, the hip, the back of the knee, knuckles, the funny bone, and so on. There was a clear sense that the location of pleasure and the erotic was not in the genitals or penetrative sex. Except for one of them (who happened to be in a heterosexual relationship), none spoke about penetrative sex or of the vagina as a location of the sensual. Myers (1982, quoted in Smith 2007, 160) describes 'pleasure in the part' of the body such as the neckline or the curve of an arm as a 'celebration of its constituent elements, giving a sense of the scope and complexity of sensual pleasure which breaks with specific genital sexual associations and with the necessity of over-determining phallic substitution in the representation of the female form' (quoted in Smith 2007, 160). My interviewees echoed this; their descriptions of sexual imagery point to a non-heteronormative idea of penetrative sex, and to intimacy in 'an eros of touch, caress and sharing' (Biswas 2011, 432).

Nita described how she would see women's bodies on the screen and started loving her own body, realizing the potential a woman's body had for sexual pleasure and attraction. She realized that she could 'take control' and 'how I should understand myself as a sexual being who could have desires and to express my feelings, while touching someone or while letting someone to touch you'. For Nita, watching pornography became a means of coming to terms with her sexuality and legitimizing her desires but it was not 'natural' and easy for her to look at naked bodies, and it took her time to get used to seeing them, moving from viewing still images of naked bodies to viewing videos of naked bodies.

Shila talked at length about her fetishization of female breasts. Although she acknowledged the multiple sizes and types of breasts represented in pornography, she clearly wanted to watch only the ones she considered normative.[12] For her, pleasure lay in the man caressing a woman's breasts. She maintained that in Indian porn women's breasts were most prominent and that the camera and her gaze desired the women's breasts alone. She constantly talked about breasts, and how the 'action' should be in and around them. She argued that it was important not to have 'fast food consumption' of the woman by directly going to the genitals, but a rather slow consumption of the woman by lingering around the breasts. Rati also desired to view 'normal' sized breasts, feeling that she could not identify with women with large breasts which gave her a sense of not matching up to the normative female body in pornography.

The gaze of the women was also focused on men – not on the genitals, but on the man in relation to the woman. Nisha saw the male body as existing to give pleasure to the woman. She did not speak about the naked male body at all, even though there were hints that some of the porn she watched might have partially naked men in it. She observed that male bodies were never 'served' in the same way as female bodies, because 'the male doesn't have a lot to show, it's only the penis, that's it'. She insisted that the penis did not turn her on. Rather, it was the caring man who touches the woman in a certain way which was attractive. Rati said that she would like to see a male body in its entirety, the 'masculine form' which includes the shoulders, the chest, and so on, and not just his penis and tongue. She insisted that the genitals should be of 'normal' size and not like a 'gun'.

As discussed by others (Smith 2007; Beggan and Allison 2009; Le Masurier 2011; Owens 2014; Beggan, Vencill, and Garos 2013), women's viewership of the naked male body can be read in a number of ways; as resistant reading, as a popular feminist expression, as an act of pleasure, or as merely re-instating patriarchal structures of inequality. My interviews with women also suggest that there is no single reading of the naked male body by women. Women expressed a degree of disinterest coupled with an active desire to reconfigure the ways in which the naked male body is represented. This concurs with Smith's (2007) reading of women's letters to *For Women*, where women show that they actively desire and are turned on by male bodies. Where Owens (2014) and Le Masurier (2011) discuss women readers' desires to see the naked male body in its entirety (including the penis), the women I interviewed went beyond that to actively construct the ways in which they would like to see this naked male body in action: caring, caressing, and being loving towards a woman. Not only did women enjoy and were turned on by naked male bodies, they had ideas about what they want these bodies to do.

The carnivalesque potential of pornography also spoke to my interviewees in various ways. For Nita, the most erotic act involved a 'different surrounding, a different position' and pornography 'develops a kind of thinking which breaks your limitations to have sex with one partner', overcoming moral barriers. Nita described a favourite scene at length where a cleaning boy in a hotel has sex with a woman. She added that every time she checked into a hotel, she was reminded of that scene and humorously 'suspected' the men there of not being entirely innocent. There was no sense of fear of sexual violence here, but a playful suspicion that the scene might repeat itself.

The shifting of the site of sexual activity outside the bedroom to a pool, the sea, in the shower, was also seen as empowering. Nita elaborated:

> In our social context, sex is all about getting into the bed, it is a very conventional understanding that if you are married to a person you will *sleep with him*. I mean the pleasure part is not there, it is always sex ... Why do you limit yourself to four walls and on a bed? [Pornography] breaks the conventional understanding of the confines of a room ... It is a very rebellious and courageous thing – because in our society it is not allowed ... [A different] space gives you the potential imagination to develop your own sexual interest. The beach, the sea, the forest, these are the potential places where you could explore yourself in a sexual manner too.

The location of the erotic outside marriage and the bedroom, among strangers, points to how space and sexual relations can be thought about differently through pornography. For Shila, place and position were deeply tied to a sense of comfort for the woman involved, because she put herself in the woman's place:

> [If] I wouldn't want that done to myself then I wouldn't want the heroine to you know also end up sharing my fate [laughter].

My interviewees also put themselves in the position of the woman on screen and seemed to enjoy watching themselves being pleasured. Their pleasures in watching pornography were intimately tied to their own bodies and to the female bodies on screen, with men's bodies seen in relation to their own bodies. Pleasure also lay outside the genitals, the norms of heterosexual monogamous marriage, and the marital bedroom. Engagements with pornography offered a sense of empowerment and sexual agency.

Women's viewership of pornography is a complex web of negotiations. The dangers and risks that they face while watching pornography include the need to maintain their reputation and respectability. The erotic is located in non-penetrative and non-genital depictions, as well as spaces that are not associated with marriage and monogamous relationships. I have explored the ways in which women actively engage with online pornography not just as a means to pleasure, but simultaneously expressing their guilt and their disappointment with particular texts. Although women voiced their displeasure with the representation of violent sex, they spoke more of the pleasures of watching pornography and of viewing female bodies. Violence was spoken about more in terms of the dangers and risks that they faced while accessing porn; of being discovered, being seen as sexually available, feeling ashamed and guilty, and not conforming to the role of the nurturing woman. They constantly reiterated their need for and pleasure in viewing non-penetrative sex.

The intention of this article was to look at pornography and its consumption and to examine closely women's experiences and narratives of consuming pornography. It aimed to address the glaring absence of women in the whole debate on pornography in India by trying to look at the complexities of women's consumption of pornography. It has attempted to look more closely at what women's pleasurable experiences of consuming porn tell us about female sexuality. I have attempted to look more closely at what women's pleasurable experiences of consuming pornography might tell us about female sexuality, in order to open up debate on women's viewership and to expand the possibilities of examining the complicated questions of gendered consumption of sexually explicit material.

Notes

1. See http://articles.timesofindia.indiatimes.com/2013-04-16/india/38584974_1_internet-laws-exploitation-service-providers (accessed 19 August 2013).
2. Nisha Susan is one of the few writers in the mainstream media to talk about women's viewership of porn; see http://www.tehelka.com/forget-the-lokpal-who-will-be-your-porn-pal/ (accessed 19 August 2013). Also see Bhattacharjya: http://thehoot.org/web/Noeasyanswersonporn/6772-1-1-7-true.html (accessed 19 August 2013).
3. Sanjay Srivastava reads 'footpath' pornography as the vast body of Hindi pornography available on the streets, or literally footpaths, of New Delhi. This genre of pornography includes 'advice' manuals of the kind one finds in 'sex clinics'. 'The booklets generally have poor production values, and it is common practice to haggle over the "official" price printed on the cover, making them quite cheap to acquire; being an intrinsic part of the accoutrements of urban footpaths, customers can, literally, obtain these on the run, or opt for leisurely perusal while killing time waiting, say, for the next bus. Cover photographs often portray either European women, in

various poses of desire/seduction or "availability" ... Both the authors and readers of these booklets would appear to be primarily male ... They are usually published by small scale, city-based presses ... and sometimes also by the publishers of provincial newspapers' (Srivastava 2004, 357).

4. See http://pornresearch.org/ (accessed 30 May 2013).
5. Women from a different location (e.g. lower classes, lower castes, or rural areas) may have similar as well as different experiences of watching pornography, something which is not addressed here. The recruitment of the six women interviewed was achieved through snowballing and random sampling.
6. Savita Bhabhi is an Indian pornographic cartoon character who is a 'promiscuous' housewife and engages in sexual encounters with a number of men when her husband is away. The comics were freely available on savitabhabhi.com before they were banned by the Indian Government. Subsequently they are available on kirtu.com. See Srivastava (2013b) for a detailed discussion of Savita Bhabhi, pornography, and modernity.
7. Metacafe.com and dailymotion.com are video-sharing websites similar to YouTube.
8. None of the interviewees spoke about specific sites of 'Indian porn'. Shila discussed the 'Indian regional variety', which she thought to be 'inferior porn' because it was recorded with a shaky camera, was dark, and was not visually enticing. Nita spoke about how she rarely visited or had any interest in any 'Indian porn' site. Once she did chance upon 'Indian porn', but she found it too 'lustful' and lacking 'grace'. Sima spoke about 'South Indian porn' being 'complete nonsense' and preferring white porn. Mala said: 'I have never liked "Indian porn" films. Call me a racist but I cannot see two Asian people kissing or making love. I squirm at it. I can see two people kissing in Hollywood films. I can see two white people making love in a porn film but when it comes to Indians, I flinch.'
9. Most preferred to watch white men and women on screen. Shila mentions that she would prefer watching 'Pierce Brosnan fucking anybody – but it can't be Halle Berry'.
10. The names of the respondents have been changed to protect their identity.
11. Shila's narratives point to a difference between suckling the breast and sucking the breast. The latter is acceptable and erotic, the former lasts longer and is associated with a baby suckling at the mother's breast.
12. Shila defines the 'normative' breast size to be between 26 and 36 inches (bra size), all the while acknowledging the ambiguity of this definition.

Acknowledgements

The author would like to thank the anonymous reviewers and the editors Clarissa Smith and Feona Attwood for their invaluable comments on various drafts.

References

Attwood, Feona. 2002. 'Reading Porn: The Paradigm Shift in Pornography Research.' *Sexualities* 5 (1): 91–105. doi:10.1177/1363460702005001005.

Attwood, Feona. 2005. 'What do People do with Porn? Qualitative Research into the Consumption, Use, and Experience of Pornography and Other Sexually Explicit Media.' *Sexuality and Culture* 9 (2): 65–86.

Attwood, Feona. 2007. '"Other" or one of "Us"?: The Porn User in Public and Academic Discourse.' *Participations: Journal of Audience and Reception Studies* 4 (1). http://www.participations.org/Volume%204/Issue%201/4_01_attwood.htm (accessed 30 June 2015).

Beggan, James, and Scott Allison. 2009. 'Viva Viva? Women's Meanings Associated with Male Nudity in a 1970s "For Women" Magazine.' *The Journal of Sex Research* 46 (5): 446–459. doi:10.1080/00224490902829608.

Beggan, James, Jennifer Vencill, and Sheila Garos. 2013. 'Vulnerable and Aloof Versus Naughty and Nice: Contrasting the Presentation of Male and Female Nude Models in Viva and Playboy.' *The Journal of Sex Research* 51 (3): 265–279. doi:10.1080/00224499.2013.776659.

Bhattacharjya, Manjima, and Maya Ganesh. 2011. 'Negotiating Intimacy and Harm: Female Internet Users in Mumbai.' In *Erotics: Sex, Rights and the Internet: An Exploratory Research Study*, edited by Jac S.M. Kee, 66–108. Association for Progressive Communications. http://www.apc.org/en/system/files/EROTICS.pdf (accessed 26 May 2013).

Biswas, Ranjita. 2011. 'Of Love, Marriage and Kinship: Queering the Family.' In *Intimate Others: Marriage and Sexualities in India*, edited by Samita Sen, Ranjita Biswas, and Nandita Dhawan, 414–435. Kolkata: Stree.

Kee, Jac S.M. 2011. 'Emerging Threads and Common Gaps: A Synthesis.' In *Erotics: Sex, Rights and the Internet: An Exploratory Research Study*, edited by Jac S.M. Kee, 6–18. Johannesburg: Association for Progressive Communications.

Le Masurier, Megan. 2011. 'Reading the Flesh.' *Feminist Media Studies* 11 (2): 215–229. doi:10.1080/14680777.2010.521628.

Malhotra, Namita. 2011. *Porn, Law, Video and Technology*. Bangalore: Centre for Internet and Society. http://cis-india.org/raw/histories-of-the-internet/porn-law-video (accessed 17 May 2013).

McKee, Alan. 2005. 'The Need to Bring the Voices of Pornography Consumers into Public Debates about the Genre and its Effects.' *Australian Journal of Communication* 32 (2): 71–94.

Owens, Andrew. 2014. 'Chicks, Dicks and Contradictions.' *Feminist Media Studies* 14 (4): 547–561. doi:10.1080/14680777.2013.824908.

Phadke, Shilpa. 2005. 'Some Notes towards Understanding the Construction of Middle-class Urban Women's Sexuality in India'. In *Sexuality, Gender and Rights: Exploring Theory and Practice in South and Southeast Asia*, edited by Misra, Geetanjali and Radhika Chandiramani, 67–81. New Delhi: Sage Publications.

Phadke, Shilpa. 2010. 'If Women could Risk Pleasure: Reinterpreting Violence in Public Space'. In *Nine Degrees of Justice: New Perspectives on Violence Against Women in India*, edited by Bishakha Datta, 83–113. New Delhi: Zubaan.

Smith, Clarissa. 2007. *One for the Girls! The Pleasures and Practices of Reading Women's Porn*. Bristol: Intellect Books.

Smith, Clarissa, Martin Barker and Feona Attwood. 2011. *pornresearch.org: Preliminary Findings*. Accessed at www.pornresearch.org on 30-05-2013

Smith, Clarissa. 2012. '"I Guess they Got Past their Fear of Porn": Women Viewing Porn Films.' In *Peep Shows*, edited by Xavier Mendik, 155–167. London: Wallflower Press.

Srivastava, Sanjay, ed. 2004. *Sexual Sites, Seminal Attitudes: Sexualities, Masculinities and Culture in South Asia*. New Delhi: Sage Publications.

Srivastava, Sanjay. 2013a. 'Introduction.' In *Sexuality Studies*, edited by Sanjay Srivastava, 1–23. New Delhi: Oxford University Press.

Srivastava, Sanjay. 2013b. 'Street, Footpath, Gated Community: On the Cultures of Indian Pornography.' In *Sexuality Studies*, edited by Sanjay Srivastava, 228–254. New Delhi: Oxford University Press.

When celluloid pornography went digital: class and race in the Bangladeshi cut-piece online

Lotte Hoek

ABSTRACT

This article investigates the fate of celluloid pornography after the end of film. With the demise of celluloid filmmaking in Bangladesh and the rapid transitioning of film projection to digital forms, bits and pieces of stray sexually explicit celluloid have migrated to digital formats. In this article, I map the movement of so-called 'cut-pieces', locally produced strips of illegal celluloid pornography, onto online forums patronized by Bengali speakers. Exploring the reception of this sexually explicit material in its new digital environment, I ask the following questions: how are the traces of 'locality' that inflected the celluloid production of cut-pieces received within digital spaces of consumption; what happens to markers of class and race when celluloid forms of pornography move onto digital platforms; and what are the cultural and technological limits to the internationalization of the aesthetic of mainstream pornography?

They are back

The mid-2000s were a high-water point for the production and circulation of sexually explicit celluloid clips known as 'cut-pieces' in the Bangladesh film industry (see Hoek 2014). A lively production of low-investment Bangladeshi action films provided the vehicle for the making and circulating of cut-pieces. Produced as part of action films but not censored for public exhibition, these short celluloid sequences were illegally produced by Bangladeshi film crews in Bangladesh, featuring Bangladeshi actors. The cut-pieces were illegally screened in the many single-screen cinema halls of Bangladesh. The arrival in 2007 of a political crisis, during which martial law was instated and a 'caretaker' government installed, pushed the phenomenon out of its existence in shadowy spaces of illegality and only semi-licit exhibition. With the excessively public arrests of producers and cinema hall owners, the paramilitary forces displayed new modes of sovereignty, including a 'cleaning up' of public and civil space (see Chowdhury 2014). Hundreds of businessmen and politicians were jailed, their bank accounts frozen. Simultaneously, the caretakers set out to beautify the city. As they jailed bankers and lawyers, they reclaimed city land on which high-rise buildings had been built fraudulently. They turned the land into lakes and ponds, with pleasant walkways and flowering bushes.

The entire city became a project of cantonmentization: to mirror the orderly and well-maintained army cantonment, with its lush greenery, that sits in the middle of the city of Dhaka. Beauty was forcefully imposed, a modern ordered polity envisioned, in which any form of spillage, any excesses of dirt and grime, had to be removed. Thus, the caretakers cleaned up the 'obscene' film industry, raided brothels and tried to stamp out 'radical' Muslim groups. Any excessive affect had to be curtailed.

On 12 January 2009, the tabloid paper *Manobjomin* announced '*Ora abar asche*' ['they have returned']. Who was the paper speaking of? The return of parliamentary democracy, restored on 29 December 2008? Were they writing about the return of the then opposition party to political dominance in the wake of those elections? The apparent restoration of secularism? No, the tabloid spoke of only one transition that accompanied the democratic regime change: '*Ora abar asche*' – the pornographers are back. The paper warned: 'together with the coming of the new government, producers, directors and artists ... who make and display obscene films are preparing to come back' (*Manobjomin* 2009, 2).

In the eerily quiet lanes of the national film studio, the sentiment was one of relief. 'Finally a political government', sighed the actresses who had waited idly for work for two years, 'shooting will start again'. The cameramen, the editors, the light men, everyone agreed that, now that there was once again a so-called 'political government', filmmaking could resume once more. And from their self-imposed exile, the makers of sexually explicit cinema returned. But as they reconvened, they found an entirely changed media landscape. While cinema halls had shut following the clampdown on popular cinema during the caretaker government, simultaneously, the participatory internet had blossomed in Bangladesh (Hussain and Mostafa 2016). Cut-pieces, the bread and butter of the Bangladeshi celluloid pornographers, had made a transition during the caretaker years, out of the cinema halls and onto the internet. Not long after, the celluloid facilities in the national film studios were shut down, taking with them the vestiges of celluloid production and circulation that had carried the cut-pieces into the rural hinterlands. Alongside these processes, the existing cut-pieces had become further detached from their parent films, decontextualized as 'microporn' (Brennan 2018) and reformed into digitally circulating goods, collected by enthusiasts, and now finding new audiences as part of a 'pirate archive' (Tanvir 2013). The production of new celluloid cut-pieces had been foreclosed in Bangladesh but the existing clips had found new digital lives.

This article maps the transition of the Bangladeshi cut-piece from their celluloid cinema hall exhibition to digital online circulation. The question I ask is what happens when this very distinctive sexually explicit material changes over to new technological platforms. I will show that the cut-pieces' distinct aesthetic, and the particular cultural and social formations in which they originated, were re-valued as they made the transition from celluloid to digital formats. As Brennan noted recently, there is a distinct 'impact of certain digital conditions on pornography' (2018, 52); however, I will show that this impact is not generic but can be decisively shaped by the *regional* specificities of the pornographic imagery under discussion. Exploring the life of this sexually explicit material in its new digital environment, I will focus my discussion around three broad themes: media specificity (what happens when pornographic fragments move between different media?); race (how might we rethink the question of race in online pornography that is not thematized for its colour and not staged for the white gaze?); and locality (how are the traces of 'locality' that inflected the celluloid production of cut-pieces received within digital spaces of consumption and how does this highlight the question of the region rather than that of the national?). In particular, I will argue that the context of exhibition and reception can determine whether particular on-screen bodies are understood as primarily marked by race or class, rather than being unambiguously anchored within the representational space of the screen. This argument is informed by anthropological ways of thinking about imagery: first, by anthropology's doubts about the capacity of the image to self-evidently and unambiguously make statements about race (Poole 2005); and, second, by (media) anthropologists' methodological tendency towards studying the social contexts of production and consumption to understand the nature of a media artefact (for example, Ginsburg, Abu-Lughod and Larkin 2002). Finally, my questions about the movement of celluloid cut-pieces onto the internet also urge a reflection on how we might document a specific historical moment in the ephemeral transitioning of particular modalities of pornography across different media platforms. The form of this article underscores this effort at documentation. I aim to contribute to a particular media archaeology in the study of South Asian cinema, in which cut-pieces and similar celluloid pornographic artefacts persist and 'remain viable beyond their historical moment' (Mahadevan 2015, 5). The article follows the cut-pieces across three different media platforms: celluloid reels, video CDs (VCDs) and online chatrooms. The ways in which the cut-pieces signify in each of these sites is markedly different, shedding light on the ways in which the material specificities of different media impact the ways in which pornography can come to excite. The sections on celluloid and VCD forms of the cut-piece are descriptive and provide the backdrop to the more ethnographically rendered account of their appearance online that follows.

Celluloid pornography in Bangladesh at the start of the twenty-first century

The cut-piece is a highly particular form of celluloid pornography. Its aesthetic and material forms are distinct and resulted from the cut-pieces' particular modes of production, circulation and exhibition in the early twenty-first century in Bangladesh. I have described all these at length elsewhere (Hoek 2010, 2014) but this bears repetition in the context of understanding the transition of this sexually explicit material to new media platforms and modes of circulation.

Cut-pieces are illegal strips of celluloid pornography that were produced as part of action films made in Bangladesh through the Film Development Corporation (FDC) from the 1990s through the 2000s. They were made as integral parts of popular action films, which had dominated the cinema screens in Bangladesh from the 1980s. The reasons for the shift to action cinema were manifold and interrelated. These included changes in the entertainment taxes raised by the government, the arrival of video and television, the abandonment of the cinema hall by female audiences, the decreasing desirability for middle-class families of leisure activities in public spaces, and the shift of young and avant-garde filmmakers to new formats, including 16-mm and later digital video. Along with the sorts of films screened, the demographic inside cinema halls changed, most prominently the withdrawal of women from the theatres. The emphasis on action cinema from the 1980s onwards (see Awwal 2018) had generated public controversy because of the ways in which these films came to be understood as 'vulgar' in the course of the 1990s. Partly, this relates to the unabashed lower-middle-class values expressed in the films and the working-class audiences that came to be associated with them, but it was also due to the prevalence of sexually suggestive and explicit cut-pieces in these films.

Cut-pieces were produced as part of action films but have always circulated with some independence from the texts of which they were part. The name derives from the practice of cutting such sequences out of the films before they were submitted to the Censor Board. Even their production, however, occurred in conditions that can best be described as a form of public secrecy (Taussig 1999). Once the film of which the cut-pieces were part was censored, the cut-pieces could be re-inserted – but weren't necessarily so. If they were reinserted, this was done on the basis of financial and social expediency by producers, distributors, hall proprietors and projectionists. The cut-piece can be understood as a hardcore 'number' (Williams 1989) that could be detached from its diegetic embedding within a particular film. Its potential for independent circulation, however, was restricted by its celluloid nature, which placed limits on its exhibition and kept it confined within the domains of theatrical film exhibition.

Despite the possibility for material disembedding, the aesthetic form of the cut-piece betrayed its origins within popular Bangladeshi action cinema. The production values of that cinema were equivalent to those of the cut-pieces. The same crew, lights, camera, laboratory facilities, editors and projectors ensured an aesthetic coherence between the main body of the feature film and its cut-pieces, even when screened independently. Celluloid pornographic clips from popular Bangladeshi feature films are therefore immediately recognizable. Their technological quality, soundscape, colour schemes, *mise en scène*, costumes, make-up and acting styles all have great specificity. The nature of the bodies on display, too, are highly distinctive, emphasizing voluptuous men and women, to the hilarity and disdain of elite commentators who appeared equally appalled and piqued by this bodily aesthetic. The aesthetic of the cut-piece emerged from the industrial context in which the films that housed the cut-pieces were produced and the imagination of the audience that animated these industrial production processes. I shall describe these in turn.

The technologies of film production at the FDC determined to a large extent the aesthetic of action cut-pieces (see Kirk 2016 for a Pakistani comparative). As the main production studio in the country, part of the Ministry of Information, the FDC rented its facilities to producers. These facilities were manned by technicians who were government employees. They deployed their craft in a highly standardized manner. The limited budgets of popular action film producers meant that the resulting films were extraordinarily formulaic. An FDC action film made in the 2000s could be recognized by such technical standards as their peculiar colour quality resulting from lighting techniques within the FDC, as well as the mix of film stock used, the limited use of colour-correcting and the long-term reuse of laboratory chemicals. Similarly, editing practices limited to jump-cuts and to sound design that heavily reused a few stock sounds produced highly specific and standardized clips. The cut-pieces betrayed their FDC origins in these aesthetic attributes, as well as being marked physically from their frequent reuse, resulting in scratched celluloid.

In terms of the diegesis, cut-pieces were also limited in their forms and highly specific in their choreography (for a more detailed discussion of this, see Hoek 2010, 2014). I name these cut-pieces pornography as they hold up to Linda Williams' use of the word 'pornography' 'to signal the focus on explicitness and "maximum visibility" of sex acts in contradistinction to obfuscation of soft core' (2014, 33). Such sexually explicit imagery contained within short sequences of detachable celluloid would mostly appear as part of a song and dance sequence or as part of a rape scene. In either, the emphasis was on the exposed female body, focusing particularly on breasts and buttocks. The sexual action was mostly explicit sex acts but could also feature simulation and involved the licking, kissing, squeezing and penetrating of exposed and fragmented female body parts, specifically the legs, breasts, nipples, buttocks and vagina of the female actress. This was generally performed by (partially) dressed male actors but sometimes by other female actresses. In cut-pieces, the camera rarely explored the male body, although in some long-shots of a couple in simulated sex, the naked male buttocks might be the centre of the image. The characters in the scenes were largely secondary to the main narrative of the film and they were either played by minor actors appearing in the rest of the action film in a subplot or by actors specifically hired for the cut-piece sequence and appearing only there. The encounters portrayed were almost always between men and women. Violent rape scenes added shots of the pinning down of female characters and their struggle against their rapist, often using the intercutting of shots of struggling exposed legs and the naked breasts of the actress. In both violent and non-violent scenes of sexual encounter, the penis remained largely out of view while the camera's gaze and the actor's activities focused solely on the female body. This is where the sight of sexual pleasure was presented, often through the facial expressions of the female actress. The soundtrack either contained Bengali songs made for the cinema or international house music and instrumental renditions of classic pop songs. Diegetic sound was dubbed in sighs and screams.

The inscribed spectators of the popular celluloid action cinema of the early twenty-first century in Bangladesh were working-class and lower-middle-class Bangladeshi men, mainly located in the rural areas and small towns of Bangladesh. Directors and producers as well as journalists were unanimous in their assessment of the audience for action cinema and its cut-pieces. They imagined a large market of poor, generally young, working-class and rural men, who would attend the cinema halls to see pornography that they would be unable to access elsewhere. Ethnographic fieldwork in the cinema halls in Bangladesh showed that this assessment was not entirely incorrect. In the mid-2000s, when I did my fieldwork, the cinema halls, and action movies in general, were frequented almost exclusively by working-class and lower-middle-class men, as well as schoolboys from middle-class families in small towns. Films that were known to contain cut-pieces were hugely popular and would draw a crowd that spanned class positions and ages. Producers, directors and scriptwriters self-consciously aimed their work at what they imagined to be an undifferentiated working-class audience located in the countryside. This is important because it meant that the sexually explicit imagery they produced was not made with any consideration of a non-Bangladeshi audience in mind. In effect, this pornography was not staged as ethnically or racially 'other' from its target audience. Race was not thematized in this material. Instead, class was a really important marker in these clips. Urban college girls wearing embroidered shalwar kameezes, doubly underscoring their middle-class status, were raped in these films. Similarly, girls who willingly engaged in sexual relations in such stories were inevitably portrayed as extraordinarily wealthy, residing in marble palaces in Dhaka. The heroes wore jeans and rode motorcycles or cars. Wealth eroticizes and encourages transgression. On the other hand, sexual violence was often perpetrated by those who drink alcohol, 'terrorists' or religious others. They are the constitutive outside of the narrative that is set within an ex-nominated and hegemonically Muslim social world. Alcoholics, gangsters, capitalists and Hindus perpetrated crimes against the proper moral order of the diegetic universe. Whilst race remained ex-nominated in these clips, it was class, and to a lesser extent religion, that was highlighted.

As a form of professionally produced, theatrically screened pornography, the Bangladeshi celluloid cut-piece was highly distinctive aesthetically and thematically due to the production values of a nationally organized celluloid cinema industry that catered to particular audiences as well as the concern with community and class that shaped its narratives. When this pornographic material traversed the digital divide and appeared on new media platforms, however, these pornographic 'numbers' came to take on completely different valences.

South Asian pornography on VCDs

When studying the circulation and exhibition of celluloid cut-pieces in cinema halls in Bangladesh in 2005, I followed the trail of the producers' assistants who travelled to remote cinema halls with film reels. Their job was to ensure the equitable division of profits, the proper exhibition of the reels, the avoidance of law-enforcers and journalists, as well as the surveillance of the theatre space to apprehend would-be pirates. Nonetheless, pirates did slip through. Entrepreneurs would set up video cameras in the cinema halls and film the screen to produce digital video versions of the films on display. Filming in cinema halls generated shareable digital forms of the cut-pieces. With editing software and the increased prevalence of cheap Chinese VCD players, and the arrival of locally produced, and therefore cheap, blank VCDs, these pirates started to produce cut-piece VCDs. Available in the markets of large cities and small towns alike, the VCD was for a while a massively available media carrier that was relatively inexpensive. Cut-piece VCDs explicitly recognized the pornographic cut-piece as a 'number' and were laid out as a music album, with the individual pieces listed as separate items on a menu. The albums would be titled *Gorom Mosla* ('hot spice') or named after a particular actress who might, or might not, appear on the VCD.

The reduction of the cut-piece to an independent number, listed alongside other numbers and now entirely divorced from the cinematic apparatus in which it originated, allowed the cut-piece to be positioned as equivalent to other, similar, bits of pornography. While on one end of the spectrum a VCD might gather a series of cut-pieces alongside songs from a particular Bangladeshi actress, on the other, the Bangladeshi cut-pieces might now be listed alongside similar but different clips from other parts of South Asia. In particular, Pakistani *mujra*, scenes from Pashto cinema, South Indian soft-porn clips and music videos from across South Asia would appear listed with the Bangladeshi cut-pieces on the VCDs. Less often, short clips of western pornography would appear on the VCDs. Now, the cut-piece imagery was positioned alongside, and equivalent to, other bits of softcore and hardcore pornography from the region and beyond. Decontextualized, the cut-pieces could appear as equivalent to other 'bits' and circulate in entirely new ways, via the marketplace and to be screened in private.

Despite such equivalences, and the erasure of the theatrical context of exhibition, the aesthetic form and language of the cut-pieces continued to make them immediately recognizable when encountered alongside other material. They stand out from western produced pornography and from the sexually explicit or suggestive material made in Pakistan, Sri Lanka and South India due to the contingencies of the context in which the cut-pieces were produced. However, to place the conventions of celluloid pornography in Bangladesh within a strict national framework limits the way we can understand this material as South Asian. While its aesthetic differences from western pornography were very clear, and perhaps explain the low levels of inclusion of western porn on these sorts of VCDs, the pornographic bits from other parts of South Asia shared some formal characteristics while differing in others. I would suggest that similarities in narrative context, bodily form, *mise en scène* or costume are due to the type of cinema that is the vehicle for cut-pieces. These aesthetic traits were shared by Bangladeshi popular cinema with other low-investment modes of film production in the region, for example Pakistan's Pashto cinema (Hulsing 2004; Khan and Ahmad 2010; Nabi 2017) and North India Bhojpuri cinema (Hardy 2010; Kumar 2016). These all drew on shared aesthetic repertoires and production conditions of what can be broadly termed the B-circuit in South Asian cinema (Srinivas 2003; Vasudevan et al. 2016), films destined for the 'segment of distribution and exhibition sectors that is characterized by low levels of investment' (Srinivas 2003, 49). In that segment, across the region, aesthetic similarities relating to editing choices, lighting practices, sound design, *mise en scène* and narrative structures of B-circuit action cinema can be discerned. The Bangladeshi B-circuit action film was heavily reliant on strong star-texts in action-heavy melodramatic narratives with stock characters and locations, taking inspiration from high-end national and international films to produce locally resonant action films (see also Hoek 2013). Visual similarities within this low-investment segment across South Asia suggest that there are shared conditions under which remarkably similar aesthetic conventions have arisen. While comparative research across South Asia is rare, even a cursory glance across Pashto and Dhaka action cinema from the 2000s reveals a remarkably similar field of cinema production and consumption. In part, these overlaps are due to the ways in which action cinema as a global form has localized itself in particular ways (Morris 2004) and, in part, this is a story of South Asian B-circuit action cinema in the late twentieth and early twenty-first century.

The transition of Bangladeshi cut-pieces from celluloid to VCD allows the similarities among South Asian sexual imagery that originates in the lower levels of the region's film industries to come into focus. It highlights the nature of what might be considered a regional cinema (see Srinivas 2015). This is a pornographic region, which is associated with particularities of narrative, aesthetic and, significantly, particular types of bodies. Studying cinematic pornography in South Asia is a way to study cinema there without letting 'political geographical boundaries generate and limit research problems, creating hermetically sealed cultures and populations' (Srinivas 2015, vii; Vasudevan 2010). Instead, as Hardy (2015) has argued for Bhojpuri cinema, it is the cinematic discourse itself that produces a cohesive regional field of pornography, crosses geographic as well as social boundaries and is delimited by its aesthetic particularities; in this case, the contingencies of the erotic pleasures located in the particular bodies, costumes, sex acts and *mise en scène* that are presented in clips of South Asian cinematic pornography. It is the transition of the cut-piece onto the VCD, enumerated in viewing lists that explicitly equate them with their regional counterparts and allow their reproduction in a single medium and distributed locally, that makes the region tangibly present. From the VCD, a leap onto the internet was short and inevitable. The transition of the cut-pieces into online environments allowed this regional element to come even more clearly into focus and to fundamentally shift the ways in which the pornographic content of the cut-pieces could be received. It is to this that I now turn, narrating the online encounter with cut-pieces in an ethnographic manner.

Cut-pieces in chatrooms

From the circulation of the cut-pieces on VCD, it was a short step onto the chatrooms of the early participatory internet. There, while the film industry itself was in lock-down during the caretaker regime, Bengali-language porn chatrooms circulated cut-pieces in their digital forms. Given the newly developing digital infrastructures, the chatrooms in the 2000s were full of patient consumers, spending long hours waiting for the download of digital videos that promised to contain Bangladeshi cut-pieces. The online chats resounded with expressions of impatience and the delayed gratifications that are native to pornography's narrative mode but were here exacerbated by very slow download speeds and frequent power cuts. In this section, I am inspired by the methodologies of digital ethnography (Horst and Miller 2012; Pink et al. 2016). This subfield is interested in 'how the digital has become part of the material, sensory and social worlds we inhabit' (Pink et al. 2016, 7) and adapts ethnographic methods and anthropological theory to study such entanglements. The discussion that follows shows how online pornography and its reception is socially and culturally embedded.

Joubon Jala and Porn Adda were two vBulletin Forums in which Bengali speakers exchanged pornographic imagery and texts in the 2000s, both are now defunct. An analysis of the conversations around cut-pieces in these forums illustrates what happened when these very particular cinematic forms of pornography arrived online and reached new audiences in new contexts, finding themselves suddenly juxtaposed with very different pornographic material. Both websites were explicitly pornographic and asked their members to be older than 21 years old. The homepage for Joubon Jala introduced the site as 'an adult community for Bangla speakers from all over the world'. Both sites set out a series of guidelines and rules for user behaviour that were continuously negotiated in practice, often through switching between languages and implicit rules of engagement. The Porn Adda forum rules stated, perhaps duplicitously, 'no obscene or controversial subject matter of any kind (this includes political commentary)'. Similarly, while calling for moderation in article 3.16 by stating 'harassment or bashing based on sexual orientation, gender, race, colour, religious views, or simply because their opinions differ from your own are not allowed', article 3.13 stated that 'no kinds of religious or political topics are allowed. No kinds of pre-teen or child porn topics/images/videos/links posting is allowed. Same goes for the animal sex & Gay related things. We have a 0 tolerance policy on this one'. When a Joubon Jala member asked whether stories can include underage porn, a moderator tellingly suggested that: 'Uncle, if the story is in BENGALI, it's alright ... but if it is in English it is impossible. And pictures/video are out of the question. [...] That would create problems for all of us' ['*Mamu, story BANGLAI hoile chole .... kintu enlish e hoite parbone. Ar chobi/video'r proshno uthena. [...] eita amader shobar jonnoi trouble korbe'*].[1] Incest, however, was a favourite topic and formed the main topic of the *choti*, written Bengali pornography, that was featured on both sites. Neither protocol seemed too strictly maintained, however, and most outlawed articles could be found. References to male homosexuality were rare but could be found, inevitably wrapped up in a discussion of its appropriateness.

The sites addressed themselves explicitly to a Bengali audience. This was apparent from their names. While *'joubon jala'* can be translated as 'burning sex', with *joubon* also meaning youth, Porn Adda relied on the quintessentially Bengali concept of *adda* to address its audience. Dipesh Chakrabarty defines *adda* as 'the practice of friends getting together for long, informal, and unrigorous conversations' (2000, 181) and argues that it is a key marker of Bengali identity and intimately linked to the middle class (2000, 183). Chakrabarty also notes that the term has come to be used online to describe chat sites for Bengalis from Bangladesh as well as India (2000, 181). Both Joubon Jala and Porn Adda allowed for the possibility of writing in Bengali fonts and full access to both forums was premised on a working knowledge of Bengali. Although most boards were self-explanatory, entries could be difficult to find if you did not understand Bengali or were not using the right search terms, such as *'joubon'* [sex] or *choti*.[2] Most contributions used Roman fonts to form Bangla words or used a mix of English and Bengali. The interface of both sites used English to name the forums although some sections such as 'Choti' or 'Deshi/Bideshi' relied on a basic acquaintance with Bengali. While everyone on the sites seemed acquainted with Bengali, the fluency with which English was used varied greatly. The main users of the websites self-identified as based in Bangladesh, the USA, India, the United Kingdom, Dubai and Australia. Muslim and Hindu, and male and female names were in use in the forums. Language use mirroring Bangladeshi inflexion (*'khaite issa kore'* [I feel like eating], *'oshadharon hoitase'* [it's going really well]) and partaking of Bangladeshi current affairs ('Were you taken by RAB?' [*'naki RAB e niya gese?'*], referring to the Bangladeshi special police branch; or 'completely djuice' [*'purai djuice!'*], quoting the Bangladeshi mobile phone company Grameen Phone) suggested a large proportion of Bangladeshi users. The prevalence of Bangladeshi national symbols such as the flag or the Liberation War Monument that were displayed by users seems to confirm this. Joubon Jala was the larger site and had 47,538 members while Porn Adda had 18,640. Joubon Jala measured time in GMT + 5.5, suggesting India, while Porn Adda maintained GMT + 6, suggesting Bangladesh. Even if there is very little that is solid in the world of the chatroom, and identities and locations are easily hidden, I am relying on these visual, linguistic and temporal indicators to posit that these particular chatrooms were used by a community that could be broadly described as Bengali oriented and geographically scattered.

Both sites hosted a range of pornography, drawn from different online sources. While Joubon Jala specifically separated out supposed *'deshi'* (meaning 'of the country') materials from *'bideshi'* (or foreign) material, Porn Adda made no such distinction. Joubon Jala had a category 'Deshi Gurl' and defined that as 'Hot "desi" girls' discussion. Girls from the sub-continent'. On the other hand, the 'Bideshi Gurl' section is marked 'Foreign (Non-Bangali) hot chicks'. The apparent gap between *deshi*/subcontinental on the one hand and foreign/non-Bangali on the other was often discussed by contributors to these sites. At Joubon Jala, a contributor asked other members to guess the origin of a girl featured in the category 'Deshi Gurl'. The thumbnails of the so-called 'Mysore Mallige' video had been uploaded under the title 'aoshadharon [amazing] deshi girl in love'. Discussing the background of the girl featured, one contributor replied by saying: 'Mama [uncle], She is not deshi. She's from mysore, India'. Another claimed inside information and corroborated that 'I also have seen a small part of the video, and I know she is not from bd'. Others disagreed, and where one exclaimed 'No way, she is desi!!!!!!!!!!' another claimed she was from Kolkata, referring this Mysore video to the Nolbon scandal.[3] Such discussions illustrate the porosity of boundaries around the identities that were so important for participants to pin down, as they struggled to put clear distinctions in place. Porn Adda did not make any distinctions between *deshi* or *bideshi* imagery but did have separate categories for 'Bangla Serial and Natok' and 'Bollywood, Dhaliwood & Hollywood'. This did not stop its members from discussing the vexed *deshi–bideshi* distinction. One contributor to Porn Adda uploaded four pictures of a brown-skinned and dark-haired girl masturbating and asked other members '*Deshi* or *bideshi* – tell me uncles' ['*Deshi na bideshi – bolento mamara*']. One member responded 'uncle, I think it is a *deshi* living abroad' ['*mama mone to hoi bideshe thaka desi*'], another suggested 'Looking, I think Indian' ['*dekhi indian monee hoitasee*]', while a third took the Joubon Jala route and concluded 'From what can be seen of her hair, I think she is from the subcontinent' ['*Chuler arale jeituk dekha jai, sub continent eri to mone hoi*']. The wealth of material on the websites was in this way divided between the porous categories of *deshi* and non-*deshi*.

Despite the confusion around the categories, members seemed clear in their preference for '*deshi*' imagery, which was at any time being viewed by far more members and guests than the '*bideshi*' material. Similarly, written pornography was always in Bengali, addressed as *choti*. Such stories generally featured aunts and uncles, mothers and children, comparable to the cheaply printed written pornography that can be found in Bangladesh and West Bengal. There was no equivalent non-Bengali written pornography, highlighting the search for Bengali pornography that members seemed to be engaged in on both websites. The cut-piece was now aligned with the *choti*, the Bengali pornographic short story that, like the cut-piece, retains narrative and formal particularities (Biswas 2013). Online, the cut-pieces were put into conversation with other forms of vernacular sexually explicit cultural production. The online space allowed the articulation of, and debate around, something particularly local, described as '*deshi*' or 'Bangali' that was sexually explicit. These were the artefacts of the pornographic region, even if much of it could not be definitively assigned to that imagined location, not 'localised' in a stable manner (see Mohan and Punthambekar 2019). Part of the pleasure here was the speculation around the material's 'proper' location and provenance.

The main forms of *deshi* pornography on Joubon Jala and Porn Adda were the written *choti* stories, posed still images – some with an amateur quality to them, others with the heads of famous actresses montaged to unknown bodies – as well as hidden camera footage from hotels and internet cafes, and mobile phone footage. Besides this, there was some professional imagery from individuals of South Asian descent working in America, such as the Bangladeshi porn actress Jazmin. Among all this *deshi* material, the cut-pieces stood out clearly from the other material on the websites due to the production values of Bangladeshi action cinema from the 1990s and 2000s. This was exacerbated by the fact that those who uploaded the cut-pieces used cheaply produced cut-piece VCDs as their source of this material; often without changing the titles given to the pieces on the VCD, uploading single songs or rape scenes via Mega-upload or Rapidshare. The quality of the VCDs meant the images often broke up. Having been taken from video cameras set up in the cinema halls, the angles in the cut-pieces were also decidedly odd, and the footage was poor quality. Scarred and bruised, the cut-pieces arrived in the digital domain, marked by their earlier circulation in the imperfect media environment of Bangladeshi cinema distribution, exhibition and piracy (see Srivastava [2007] on the pleasures of such imperfect images).

The cut-pieces were uploaded into specific video sections on both bulletin boards, marked 'BD movies' on Joubon Jala and part of the video-forum on Porn Adda. Here, a relatively small group of members uploaded Bangladeshi cinema pornography. The individuals behind the names 'BDhotguy', 'TrInItY', 'kOlkaTar_SayTan' and 'Helaloop' were prominent posters on both sites. They titled their contributions 'Uncensored BD Movie Scene', 'Hot bangla song', 'BD movie nude clip' or just 'Bangla Cinema'. Despite these titles, the uploaders of the clips frequently revealed their distance from the industry and lack of involvement in the culture of cinema hall attendance or reading film magazines. They sometimes speculated on the origin of the clips, indicating a vague awareness of the industry based on newspaper reports that circulated in Bangladesh. For example, when asked the name of the film from which a clip had been uploaded, Helaloop replied: 'Uncle, I don't know the name … where would I get that?' ['*mama nam jani na … pamu koi?*']. kOlkaTar_SayTan, whose handle suggests a link to Calcutta, asked 'Have a look, do you know them, are they really Bengali cinema actors/actresses?' ['*dekhen eder chen kina, era ki realy bengali cinemar abhineta/netri*']. This lack of acquaintance with the industry and the city of Dhaka was also apparent when kOlkaTar_SayTan commented on a clip set in a nightclub. Nightclubs are common backdrops to cabaret-type song sequences across South Asian cinema and feature heavily in Bangladeshi action films. There is a standard set involving a stage and a bar made out of cardboard used at the state-owned FDC studios in Dhaka. kOlkaTar_SayTan, however, asked: 'Uncle, are all these nightclubs in Dhaka or what?' ['*Mama ei saab Night Club gula ki Dhakay naki?*']. The lack of acquaintance with cut-piece materials was not only apparent among the uploaders of the footage. Those who downloaded and commented on the clips were equally amazed by them. Mituctg asked: 'are Bangladeshi cinemas gaan [songs] – I dont believe' (*sic*). Rajon_dhk asked: 'is that really a Bangla movie?' ['*eita ki asholeo bangla movie*']. Also, m626 on Porn Adda exclaimed: 'Are they really shown on cinemas in Bangladesh?????????' (*sic*). Sayeed on Joubon Jala was even more explicit: 'unlce, if you didn't post this stuff, I would never understand what happens at the FDC' ['*mama apne agulo post na korle kono din bujhtam na FDC te ke hoy*']. From such statements it is apparent that those who uploaded and downloaded Bangladeshi cut-pieces operated at quite a distance from the circuits of production and consumption of the celluloid industry from which these clips were originally taken.

This distance is not completely surprising. It can be understood in relation to both class position and location. From their presence online in this period of the 2000s (before the spread of smartphones and the broadening of access to the internet across the region), it is clear that these were educated and relatively wealthy Bengali speakers, most probably from middle-class households, located in South Asia and elsewhere. Their exposure to Bangladeshi action cinema was likely to be limited. Mainstream Bangladeshi action cinema of the period, as discussed earlier, was working-class cinema, aimed at semi-urban and rural audiences. This explains why educated and middle-class Bangladeshis should have expressed their surprise at finding sexually explicit material appearing from Bangladeshi cinema halls. They were unlikely to have had much exposure to the cinema halls, let alone to have frequented them. On top of this, the action cinema within which cut-pieces were produced was largely consumed nationally. Although some pirated cut-piece VCDs could be found in Calcutta, London and Dubai, Bengalis not resident in Bangladesh would have had little opportunity to see sexually explicit Bangladeshi cinema. As Labony, apparently based in the USA, asked on Porn Adda: 'who are the viewers of these movies?' [*'accha, ei movie gular viewers kara?'*].

The distance of the online audience from the cut-pieces can also be read in other comments. Sumon711, who says he is based in Dhaka, responded to an entry titled 'Hot bangla song' that 'Bangla cinema is in such a state, it is impossible to watch it with your family. [...] The target audience for these directors are rickshaw-wallahs who are unmarried or whose wives reside in the village' [*'bangle cinemar ja obostha, family nia dekhar kono sujog nai. [...]. Ei somosto porichalok der target audience hoilo rickshaw ala jara unmarried ba bou thake deshe tader jonno'*]. Rehearsing a common complaint about Bangladeshi mainstream cinema, Sumon711 also clearly sets himself off from the 'real' audience of these clips, namely poor labour migrants in menial jobs. The purportedly female uploader of a sexually explicit song sequence clip named Nisha titled her entry 'Ugly nude song in Bangla film' and introduced it by writing in perfect English: 'Don't know what to say about this ... thought you guys might wanna see it, but don't enjoy it. There is nothing to enjoy .. *odhopoton e gese*!' The last part means 'it is morally depraved'. This judgement of 'ugliness and depravity' should be read in line with the class distinction imagined between the 'real' audience for the clips, the 'morally depraved' rickshaw-wallah, and the community of readers gathered for the pornographic *adda* taking place online.

With the movement of cut-pieces from small-town cinema halls to the long-distance *addas* of internationally dispersed Bengalis, the audience and the context of reception is completely transformed. Where before the cut-pieces were embedded in the diegesis of action movies and an integral part of the movie theatre experience, now they are embedded in chatsites, alongside other Bengali and international pornography, watched from private computer screens or in internet cafes. Alongside this, however, is a sudden emergence into visibility of the racial and ethnic qualities of the imagery. Take the following example: Sumon_hoq2005 expresses the common sentiment that 'the taste of BD chicks is different' [*'BD maal ar shaad e alada'*].[4] Khara_dhon, supposedly based in Sydney, agrees: 'I want more. [...] Watching things from your own country has a different pleasure' [*'aro chai. [...]. Shodeshi jinish dekhar mojai alada*]'. Vuka also agrees and says 'uncle, the pleasure in seeing the breasts of Bengali girls is different. I feel like I am the hero' [*'mama, bangali meyeder dudh dekhar mojai alada. Mone hoi ami hero'*]. Besides the idea of local flavour, there is also a suggestion of the possibility of identification with the imagery, mediated by a sense of ethnic or linguistic similarity that is apparently different from the identificatory process with other types of pornography. Within the context of cinema viewing in Bangladesh, this sort of utterance would be very difficult. Class boundaries make identification with mainstream cinema unlikely, while racial or ethnic identification remains unremarked within an industry that is Bengali dominated and screened for largely Bengali audiences.[5] Here in vuka's comment, markers of class, attached to the theatrical context of consumption, recede in favour of markers of race and ethnicity that are imagined to be specific to the body, available on screen in the online context of consumption.

The comments illustrate the shift in emphasis from class to race. Intimacy is produced out of the possibility of identifying the visual markers of race at the site of the body, while this attribution remains continuously beset by doubts as the visual cannot offer 'sufficient' clues or bolster claims about the nature of the body represented (Poole 2005). Clues about who a person is racially or ethnically are continually sought as a means to heighten the pleasure the clips offer, but cannot be definitively found because of 'the forms of suspicion that surround visual representations and race' (Poole 2005, 161). Here, race acts as a medium; as Mitchell argues, 'a vehicle for *both* fantasy *and* reality' (2012, 14; emphases in original). This is why much time is spent online in parsing the location of the representational content, the origin films, the probable provenance of the imagery and the identity of the actors, and the continuous debate about *deshi* or *bideshi*. There is a desire to fix these bodies as Bangladeshi or Bengali, which heightens the pleasure in consuming the material, but is continually beset by doubt.

This emphasis on the pleasures of all things Bengali is also to be found in the commentary on mobile phone footage or personal photography of Bengali subjects. However, the production of cut-pieces within the formalized cinema industry allows these clips to be discussed as national products. In fact, part of the pleasure that the cut-pieces provided is the possibility to use them to illustrate the advanced position of Bangladesh and Bengalis within the progress of nations. Replying to a clip titled 'BD Movie the most explosive Nudity Clip 19 – Nishidho Nari', someone named RestLess replies: 'Amazing, :D. Bangladesh is getting much ahead. The future of the porn industry is very good' ['*Oshadharon, :D. Bangladesh onek egiye jacche. porn industry er future onek valo samne*']. Similarly, Olash says: 'Bangladesh has gotten ahead a lot now, uncle, these sort of scenes are as common as milk and rice' ['*bangladesh ekhon onek agaya geche mamu, eai sob scene ekhon dud bhat*']. Such narratives of progress invoke plenitude. KalamamaAUS, said to be based in Australia, says on Porn Adda: 'today everything is possible in the country' ['*ajkal deshe shobe shombhob*']. Shonaa812 explicitly measures Bangladesh with the rest of the world by quoting a favourite political one-liner in an ironic manner: 'the country is moving in rhythm with the world' ['*bissher shathe tal miliye desh agiye jacche*']. On Porn Adda and Joubon Jala, sexually explicit cinema clips are discussed by way of a middle-class discourse of progress vis-à-vis other nations that leans heavily on the development narratives of institutions such as the World Bank and the UNDP. Both have a strong presence in Bangladesh. Women are targeted in such development narratives and it is no coincidence that many contributors to Porn Adda and Joubon Jala invoke this in their analysis of the cut-pieces. As rajarshi5 states: 'Bangladeshi Bengali girls are very mentally advanced' ['*bangladesher Bengali meyera manosik bhabe onek advanced*']. The use of 'mentally' here means 'socially forward' or 'liberated'. Here, we see the international development discourse, with its emphasis on female sexual health, women's rights and family planning, reproduced as pornography. The pornographic cannibalizes other discourses, including nationalist or developmentalist ones.

National progress is also measured against other places, especially those generally seen as well ahead of Bangladesh in terms of development. It is here that ethnicity becomes wedded to national belonging and progress. Responding to Nisha's suggestion of moral depravity, a member of Porn Adda named helloblue says: 'who says odhopoton [depravity] I think it's opposite don't you know we have rided on [*sic*] the train which is driving by USA'. Nunu_mia ('Mr. Penis') wonders 'why can't you get as much nude in Hindi cinema as you can in Bangla cinema' [*'bangle cenema to joto khani nude pai hindi te oto khani pai na ken'*]. When a song sequence from the film *Noya Mastan* ('New Gangster', dir. Opurbo-Ranaa, 2005) appeared on the Indian website Debonairblog, its Indian users there lamented: 'I have not seen any such thing in the Indian soft porn movies. This is quite natural and the girl has acted without any inhibition. Something which is lacking in Indian movies'. Thankfully, the commentator could reinstate the proper hierarchy between the 'rising superpower' and its poor neighbour by explaining the bad quality of the clip, stating that 'in Bangladesh they normally don't come out with DVD/VCD quality versions'. Another Indian contributor is willing to solve the problem by imagining a trip to one of India's neighbouring countries, of which 'many Indians choose to live in mortal fear' (Nandy 1998, 4): 'really I wanted to go to bangledesh [*sic*] after seeing this clip'. Closer to home, KOlkaTar_SayTan asks who says that it is only Hollywood which produces films containing nudity. Polash responds by saying: 'uncle, actually Bangla movies are leaving Hollywood behind'. KOlkaTar_SayTan replies to Polash by saying 'yes, yes, uncle, well said, we will stop watching those white ones, we can get naked better than them' [*'han, han, mama thik bolsen, aamra oi goragula re dekhay charbo aamra oder thekey bhalo nengto hate pari'*]. Nationality and ethnicity thus become mobilized within narratives of progress to discuss Bangladeshi pornography online.

The surpassing of other nations is not without its flipside, however, and not everyone was equally celebratory. Labony recounted on Porn Adda:

> One of my friends saw it, she is american, and she said ... bangladeshi movies r the most explicit among all the counties in Indian subcontinent ... bollywood, tallywood, lollywood nothing can override BD films ... I was like saying to myself..should I feel ashemed [*sic*] or proud??

Labony is not the only one with this concern. Sayeed wonders: 'in which direction is our country advancing/retreating?' [*'amader desh ta kon dike agacche/pechacche?'*]. Such misgivings pitch the cultural worth of the nation against the boons of 'progress'. Others see the hand of God. 'May Allah bless you with more such stuffs [*sic*]', says one contributor, while another cries appreciatively: 'masha-allah ... good work man ... keep it up'. Ethnic markers and national belonging are mobilized both in favour of the clips shown and against them.

In the online worlds of Bengali chatrooms in the later 2000s, cut-pieces were positioned within discussions of the fate of culture and the nation in the drive towards progress and the march of modernity. They featured in such debates in a manner very similar to the fraught discussions about cultural change incurred by playing Hindi movie songs at Bangladeshi weddings or the use of particular oils to prepare Bengali food. As Laura Kipnis has already suggested, pornography features within the boundary-marking of culture and identity no differently than in other cultural production (Kipnis 1996, viii). On Joubon Jala and Porn Adda, the cut-pieces were the foil to debates about identity, belonging and modernity, belaboured by anonymous, Bengali-speaking, internet users. They had travelled a great distance from the single-screen rural cinema halls in which they might have originally been screened and came to mark an entirely different set of boundaries as they reached the internet.

Race and class in cut-piece pornography

While pornography in general may be good at marking cultural boundaries, as Kipnis (1996) notes, the type of boundary that is marked by a particular artefact of pornography cannot be predicted from its representational content. As I have shown, the meaning of the cut-pieces was fundamentally transformed as they traversed celluloid and digital formats and were made available in very different reception contexts. The boundary marked online in the discussions generated by the cut-pieces was a very different one to the boundary marked in debates about the cut-pieces in Bangladeshi cinema halls. In the context of theatrical exhibition, the debates generated by cut-pieces were about class and the nature of the audience for cinematic entertainment, while online they generated discussions about the place of Bengali culture and Bengali bodies within a larger global framework of cultural and national value. Also, where theatrical exhibition produced anxieties and excitement about men (rural men, working-class men, men without 'proper' outlets for their sexual and entertainment needs; in a word, 'other' men), online the discussions were largely about the women who featured in the cut-pieces. In the cinema halls, these clips marked the boundaries between classes and between the urban and the rural via the figure of the male spectator, but online the boundaries marked were between nations and ethnicities through the figure of the female actress. Finally, the question of the ethnically marked body, a body understood to be the site of the articulation of race, only emerged significantly in the online context, where presumably the hegemonic form of pornography features white bodies. In the Bangladeshi cinema halls, with Bangladesh's longstanding controls on foreign cinema, the white body is largely absent and films are made in a hegemonically Bengali film industry, catering to an almost entirely Bengali audience.

The transition of the cut-pieces from cinema halls to online chatrooms brings sharply into focus the ways in which our thinking around pornography is ill-adapted to think through the question of race in online pornography that is not thematized for its colour and not staged for the white gaze. Much academic discussion of race in pornography, online or otherwise, has approached the question from an ethnic minorities and western race-relations perspective (Alloula 1986; Hoang 2004; Mahawatte 2004; Williams 2004; Cervulle and Rees-Roberts 2009). Studies of non-western pornography, on the other hand, emphasize the coherent cultural universe within which 'other' expressions of sexuality are embedded in radically different cultural worlds, incommensurable with western pornographic arenas (Shamoon 2004). Although insightful and critical, neither of these approaches fully captures the possibility of a pornography not staged for an imagined white audience yet participating in the aesthetics of international mainstream pornography. It is the possibility of a mode of pornography that is both in conversation with international genres while remaining locally resonant which the cut-piece inherits from its B-circuit, action cinema, parent films. Realizing such a regional pornographic aesthetic is what has given cut-pieces their longevity and allowed them to outlive the celluloid world from which they originated.

What is more, the movement of the cut-piece from celluloid to digital platforms, and the transformed response they find there, provides an important impetus to rethinking the ways in which questions of race and class have been approached in the study of pornography. Ground-breaking studies in this field (Kipnis 1996; Penley 2004; Williams 2004) have tended to locate the racialized or 'classed' appeal of particular modes of pornography within its imagery. That is, pornography that mobilizes race or class as the means to generate bodily responses in its audience is often understood to use bodies that are marked in particular ways, specific *mise en scène* and particular forms of language, to generate that response. What the movement of the cut-pieces shows, however, is that how the pornographic imagery is received as classed or racialized, and therefore desirable or exciting, is also dependent on the form of exhibition or distribution and its attendant context of reception. This is a hugely significant addition to existing conversations, and one that has obvious implications for thinking about where we may 'locate' the questions of class and race in the operations of pornographic texts.

This article is set at a particular historical moment, the mid-2000s, which saw the simultaneous high-water point for the production of celluloid pornography in Bangladesh and the imminent disintegration of the celluloid film industry in Bangladesh. This moment produced the end of the illegal production of celluloid pornographic clips as well as its revival online. In this article I have documented that moment of transition. Tracking the appearance online of celluloid cut-pieces has allowed me to make three interventions with regard to the study of pornography in South Asia. First, I have shown how the contexts of exhibition and reception are hugely significant for understanding the operation of race and class in this type of pornographic material. Second, I have suggested that, once emancipated from its celluloid form, the nature of the cut-pieces as part of a regional form of sexually suggestive or explicit cinema also came more forcefully into view. This suggests that the nature of the 'regional' can be expanded in significant ways to encompass localized forms that share significant similarities, not with what is most geographically near but what is aesthetically and socially near within a certain field of filmmaking. Finally, the cut-pieces, pornographic ephemera even when they were blossoming in Bangladesh at the turn of the century, have paradoxically come to find their archive outside of their native habitat of exhibition and circulation. It is as digital clips that they have come to be archived, not unlike the vast domain of South Asian screen culture that falls between the gaps of legal, formal and respectable archives and repositories (Tnavir 2013; Bull 2014; Mini 2016).

Notes

1. I have copied the Bengali wording of these citations as they appear online, without 'correcting' the transliteration of the Bengali as presented there.
2. For example, searching the internet for 'Bangladesh' and 'Sex' leads you to numerous non-governmental organizations and charities concerned with the health of Bangladeshi sex workers, the correlations between tuberculosis outbreaks and gender, as well as sex discrimination in birth rates.
3. Both the Mysore Mallige and the Nolbon sexually explicit home videos created a scandal in India, where they were made and distributed. These videos were purported to have been accidentally made public. Both videos have reached a certain cult status and continue to circulate online. See Baishya (2017).
4. The multivalent *maal* is difficult to translate. Meaning anything ranging from piece to load or cargo, it is often used to address a desired person in an objectifying way. In this case, 'chicks' seems to come closest to the implied meaning. See Ramaswami (2006).
5. The complex question of non-Bengali Bangladeshis and their identification with Bangladeshi cinema is beyond the scope of this article.

Acknowledgements

The author is very grateful for the encouragement and patience of Darshana Sreedhar Mini and Anirban Kapil Baishya as well as the helpful comments by Feona Attwood and two anonymous reviewers.

Disclosure statement

No potential conflict of interest was reported by the author.

References

Alloula, Malek. 1986. *The Colonial Harem*. Translated by Myrna Godzich and Wlad Godzich. Minneapolis: University of Minnesota Press.

Awwal, Aprana. 2018. 'From Villain to Hero: Masculinity and Political Aesthetics in the Films of Bangladeshi Action Star Joshim.' *BioScope: South Asian Screen Studies* 9 (1): 24–45.

Baishya, Anirban K. 2017. 'Pornography of Place: Location, Leaks and Obscenity in the Indian MMS Porn Video.' *South Asian Popular Culture* 15 (1): 57–71.

Biswas, Hardik Brata. 2013. 'The Obscene Modern and the Pornographic Family: Adventures in Bangla Pornography.' In *The Sexual History of the Global South: Sexual Politics in Africa, Asia and Latin America*, edited by Saskia Wieringa, and Horacio Sívori, 44–64. London and New York: Zed Books.

Brennan, Joseph. 2018. 'Microporn in the Digital Media Age: Fantasy Out of Context.' *Porn Studies* 5 (2): 152–155.

Bull, Sarah. 2014. 'Digital Archives and the History of Pornography.' *Porn Studies* 1 (4): 402–405.

Chakrabarty, Dipesh. 2000. *Provincialising Europe: Postcolonial Thought and Historical Difference*. Princeton: Princeton University Press.

Cervulle, Maxime and Nick Rees-Roberts. 2009. 'Queering the Orientalist Porn Package: Arab Men in French Gay Pornography.' *New Cinemas: Journal of Contemporary Film* 6 (3): 197–208.

Chowdhury, Nusrat. 2014. '"Picture-Thinking": Sovereignty and Citizenship in Bangladesh.' *Anthropological Quarterly* 87 (4): 1257–1278.

Ginsburg, Faye D., Lila Abu-Lughod and Brian Larkin, eds. 2002. *Media Worlds: Anthropology on New Terrain*. Berkeley: University of California Press.

Hardy, Catherine C. 2010. 'Mediating *Bhojpuriya*: Migration, Circulation, and Bhojpuri Cinema.' *South Asian Popular Culture* 8 (3): 231–244.

Hardy, Catherine C. 2015. 'Constituting a Diffuse Region: Cartographies of Mass-Mediated Bhojpuri Belonging.' *BioScope: South Asian Screen Studies* 6 (2): 145–164.

Hoang, Nguyen Tan. 2004. 'The Resurrection of Brandon Lee: The Making of a Gay Asian American Porn Star.' In *Porn Studies*, edited by Linda Williams, 223–270. Durham: Duke University Press.

Hoek, Lotte. 2010. 'Cut-Pieces as Stag Film: Bangladeshi Pornography in Action Cinema.' *Third Text* 24 (1): 135–148.

Hoek, Lotte. 2013. 'Killer Not Terrorist: Visual Articulations of Terror in Bangladeshi Action Cinema.' *South Asian Popular Culture* 11 (2): 121–132.

Hoek, Lotte. 2014. *Cut-Pieces: Celluloid Obscenity and Popular Cinema in Bangladesh*. New York: Columbia University Press.

Horst, Heather and Daniel Miller. 2012. *Digital Anthropology*. London: Berg.

Hulsing, Milan. 2004. 'Pashto Horror Films in Pakistan.' *Wasafiri* 19 (43): 53–57.

Hussain, Faheem and Mashiat Mostafa. 2016. 'Digital Contradictions in Bangladesh: Encouragement and Deterrence of Citizen Engagement via ICTs.' *Information Technologies & International Development* 12 (2): 47–61.

Khan, Ali and Ali Nobil Ahmad. 2010. 'From *Zinda Laash to Zibahkhana*: Violence and Horror in Pakistani Cinema.' *Third Text* 24 (1): 149–161.

Kipnis, Laura. 1996. *Bound and Gagged: Pornography and the Politics of Fantasy in America*. Durham: Duke University Press.

Kirk, Gwendolyn. 2016. '"A Camera from the Time of the British": Film Technologies and Aesthetic Exclusion in Pakistani Cinema.' *Screen* 57 (4): 496–502.

Kumar, Akshaya. 2016. 'Bhojpuri Consolidations in the Hindi Territory: Infrastructure, Aesthetics, and Competing Masculinities in North India.' *BioScope: South Asian Screen Studies* 7 (2): 189–206.

Mahadevan, Sudhir. 2015. *A Very Old Machine: The Many Origins of the Cinema in India*. New York: SUNY Press.

Mahawatte, Royce. 2004. 'Loving the Other: Arab-Male Fetish Pornography and the Dark Continent of Masculinity.' In *More Dirty Looks: Gender, Pornography and Power*, edited by Pamela Church Gibson, 127–136. London: BFI.

Manobjomin. 2009. "They Are Coming Back" [Ora abar phirchhe]. January 12.

Mini, Darshana Sreedhar. 2016. 'The Spectral Duration of Malayalam Soft-Porn: Disappearance, Desire, and Haunting.' *BioScope: South Asian Screen Studies* 7 (2): 127–150.

Mitchell, W. J. T. 2012. *Seeing Through Race*. Cambridge: Harvard University Press.

Mohan, Sriram and Aswin Punathambekar. 2019. 'Localizing YouTube: Language, Cultural Regions, and Digital Platforms.' *International Journal of Cultural Studies* 22 (3): 317–333.

Morris, Meaghan. 2004. 'Transnational Imagination in Action Cinema: Hong Kong and the Making of a Global Popular Culture.' *Inter-Asia Cultural Studies* 5 (2): 181–199.

Nabi, Hira. 2017. 'Transient Space and Places: Inside an 80s Cinema Hall in Lahore.' *BioScope: South Asian Screen Studies* 8 (2): 268–279.

Nandy, Ashis. 1998. *The Secret Politics of Our Desires: Innocence, Culpability and Indian Popular Cinema*. Delhi: Oxford University Press.

Penley, Constance. 2004. 'Crackers and Whackers: The White Trashing of Porn.' In *Porn Studies*, edited by Linda Williams, 309–331. Durham: Duke University Press.

Pink, Sarah, Heather Horst, John Postill, Larissa Hjort, Tania Lewis and Jo Tacchi. 2016. *Digital Ethnography: Principles and Practice*. London: Sage.

Poole, Deborah. 2005. 'An Excess of Description: Ethnography, Race, and Visual Technology.' *Annual Review of Anthropology* 34: 159–179.

Ramaswami, Shankar. 2006. 'Masculinity, Respect, and the Tragic: Themes of Proletarian Humor in Contemporary Industrial Delhi.' *International Review of Social History* 51 (S14): 203–27.

Shamoon, Deborah. 2004. 'Office Sluts and Rebel Flowers: The Pleasures of Japanese Pornographic Comics for Women.' In *Porn Studies*, edited by Linda Williams, 77–103. Durham: Duke University Press.

Srinivas, S. V. 2003. 'Hong Kong Action Film in the Indian B Circuit.' *Inter-Asia Cultural Studies* 4 (1): 40–62.

Srinivas, S. V. 2015. 'Region in Focus.' *BioScope: South Asian Screen Studies* 6 (2): vii–ix.

Srivastava, Sanjay. 2007. *Passionate Modernity: Sexuality, Class and Consumption in India*. London: Routledge.

Tanvir, Kuhu. 2013. 'Pirate Histories: Rethinking the Indian Film Archive.' *BioScope: South Asian Screen Studies* 4 (2): 115–136.

Taussig, Michael. 1999. *Defacement: Public Secrecy and the Labor of the Negative*. Stanford: Stanford University Press.

Vasudevan, Ravi. 2010. 'Geographies of the Cinematic Public: Notes on Regional, National and Global Histories of Indian Cinema.' *Journal of the Moving Image* 9: 94–117.

Vasudevan, Ravi, Rosie Thomas, S. V. Srinivas, Debashree Mukherjee and Lotte Hoek. 2016. 'Infrastructures and Archives of the B-circuit.' *BioScope: South Asian Screen Studies* 7 (2): vii–xi.

Williams, Linda. 1989. *Hard Core: Power, Pleasure, and the 'Frenzy of the Visible'*. Berkeley and Los Angeles: University of California Press.

Williams, Linda, ed. 2004. *Porn Studies*. Durham: Duke University Press.

Williams, Linda. 2014. 'Pornography, Porno, Porn: Thoughts on a Weedy Field.' *Porn Studies* 1 (1-2): 24–40.

Transgressions in Toonland: *Savita Bhabhi*, *Velamma* and the Indian adult comic

Darshana Sreedhar Mini and Anirban K. Baishya

ABSTRACT

While India is no stranger to titillating imagery, its pornographic circuits remain underground due to stringent laws. The emergence of Indian pornographic comics under the aegis of the adult entertainment company Indian Porn Empire has destabilized this framework through their dispersed production practices and viral circulation. This article examines two of the most popular comic book titles, *Savita Bhabhi* and *Velamma*, that feature married women as their protagonists. While interrogating these comics in terms of their content and effects, we suggest that the affordances of the comic book medium allow them to display a wider range of fantasies than both the amateur and soft porn that circulates in India. Thus, these comic books become sticky objects that absorb and express the dynamics of class, gender and taboo. The adult comic book visualizes sexual and moral anxieties on the two-dimensional plane of the comic book panel and becomes a canvas of fantasies that allows for vicarious boundary-crossing.

Introduction

In 2016, during a conversation about pornography with an American friend, we were asked what is a '*bhabhi*?' Our mutual friend had encountered the term on some internet forum where one of the threads was an ongoing conversation between Indian men about their sexual fantasies. Not being conversant with Hindi, he had subsequently associated the term with something to do with sex. While we later explained to him that *bhabhi* simply meant sister-in-law in Hindi, our brief conversation got us thinking about what this said about Indian sexual culture.[1] Indeed, even a cursory look at any Indian pornographic website would reveal a plethora of material – both stories as well as videos – that are tagged with the term *bhabhi*, and this is rivalled only perhaps by the taxonomic category of the 'aunty'. Together, both '*bhabhi*' and 'aunty' point towards a shared sexual fascination with married women – usually (but not necessarily) middle-aged – who present a window to the latent cultures of sexual transgressions in an otherwise censorial and strictly regimented social fabric. As pornographic forms, however, the figures of both the *bhabhi* and the aunty have rarely been the focus of sustained textual effort, by which we mean that there has not been a single character that has consistently represented transgressive sexual fantasies.

Instead, the *bhabhi* and the aunty have usually circulated as archetypes, appearing mostly as tags or taxonomic markers for fragments of videos and hurriedly written online stories, or as the stuff of cheap pulp fiction. Thus, while these figures are durable across time, they have usually eluded being fixed onto a particular face or a character.

Things changed in the 2000s, however, with the emergence of Indian pornographic comics under the aegis of the adult entertainment company, Indian Porn Empire. While Indian Porn Empire also includes 'live' porn websites such as the amateur porn sites Free Sexy Indians (FSI Blog), Antarvasana and Indian Porn Videos, we turn our attention to the comic books produced under the Indian Porn Empire banner. These sex comics include a wide range of titles, but can be broadly divided into two labels, Kirtu and Velamma. While the Kirtu label boasts of titles such as *Priya Rao*, *XXX Apartments* and *Kinara Lane*, its flagship title is the famous *Savita Bhabhi* series. On the other hand, the Velamma label is spearheaded by the eponymous *Velamma* series, but also has a spin-off titled *Veena* (Velamma's daughter). The rapid rise in the popularity of both *Savita Bhabhi* and *Velamma* has sent the circuitries of censorship and moral judgement into a tizzy, particularly because they proliferate through the 'unruly' medium of the internet. Originally, it was *Savita Bhabhi* that appeared and kicked off controversies regarding pornography, obscenity and legality in India's public sphere, partly due to its shockingly frank depiction of sexual acts and partly due to its immense popularity. Recently, the *Velamma* series has also attained immense popularity, offering a 'South Indian' counterpart to the apparently 'North Indian' Savita. We suggest that comic book characters such as Savita Bhabhi and Velamma are what Sara Ahmed calls 'sticky objects' – objects that are 'saturated with affect, as sites of personal and social tension' (2014, 11). If *Savita Bhabhi* and *Velamma* constitute a genre of pornography – call it the pornography of transgressive domesticity – we would be well served to heed film historian Rick Altman's (1996, 285) suggestion that genres express the constitutive contradictions of a society and offer imaginary solutions to them. Comic books like *Savita Bhabhi* and *Velamma* offer imaginary solutions to the contradictions between tradition and modernity, between monogamy and a new libidinal economy of endless possibilities.

In reading *Savita Bhabhi* and *Velamma* as *loci classici* of the genre, our argument is twofold. First, we argue that, as a particular genre of sexual fiction, *Savita Bhabhi* and *Velamma* offer new forms of imagining sexual transgression that can bypass the spatial logic of national censorial regimes. As pornographic objects that originate outside the boundaries of India and travel within the viral pathways of the internet, such comics occupy a trans-spatial zone of sexual fantasy. Deshmukh, one of the creators of *Savita Bhabhi*, describes it as 'the creation of a couple of second-generation Indians' (Swarup 2009), and while the exact creators of *Velamma* are more difficult to place, the authorship of *Velamma* and *Savita Bhabhi* overlaps. Deshmukh is credited as an author on some *Velamma* issues (Episode 3 and Episode 4, for example), and there are narrative crossovers featuring Velamma and Savita in the same issue (*Savita Bhabhi* Episode 43 and *Velamma* Episode 6). However, even as the comics may be produced and distributed by writers and artists based outside India, there is an active imagination of an 'Indian' erogenous space that appears quite strongly in the narrative and the visual content of the comics. This erogenous space is contained within the space of the comic book, which becomes an interface between the libidinal spaces of the internet and the physical spaces of the reader/user. Second, and relatedly, we argue that the form of the comic book itself lays the ground for this trans-spatial circulation, because the drawn form, as opposed to live action, allows the sexual fantasy to come to the fore in a sustained fashion without the risks of a performer's sole attachment to the character. This is a significant aspect in a country like India, where the production and circulation of pornography is illegal. As two-dimensional representations of sexual encounters, the comic book medium becomes a canvas of fantasies on which desires and explorations are played out.[2]

Thus, figures such as Savita Bhabhi and Velamma are a graphic spatialization of sexual fantasies and taboo. Both figures are represented as married women and domestic space becomes essential to the imagination of transgression and sexual exploration. The panels in the comic book become the spaces of the domestic interior where the narrative unfolds. If domestic space is the space of the sexual encounter in these comics, then the comic book panels allow for the visual manifestation of the sexual imaginary. Here, the comic book form supplements the sexual imaginary – it is an extension of the imagined spaces of the domestic everyday – one that can potentially exist in real space, but under constant threat of closure by way of social norms and legal censorship. Thus, the comic book presents itself as a virtual appendage for the libidinal possibilities of real domestic interiors. The domestic becomes both a metaphor as well as an important representational element in these comics. The homepages for both of the characters, Kirtu.com (Savita Bhabhi) and Velamma.com (Velamma), feature banners with the central characters in different stages of undressing, while declaring 'Welcome to my home' as an invitation to visitors. The status of *Savita Bhabhi* and *Velamma* as digital comics spatializes this imagination of domestic space within the fast-moving sphere of internet circulation. Just as domesticity is destabilized on a representational level within the transgressive narratives of the comics, the digital renders the domestic doubly unstable by spatializing it within the non-space of the internet.[3] Thus, while *Savita Bhabhi* and *Velamma* are representations of carnal fantasies, they are marked by non-material erotics – i.e. the erotic charge of two-dimensional, non-fleshy bodies as well as an immaterial domesticity within the internet. This is not to say that it is the internet itself which is non-material, as computer networks, of course, constitute computer hardware and fibre-optic cables. When we invoke the non-material erotics of *Savita Bhabhi* and *Velamma*, we speak essentially of a fantasy space that is composed of libidinal energies and desires that are enabled by cybernetic virtuality.

This fantasy space, again, is not the sole domain of the internet. For sure, such fantasy spaces (and the spaces where they are peddled) have existed without the medium of the internet. In the context of India, Sanjay Srivastava (2013, 231), for example, talks of 'footpath pornography' – cheap, poorly-bound Hindi print materials that are sold in transient spaces and offer the urban poor fantasies of transgressive desires, seductive 'Western women' and extramarital affairs. Srivastava posits *Savita Bhabhi* as a part of '"middle-class" sexual cultures' (2013, 228), something opposed to footpath pornography. While Srivastava's analysis is largely useful for understanding the transient spaces of Indian pornography, its delineation as the domain of the urban poor is more ambiguous. As Rini Barman (2015) writes, 'we cannot categorise the consumers of these pulp porn magazines into one. The fact that they come in cheap, pulp paper with very low costs, doesn't really say anything about the class of the consumers.' As fantasy spaces, the storylines and narrative drives of 'urban poor' and 'middle class sexual cultures' can often overlap. There is no clear outside or inside when it comes to readership, and the footpath aesthetic is something that is common to both middle-class and lower-class consumption. The surreptitious pleasure that is associated with the consumption of erotic material is also marked by India's obscenity laws that disallow the production and circulation of sexually explicit material. It is part of the logic of occlusion or partial visibility that lends pornographic cultures their 'footpath' or 'underground' nature. Laws against pornography translate moral anxieties into legal dictums that further marginalize sexual cultures in the region of the footpath. In this context, the platform of the internet and digital adult comics complicate the stringent framework of legality.[4]

What we see in comic books such as *Savita Bhabhi* and *Velamma*, then, is an appropriation of the footpath aesthetic that is transposed onto the mobile space of the internet. *Savita Bhabhi* and *Velamma* transform footpath pornography into internet chic. To borrow a term from Steven Marcus' work on Victorian pornography, this constitutes a kind of a pornotopia – 'the imagination of the entire universe beneath the sign of sexuality' (2017, 242). According to Marcus, pornotopias' 'true existence is not in the world [...] They truly exist behind our eyes, within our heads' (2017, 268). In Marcus' conception, pornotopia erases clock-time in favour of the time of the erotic encounter. In some senses, then, pornotopia is always a virtual space. The fantasy spaces of *Savita Bhabhi* and *Velamma* are pornotopic to the extent that they insert the work of the libidinal imagination into the parallel space of the network. If, as Wendy Chun (2006, 83) reminds us, 'online pornography can be pervasive without being extensive' – that is, if they can reach vast audiences without necessarily being massive in scale – then online porn's non-material erotics can have actual social impact. What comes across both in the content of these adult toons and in their reception is the playing out of surreptitious pleasures of watching contraband material, or what Shohini Ghosh (2017) calls the 'dissident pleasures of pornography'.[5] Ghosh describes pornography as a 'phantasmatic arena [that] does not reflect people's "real" sex lives so much as it articulates the desires and aspirations for imagined ones'. In doing so, she places *Savita Bhabhi* as an extension of the sensuous bodies of women presented in mythological and historical comics such as *Amar Chitra Katha*, but without any of their monogamous, pious and heroic trappings.[6]

Our examination of *Savita Bhabhi* and *Velamma* oscillates between these various spaces – the representational space of the narratives, the formal space of the comic book, the spaces of circulation over the internet and the social spaces where debates over legality and morality are played out. In this we follow Susanna Paasonen's assertion that any investigation of pornography must account for 'how the images have been put together, what kinds of representational conventions have been used, and how these may have evolved and traveled from one medium to another' (2011, 258). In what follows, we examine *Savita Bhabhi* and *Velamma* both in terms of form and content to demonstrate how their images and texts speak to us, how they resonate and through what channels they travel and accumulate meaning. 'Meaning', as Paasonen (2011, 256) reminds us, 'is not a property of pornographic images, texts, or videos but is something that is made possible through specific material practices'.

In the region of the comic book: spatializing fantasy in *Savita Bhabhi* and *Velamma*

The lead protagonists in both *Savita Bhabhi* and *Velamma* are portrayed as well-endowed buxom figures. Fantasies of sexual plenitude crowd the panels, with the women taking charge of the situation. *Savita Bhabhi* and *Velamma* appeal to different variants of the 'married woman' sexual fantasy in India. Ethnic identity is prioritized, even fetishized in these comics through the use of linguistically specific suffixes to denote the status of their protagonists as married women – *'bhabhi'* meaning sister-in-law in Hindi, and *'amma'* being a common way of referring to a mature or married woman in Tamil. The instructions for artists and authors on the Kirtu.com submission portal emphasize that the comics must 'contain nudity, hardcore sex and at least one *central character of Indian ethnicity* who will be involved in sex' (emphasis added).[7] However, this idea of 'Indian ethnicity' remains nebulous.

In the initial discussions on *Savita Bhabhi*, one of the main ideas that the creators played with was the regional identity of Savita – whether she should be a young Gujarati woman or a South Indian Aunty (Khan 2013). The question was resolved when the creation team posted the query on a few discussion forums where the idea of the Gujarati woman won by popular vote. In *Savita Bhabhi* Episode 3, 'The Party', Savita's husband is introduced as 'Ashok Patel' and Savita is referred to as 'Mrs. Patel'.[8] In the character description for the *Savita Bhabhi* movie, she is again described as a 'young gujarati housewife who is very very attracted to one thing. Sex!'[9] Although this does mark her out as Gujarati, the reference to the surname is seen only in a few episodes and the Gujarati identity lurks in the background most of the time. There is little visual reference to specifically 'Gujarati' traits and a new reader of *Savita Bhabhi* might begin reading a later episode with no mention of the surname. The episodes are not sequential, there is no narrative flow between one episode and the other even though characters reappear. Thus, for a reader of a later episode, identification with the surname might not even be a factor. Even on the Kirtu.com website, the description of the comic reads 'Savita Bhabhi is an adult toon featuring explicit depictions of the sexual adventures of a housewife named Savita', making no reference to the surname.[10] In an interview with 'Savita Bhabhi' (where the creators speak in the persona of Savita), the response to the interviewer's question about her regional identity goes: 'I like to think of myself as a complete Indian woman, not necessarily from one part of India' (Shekhar 2009). Since the Hindi referent *'bhabhi'* could be located in any of India's Hindi-speaking states, Savita Bhabhi is not intrinsically connected to one specific region and thus the character remains translatable for the most part.

On the other hand, Velamma's depiction and the diegetic world of the comic is structured by 'South-Indian' references that situate it as some place in southern India. On the homepage for the official *Velamma* website, her description runs: 'Mrs Velamma Lakshmi, or Vela as her loved ones like to call her is a loving and innocent South Indian Aunty'.[11] Thus, while there is an effort to regionalize Velamma, the descriptor 'South Indian' could refer to any of the states in India's southern region that, despite linguistic differences, share a number of cultural traits. Also, the vocabulary in the comics is spattered with Hindi, as in the reference to *devar* (brother-in-law), *beta* (son) and so on, which are sporadically mixed in with the Tamil word *'amma'* (usually mother, but also any mature woman) or the Malayalam referent *'chechi'* (elder sister).

The issue of regionality is rendered more complex if one considers the fact that the creators of these comics are not located in India. Some reports indicate that *Savita Bhabhi* is published in 10 different languages with regional language translations also being solicited (Overdorf 2009). We have also come across translations of *Savita Bhabhi* in Bengali and of *Velamma* in Malayalam floating around on blogs and document-sharing sites. Such linguistic and cultural flexibility make *Savita Bhabhi* and *Velamma* a kind of a pan-Indian amalgamation of sexual fantasies related to boundary-crossing and clandestine pleasure. Regional markers become 'some place' in northern or southern India and are easily transposed to local contexts through textual translation. When translated into regional languages, *Savita Bhabhi* and *Velamma* become bearers of cultural verisimilitude. Thus, the comic book characters become malleable surfaces onto which specific fantasies can be projected.

We suggest that the form of the comic book and this linguistic/regional malleability go hand in hand. We draw on Scott McCloud's (1993, 20) definition of comics as 'juxtaposed pictorial and other images in deliberate sequence, intended to convey information and/or to produce an aesthetic response in the viewer'. Language in comic books appears as textual and graphic elements, but never in its auditory aspect. So, the 'spoken' nature of the language of comic book speech remains tethered to the imagination and subjectivity of the reader. While this may appear to be a constraint, it makes the comic book format much more open to translation. Unlike a dubbed film where the gap between the movement of the mouth and the uttered sound are not in sync, making the audiovisual experience awkward, the lack of any sonic element in the comic book makes the transposition of the fantasy element much smoother. In the comic book format, language is textual or graphic and the spoken sound of language is always a matter of the reader's imagination. Thus, the cultural translation of *Savita Bhabhi* and *Velamma* is a matter of replacing Hindi or English text in thought and speech bubbles with the script of another language.

The fact that *Savita Bhabhi* and *Velamma* feature drawn rather than 'live' action figures is central to the malleability of their fantasy space. Unlike live-action figures, the drawn figure is only limited by the imagination of the author or the illustrator. The Kirtu website recommends Scott McCloud's (1993) *Understanding Comics* to potential writers who may have story ideas but not be conversant in the language of comics, pointing out that the fantasies that are scripted have to adhere to a certain form and aesthetic style.[12] In an interview with the *Erotic Review*, Deshmukh states:

> Comics are a medium through which we can really allow our creativity to go unbridled [...] it is a unique medium in the context of Indian porn. We've had multimedia text messages, videos, stories: but no porn comic. Also a comic strip allows us to explore the fantasy in a much more vivid way than any other medium. (Khan 2013)

The comic book format allows for fantasy projection in *Savita Bhabhi* and *Velamma* in two ways. First, by rendering the object of desire as a two-dimensional surface, these comics remove references to 'real' bodies of flesh and blood. An argument could be made that printed pornographic images or moving images are also accessed as two-dimensional images; but in the case of live-action porn, the bodies on the screen always have a three-dimensional referent in the physical world. On the other hand, comic book characters such as Savita and Velamma only exist as two-dimensional surfaces. Whenever real-life associations can be drawn, this works through cultural referentiality and intertextual knowledge, instead of an indexical relationship between the drawn body and the real world. For instance, *Savita Bhabhi* Episode 10, 'Banungi Mai Miss India' ['I Will Be Miss India'], features a 'famous yesteryear's film star' named Jeet Kumar, which is a thinly-veiled visual reference to Bollywood superstar Amitabh Bachchan. In this case, the similarity of the character to Bachchan's character in the Hindi film *Kabhi Alvida Na Kehna* (2006) ruffled some feathers, such as, for instance, when the director Karan Johar alleged that the makers of *Savita Bhabhi* exploited the actor's look, over which the production house claimed complete rights (Durham and Sharma 2009).[13] However, these cultural references are pinned on peripheral or supporting characters, while Savita Bhabhi and Velamma themselves remain character types.

Second, since the drawn body is only limited by the artist/author's imagination, the comic book panel becomes a display surface. While explicit material is not alien to India's pornographic landscape, two of the most widely circulated variants of 'Indian pornography' – soft porn and amateur cellphone pornography – are marked by varying levels of invisibility or occlusion. While soft-porn films do show naked, copulating bodies, they work more through titillation and depictions of foreplay rather than genital display. On the other hand, while amateur cellphone pornography can show more explicit sexual acts, they are often marked by pixellation, blurry camera movement and bad lighting (Baishya 2017, 59). In both cases, the depiction of sexual intercourse is less visible than in industrially produced hardcore pornographic films. The comic book panel is a unique intervention in this landscape, as it allows for a graphic demonstration of the sex act as if to declare 'this is what penetration looks like'. Often, the copulating bodies in *Savita Bhabhi* and *Velamma* are placed in exaggerated physical postures to emphasize that the centre of the scene is the area of genital contact. As Deborah Shamoon (2004, 88) points out in the context of Japanese pornographic comics, 'drawings can show things that would not be visible on film, in particular vaginal penetration'. Sometimes full panels are filled with images of genitals only, not unlike close-up shots of genitals in hardcore pornography. However, while the motion-picture close-up is an optical function of the camera's lens, these full-frame comic panels are an imaginary projection of the mental image of penetration – here, the panels foreground themselves as surfaces to be read. Often, these panels are presented as sequences of twos and threes bound together by sonic text that simulates hardcore pornography's 'articulate and inarticulate sounds of pleasure [...] the slurp of fellatio and cunnilingus, the woosh of penetration [...] the clichés of "fuck me harder" and "I'm going to come"' (Williams 1999, 123). This simulation of hardcore pleasure renders pornographic comics such as *Savita Bhabhi* and *Velamma* as hypervisible surfaces that defy the censorial logic of occlusion. As we now see in the debates around the censorship of *Savita Bhabhi*, it is the medium of the comic book itself that becomes the site of struggle.

Censorship and *Savita Bhabhi*

Savita Bhabhi was created by a trio who used the pseudonyms Deshmukh, Dexter and Mad in March 2008 and hosted on the website Savitabhabhi.com. This has now been replaced by Kirtu.com, with the brand name 'Kirtu' also hosting other comics such as *Kinaara Lane* and *XXX Apartments*.[14] The original website also had a feedback section, a discussion board, a submission area for story ideas, a suggestion box, a fan club and live sex chat (Prema 2009). Thus, the Savita Bhabhi website created an interactive platform to connect the fans with the team. But, for all its novelty, *Savita Bhabhi* ran into trouble when the Indian government blocked the website under the instructions of the Department of Telecommunications of the Ministry of Communications and Technology in July 2009. This came up as a part of the amendments to the Information Technology Bill that authorized the Government of India to institute measures to censor electronic information, including the freedom to block any website without allowing a fair hearing to the aggrieved parties.[15] The moderators of the site, who were based in Europe, had no inkling of what was coming and were not informed before it was banned. The ban drew the ire of both fans and anti-censorship proponents. Deshmukh, one of the founders of the site, floated the 'Save Savita Project', calling it 'an attempt to give a voice to [...] SB fans' and a resistance against 'selective internet censorship'.[16] The website Savesavita.com also featured links to proxy and anonymizing tools and solicited guest submissions in the form of graphics and banners. Nishant Shah points out that this led to a kind of a distributed archiving practice that defied the law's containment drive. Shah writes that, 'instead of Savita Bhabhi disappearing from digital storage and public memory, multiple archives emerged across the peer-to-peer networks of the web' (2015, 23). Thus, the ban had the reverse effect of ensuring viral circulation and a more widely distributed presence. The Save Savita campaign was withdrawn when Deshmukh's real identity was revealed, but the campaign echoed some of the major concerns about internet censorship that were coming to the fore in India at the time.[17] The journalist Pritish Nandy (2009), for instance, wrote that with the ban on Savita Bhabhi, the 'I&B Ministry has demonstrated (yet again) how men want to control women all the time', while graphic novelist Sarnath Banerjee said that, with the ban, India had joined 'the elite club of China, Iran, North Korea and suchlike in the area of Internet censorship' (Sruthijith 2009).

Such responses also found resonance in a *Savita Bhabhi* animated film that was released in 2013. The film was marketed as India's first animated porn film and was set in a future version of India in 2070. The film was marketed with, among other things, a Vine that was described as 'India's first "tweaser"' (Chaturvedi 2013). The six-second looping Vine with its music, dialogue and scenes from the film was a way of marking out the convergent media landscape that *Savita Bhabhi* now occupied.[18] The promotional website for the film (where the film can also be downloaded for a fee) also featured content such as t-shirts for sale, free desktop backgrounds, posters and Facebook banners, and two 'interactive games', one of which allowed users to upload their photograph and get a composited image with Savita Bhabhi. The makers of the film clearly capitalized on the publicity that followed the banning of the website in India, and *Savita Bhabhi* became a kind of an icon that stood in for the censorship issue. The makers of the film promoted the film as 'a movie with a message – it's time Savita fought back against the people who banned her!'.[19]

Here, Savita Bhabhi herself emerges as a saviour figure who intervenes to save society from the Department of Telecommunication's newly devised Net Protection Act that clamps down on citizen's free speech. This fictional 'Net Protection Act' is a thinly-veiled reference to the actual censorship of *Savita Bhabhi*. The film begins with a youngster, Suraj, ranting against the government's censorship when he chances upon contraband material from the past (2000s) – *Savita Bhabhi* comics to be precise. We see Suraj in awe of what he sees as the opening credits begin. The credit sequence features actual panels from *Savita Bhabhi* comics that roll out as a series of moving screens, seen sometimes in a grid and at other times overlaid on top of each other. We zoom into the screens, focusing on scenes from *Savita Bhabhi* episodes. The dynamically moving panels are diegetically linked to the temporal world of Suraj's encounter with the *Savita Bhabhi* comics, but are also directly connected to the actual censorship of the *Savita Bhabhi* website. The movement of these panels across Suraj's computer screen connects the temporality of contemporary India and its censorship regulations to the fictional temporality of the censored world in the film.

In the film, Suraj and his friend Hari have devised a virtual reality simulator machine that can transport people to a different time period. But the machine malfunctions, dropping the naked Savita Bhabhi to the same temporality as that occupied by the two youngsters. In order to repair the machine that can allow Savita to return to her world, they need to get equipment that requires the Information Technology minister's biometric details. Savita Bhabhi is sent as a press reporter, and the minister ultimately ends up having a tryst with her, confirming her earlier suspicions that his censorship of sexual material arises from sexual frustration. She helps to expose the hypocrisy of the minister by filming their sex. The film concludes with Savita's return to her world after partaking in a task to support the 'greater good of mankind'. This image of Savita as a saviour figure is also seen in the comic books; for instance in 'Savita in Shimla' (Episode 11), where she helps to nab a *dacoit* (an armed robber) by luring him with her sexual charms.[20]

This idea of Savita as a saviour is also reflected in a rock song titled 'Savita Bhabhi'. Performed by the Mumbai-based band Shor Bazaar, the song features a fictional protagonist whose social class and lack of affluence make him unlucky with women. The lyrics of the bilingual song portray *Savita Bhabhi* as a site of relief and a leveller of class – a fantasy space where one can live the life of the characters in the comic book. This is also reflected in the film when Suraj and Hari are teleported into Savita's world, living out the lives of the comic book characters Tarun and Varun before the machine malfunctions, sending both of them back with Savita to their world. In one way, Suraj and Hari re-enact the sexual acts that are already scripted for them as comic book characters, encouraging a slippage between the idea of the reader and the character in the comic. This ability to transform into the 'hero of your favorite movie' through the endless possibilities offered by teleportation is premised on taking the place of someone who is already narratively placed in the diegetic space.[21] The dialogues in the film reiterate the '*Bhabhi*' image, with Savita referring to herself in the third person as '*Bhabhi*'. The temporal logic of teleportation in the film is echoed by Shor Bazaar's song where the lyrics run 'in such dire circumstances [...] its best to go online'.[22] While the song was certainly inspired by the comic book character, it was not commissioned by the creators. Nevertheless, the song ended up in the opening credits of the *Savita Bhabhi* animated film, marking the entire film as a kind of a meta-text about sexual freedom and resistance against censorship.

Interestingly, the logic of identification used in the film – of transforming into the 'hero of your favorite movie' – also cropped up in relation to the censorship issue. For instance, with the initial ban on *Savita Bhabhi*, one of the allegations was that comics are 'a more participative medium [where a reader] imagines himself as the character' and, as one critic of the comic book suggested, this kind of participatory reading would even allow a young child to 'see a Savitabhabhi among his relatives' (Sruthijith 2009). Elsewhere, Deshmukh (2011) has responded to this line of criticism by writing: 'To say that Savita Bhabhi would inspire married women to become promiscuous is like saying Batman would inspire rich men to become nocturnal, cape-wearing vigilantes.' Thus, the debate over the censorship of *Savita Bhabhi* was also a debate about the medium of the comic book and its possibilities as a 'phantasmatic arena' (Ghosh 2017). As we pointed out earlier, the phantasmatic arena is slightly different in the case of the two comics. While both of them share similar comic styles, there is a stark difference in the fantasies of the female body associated with them. In the next section, we explore how the body politics of *Velamma* differ from those of *Savita Bhabhi* and what these different imaginations allow the comics to do.

Body aesthetics: *Velamma* versus *Savita Bhabhi*

Unlike the hourglass figure depicted in *Savita Bhabhi*, Velamma's figure is depicted with its folds of fat intact. Her bodily contour reflects a sense of everydayness and gives her the impression of a next-door neighbour. Layers of flesh and prominently drawn trails of curly pubic hair give Velamma a look that is distinct from Savita Bhabhi's air-brushed, model-like appearance. For instance, in *Savita Bhabhi* Episode 10, the entire fantasy revolves around the fact that she possesses an impeccable figure that allows her to take part in a fictional beauty contest. The title of the episode 'Banungi Mai Miss India' ['I will be Miss India'] reflects the world of conspicuous consumption that Savita inhabits. In the Indian context, Radhika Parameswaran (2005, 421) sees the figure of the beauty queen and its mass media projection as the 'ideal professional worker of a global economy', while Susan Dewey (2008, 205) connects the Miss India pageant to the 'postliberalization creation of a vastly expanded consumer culture in a new market economy'. Sanjay Srivastava's (2013, 251) description of Savita Bhabhi posits that, despite her marital markers such as the *mangal sutra* (traditional Hindu wedding necklace), she is 'an active subject of consumerism'. Savita is often depicted in outside spaces or white-collar workplaces that posit her as a subject of the neoliberal economy where work and pleasure intermesh. Thus, the easy association of Savita Bhabhi with 'Miss India' points out a certain representational aesthetic that draws on her mooring in consumer culture, as well as a certain bodily aesthetic that prioritizes the fetish of the perfect body.

While Velamma's world is also one of disposable income and she is also clearly depicted in middle-class moorings, her body does not conform to this aesthetic. Thus, Savita and Velamma's different body types also depict two different visions of the urban Indian woman – one is mobile, outgoing and willing to partake in the pleasures of neoliberal capitalism, while the other is the epitome of middle-class traditionalism that is rooted in the family. While both characters are located within the spaces of the domestic, Savita's choice of entry into public space and mobility situates her within a certain sense of privilege. In contrast, Velamma is someone who takes up domestic chores and plays the ideal host, whether it is to host her friend's son or to make compromises for the sake of keeping the family together. Savita's sexual escapades are always marked by a sense of her control and the fantasies of sexual boundary-crossing are regulated by her autonomy. For Savita, home and tradition do exist, but as something to return to once the deed is done; even when Savita is shown having sex with different men, we sometimes see her wedding photograph in the background, a clear indication that she chooses to engage in the act despite her marriage. But Velamma's urge to keep the familial and domestic space in order is what leads her into being an unwilling sexual partner in many instances. Unlike Savita, Velamma constantly seeks assurance from her male partners that no one should ever know what has transpired between them.

Velamma's visual depiction corresponds to the trope of the 'Aunty' figure who is sexually available for initiating young men into the pleasures of lovemaking. This was part of earlier traditions of pornographic representation as well; erotic fiction and soft-porn films exploited this generic feature and have been popularly described as 'Aunty films' (Mini 2016, 142).[23]

Bhaskar Mukhopadhyay (2012, 147) points out that the '"Aunty" is clearly an Indian innovation and the metropolitan categories ("BBW," "MILF," "chubby," "mature" etc.) do not quite correspond to the vernacular "aunty"'. Mukhopadhyay sees the 'aunty' as a generic category that encompasses other categorizations such as the sister-in-law (*bhabhi*), the elder sister, the housewife or the maid. This is true to some extent as the categories of '*bhabhi*' and 'aunty' often have the imagination of similar social and body types – 'the flab and flesh of the maternal figure', as Mukhopadhyay (2012, 147) puts it. But the figure of Savita Bhabhi diverges from this fetish for the maternal female body, despite the suffix '*bhabhi*'. On the other hand, Velamma plays into this stereotype of 'flab and flesh' and accommodates a more deeply entrenched imagination of the married woman who is concerned with the transgression of the maternal boundary, if not always the marital one. While both *Savita Bhabhi* and *Velamma* are depictions of non-normative social orientations, they play into different imaginations of class and mobility that are also reflected through the design of their two-dimensional bodies.

Hardcore, beyond the lines

What, then, is the appeal of erotic comics such as *Savita Bhabhi* and *Velamma*? Clearly, although their storylines are fuelled by earlier entrenched fantasies of taboo and boundary-crossing, their visual aesthetic is clearly non-indexical. These are not still photographs or moving images that have a direct referential relationship to any living, identifiable person. Following Susanna Paasonen (2011, 16), we suggest that *Savita Bhabhi* and *Velamma* are manifestations of a carnal resonance in the imagination of Indian online pornography. Paasonen (2011, 17) defines carnal resonance as both the affective power of pornography – 'its visceral appeal and power to disturb' – as well as the 'connections and movement between porn and its audiences that are always imprinted and marked by contexts and technologies of production, distribution, and circulation'. Comics such as *Savita Bhabhi* and *Velamma* are essentially translations. They translate sexual imaginations, taboos and desires into consumable texts that can be distributed and exchanged. At the same time, they themselves remain translatable both in terms of their own variations as well as derivations. Take, for instance, the issue of sonic presence in *Savita Bhabhi*'s intra-textual world, or the Savita Bhabhi 'universe' that is shared by the various comic book episodes, crossover issues and the film. The *Savita Bhabhi* comics do not have any sound elements, but there are voice-actors in the animated film. The website for the *Savita Bhabhi* movie features a 'Characters' section in which the characters in the film are introduced textually, visually and sonically.[24] The section features a thumbnail image, a blurb and a brief sound clip from the movie that attaches a voice to the figure. The change of medium necessitates a sonic voice that replaces the way that readers might imagine the voice in the comic book.

If the intra-textual is one arena of translation, another can be seen in derivative forms that borrow from the *Savita Bhabhi* and *Velamma* imaginaries. On porn-aggregator websites such as Xvideos, Xhamster, Xnxx and PornHub, the search terms 'Savita Bhabhi' and 'Velamma' lead to sequential videos of the comic book pages and live-action porn. In most cases, these are amateur videos that are tagged with the keywords 'Savita Bhabhi' and 'Velamma', inserting the comic book imaginary into an existing economy of sexual fetishes. However, there are also stand-alone websites that cater to specifically live-action versions of the Savita Bhabhi and Velamma fetishes. For instance, the website Velammabhabhi.com features a masked, live-action porn performer who plays the role of Velamma. This 'live' Velamma is described on the homepage of the website as 'a big tits south Indian MILF [...] with a plump body', playing into the 'flab and flesh' imaginary that Mukhopadhyay describes.[25] On another website, MySexySavita, a similar representational strategy is used to present another masked porn performer. Unlike the earlier website where the association with the *Velamma* comics is through the name only, MySexySavita goes on to declare that it is the 'home of Savita Bhabhi Indian cartoon character [that] turns into reality' and videos within the website also feature her 'husband' Ashok.[26] The videos on the two websites are typical of low-budget porn and have almost no relationship to the *Velamma* or *Savita Bhabhi* stories, but draw directly from the popularity of the series. Both are pay-sites (although their content floats around on porn aggregator sites) and are owned and operated by the Cyprus-based company Yellowplum that describes itself as a 'global leader in adult entertainment, consulting, technology and billing solutions'.[27] No other information about the two websites is available, but the nomenclature of the '*bhabhi*' figure and the use of the names 'Velamma' and 'Savita Bhabhi' displays a translation of the two-dimensional comic book imaginary into a live-action form that becomes monetized in the exchange economy of the web. Here, the 'carnal resonance' of Savita Bhabhi and Velamma is both a factor of what imaginaries the comic books play with as well as the fantasies and systems of exchange and circulation that they foster. The immaterial bodies of Savita and Velamma are given shape and form by actual human bodies that reflect their potentialities.

In this sense, *Savita Bhabhi* and *Velamma* are sticky objects – they are texts that absorb the peaks and falls of sexual cultures in India and, at the same time, new formulations and articulations of sexual expression also attach themselves to them. Boundary-crossing in these comics, to use a pun, is an orgiastic assemblage of the pulse of contemporary Indian society. As Eva Illouz writes, 'Literature – good or bad – puts into form what is often at the level of inarticulate social experience' (2014, 21). If *Savita Bhabhi* and *Velamma* resonate with contemporary readers of sexual fiction, it is only because the depictions of hardcore sex and transgression in these comics are expressions of anxieties about new arrangements of family, class and tradition. To take a cue from Illouz (2014, 23), *Savita Bhabhi* and *Velamma* resonate with their readers because they articulate 'a social experience that is baffling, that presents itself as a repeated cognitive and emotional challenge'. If morality and law respond to changing social arrangements by delimiting the sexual within the realm of the obscene and the illegal, *Savita Bhabhi* and *Velamma* explore these arrangements by stretching them to their most extreme libidinal limits.

Notes

1. We would like to thank N. Trace Cabot for allowing us to refer to our casual conversation on the topic.
2. While we use the term 'comic book' throughout the article, we are aware that the term is a bit of a misnomer. These comics exist as digital files that are not physically printed books. So, the term comic book is meant to point towards a certain arrangement of text and images that replicates the structure of the printed comic book without sharing its materiality.

3. We use the term non-space here to denote the impossibility of locating cyberspace as geographical space. Although the internet can be regulated through techniques such as geo-blocking, this is not the same as marking out boundaries on a map or fencing around a house. For instance, when websites hosted by servers in one location are accessed in another, the 'site' becomes a two-way mirror that connects the space of the user to the space of the server. Although disrupting the server would disrupt access in the other location, at the moment of access the website becomes a fluid space that allows interaction between the user and the server.
4. The Indian Information Technology (Amendment Act) came into force in 2008. While the 'Information Technology Act 2000' (2000) had only one provision – clause 67 pertaining to the 'Publishing of information which is obscene in electronic form' – the 'Information Technology (Amendment) Act 2008' (2016) expanded upon it by including two separate clauses – 67A and 67B. While 67A was a separate clause for 'publishing or transmitting of material containing sexually explicit act, etc. in electronic form' (the 2000 Act had no separate clause), 67B dealt with 'material depicting children in sexually explicit act, etc. in electronic form'. Section 67 warrants punishment of five-year imprisonment and a fine of Rs.10 Lakhs (US$1573 approximately) for publishing any electronic material that contains sexually explicit acts. Section 69 A (1) bestows the Controller of Certifying Authorities, with the power to intercept, monitor and decrypt material transmitted, received or stored in the interest of nation's sovereignty and public order or for preventing incitement to the commission of cognizable offence.
5. 'The Dissident Pleasures of Pornography' is the title of Gosh's reprinted article in *Himal South Asian*. The original article was titled 'The Pleasures and Politics of Pornography' and was published in *Himal Southasian,* September 2009.
6. We must mention here that the representational politics of *Savita Bhabhi* and *Velamma* are slightly different, as Velamma's illustrations are reminiscent of the buxom figures of Malayalam soft-porn stars such as Shakeela.
7. For the full list of instructions, see 'Artist Submission'. See also 'Author Submission' in the 'Submissions' section on the Kirtu website. Accessed 12 November 2017. https://www.kirtu.com/submissions/
8. Patel is a prominent Gujarati surname.
9. The character description for Savita Bhabhi and the other characters can be found on the official website for the film. Accessed 29 November 2017. http://www.savitabhabhimovie.com/category/characters/
10. See the homepage for the Kirtu website. Accessed 10 October 2017. https://www.kirtu.com/
11. Like the Savita Bhabhi message, this welcome message also appears on the homepage for Velamma comics. Accessed 10 October 2017. https://www.velamma.com/
12. See 'Writer Submission' (n.d.) on the *Kirtu* website for more details. Accessed 12 November 2017. https://www.kirtu.com/writers-submission/
13. This is ironic if one considers that one of the final instructions given to potential authors on the Kirtu website forbids the submission of 'stories containing celebrities or characters and settings' that the writers do not themselves have proprietary rights over. Accessed 12 November 2017. https://www.kirtu.com/writers-submission/
14. Accessed 10 December 2017. https://www.kirtu.com/all-kirtu-series/
15. See endnote 4.
16. The original website for the Save Savita campaign is no longer accessible. Archived webpages can be accessed via the Internet Archive's Wayback Machine. Accessed 2 January 2018. https://web.archive.org/web/20090627223958/http://www.savesavita.com:80/
17. The original press release can be found archived on a webpage snapshot by the Internet Archive's Wayback Machine, where Deshmukh writes: 'Unfortunately, due to personal and family issues arising from my going public last week, I am forced to take this decision. I will be taking down all links and posts subsequent to releasing this statement. I apologize for any inconvenience caused to bloggers/tweeters that are linking to the content on the Save Savita website' (Deshmukh 2009).
18. Savita Movie (2013). Accessed 16 December 2017. https://vine.co/v/bPWBUiUHmtu/.

19. The complete article can be accessed on the website for the *Savita Bhabhi* movie in a section titled 'Why We Made the Movie?' (Deshmukh 2016). The article also mentions 6 December 2017 as the exact date when the idea for the *Savita Bhabhi* comics emerged. Accessed 8 November 2017. http://www.savitabhabhimovie.com/the-story/why-we-made-the-movie/
20. The idea for the episode 'Savita in Shimla' was contributed by a guest author, Sumit Kumar. Kumar is a comic book author who later came to prominence with his autobiographical work *An Itch You Can't Scratch* (2011). Although uncredited in the episode, he started his writing with *Savita Bhabhi*. The idea that he pitched about Savita Bhabhi in Afghanistan trying to lure Osama bin Laden on behalf of America was fine-tuned to Savita's attempt to nab a *dacoit* (Biswas 2016).
21. The original dialogues are in Hindi, but these are the words used in the English subtitles for the film. When Hari explains how his virtual reality simulator works, he tells Suraj: 'You can be the hero of your favorite movie […] The possibilities are endless.'
22. The exact lines we refer to are in Hindi. The original lines are: 'Aise in halaat mein, Majboori ke saath mein, Best to go online … Leke apne haath mein.' Full lyrics can be found on Shor Bazaar's website. The Doc (2009). Accessed 21 December 2017. http://bazaarshor.blogspot.com/2009/07/savita-bhabhi-lyrics.html
23. For instance, the storylines of many Malayalam soft-porn films feature an 'aunty' protagonist and when clips from earlier Malayalam soft-porn films find their way into the internet they are often tagged as 'Mallu Aunty Films'. Thus, the imagination of the sexually experienced and mature 'aunty' is an integral feature of India's pornoscape.
24. Accessed 29 November 2017. http://www.savitabhabhimovie.com/category/characters/
25. This description appears on the homepage for the Velammabhabhi website. 'VELAMMA BHABHI' (n.d.). Accessed 3 January 2018. http://velammabhabhi.com/
26. The description appears on the homepage for MySexySavita. Accessed 3 January 2018. http://mysexysavita.com/
27. See the 'About Us' page on the Yellowplum website. Accessed 3 January 2018. http://www.yellowplum.org/aboutus.html

Disclosure statement

No potential conflict of interest was reported by the authors.

References

@kirtuepisodes. 2016. 'http://goo.gl/tTfDiQ Velamma Episode 10: The Loving Wife.' *Twitter*. June 1. https://twitter.com/kirtuepisodes/status/737931512973139968.

@SavitaMovie. 2013. 'Do you want this 2 happen 2 u just 4 Choosing Adult Entertainment?!' *Twitter*. April 16. https://twitter.com/SavitaMovie/status/324403780739272704.

'About us.' *Yellowplum*. Accessed December 29, 2017. http://www.yellowplum.org/aboutus.html

Ahmed, Sara. 2014. *The Cultural Politics of Emotion*. 2nd ed. Edinburgh: Edinburgh University Press.

'All Kirtu Series.' *Kirtu*. Accessed November 19 2017. https://www.kirtu.com/all-kirtu-series/

Altman, Rick. 1996. 'Cinema and Genre.' In *The Oxford History of World Cinema*, edited by Geoffrey Nowell-Smith, 276–321. Oxford: Oxford University Press.

'Artist Submission.'*Kirtu*. Accessed November 19 2017. https://www.kirtu.com/artists-submission/

Baishya, Anirban K. 2017. 'Pornography of Place: Location, Leaks and Obscenity in the Indian MMS Porn Video.' *South Asian Popular Culture* 15 (1): 57–71.

Barman, Rini. 2015. 'Why Porn Ban won't Stop a Savita Bhabhi from Fulfilling India's Sexual Desires.' *Daily O*. Accessed December 22 2017. https://www.dailyo.in/politics/porn-ban-kamlesh-vaswani-porntoons-magazines-freedom-of-expression/story/1/5471.html.

Biswas, Sreejita. 2016. 'From Naughty to Naxalbari.' *Bangalore Mirror*. Accessed November 19 2017. http://bangaloremirror.indiatimes.com/columns/sunday-read/from-naughty-to-naxalbari/amp_articleshow/50607179.cms.

'Characters.' *Savita Bhabhi Movie*. Accessed January 3 2018. http://www.savitabhabhimovie.com/category/characters/

Chaturvedi, Vinita. 2013. 'India's first Tweaser for Savita Bhabhi.' *The Times of India*. Accessed November 19 2017. https://timesofindia.indiatimes.com/entertainment/hindi/bollywood/news/Indias-first-Tweaser-for-Savita-Bhabhi/articleshow/19725657.cms.

Chun, Wendy Hui Kyong. 2006. *Control and Freedom: Power and Paranoia in the Age of Fiber Optics*. Cambridge: MIT Press.

Deshmukh. 2009. 'The Save Savita project closed down.' *The Save Savita Project*. (*Internet Archive*, 2010). Accessed December 17 2016. https://web.archive.org/web/20100124202922/http://www.savesavita.com:80/.

Deshmukh. 2011. 'Indian Women are on the Road to Sexual Liberation.' *India Today*. Accessed November 19 2017. https://www.indiatoday.in/magazine/cover-story/story/20111205-savita-bhabhi-safe-sex-aspects-of-sex-749788-2011-11-24.

Deshmukh, dir. 2013. *Savita Bhabhi Movie*. India.

Deshmukh, 2016. 'Why we Made the Movie?' *Savita Bhabhi Movie*. Accessed December 6 2016. http://www.savitabhabhimovie.com/the-story/why-we-made-the-movie/.

Dewey, Susan. 2008. *Making Miss India Miss World: Constructing Gender, Power, and the Nation in Postliberalization India*. Syracuse: Syracuse University Press.

Durham, Bryan, and Amul Sharma. 2009. 'KJo Wants to Check Out Savita Bhabhi.' *Mid-day*. Accessed November 19 2017. https://www.mid-day.com/articles/kjo-wants-to-check-out-savita-bhabhi/39197.

Ghosh, Shohini. 2017. 'The Dissident Pleasures of Pornography.' *Himal Southasian*. Accessed December 15 2017. http://himalmag.com/the-dissident-pleasures-of-pornography/.

Illouz, Eva. 2014. *Hard-Core Romance: Fifty Shades of Grey Best-Sellers and Society*. Chicago and London: The University of Chicago Press.

Johar, Karan, dir. 2006. *Kabhi Alvida Naa Kehna*. India.

Khan, Divya. 2013. 'India's First Porn Star: An Interview with the Creator.' *Erotic Review*. Accessed November 14 2017. http://eroticreviewmagazine.com/articles/indias-first-porn-star-an-interview-with-the-creator/.

Marcus, Steven. 2017. *The Other Victorians: A Study of Sexuality in Mid-Nineteenth-Century England*. London and New York: Routledge.

McCloud, Scott. 1993. *Understanding Comics: The Invisible Art*. New York: Harper Perennial.

Methil, Renuka. 2002. 'Cinema, Shakeela Khan: Southern Comfort.' *India Today*. February 11, 65.

Mini, Darshana Sreedhar. 2016. 'The Spectral Duration of Malayalam Soft-porn: Disappearance, Desire, and Haunting.' *BioScope* 7 (2): 127–150.

Ministry of Electronics and Information Technology. 2016. IT (Amendment) Act 2008. Ministry of Electronics and Information Technology. Accessed October 28 2017. http://www.meity.gov.in/writereaddata/files/it_amendment_act2008%20%281%29_0.pdf.

Mukhopadhyay, Bhaskar. 2012. *The Rumor of Globalization: Desecrating the Global From Vernacular Margins*. New York: Columbia University Press.

'My Sexy Savita: 100% Real Bhabhi.' *MySexySavita*. Accessed January 2 2018. http://mysexysavita.com.

Nandy, Pritish. 2009. 'The Assassination of Savita Bhabhi.' *The Times of India*. Accessed November 19 2017. https://blogs.timesofindia.indiatimes.com/extraordinaryissue/the-assassination-of-savita-bhabhi/.

Overdorf, Jason. 2009. 'Meet India's First Porn Star.' *Public Radio International*. Accessed November 19 2017. https://www.pri.org/stories/2009-05-04/meet-indias-first-porn-star.

Paasonen, Susanna. 2011. *Carnal Resonance: Affect and Online Pornography*. Cambridge: MIT Press.

Parameswaran, Radhika. 2005. 'Global Beauty Queens in Post-Liberalization India.' *Peace Review: A Journal of Social Justice* 17 (4): 419–426.

Prema, K. 'Savita Bhabhi Reloaded,' *The Hindustan Times*, December 28 2009.

Savita Movie. 2013. 'Savita Bhabhi Movie Teaser.' Vine. Accessed January 13 2017. https://vine.co/v/bPWBUiUHmtu/.

Shah, Nishant. 2015. 'Of Heathens, Perverts and Stalkers: The Imagined Learner in MOOCS.' In *The Europa World of Learning*, edited by Europa Publications, 21–25. London: Routledge.

Shamoon, Deborah. 2004. 'Office Sluts and Rebel Flowers: The Pleasures of Japanese Pornographic Comics for Women.' In *Porn Studies*, edited by Linda Williams, 77–103. Durham and London: Duke University Press.

Shekhar, Shashank. 2009. 'I'll Come on Film: Savita Bhabhi.' *Mid-day*. Accessed November 14 2017. https://www.mid-day.com/articles/i-ll-come-on-film-savita-bhabhi/34594.

Srivastava, Sanjay. 2013. 'Street, Footpath, Gated Community: On the Cultures of Indian Pornography.' In *Sexuality Studies*, edited by Sanjay Srivastava, 228–253. New Delhi: Oxford University Press.

Sruthijith, K. K. 2009. 'Govt bans popular toon site.' *The Hindustan Times*. Accessed November 19 2017 https://www.hindustantimes.com/entertainment/govt-bans-popular-toon-porn-site/story-M7UO7XgStS9Cfrvfziok6J.html.

Swarup, Shubhangi. 2009. 'The Secret King of Indian Porn.' *Open Magazine*. Accessed November 19 2017. http://www.openthemagazine.com/article/art-culture/the-secret-king-of-indian-porn.

The Doc. 2009. '"Savita Bhabhi" Lyrics.' Accessed November 24 2017. http://bazaarshor.blogspot.com/2009/07/savita-bhabhi-lyrics.html.

'The Information Technology Act 2000.' 2000. Accessed August 1 2018. http://www.wipo.int/edocs/lexdocs/laws/en/in/in024en.pdf.

'The Information Technology (Amendment) Act, 2008.' 2008. http://www.eprocurement.gov.in/news/Act2008.pdf

'VELAMMA BHABHI.' n.d. *Velammabhabhi*. Accessed November 19 2017. http://velammabhabhi.com.

Williams, Linda. 1999. *Hard Core: Power, Pleasure and 'Frenzy of the Visible'*. Berkeley: University of California Press.

'Writers Submission.' n.d. *Kirtu*. Accessed November 19 2017. https://www.kirtu.com/writers-submission/

OPEN ACCESS

Capitalizing on desire: (re)producing and consuming class in Indian 'gay' pornography

Michiel Baas

ABSTRACT

This article investigates the emerging popularity of same-sex pornographic content in India featuring fitness trainers and bodybuilders. The article argues that its production and consumption is governed by socio-economic difference that is revealing for the resilience of (middle-)class boundaries. Drawing on long-term ethnographic research, the analysis is complemented by engaging with informants' social media updates and the un/intentionality of their homoerotic layering. By focusing on the trajectory of one trainer who now provides escort services and features in pornographic movies, the article shows that such productions need to be understood as amalgamated with and indivisible from non-pornographic content depicting near-naked muscular men. It treats homoerotically suggestive social media updates, YouTube productions that warn men against the pitfalls of male modelling and the risk of sexual abuse and exploitation, and actual same-sex 'porn' as existing within a shared continuum through which we can understand different productions of desire and desirability.

Introduction

Before boarding his flight, Selvam[1] had texted me that he expected traffic from Chennai airport to be unpredictable and that he might be late for our appointment at TGI Fridays in the suburb of Teynampet. As a heterosexual gay-for-pay actor and model, Selvam makes money out of porn work (Lee and Sullivan 2016). He supplements this with performing as a go-go dancer at gay parties and providing various sexual services on an escort basis. Having just finished a pornographic videoshoot in Mumbai, he had planned to go home and freshen up first. Usually in firm control of all logistics, for this shoot he was collaborating with a third party and had not been altogether sure of the facilities beforehand. Somewhat relieved, he had texted me that the shoot had taken place in a five-star hotel room and he had been able to take a shower afterwards.

Dressed in a loose-fitting red Adidas track suit, his muscular build still manages to stand out as we make our way inside, security guards sizing him up and patrons briefly resting their gaze on him. Considering his looks and physique, I had once asked whether he had ever considered a career in Kollywood – Tamil Nadu's film industry named after the suburb of Kodambakkam – a suggestion which he found flattering although ludicrous, considering his lack in terms of connections and socio-economic background. 'It's not a system based on talent. Or not purely on talent', he explained. Surely I had noticed the number of sons and cousins of actors who also featured in the movies? Considering the small town he had grown up in located on the outskirts of the Greater Chennai region and his impoverished family, he felt that he had to live with the chances he had been meted out on the day he was born. It partly explained why he was now making money out of porn and sex work, but it was not the entire story. Bluntly he had put it as follows: 'What's the point of having a hot body if you cannot enjoy or make others enjoy … It's not going to be a museum piece'. It was definitely a more outspoken view than I had encountered in the near-decade I had spent conducting anthropological research among Indian fitness trainers and bodybuilders. Sharing my surprise, he had responded 'it's all in your mind … for me I just think someone is enjoying my body'.

After having come across Selvam's erotically suggestive social media updates a year earlier – posing in tiny swimwear and using banana and eggplant emoticons to get his message across – I had approached him with the idea of including his life-story in a chapter for a book I was working on at the time. This book – *Muscular India: Masculinity, Mobility and the New Middle Class* (Baas 2020) – which has since come out, takes as a point of departure the popularity of the lean, muscular bodily ideal and the emerging profession of fitness or personal trainer in urban India. It investigates the possibilities for upward socio-economic mobility for men of lower middle-class backgrounds who have received most of their education in a vernacular language. This new middle class contrasts with an older 'upper' middle class who tend to take the position of custodians of socio-cultural capital in Indian society and who are educated in English (Van Wessel 2004; Fernandes 2006; Brosius 2010; Baviskar and Ray 2015; Srivastava 2015).[2] Drawing upon theorization by Bourdieu (1977, 1984) and Wacquant (2001), *Muscular India* argues that, to a certain degree, bodily capital can substitute a lack in social and cultural capital otherwise, although this is contextually bound by the gym itself. Even if this bodily capital equates a muscularity and vascularity popularized by Bollywood actors and is framed as (sexually) attractive to the opposite sex in popular media, my interactions with trainers and bodybuilders suggested that this was rarely enacted upon. Selvam was a notable exception here. Over time he had shared snippets of his life with me via WhatsApp and Messenger, because of which I had been able to sketch a fragmented picture of his trajectory from 'fitness work' to porn and sex work. Meeting him that evening at TGI Fridays was the last opportunity I had to fill the holes in his life story as he had shared it with me so far. While *Muscular India* is mainly interested in Selvam's life-course trajectory, what I seek to interrogate in this article instead is my quest for completion itself. With reference to Selvam's case, what I mean by this is that initially my interest in his life story mainly revolved around developing an understanding of what had led him to transition from personal training to capitalizing on his erotic and sexual potential and catering to an all-male clientele. However, I gradually came to realize that inevitable to such an approach is the elusive idea of arriving at a 'complete' understanding of such a transition, which therefore relies on clearly predetermined and opposing start and end points; from fitness/personal trainer to porn and sex worker. Instead, I found that if we want to understand what might motivate a trainer to become involved in sex and porn work, it makes more sense to treat these fields as forming part of the same continuum[3] in which the body is already layered with multiple and often incongruous notions of what makes it (sexually) attractive. To explore this in greater detail, I will examine how the muscular male body is interpreted and consumed along socio-economic/class lines. For this, it is crucial to better appreciate how this body is 'narrated' in popular Indian movies, what it is associated with in lifestyle magazines such as the Indian edition of *Men's Health*, and the way trainers and bodybuilders themselves use hashtags to communicate various ideas and possibilities about their bodies.

This article draws upon a decade-long research involvement through participant observation among and semi-structured interviews with male trainers, bodybuilders and others involved in India's burgeoning fitness and health industry. In particular, the article focuses on Selvam and two other men he regularly collaborates with for explicit photoshoots and videoshoots. Their experiences will be brought into dialogue with the ostensive homoerotic layering of the social media updates of informants who are not involved in porn or sex work. These social media updates rarely intentionally or explicitly reach out to a possible gay fanbase. Yet the way such updates get interpreted by and shared among men interested in same-sex contact points to entrenched notions of socio-economic difference. My Indian gay friends' experiences with and fantasies about the availability of my informants for sexual services underline this. Investigating the production and consumption of porn within this broader context allows us to build a nuanced understanding of its emergence in India and what it signifies. It paves the way to discuss porn (and sex) work in a way that relies less on 'extreme positions' (for instance, seeing Selvam as an outlier in terms of the transition he has made) and more as part of a momentum that knows manifold but not hierarchically sorted dimensions in terms of acceptability or commonality.

Gay for pay and desire

Before coming to Chennai, I had discussed Selvam's case with a gay friend[4] from Delhi. Even if I had not shared Selvam's actual name, my friend instantly guessed who I was meeting. Without further ado, he had opened a folder on his laptop which contained numerous pornographic clips, some featuring Selvam seductively gazing into the camera and showing off his body, while in others he was involved in oral and anal intercourse with similarly muscular men. The research project I was involved in focused primarily on questions of upward socio-economic mobility and therefore I saw no use for the actual videos, declining the offer to copy them onto my laptop. In my interactions with Selvam I had always emphasized that my interest in him and his work was strictly professional. Conducting research among men whose bodies approximate an ideal type among gay men, I had often found myself confronted by my own gaze. What precisely was I seeing when I encountered these men in the gym, meeting them for coffee at Starbucks or observing them perform on stage at a bodybuilding competition? At first glance, Selvam's case contrasted markedly with that of other trainers and bodybuilders whose life-course trajectories I had mapped. Sex and sexual desire seemed explicitly and decidedly absent from their lives. A girlfriend, I was repeatedly told, would just get in the way of workout routines, while a wife would make following through on rigorous diets extremely complicated.[5] There were some who had explored sexual liaisons with female clients but not only was this a no-no for the gyms that employed them, it almost always seemed to end badly.[6] At the same time, these men's social media updates indicated an awareness of the erotic qualities of their bodies. Flexing their muscles while capturing themselves in the mirror or having asked a buddy to snap a picture, social media uploads were frequently embellished with hashtags such as #sexybeast, #hunk, #hotboy and #humpday.

Almost all of the men I interacted with and interviewed over the years identified as heterosexual, which contrasted with the explicit homoerotically saturated photoshoots they engaged in. Asked about these, informants would hold that such photoshoots were merely an opportunity to showcase what they had achieved in terms of bodily transformation. The suggestion that the audience's gaze at a bodybuilding competition might venture beyond an appreciation of the physical dimensions on display was ardently dismissed. If it had occurred to them at all, they vowed that their focus was determinedly on their posing, making sure that the jury got to see the best of their muscularity and vascularity. In contrast, the explicit comments that social media posts generated did confirm that there was a rather blatant sexual dimension to their followers' appreciation. Could not the same be argued about the applause, cheering and whistling their bodies received while on stage? As with my quest for 'completion' in terms of Selvam's life-course trajectory, I came to realize that these questions rested too firmly and too narrowly on the idea of difference informed by my interaction with gay friends who themselves belonged to the English-speaking upper middle class, and thus a very different stratum of society than most of my informants. Often these friends had mocked me, suggesting that rather unscrupulously I had found the perfect research project to involve myself in. Probing me for gossip about the sexual availability of my informants, I was assured that 'such men' were 'easily to be had'. In the context of Delhi, Jat men[7] were always in for it, 'not even necessarily for money', as a Delhi friend had put it. Having resided in Bangalore as well, he assured me that his experiences with Malayali men compared favourably as well. Well hung, physically strong and muscular, he swore that 'they are quite the meat eaters', a double-entendre he assumed I would understand for all its intent and purposes. Most importantly, 'they' were not particularly perturbed by same-sex contact. As another gay friend had confided in me: 'It doesn't mean much to them ... They don't think of it as an issue'.

Speaking of porn, sex and attraction

In an editorial to *Porn Studies*, Attwood, Maina, and Smith (2018) suggest that even if there is ongoing incitement to speak about sex, the way we approach the topic of sexual issues is strongly policed. A scholarly approach offers some legitimacy but, as the editors' note, it remains a problematic area of study to strike a proper attitude (2018, 1). This is complicated by the persistence of anti/pro voices that not only divide the audience but also infer that pornography requires a standpoint that exists in stark opposition to another; it either judges or responds to judgement. Whereas academic work offers an alternative to this kind of rhetoric with its emphasis on objectivity, '[t]he detailed examination of the texts, images and fantasies of sex may feel dangerously close to self-revelation ... ' (2018, 1). It is therefore not surprising that research into pornography and porn work continues to be met with suspicion, disdain and hostility, even facing explicit rejection as a valid field of study (2018, 2 drawing on Gabriel 2017, 308).

In a crucial contribution to *Porn Studies*, Nathaniel Burke (2014) discusses a researcher's positionality vis-à-vis pornography when it is the object of one's study. Noting how one's position has a bearing on the final written product, he found that the relationship between his writing and the people he studied put him in a complicated spot (2014, 71). As a feminist, he felt it necessary to address gender and sexual inequality in the way they are constituted in the product of a gay adult film through hiring and directing processes (2014, 71). However, he also realized that his research questions with respect to this could be understood to render porn workers as complicit in the kind of inequalities he was seeking to highlight (2014, 71). Considering the already stigmatized professional occupation he was looking into, would he not be contributing to this? The introduction to a special issue on 'audiences and consumers of porn' for *Porn Studies* edited by Sharif Mowlabocus and Rachel Wood provides important perspective here as well. Their opening question 'who are pornography consumers?' (Mowlabocus and Wood 2015, 118) immediately evoked my response: are not we all? Studies of the sheer volume of online pornographic content underlines how omnipresent 'porn' is, yet its consumption is rarely directly admitted to. Who knows the pornographic preferences of friends and family? The moment a researcher acknowledges having an interest in porn, this suggests viewership and inside knowledge. Florian Vörös' (2015) study resonates with Burke's feminist concerns here. Offering a self-reflexive account of an audience reception study that examines gay, bisexual and heterosexual cisgender men's everyday uses of pornography, Vörös turns to the notion of ethnographic complicity and the tensions that emerge from this navigation of a treacherous terrain of pornographic pleasure and academic scientism. This article, therefore, responds to the need for further reflexivity for which auto-ethnography has been suggested as a useful way to approach the matter in hand (Blinne 2012). However, even considering the readers of this journal, this entails a risk of sorts. It requires a dedication that embraces feelings of the body, heart and mind, eventually resulting in a safe space where sexual stories can be expressed freely regardless of the self-pleasure (potentially) involved (Blinne 2012, 954-955). Therefore, the unease I experienced because of my friends' jocular remarks, and them forwarding Selvam's (and other's) pornographic material (thus seeing him and colleagues at work, so to speak), should be unpacked for what it signified about my own position in the field as a gay male and the way I relate to my research material.

Initially, the observation that had had led me to develop an interest in Indian fitness and bodybuilding scene was its rather abrupt centrality in Bollywood movies. This development can be traced to *Om Shanti Om* (Khan and Puri, dirs 2007) in which the lead actor Shah Rukh Khan reveals his six-pack abdominals in one of the movie's hit songs. His dramatic bodily transformation was discussed extensively in mainstream media at the time. While for an older generation of fitness trainers Salman Khan's hit-movie *Pyaar Kiya to Darna Kya* (Khan, dir. 1998) had already given them an inclination of what could be achieved with their (Indian) bodies, its appeal did not immediately resonate with a middle-class audience. Shah Rukh Khan's transformation was followed by that of Aamir Khan, who took this to another level of muscularity altogether in the action blockbuster *Ghajini* (Murugadoss, dir. 2008). It fuelled a rapid growth of the fitness industry and when I conducted fieldwork in a small neighbourhood gym in South Delhi in 2013–2014, gyms had already become an indelible part of India's urban landscape.

Questions that had initially propelled my research included what this muscular body was precisely about and why it had seized the imagination of middle-class men in the way that it had. This had also led me to wonder where these trainers who had now found employment in the burgeoning fitness industry had emerged and originated from. The questions that I would later come to explore in relation to sex and porn work did not arise from the field itself but instead found expression through the commentary that my research received over time. Gay friends had repeatedly suggested that, rather opportunistically, I had situated my research in a candy store with the owner absent and the *ladoos* up for grabs. This aligned with the feedback I received from (male and female) academic audiences over time. At lectures and conferences the question would come up of whether these men were also involved in sex work. Were they preyed upon by female clients for sexual services? The relative absence of experiences of sexual conquests or even an understanding of their masculine bodies as embodying a potential for sex in personal narratives (something which in itself already contrasted with the way they would label their bodies with various hashtags) thus juxtaposed with the way these men were reflected on by others.

When I first encountered Selvam online and realized that he was in fact capitalizing on his sexual or erotic potential, my first inclination was to treat this as a deviation from the norm. Interacting with him, however, forced me to reconsider this assumption. Instead, I realized that the way I approached his life-course trajectory rested too firmly on the assumption that this was in fact a deviation. Being gay myself, my attempt to communicate 'professionalism' (convincing my friends that I was not interested in these men; repeatedly reconfirming to Selvam that I was only interested in him in a research capacity) had added to this in an unproductive way. More than once Selvam suggested that he saw his sex and porn work as a 'natural' outcome of providing personal training. In rough brush strokes he painted a picture of not nearly making the income he required to pay for his own fitness ambitions and taking care of his family, to getting involved in photoshoots to build up a modelling portfolio and potentially supplementing his income this way, to being asked to perform as a go-go dancer and, finally, this leading to paid-for 'muscle worship' and 'light' sexual services as being masturbated by a client. The way he presented the decision-making process that had characterized his trajectory made it seem profoundly logical. Questioning my own unease helped upset and question a more normative approach to the matter that had unwittingly made me think of Selvam – who identifies as heterosexual and who is married and has a young daughter – as a victim instead of an agent who was firmly in control of the business that his body represented.

Porn in India/Indian porn

While my interest in the emerging field of (self-produced)[8] gay pornography in India originates from earlier work on the emerging fitness and bodybuilding scene in the country, the focus on India should not be read as one simply oriented towards gaining insight into regional difference, as Baishya and Mini (2020) also caution against. In doing so, one would run the risk of othering and exoticizing a field that nowadays relies on shared online technologies that makes content globally accessible. At the same time, it would be a mistake to think of the productions Selvam and colleagues feature in as one-on-one copies from Western counterparts. Studies that have looked into pornographic content creation in a Western context therefore do not always offer deeper insight into what is at stake in India. As Jacobs, Baudinette, and Hambleton (2020, 251) note, when Asian bodies are discussed in porn studies research, the focus on North American cultural productions means that the analysis often touches upon regionally specific racial logics and concerns. In the case of India, the question of socio-economic/class difference is not just relevant for understanding its production and consumption but also how its emergence relates to broader societal developments. While scholars have noted the legal constraints which have sought to curtail accessibility and creation of pornographic content in India (Baishya and Mini 2020, 3–4), this study's mode of inquiry seeks to invert the ostensible interest in 'Indian' morality (pointing at abjection and rejection) and asks why 'an' Indian audience would be so keen to have it confirmed (by me) that 'it' exists. Moving away from a fetishist approach to regional difference as a way to explain why porn 'looks' the way it does, it is more productive to train our attention to issues of class and vernacularity as they play out within the context of rapid urban change and the idea of an emerging 'new' India.[9] This approach deviates from contributions to a previous special issue which sought to engage with the problem of how to speak about sex and sexuality in the South Asian context in terms of legal, moral and censorial issues. Such work draws upon Srivastava's (2006; 2013) pathbreaking work on footpath pornography as well as Bhattacharjya and Ganesh's (2011) internet-focused study that discusses the way sexual rights are expressed and engaged with online.[10] While Srivastava's work offers an important locus to understand issues of (middle-)class difference in urban India, the latter's focus takes us in a direction which holds little relevance to understand Selvam's trajectory and that of his collaborators. Contrary to the question of how pornographic material challenges cultural conventions and normativities, or for that matter how it speaks to notions of (hidden/veiled) sexuality and pleasure, the expectation of its existence and the way Selvam himself sought to 'naturalize' his journey point to its 'mundaneness', for lack of a better term. By treating pornographic content as amalgamated with, and indivisible from, the production of non-pornographic content depicting near-naked men, the notion of a continuum through which we can understand different productions of desire and desirability helps encapsulate this. The way intentionality of (homo)erotic layering is explained and interpreted is crucial for penetrating this and understanding how it draws in a hierarchical interpretation of middle-class belonging that revolves around notions of access, consumption and positionality.

In understanding the way (the bodies of) trainers and bodybuilders in India are perceived, utilized and ultimately consumed through different lenses and modes of production, it is paramount to delineate a hierarchical ordering in terms of the way those belonging to the middle classes reflect on each other. On the one hand are there those who consider themselves the upper and older (thus more entitled) middle class. This is informed by a generational history with being middle class (for example, Misra 1961; Joshi 2001). In general, its members have grown up speaking and receiving most of their education in English, often from privileged so-called convent institutions. Considering the long-standing networks they are part of and the neighbourhood that upper middle-class members reside in, these are families who are not just financially well-off but also hold an excess of social and cultural capital. This contrasts with a group of newcomers to middle-class ranks who are described as 'lower' and whose upbringing and education is characterized by the fluency in a vernacular language instead (for example, Van Wessel 2004; Baviskar and Ray 2015; Srivastava 2015). The role caste plays in this needs to be thought of as byzantine rather than hierarchically clear-cut. As much as I agree with recent publications that have underlined that caste continues to matter (Yengde 2019), its conflation with class hierarchies is less obvious than is often assumed. The way semi-rural/urban North Indian caste communities such as the Jat and Gujjar have been able to capitalize on increased land values and the rapid growth of the National Capital Region (of which Delhi as well as satellite cities Gurgaon and Noida are part) means that that their monetary capital occasionally exceeds that of older/upper middle-class communities in South Delhi who are more commonly associated with the 'upper caste'. Parallels can be drawn with the Thevar and Gounder (Kongu Vellalar) castes and presence in the greater Chennai Region of Tamil Nadu, the Lingayats and their importance to Bangalore (Karnataka) and Maharashtra's Marathas. While none of these comparisons are ideal and this article certainly does not offer the scope to enter into detail with respect to these differences, what it sketches is a caste-class predicament that is less about financial wealth and more about sociocultural capital. This corresponds with a dyadic way of understanding middle-class difference – as in lower/newer versus upper/older – and the way it reflects notions of rural versus urban, tradition versus modernity and provincial versus cosmopolitan. This kind of imaginary dyadic–hierarchical ordering and reasoning draws the contours which help understand the way lower/new middle-class fitness professionals like Selvam are consumed, perceived and treated by upper middle-class men. I argue that there is no intrinsic difference whether this concerns men who utilize Selvam for his expertise as a personal trainer, seek out his escort services, consume and share his pornographic images or videos, or merely follow and appreciate his social media updates. It is therefore important that we remain careful in the way we treat 'actual' sexual intercourse as a boundary of significance here.

Homoerotic layering and showcasing the body

The homoerotic layering of photographs of muscular men has long been a topic of fascination for historians and aficionados alike, yet its intentionality is rarely thoroughly interrogated. Instead, studies tend to evoke a certain inside knowing, as if those who are 'in the know' understand and appreciate something about these pictures that those who feature in them were not aware of. This seems especially true for early photography of muscular men. In *Universal Hunks*, for instance, David L. Chapman (2013) brings together the photographic history (1895–1975) of muscular men from around the world. Douglas Brown, who penned the foreword, asks what a hunk actually is, noting the subjective qualities of hunkiness itself. This kind of subjectiveness continues to inform how the homoerotic layering of imagery is interpreted and understood. The photographs included in *Universal Hunks* are all of muscular men whose framing conveys both admiration and adulation. The male gaze, one informed by same-sex desire, is obliquely present and seems to have left a mark on the curation of the book. The use of the word 'hunk' itself is already an indication of this, something magazines like *Men's Health* staunchly avoid, having always made sure not to be seen as a 'gay magazine'. Almost all muscle men featured wear some form of underwear or have their private parts covered with a leaf. Douglas Brown argues that these images were produced as material objects that served a different purpose according to the context. However, he warns that like literary texts they should not be regarded as unique and autonomous entities but instead build on various pre-existing codes, discourses and other texts: '[E]ach photograph is inter-textual and, at any moment in time, is admired or scrutinized according to a multitude of shifting ideas about health and fitness, male beauty, masculinity, sexuality, pleasure, and desire' (Brown 2013, 9–10 as quoted in Chapman 2013). The analysis Erick Alvarez (2008) provides in his book *Muscle Boys. Gay Gym Culture* reflects this. In it, Robert Mainardi – author of *Strong Men: Vintage Photos of a Masculine Icon* (Mainardi 2001) – argues that most of these pictures were in fact meant to be sold to women but that many eventually ended up in the collections of men.

The difficult relationship between the appreciation of a muscular physique and the way such images appealed to those interested in same-sex contact has a century-long history. Up until the 1920s it appears to have been relatively unproblematic for men to appreciate other men for being handsome. The arrival of public figures such as Charles Atlas (1892–1972) conjured a shift in thinking about this, however. As an Italian-American bodybuilder, Charles Atlas contrasted scrawny 'sissy'-type guys with far more successful muscular 'real' men, in a well-known marketing campaign. By doing so, he suggested that a muscular body could be thought of as an antidote for masculine underperformance (Alvarez 2008, 57). This provides a glimpse into the continued ambivalent relationship between same-sex desire, something Alan Klein's (1993) classic study *Little Big Men* also emphasizes. Building on extensive fieldwork in the West Coast bodybuilding scene, his study was revealing for the way bodybuilders supplement their income by offering services such as (sexualized) muscle worship to male clients. Yet Klein found that same-sex desire and homosexuality remained topics of taboo in the gym. Ellexis Boyle (2010, 156) argues that this is where we encounter a homoerotic paradox that arises from the fetishization of the male body and the intimate relationships that men develop with each other in all-male sporting cultures. A dialectic, although not necessarily amicable, relationship can be dissected between homosocial bonding and what fuels and sustains homoerotic desire.

Such analysis as already provided builds upon a reasoning that places the consumer as if in direct opposition to the one consumed. There is an innocence at play (or assumed to exist) in these pictures that is 'sinfully' distributed and 'polluted' by a gaze that begs to differ. It not only sexualizes imagery that may not have been intended as such, but this reasoning in itself also puts the consumer in control of the narrative. I was not unfamiliar with doing so myself. Like my friends, I had interpreted these social media updates not just homoerotically or even as sexually charged but simultaneously denied them their intentionality. In fact, that was precisely what made it the most interesting, so it seemed. Personal trainer Bikram's social media updates, which I discuss in the following, speak to this. While Bikram is not involved in porn or sex work, I will bring his experiences in line with those of two men – Daniel and Prashant – who are, and who often collaborate with the earlier-mentioned Selvam.

The potential for appreciation and 'fun'

Long-term informant Bikram, a personal trainer who mainly provides online training, is often approached for modelling assignments. After having competed successfully in the Mumbai edition of the male modelling competition that was held as part of Muscle-Mania, he had received numerous inquiries from Bollywood recruiters. However, '90% of these are fake'. They will help you develop a portfolio for which you have to pay, but if you are short on cash, payment can be done in nature. In contrast, Bikram's regular updates on social media do suggest that the notion of sex is not altogether disjointed from the way he envisions himself. In a striking picture, he can be found gambolling on a Goan beach, a tiny pair of red swimming pants leaving little to the imagination. In another, he is wearing a pair of silver-coloured bikini briefs with a rather unnecessary zipper lining his crotch. In his understanding, all he is doing is showcasing his bodily accomplishments. He interprets the sexually explicit comments online as confirmation that his body is appreciated for what he had accomplished with it. His experiences resonated with other informants who had attempted to generate an additional income out of modelling, although building up a portfolio itself had often cost them more than it had ever generated. Almost none regretted this in itself but did voice their disappointment in how promising leads for lucrative assignments often turned out to be about sex instead. That their bodies were desired by other men was of little importance in this since they held their bodies to elicit admiration and envy in any case. Instead, what bothered them was their own lack of sociocultural capital to anticipate this situation. They felt blindsided not by (same-sex) desire but the inherent treacherous aspects of moving up the (middle-)class ladder. Those who did get involved in porn work invoked the 'sexualized' appreciation of their bodies as a way to explain it as a logical continuation of what they imagined their bodies to be about already. While money played an important factor in the way informants negotiated the stigmatized dimensions of porn work, it was ultimately the way they understood it as a continuation or extension of appreciation and male desire of their muscular bodies that allowed them to follow through on it.

Two men Selvam regularly collaborates with are 34-year-old Daniel from Cochin (Kerala) and 29-year-old Prashant who hails from a small town in Andhra Pradesh. While Daniel continues to work as a security guard for a multinational company and Prashant provides personal training to a select number of clients, both supplement their income by featuring in pornographic productions on a semi-regular basis. Recruited by Selvam on the basis of their social media updates, it took some convincing before they agreed. Initially their videos were of solo performances, whereby their showed off their bodies fully naked and/or masturbated on camera. Once they became more comfortable in front of the camera Selvam would pair them with other 'trainers' and they would engage in sexual intercourse as well. Especially, Prashant was worried about the consequences for his career as a professional bodybuilder, because of which he does not allow his face to be filmed. Both identify as straight or heterosexual, but when it comes to porn work describe themselves as bisexual. Deviating from its more regular interpretation, the way they employ 'bisexuality' does not relate to the idea of a sexual identity per se but to their ability to not only have but also enjoy sex with a same-sex partner. From the age of 19 years, Daniel 'did fun with boy and girl', as he put it. He prefers girls and envisions himself married with a wife and children, but at this stage of his life a girlfriend would require him 'to spend more time for chat, out, spend money for all etc.'. It is not something he can afford now. To this he added that 'I respect girl who accept me for fun', meaning casual sex. However, when it comes to porn work he would not like to involve girls since 'they trust and have fun with me so am respect them'. With male sex partners it is different since he can think of them as colleagues who have a similar objective, which is to generate an additional income on top of their day-to-day professions. Studies on homosexuality and same-sex activity in India often argue that it is crucial not to confuse the two with each other. As Sudhir and Katharina Kakar argue: 'Sex between men, especially among friends or within the family during adolescence and youth, is not regarded as sex but masti, an exciting, erotic playfulness, with overtones of the mast elephant in heat' (Kakar and Kakar 2007, 101). Yet for Daniel, thinking of it as a 'fun' thing which references meaningless sexual pleasure ('fun') also helps understand how he thinks of himself as bisexual as a necessary aspect of porn work.

Prashant's experiences and reasoning resonate with Daniel's. Working out since a young teenager, his aspirations to become a professional bodybuilder means that his body requires continuous investment. With his father a factory employee and his mother a homemaker, this is money his family cannot provide him with: 'Because every month I have to invest at least 20k on my body ... Only Fans was last option for me'. When Selvam recruited him he therefore understood this as way out of his financial predicaments first and foremost. Like Daniel, it is his muscular body that he imagines to be the main lure for those who subscribe to his OnlyFans channel. Even though he was concerned about his family finding out, featuring without his face being recognizable reduced the risk of this and made it possible to capitalize on what he imagined other men to find attractive about his body: 'For me there is no problem there'. In fact, he enjoys porn work, especially when 'the men are good looking like me'. He is used to his body being admired in the gym and his Instagram has thousands of followers. That he sees an increasing number of men like himself active on OnlyFans serves as confirmation of porn work as an extension of his involvement in bodybuilding and modelling.

Understanding the transition as continuum

While Daniel and Prashant are relative newcomers, Selvam has been generating an income out of porn work for at least two years now. He explained his trajectory as follows: 'When I started with fitness modelling some photographers wanted to have sex with me. Or some followers in social media'. Yet he was well aware that this might happen. Speaking in the plural he added that: 'So we take it lightly. Just close your eyes and let your dick be sucked. A mouth is a mouth at the end of the [day]'. If the guy he was performing with or rendering sexual services to was good-looking he might even enjoy it, he said.

Selvam describes himself as 'basically straight' but 'bisexual due to exposure'. He believes the same goes for other trainers who are involved in porn and sex work. Over dinner with two other trainers at a fitness event in Goa in which they had all competed in the male modelling category, the conversation had turned to the topic of sex work. The position the other two trainers had taken was that 'if someone from the organisation wanted to enjoy with them in exchange for some benefits they were open to it'. It has not surprised Selvam that most of the participants were already known to the organization. Selvam made it a point, however, to underline that 'they' did not see it as something gay: 'It's just the way it is ... in fitness case it's also the acknowledgement that people are ready to pay to enjoy your body'. To this he added: 'If you are sexy you keep getting this offers from eager men. And if one day it hits you in a low financial moment you just go for it'. Yet he did not deny that there was still a sigma associated with it: 'It's kinda of a shameful activity for many', since 'your manliness might be question', as 'everybody knows that with a client you need to be flexible ... some things you wouldn't do as a straight macho man'. Ultimately, however, considered it a performance: 'But as in every performance sometimes might be more or less pleasant'.

Conclusion

When I met Selvam that evening in Chennai we talked at length about the sexual services he provides and the sex with men he has on camera. Reflecting on his humble upbringing and the upward mobility he concludes that, in the end, 'We are tissue papers for clients to blow their noses in and then toss away'. He let it sink in for a minute to make sure I had understood what he meant. It was something that reverberated with other accounts of fitness trainers as well: as unique as their bodies may be perceived, they often thought of themselves as replaceable or even disposable. The impression that trainers were easily available for sexual encounters, whether of the straight or same-sex variety, spoke to this quite clearly.

This article has put forward that socio-economic (class) difference is crucial in understanding what informs the production as well as consumption of desire (for the male muscular body) in India. Regularly sharing publications with Selvam over time proved particularly insightful into how he reflected on this himself. In one such article I had discussed the role the body can play as an equalizer for a lack of sociocultural capital otherwise (Baas 2017). On the basis of it, Selvam had drawn the conclusion that he himself could be considered a person who was attempting to bridge 'the ostensible gap in middle-classness' (2017, 11). While he liked the idea of it, he was not convinced that he could ever fully cross over from a lower/vernacular middle-class status to an upper middle-class one, even if he had an income to match. In a tongue-in-cheek kind of way he would sometimes use quotes from my book as part of his social media updates, flaunting his muscular body in some aspirational context such as a five-star pool or hotel room. While his fanbase was not likely to engage with the double entendre, I knew it was a way for him to reflect on the opportunities as well as constraints that the idea of a new India offered. In our ongoing interactions Selvam has repeatedly suggested not to overthink his involvement in porn and sex work, and this is also how I imagine him to respond to this article as well. But that encouragement in itself has also greatly contributed to the conceptualization in this article. Consequently, the article argues that the transition from fitness to porn and sex work should be thought of less as taking place between end points and more in terms of forming part of a continuum whereby the body is already layered with multiple and often incongruous notions of what makes it attractive for consumption. Porn work is not a complication but an affirmation and continuation, as such.

After the launch of *Muscular India* (Baas 2020), Indian gay friends continued to share insights with me regarding the sexual availability of trainers. Rarely did it concern direct experiences. Instead, I could not help think of it as an urban fantasy that was revealing for the way the upper middle class reflects on upwardly mobile new entrants to middle-class ranks. For most of their lives my gay friends had been used to 'servants' catering to their every need; as drivers, cooks, gardeners, security guards, tutors and so on. With the emergence of the lean and muscular bodily ideal, a new group of service professionals had emerged who were bringing bodily capital to the table as a way to compensate for a lack in social and cultural capital otherwise. Albeit metaphorically, often demeaning or disparaging assessment of sexual availability seemed to reaffirm middle-class boundaries. However, employing a dyadic interpretation in terms of the un/intentionality to ostensive homoerotically suggestive social media updates also meant reproducing socio-economic/middle-class difference in a way that I knew men like Selvam to challenge actively and directly. Their upward trajectories were characterized by challenging middle-class boundaries in which they utilized their bodily capital as leverage. Capitalizing on the desire their bodies elicit is therefore not just a matter of economics but should also be understood as an engagement with the way these men understand their bodies to be perceived, engaged with and ultimately consumed.

In this article I aimed to show that the emergence of self-produced pornographic material in India that is made available through online platforms such as OnlyFans needs to be understood as existing in a continuum with other productions that appear saturated with homoerotics. The question of intentionality and even the predicament of absence/presence of sexual desire in trainers' day-to-day lives speaks to a dyadic hierarchical ordering that ultimate negotiates agency as part of a (middle-class) schema that pits new versus old(er), lower versus upper, vernacular versus cosmopolitan, tradition versus modernity and rural versus urban. In our continued effort to understand the production and consumption of pornography we need to reflect actively on the context it emerges from as well as the way our questions and modes of inquiry speak to pre-held assumptions.

Notes

1. All names of informants are anonymized. In some cases, additional details have been changed to provide additional privacy.
2. This article builds on an extensive analysis of publications about the Indian middle-class and new middle-class formations. I have cited a number of central works here, but for a longer and more detailed analysis I refer to the first chapter of *Muscular India* (Baas 2020, 24–54).
3. Although this idea resonates somewhat with Sedgwick's notion of a continuum between homosociality and homosexuality, for its conceptualization this article does not draw directly on this work.
4. All friends mentioned here are originally from India and identify as gay or homosexual. Since I identify as gay myself and have stayed and lived in India over long periods of time, I have built up an extensive network of gay friends who often host me when I am travelling around. As English-educated highly skilled professionals they form an important sounding board to my research, and in this article I build upon their responses in an anthropological fashion forming part of a thick(er) Geertzian description (Geertz 1973).
5. This comment needs to be understood primarily in terms of the first year of marriage when the newly married couple is expected to be hosted for dinner by a wide array of family members. Moreover, the wife is expected to dote on her husband by showing off her cooking skills and feeding him snacks and sweets.
6. Strikingly, most such accounts revolved around misunderstandings whereby the female client appears to have thought of 'it' as a one-night stand while the trainer in question had hoped/expected more.
7. An agricultural and influential caste in North India.
8. Almost all same-sex-oriented porn in India is self-produced and made available through sites such as Pornhub and OnlyFans.

9. See, for a particularly insightful study, Ravinder Kaur's *Brand New Nation* (2020). For a more extensive discussion of the vagaries of labelling India with the prefix of new, see *Muscular India* (Baas 2020).
10. See also Ketaki Chowkhani's (2016) pathbreaking work in this regard.

Disclosure statement

No potential conflict of interest was reported by the author.

Funding

The author reported there is no funding associated with the work featured in this article.

References

Alvarez, Erick. 2008. *Muscle Boys. Gay Gym Culture*. New York and London: Routledge.
Attwood, Feona, Giovanna Maina and Clarissa Smith. 2018. 'Conceptualizing, Researching and Writing About Pornography.' *Porn Studies* 5 (1): 1–5.
Baas, Michiel. 2020. *Muscular India: Masculinity, Mobility and the New Middle Class*. Delhi: Context (Westland).
Baas, Michiel. 2017. 'Bulging Biceps in Urban India. A Middle Class Goes to the Gym.' *IIAS Newsletter* 77: 10-11.
Baishya, Anirban K. and Darshana S. Mini. 2020. 'Translating Porn Studies: Lessons from the Vernacular.' *Porn Studies* 7 (1): 2–12.
Baviskar, Amita and Raka Ray. 2015. *Elite and Everyman. The Cultural Politics of the Indian Middle Classes*. Delhi: Routledge.
Bhattacharjya, Manjima and Maya Indira Ganesh. 2011. 'Negotiating Intimacy and Harm: Female Internet Users in Mumbai.' In *Erotics: Sex, Rights and the Internet: An Exploratory Research Study*, edited by Jac S. M. Kee, 66–108. Association for Progressive Communications. Available online: https://www.genderit.org/resources/erotics-sex-rights-and-internet-exploratory-research-study (accessed September 21, 2021).
Blinne, Kristen C. 2012. 'Auto(erotic)ethnography.' *Sexualities* 15 (8), 953–977.
Boyle, Ellexis. 2010. 'Marketing Muscular Masculinity in *Arnold: The Education of a Bodybuilder*.' *Journal of Gender Studies* 19 (2): 153–166.
Bourdieu, Pierre. 1977. *Outline of a Theory of Practice*. Cambridge: Cambridge University Press.
Bourdieu, Pierre. 1984 [1979]. *Distinction. A Social Critique of the Judgment of Taste*. Cambridge: Harvard University Press.
Brosius, Christiane. 2010. *India's Middle Class: New Forms of Urban Leisure, Prosperity and Consumption*. New Delhi: Routledge.
Burke, Nathaniel. 2014. 'Positionality and Pornography.' *Porn Studies* 1 (1-2): 71–74.
Chapman, David L. 2013. *Universal Hunks. A Pictorial History of Muscular Men Around the World, 1895-1975*. Vancouver: Asenal Pulp Press.
Chowkhani, Ketaki. 2016. 'Pleasure, Bodies and Risk: Women's Viewership of Pornography in Urban India.' *Porn Studies* 3 (4): 443–452.
Fernandes, Leela. 2006. *India's New Middle Classes: Democratic Politics in an Era of Economic Reforms*. Minnesota: University of Minnesota Press.
Geertz, Clifford. 1973. *The Interpretation of Cultures*. New York: Basic Books.
Jacobs, Katrien, Thomas Baudinette and Alexandra Hambleton. 2020. 'Reflections on Researching Pornography Across Asia: Voices from the Region.' *Porn Studies* 7 (3): 250–257.
Joshi, Sanjay. 2001. *Fractured Modernity: Making of a Middle Class in Colonial North India*. New Delhi: Oxford University Press.

Kaur, Ravinder. 2020. *Brand New Nation: Capitalist Dreams and Nationalist Designs in Twenty-First-Century India*. Pala Alto: Standford University Press.

Kakar, Sudhir and Katharina Kakar. 2007. *The Indians. Portrait of a People*. New Delhi: Penguin.

Khan, Farah and Mayur Puri, dirs. 2007. *Om Shanti Om*. India.

Khan, Sohail, dir. 1998. *Pyaar Kiya to Darna Kya*. India.

Klein, Alan M. 1993. *M. Little Big Men. Bodybuilding Subculture and Gender Construction*. Albany: State University of New York Press.

Lee, Jiz and Rebecca Sullivan. 2016. 'Porn and Labour: The Labour of Porn Studies.' *Porn Studies* 3 (2): 104–106.

Mainardi, Robert. 2001. *Strong Men: Vintage Photos of a Masculine Icon*. Chicago: Council Oak Books.

Misra, Bankey Bihari. 1961. *The Indian Middle Classes: Their Growth in Modern Times*. London, etc.: Oxford University Press for the Royal Institute of International Affairs.

Mowlabocus, Sharif and Rachel Wood. 2015. 'Introduction: Audiences and Consumers of Porn.' *Porn Studies* 2 (2-3): 118–122.

Murugadoss, A. R., dir. 2008. *Ghajini*. India.

Srivastava, Sanjay. 2006. *Passionate Modernity Sexuality, Class, and Consumption in India*. Delhi: Routledge.

Srivastava, Sanjay. 2013. 'Street, Footpath, Gated Community: On the Cultures of Indian Pornography.' In *Sexuality Studies*, edited by Sanjay Srivastava, 228–254. New Delhi: Oxford University Press.

Srivastava, Sanjay. 2015. *Entangled Urbanism. Slum, Gated Community and Shopping Mall in Delhi and Gurgaon*. New Delhi: Oxford University Press.

Van Wessel, Margit. 2004. 'Talking About Consumption: How an Indian Middle Class Dissociates from Middle-Class Life.' *Cultural Dynamics* 16 (1): 93–116.

Vörös, Florian. 2015. 'Troubling Complicity: Audience Ethnography, Male Porn Viewers and Feminist Critique.' *Porn Studies* 2 (2-3): 137–149.

Wacquant, Loïc. 2001. 'Whores, Slaves and Stallions: Languages of Exploitation and Accommodation among Boxers.' *Body & Society* 7 (2-3): 181–194.

Yengde, Suraj. 2019. *Caste Matters*. Delhi: India Viking.

OPEN ACCESS

'Grindr is basically interactive porn': Ethnographic observations from Kolkata on queer intimacies and 'pic exchange' on Grindr and PlanetRomeo

Rohit K. Dasgupta

Introduction

This Forum article is based on an ethnographic analysis of social media usage by young queer men in Kolkata, India between 2012 and 2018.[1] I conducted digital ethnography during this entire period with extended field work in 2013, 2014 and 2017. Interviews were conducted during the entire period both online and offline. This ethnographically informed research on queer social media offers a new perspective on porn consumption and representation. It also asks how the use of platforms such as Grindr and PlanetRomeo affects the way people interact sexually through self-made pornographic images. Whilst many of these images are impregnated with pornographic representations and stereotypes, it also offers a new site for interrogating issues of porn aesthetics within profile images and the visual dialogue of queer Indian males on digital platforms. By porn aesthetics I refer to the potential value and affective gestures that imbibe these images – one that brings together the hyperreality of sexuality with the authenticity of South Asian identities (markers of class, caste, religion). The context of Kolkata is especially important too, as masculinity has a vexed and complex history in West Bengal where concomitantly Bengali men were often constructed as lacking in power and, hence, as effete and emasculated (Boyce and Dasgupta 2021; Sinha 1995). This in turn outlines some of the visual practices employed on platforms such as Grindr and PlanetRomeo. Whilst the fixity of masculine identities has destabilized in recent years, there still remains a dominance of heteronormative masculinity, especially in gay porn (Mercer 2017).

The profile image

It is a late Saturday afternoon in Kolkata. In the last few weeks there have been a number of 'gay parties' being advertised on Facebook groups. These parties, which are organized

---

[1]This article draws on the author's earlier chapter 'Keep It Classy: Grindr, Facebook and Enclaves of Queer Privilege in India' in *The Routledge Companion to Media and Class* edited by Erika Polson, Lynn Schofield-Clark, and Radhika Gajjala (Routledge 2020). This article uses a different argument and narratives.

This article has been published with minor changes. Two figures have been removed as copyright permissions could not be obtained. These changes do not impact the academic nature of the article and the figures can be accessed in the original article.

by both individuals and community groups (Pink Party Kolkata, Kolkata Rainbow Pride Festival Party), are mostly advertised via email, social media, text messages and word of mouth. There is an air of jubilation since the Supreme Court decision to unanimously rule that Section 377 was unconstitutional, thus removing a cloud of uncertainty and fear from the lives of LGBTQ people in India. Within days, a number of marches, talks and parties were organized and publicized on social media. After scrolling through some of these invites for a while I decided to log in to my Grindr account. After a few anonymous tiles I started chatting to Andy. Andy had an interesting profile and was only a few minutes away from me but what particularly caught my eye was the display of his *upanayan* (sacred) thread against his chiselled body displayed in his underwear. The thread signified his upper caste status in India, which along with his profile information 'sophisticated' and 'love art, culture, music' also signified his class status.

Andy and I started chatting straight away. We both had a similar background having studied in Christian missionary schools and a few common friends. After a few minutes of flirty chats, we decided to meet up. I told him how intrigued I was by his sacred thread on his profile picture and asked if it was deliberate. Andy was actually quite honest in describing that it was deliberate as it was considered erotic by several people he met on the app who fetishized his caste background (as an upper caste

Brahmin with a thread). Even though it remained unsaid, Andy was also signalling his own caste desire in his potential partners. Over the course of that month I met Andy a couple more times. Given our backgrounds – we both went to private Christian missionary schools and had a few acquaintances in common – I became a regular person who he started including in his social life. My own class privilege and caste identity played a role in this acceptance. For Andy I was recognized as 'one of them'. Albury et al. (2017) have discussed that the convergence of public and private life associated with social media technologies which mediate dating, relationships and sex is also connected to other aspects of our lives and identities.

The Grindr profile is created through an assemblage of written text and visual cues. Mowlabocus (2010, 81) asserts that, 'If gay male digital culture remediates the body and does so through a pornographic lens, then it also provides the means for watching that body, in multiple ways and with multiple consequences'. The profile picture identifies the user, evidences his desires and implicates his intentions. McGlotten (2013, 127) calls it 'image labour', explaining that profile creation is a process laden with affective demands entering one into a 'market place of desire, of sexual value and existing hierarchies'. Mowlabocus (2021) more recently argues how apps such as Grindr have proliferated a form of 'sexual racism' which essentializes race and desire, and on being confronted on their practices argues that this is about 'desire' and not 'discrimination'. We see a similar pattern in the case of Kolkata too, where practices such as class, religion and caste preference are defended as desire and 'wanting others like me' (Andy) rather than recognizing the privilege at play.

Andy described Grindr as 'interactive porn'. He did not necessarily log in there to hook up. He used his profile image as a thirst trap to chat to other users, join in sexual conversation and for quickly 'getting off'. As he said:

> Why pay for onlyfans when I can have an erotic chat session with someone, exchange pictures and get the 'real thing' online?

Race (2018, 1328) argues that pornography is no longer just the 'production of sexual arousal through representation practices'. Rather, interpersonal exchanges such as sexual chatting activities – for example, the exchange of intimate pictures (privately or publicly as thirst traps which encourage interaction) or videos – characterize the kind of 'interactive porn' that Andy refers to. These forms of self-pornography have become an essential part of the sexual grammar that govern how users I have spoken to in my research consume porn and participate in sexual activities online.

Pic exchange

In addition to the textual component of chatting, private sharing of pictures is another way through which my respondents participate in intimate encounters. 'Pic exchange' remains a process laden with affective demands which Campbell and Carlson (2002, 591) call 'exchanging privacy for participation'. Picture sharing can take place at various points of an encounter. This could take place at the very beginning where a connection is being established and when users do not want to initiate conversation with someone without at least some kind of a face or body picture. It was not uncommon to see profiles with 'no pic no dic' (*sic*) during my research. Other times, exchange of intimate or 'fun' could happen much earlier even before any other conversation. Whilst scholars such as Jones (2005) and Tziallas (2015) argue that in online interactions information emerges incrementally sometimes with a form of strategic ambiguity, this has not always been the case with my research informants. Neel, for example, described how he often began a conversation by sending a couple of pictures including erotic ones and asking for reciprocity even before any other conversation:

Neel: I send a few of my pictures and ask for 'Ur Pics'. There is no point in even having a conversation if I am not sexually interested is there?
R.K.D.: What if they want to have a conversation and not send you pictures right away.
Neil: depending on what I am looking for at that time I might chat but I would usually just block them and move on. You're on grindr not shaadi.com

McGlotten (2013) argues that the erotic representations and exchange of pictures is part of the visual market of gift economy. The smartphone screen acts as an affective device bringing sexual gratification as Andy and I chatted about the city's gay scene interspersed with flirtatious erotic innuendos and exchange of pictures. The act of 'pic exchange', Jones (2005) argues, is based on subtle choreography and reciprocity and one of the many ways through which gay men organize their sexual lives. The act of pic exchange whilst offering 'the wordless suggestion of intercourse' (Paasonen, Jarrett, and Light 2019, 77) also signals different forms of sexual intimacy. As Andy reminded me:

> I don't have 'place' most of the time. Ever since my parents retired I don't really have the house to myself anymore so I have to plan my meetings quite carefully. There is a lot of time investment in this. Through exchanging 'fun pics' I want to get to know the other person, see if we sexually turn each other on. It is the first step towards what will happen next.

On apps such as Grindr and PlanetRomeo, the type of pictures exchanged is associated with the purposes of the conversation during that given time, with sexualized images in different forms of undress being common. In fact, Race (2015) rightly points out that 'dickpics' or familiarity with a person's genitalia might happen well before any other social acquaintance.

Receiving a 'dickpic' through a pic exchange is more erotic than finding it online, as another user SweetLuv, who I met on PlanetRomeo, explained to me:

> If I have shared dickpics with someone it means he is quite near. It is 'more real' than sourcing it from pornhub or xvideos which doesnt really have that many desis anyway.

Proximity through networked communication, as SweetLuv explains, creates affective bonds. These are further strengthened through the sharing of erotic pictures. It was interesting that Andy and SweetLuv both referred to the 'real thing' or 'more real'. Tziallas (2015) argues that platforms such as Grindr and Scruff double down as DIY (do it yourself) amateur porn platforms where meeting up is not always the main goal for users. This is a very similar position several of my respondents take. For users such as Andy and SweetLuv, Grindr was not simply about facilitating a sexual encounter but, rather, through the use of text and visual cues engineering a form of instant sexual pleasure. Grindr is also acutely aware of issues around poor data and slow smartphones in India, launching a 'lite' version specifically for its Indian users since 2020, thus also addressing the issue of having to stream porn videos as both Andy and SweetLuv further explained:

> I am often on my 3G which isn't that great most of the time in my neighbourhood. Often it is difficult to quickly stream a video especially if I am on my own. Time is precious. Exchanging pictures and having a sexy chat session is much faster. (SweetLuv, 23 May 2016)

Robby, another user, also described the use of emoticons and footprints on platforms such as PlanetRomeo. Footprints are graphic animated images which are used to convey certain meanings – these range from 'gorgeous face' and 'cool' to more explicit and sexualized messages such as 'hot cock', 'hot butt' and 'horny pig'. These fleeting messages are an example of phatic communication which is a form of verbal or non-dialogic communication. Footprints are ephemeral gestures seeped in intimacy. Robby explained that he used footprints more than actual texts when communicating his desire for other users:

> I don't want to come out too needy with long messages. We have already sent the pictures. We have seen our nude bodies. Sometimes it can feel awkward so I move to footprints like 'great body' 'sex now' or 'hot cock'. I have had some great 'hot sessions' just through exchanging nudes and footprints! I am always doing this on Grindr and Planetromeo when I am bored.

One of the ways in which one can make sense of footprints is by employing Miller's (2008) concept of phatic culture, a form of communication that Miller identifies as non-dialogic and non-informational. While I do not agree with Miller's argument that this form of communication is non-informational, I do, however, think it provides a useful framework to think about this form of non-dialogic forms of erotic and intimate conversation. Footprints are an ephemeral way of sending messages on PlanetRomeo. They are transient, lasting only for a short while. The user cannot save them, and they only remain a fleeting gesture and reminder of an intimate, often non-dialogic, encounter with another person of sparing linguistic play of erotic gestures. It is a way of reminding another user you are thinking of them, to say hello and to register sexual interest, as Robby mentions.

Berlant (2004) argues that intimacy is about being able to communicate with the sparest of signs and gestures. Robby's use of footprints seems to fall within the same territory. He is cautious about not wanting to come on too strongly, and so he uses subtle methods such as leaving a footprint to make his presence felt and his intentions known. Jean Burgess (2006) uses the term 'vernacular creativity' to talk about these everyday creative practices on new media where users such as Neel, SweetLuv, Roby and Andy situate their textual and visual strategies to engage in a form of eroticization. This, according to Burgess, reduces cultural distance and creates an affective form of erotic intimacy.

Conclusion

Grindr and PlanetRomeo are constructed as a haven for mostly gay men looking for sex and casual hook-ups with the possibility of finding romance. It is where gay men are going when they are bored, horny and in need of some instant gratification. As my research shows, Grindr and PlanetRomeo are being used by many of my respondents in more ways than just as a way to 'get off'. The images, texts and footprints circulating here, whether created with the intent to be erotic or leading to an offline encounter, are 'interpellated within the regime of pornography' (Tziallas 2015, 771). There are different interaction norms and, as we can see, they can be racialized, class-ed and cast-ed. On Grindr we face a constant rotation of bodies and faces updated by users setting up information about themselves but also hinting at what 'they want', thus allowing one to participate in objectified media images. Face-to-face contact and offline encounter are not necessarily the end goal of the interaction taking place on these platforms. As I have described earlier (Dasgupta 2017, 2018, 2020), being on queer social media platforms such as Grindr and PlanetRomeo is serious emotional labour – the anxiety, intimacy and sexual tension offer various kinds of possibilities and exclusions. Whilst academics have studied these digital queer spaces in India as potential for activism, community formation and intimacy, the opportunity to see the role played by the circulation of erotic images and texts offer a different lens to understanding gay men's culture and sexual politics in contemporary India.

Acknowledgements

This paper was presented at the Ashoka University Summer of Ishq Webinar on 14 July 2021. The author would like to thank Prof. Madhavi Menon and Sam McBean for their feedback and conversation. The author would also like to thank Darshana Sreedhar Mini and Anirban K. Baishya for their insightful comments on the drafts that preceded this article which helped clarify much of the author's argument.

Disclosure statement

No potential conflict of interest was reported by the author.

References

Albury, Kath, Jean Burgess, Ben Light, Kane Race and Rowan Wilken. 2017. 'Data Cultures of Mobile Dating and Hook-up Apps: Emerging Issues for Critical Social Science Research.' *Big Data and Society* 4 (2): 1–11.

Berlant, Lauren. 2004. *Compassion: The Culture and Politics of an Emotion*. Abingdon: Routledge.

Boyce, Paul and Rohit K. Dasgupta. 2021. 'Joyraj and Debanuj: Queer(y)ing the City.' *Contemporary South Asia* 28 (4): 511–523.

Burgess, Jean. 2006. 'Hearing Ordinary Voices: Cultural Studies, Vernacular Creativity and Digital Storytelling.' *Continuum: Journal of Media and Cultural Studies* 20 (2): 201–214.

Campbell, John Edward and Matt Carlson. 2002. 'Panopticon.com: Online Surveillance and the Commodification of Privacy'. *Journal of Broadcasting & Electronic Media* 46 (4): 586–606.

Dasgupta, Rohit K. 2017. *Digital Queer Cultures in India: Politics, Intimacies and Belonging*. London: Routledge.

Dasgupta, Rohit K. 2018. 'Digital Outreach and Sexual Health Advocacy: SAATHII as a Response.' In *Queering Digital India: Activisms, Identities and Subjectivities*, edited by Rohit K. Dasgupta and Debanuj Dasgupta, 112–131. Edinburgh: Edinburgh University Press.

Dasgupta, Rohit K. 2020. 'Keep It Classy: Grindr, Facebook and Enclaves of Queer Privilege in India.' In *The Routledge Companion to Media and Class*, edited by Erika Polson, Lynn Schofield-Clark and Radhika Gajjala, 90–98. London: Routledge.

Jones, Rodney H. 2005. ''You Show me Yours, I'll Show you Mine': The Negotiation of Shifts from Textual to Visual Modes in Computer-Mediated Interaction among Gay Men.' *Visual Communication* 4 (1): 69–92.

McGlotten, Shaka. 2013. *Virtual Intimacies: Media, Affect and Queer Socialities*. Albany: SUNY Press.

Mercer, John. 2017. *Gay Pornography: Representations of Sexuality and Masculinity*. London: Bloomsbury.

Miller, Vincent. 2008. 'New Media, Networking and Phatic Culture.' *Convergence: The International Journal of Research Into New Media Technologies* 14 (4): 387–400.

Mowlabocus, Sharif. 2010. *Gaydar Culture: Gay Men, Technology and Embodiment in the Digital Age*. London: Routledge.

Mowlabocus, Sharif. 2021. 'A Kindr Grindr: Moderating Race(ism) in Technospaces of Desire.' In *Queer Sites in Global Contexts: Technologies, Spaces and Otherness*, edited by Regner Ramos and Sharif Mowlabocus, 33–47. New York: Routledge.

Paasonen, Susanna, Kylie Jarrett and Ben Light. 2019. *NSFW: Sex, Humour and Risk in Social Media*. Cambridge: MIT Press.

Race, Kane. 2018. 'Towards a pragmatics of sexual media/networking devices.' *Sexualities* 21 (8): 1325–1330.

Sinha, Mrinalini. 1995. *Colonial Masculinity: The Manly Englishman and the Effeminate Bengali*. Manchester: Manchester University Press.

Tziallas, Evangelos. 2015. 'Gamified Eroticism: Gay Male "Social Networking" Applications and Self-Pornography.' *Sexuality & Culture* 19: 759–775.

Part IV

Feminist and minor approaches to South Asian pornographies

#PatriarchyKaPackup: mediating sexual discourse and the casteless feminist subject in Indian performance poetry

Pallavi Rao

ABSTRACT

Exploring the formations of gender, caste, sexuality, and class in India, this article examines the seemingly casteless discursive and material fields in the poetry of upper-caste female slam poets performed live in Mumbai and hosted on YouTube channels. I approach these texts as a form of mediated erotics occupying media sites contentiously marked as obscene and pornographic by the state while nuancing how these mediums harness language, sound, and speech for confessional sexual articulations. Studying these poets' discursive strategies towards pleasure and desire and their digital circulation on a transnational scale, I argue that slam poets theatrically channel (out)rage against conservative Brahminical attitudes that treat articulations around women's bodies as continually verging on the pornographic, whilst obscuring how caste is implicated in sexual discourse. Finally, I argue that casteless Anglophone spoken word can be contrasted with anti-caste vernacular performances by Dalit artists who articulate possibilities for a futurist Ambedkarite castelessness.

Introduction

Slight applause punctuates the beginning of a YouTube video, as the logo of 'UnErase Poetry' appears in a circle on the screen. A title card appears on a black background, saying:

> Right to Pleasure ~ Priya Malik ~

The word 'Pleasure' is in pink, the rest in white. The video opens with an off-centre medium shot of Priya Malik, an Indian poet, in front of a mic on a small stage with a chalkboard with the same UnErase Poetry logo on it. A soft overhead lights up Malik on stage, who is dressed in a bright pink kurta, long earrings, and loose hair, facing an audience we cannot see. As light guitar music begins to drift in, she begins to recite her English-language spoken word poem. 'Dear men, here are a few definitions that might help', she begins. As she recites a poem asserting a woman's right to pleasure, the guitar strumming in the background builds up to an agitated rhythm, its loudness almost drowning out Malik's voice. With her poem framed as a 'lesson' that alternately addresses men and women, Malik says 'Your body is not a temple, neither sacred nor holy, it is a graveyard of societal conventions, tombstones inscribed with centuries of shame, of being told that being sexual is a bad thing, haha.' Malik's gaze slides across her small audience as she speaks, and the video camera periodically changes angles, sometimes facing her straight or sometimes profiling her from the side. The camera also captures the guitarist Pranav Kakkar, as well as the logo of the Mumbai performance venue, the comedy and music café The Hive. Malik concludes her poem stating: 'That it is our right to exercise our pleasure, and our pleasure to exercise that right. Your lesson is now complete' (Malik 2017).

Moving from the imagination of a woman as an erotic object to the woman as an erotic subject with a right to exercise pleasure and to take pleasure in exercising their rights, Malik's performance illustrates the embodied caste-gender politics of upper-caste women reciting spoken word through popular feminism and a pop-cultural performance practice in urban India today. Pleasure and desire in South Asia occupy a nebulous space in public culture, caught between repressive caste and religious orthodoxies and contentious legal discourses of obscenity and vulgarity. Sexual articulations, especially by women, are mediated through cultures of social surveillance, moral policing, legal regulation, and self-censorship, so that performances of the erotic in public culture require a tense balancing act between not being easily identifiable as 'pornographic' while remaining legible as expressions of desire and pleasure intended for public consumption. In such a context, scholars studying the pornographic may have to seek gradations of the erotic in content widely marked as 'obscene' or 'vulgar' as a kind of pornographic lexicon and develop inventive ways of reading the 'pornographic' in public culture. Purnima Mankekar (2012, 185) thus argues for a reading of desire in public culture, which is a densely visual interlocular field that is 'intertextual' and is constituted by 'a range of texts' across popular media from print magazines and advertising to television and popular cinema.

Exploring the formations of caste, gender, class, and sexuality in Mumbai's performance poetry scene and its digital counterparts, this article examines the seemingly casteless discursive and material fields that the poetry of female slam poets engage with in contemporary Indian popular culture. Reading the spoken word performances of several women poets hosted since 2017 on YouTube and Instagram channels, I ask, what forms of mediation are female slam poets utilizing in urban performance spaces and through digital media technologies to script and narrate sexual violence, harassment, and sexism that are devoid of any mention of caste, class, or other vectors of identity? I approach these women's performance confessions as exemplars of castelessness, which nonetheless theatrically channel feminist (out)rage against patriarchy and confront conservative attitudes in India's caste-riven society that treats most subject matter concerning sex as taboo and pornographic. However, in locating the caste and class (and to a limited extent racially) implicated performances of gender and sexuality through these social media platforms, I contrast these urban women's performances that disavow any recognition of their caste identities with the vocal anti-caste articulations of Dalit-Ambedkarite women who are also performance poets and singers albeit in different venues and media platforms. Juxtaposing the universalized casteless feminist subject in spoken word with the specificity of a caste-annihilating castelessness articulated by Dalit women performers, I locate how digital media performances illuminate the continuing frictions between a cosmopolitan neoliberal feminism and localized anti-caste women's politics in India.

The elastic sphere of what constitutes the erotic in urban Indian culture and new media is where I situate the sexual confessions of performance poetry that are mediated through the internet; that is, a form of 'mediated erotics' (Mankekar and Schein 2012). While spoken word's articulations punctuate the aural and verbal realm more than the scopic and visual, and with formal registers not identifiable as pornography in the Euro-American sense, they nonetheless occupy highly mediated fields within which erotic discourse proliferates in India's cultural spheres. Digital circulations of performance poetry are dispersed in an arena rife with debates about vulgarity, obscenity, and pornographic content via moral panics about globalization in India and the unregulated spread of media texts over cyberspace (Shah 2007). Content platforms confronted by the Indian state's censorial gaze must navigate highly regionalized interpretations of the obscene, from kissing and nudity to profanity to the reference of body parts. Performance poetry's exploration of sexuality, its explicitly worded yearnings for erotic pleasure on selective public stages and media platforms, and its circulation among seemingly 'liberal' spaces for content considered taboo or obscene by mainstream media reflect its deep imbrications within both the sensorium of India's public culture and its digital media platforms. As Anirban Baishya and Darshana Mini (2020, 6) ask, are erotic cultures in South Asia 'also untranslatable vernaculars that require us to constantly recontextualize the meanings of pornography in its historical and cultural particularities?' If we do treat performance poetry as non-pornographic yet localized articulations of mediated erotics, then the vernacular inflections that construct its contours deserve to be examined closely. These include the 'social locations of producers and consumers, the politics of enunciation refracting the diverse modes of address deployed by specific genres of media, the narrative repertoires on which media texts draw, and the semiotic skills of audiences and consumers' (Mankekar and Schein 2012, 4). It is these detours, overlaps, edges, and deviations of erotic performance in spoken word poetry which concern my analysis in this article, and which I consider illustrative as evocations of sexual desire and sexual freedom in urban performance culture.

Performance confessions and the sexual imaginary

Malik's (2017) spoken word performance, like many other performances curated by event organizers such as UnErase Poetry, Kommune India, and Tape a Tale, utilizes multiple formal elements of literary-poetic conventions of rhythm and verse, of the musical, vocal, and bodily conventions of spoken word poetry, and of the digital modes of video production and circulation of performance poetry through social media. English and Hindi-language poetry has seen a resurgence in the Indian urban public sphere in the past five years, where slam poetry (as referred to in the USA) or spoken word poetry has emerged as a popular urban form of performance art, with poets gaining microcelebrity status despite being underpaid – if paid at all, which remains unclear – for their performances. In performance venues across metropolitan cities, urban women – predominantly upper-caste and upper-middle-class – have taken to scripting and performing spoken verse concerning sexual trauma, (out)rage against sexual violence, and explorations of sexual desires, pleasures, and agency. Recorded clips of these performances are subsequently mobilized through YouTube and Instagram, locating these female poets, some of whom already have burgeoning acting careers, in expanding feminist performance spaces, digital media circuits, and celebrity culture in Indian cities. UnErase Poetry's YouTube video of Malik's performance, for instance, circulated with the hashtag #MyBodyIsNotATemple, has gathered 1.78 million views since its upload in September 2017.

As a regionally and culturally specific variant of performance poetry, Indian women's spoken word poetry connects how the cis-woman's body is experienced and ideologically invested to her articulations of pleasure and desire. For one, poems describing sexual assault, cultural conservatism, and bodily autonomy feature significantly in these poets' orations, channelling what Lynda Goldstein (1999, 102) terms 'performance confession', which are a 'no-holds-barred confession of/from the sexualized body that operates against the "outrage" generated by the reception of their work' and a 'shifting play among *rage, outrage,* and *out/rage*' amongst poetry audiences (1999, 103; original emphases). While Goldstein's essay examines American performance artists whose theatrical repertoire extends far beyond just the recitation of verse and involves enacting and choreographing a variety of narrativized movements on the stage that accompany their oral performance, Indian spoken word poets remain mostly stationary, relying on instrumental back-up and their poetic enunciation to convey narrative and emotion. This limited yet bodily mode of recitation still borrows heavily from the American slam scene, where the dominant mode of the slam remains a 'relentless focus on the ego', so that the immediate presence of the poet with little else on stage creates a charged intimacy with the audience members (Hoffman 2013, 224). Kathleen Crown (2002, 216) notes that spoken word poetry 'testifies to a popular demand for a return to "voice" and "presence" as fundamental principles of lyric poetry' and that it 'seems at times to exalt the authoritative presence of the poet's body and the esoteric aura of the poem's voiced body prior to any technology of reproduction (whether the printed page or a tape recording)'. Through the corporeality of the poet, the poem too gains a charged presence in its recitation.

In Aranya Johar's (2017) 'A Brown Girl's Guide to Gender', the poem's sexualized protagonist voices a rage against the boiling down of women's subjectivity to sexual interaction. Johar's breathless recitation traces a social minefield of misogynist behaviour targeting young women whose articulations of menstruation are rendered taboo, but whose bodies are acceptable to be sexualized by the male gaze and initiated into sexual activity, sometimes consensual and sometimes not. Johar's (2017) sexual speech also references the hypermediated event of Jyoti Singh Pandey's rape and murder in New Delhi in 2012, when she says 'My mom telling me to wear skirts out less often, Nirbhaya and more, left forgotten, we don't want to be another of India's daughters, do we?' Krupa Shandilya (2015, 466) has referred to how Jyoti Singh Pandey's rape and murder, condensed within the term 'Nirbhaya' in popular culture, has generated a cultural legacy that portrays her as an 'everywoman'. This marking of Pandey as an everywoman allows her life both to serve as a warning to all Indian women about the perils of exercising freedoms while also recalling her specific identity as 'middle-class' and 'urban' (2015, 470). In contrast to upper-caste poets universalizing Pandey's experience in this way is the silence around the non-universal lower-caste women subjects in the digital media sphere who have never been afforded the space to claim a similar castelessness or universality of Indian womanhood because their media appearances are often predicated on the politicization of their identities as Dalitbahujan women. Johar's (2017) verse both recites and re-cites 'Nirbhaya', the fearless one, as a popular cultural script that indexes both the upper-caste Indian woman's courage in pushing back against patriarchal violence as well as their continued vulnerability to the violence that upholds caste patriarchy's structures, while the Dalitbahujan woman subject remains unreferenced.

Nearly a decade after 2012, Pandey thus remains a discursive (and often an exclusionary) placeholder for the anxieties of Hindu upper-caste urban women, who have laboured visibly in public culture to assert themselves as 'India's daughters', and lay claim to their everyday bodily autonomy and their right to movement in public spaces. Such citationality also allows Johar to socially reposition her own Punjabi Khatri (upper-caste) subjectivity on to the 'I/we' of the poem, where she can script powerful confessions of surviving a culture of sexual assault and sexism, while also expressing a sexual awakening that inevitably seems to operate against mainstream culture's respectability politics. In fact, Johar's narrative constructs a burgeoning sexual awareness that is a consequence of histories of past violence against a collectively recognizable 'womanhood'. In this kind of discourse, sexual pleasure and desire seem to be constructed as learned and developed through sexual violence against upper-caste women, with pleasure and pain rendered relational and educational through violence enacted on their bodies.

Moreover, this format of the sexual confessional generalizes pleasurable sexual acts in the plural – 'vaginas only meant to be fucked, breasts only meant to be sucked' – while also displacing sexual action off-stage, into the past, only to be brought forth through the erotically charged gasps and quiver, simulating a softcore pornographic subtext. Johar's reliance on the aural and vocal simulation of sex – a 'pornosonic' – generates a sonic public in performance poetry 'refashioned through the absent-presence of the actual sexual act' (Mini 2019, 7). The confessional thus supplants the visuality of the sexual act with an aural component, tactics that Mini (2019, 4) suggests 'are developed in response to censorship and a culture of redaction'. Further, Sharif Mowlabocus and Andy Medhurst (2017, 210) suggest that 'accent, timbre, pitch and register all play a role in the success (or failure) of the narrator in constructing a "believable" erotic encounter'. Johar's south Mumbai-inflected English and her simulation of a little slice of pornosonic fantasy – that of the woman who cannot get enough – imitate the idealized female erotic object in pornography to stage a critique of patriarchy's normative expectations of femininity.

Taranjit Kaur's (2019) 'I Am Not a Virgin' follows a trajectory similar to Johar's in its evocation of assault and with Kaur's poetic persona speaking to the audience about the violent expectations of virginity imposed upon women who need to demonstrate it on their wedding night. Kaur's poem maps a number of discursive routes that demarcate the speculative boundaries of sexual anxiety, consent, confession, and pleasure for the contemporary urban woman trapped within the ideological apparatuses of patriarchy. Her narrative relies upon the normativity of arranged marriage as an initiation into sexual activity, with the wedding night lending weighty significance to the bride losing her virginity. The poem also points to the limits of consent in such a sexual set-up through the visual metaphor of the spotless white sheet standing in for the chaste woman's blank sexual past. The sexual act itself is condensed into three speculative lines, 'He would come, undress, and once he is done … ', with all of the agency enacted by the husband, and the wife merely a passive object, with no pleasure being anticipated in the act. Then, her poem speculates that the collective discovery that the poem's female subject may not be a virgin is akin to a kind of social death, converting the spotless sheet into her shroud, where her body – in fact, her blood – disappears, but crucially it is her voice, her speech, that can still be heard. Kaur's detailing of her poetic persona's fear and rage offer an interiority to the woman as sexualized object in India's traditional caste society, but it is ultimately this persona's undying 'voice' that has to be recuperated for the construction of a feminist sexual subject who rejects purity tests. The poem subsequently goes on to ask:

> Can I just call her Mary and not virgin?
>
> Can Sita stop proving her integrity?
>
> Can I say no before giving this virginity test? (Kaur 2019)

Such 'autobiographical' discursive manoeuvres in performance poetry operate in a complex terrain of power relations in the domain of popular culture, both enabling the formation of a sexual subject – albeit incoherent and unstable – who can confess about the violence her poetic persona is subjected to as a truth-claim while also functioning as a constraining mechanism for the kind of confessional narratives women can articulate within patriarchy. Crucially, as Michel Foucault (1978, 62–63) notes, such truth claims within sexual confession also rely on a validating authority 'who requires the confession, prescribes and appreciates it, and intervenes in order to judge, punish, forgive, console, and reconcile', in this case the audience for women's performance poetry. As spoken word poets like Malik, Johar, and Kaur participate in confessional modes of address, the foregrounding of female sexuality and the recuperation of the silenced woman's 'voice' in performance poetry reinstates the (upper-caste) woman poet as the interlocutor who is capable of doing so, but with the validating power residing with the listening and viewing audience as well. Any claims to truth, as a result, have to be witnessed and 'verified' through performance poetry's audience, their snapping, verbal encouragement, and applause.

In the years since Pandey's rape and murder in December 2012, popular Hindi cinema has been a site rife with narratives of gender-based violence, addressing the scale of sexual assault in India and interrogating notions of justice. Hindi films such as *Mardaani* (Sarkar, dir. 2014), *Pink* (Chowdhury, dir. 2016), *Bhoomi* (Kumar, dir. 2017), *Mom* (Udyawar, dir. 2017), and *Simmba* (Shetty, dir. 2018) feature plotlines involving the sexual assault of peripheral female characters, with the films often resorting to vengeful cathartic resolutions generated by 'saviour' protagonists who are related to the survivor. In films like *Mardaani* and *Mom*, the revenge/justice arc is specifically executed by enraged maternal protagonists, so the climactic 'saviour' today can also be imagined as a powerful guardian-like female figure. Meanwhile, the newly minted genres of online comedy through collectives such as All India Bakchod and Girliyapa have also scripted YouTube sketches that satirize rape culture and gender-based violence. Digital feminist initiatives such as Blank Noise and the Indian chapter of #MeToo have proliferated scripts across Facebook, Twitter, and Instagram as sites where women participate in rituals of sexual confession about their experiences of sexism, misogyny, and sexual freedom and such confessions receive public validation in this discursive terrain.

Performance poetry centring sexual assault and agency therefore locates itself within this domain of popular culture and its mediatized mainstream discourses, where the death of Jyoti Singh Pandey haunts the sexual anxieties writ large across poems, but in the spirit of 'Believe All Women', imaginations of sexual violence also emerge as performative truth-telling mediated through a truth-teller, a stage, and an audience. In the case of UnErase Poetry, Kommune, and Tape a Tale, this validating authorizing audience is not just limited to the people present in upscale venues such as The Hive and The Cuckoo Club,[1] but also virtual social media audiences who become imbricated in this mediatization of sex as discourse. Spoken word artists' double-edged discursive deployment of sexual confession thus seems to articulate a sexual subject always under threat of erasure in an oppressive regime, while also producing the upper-caste feminine subject through performative repetitions of survivor stories, which then go on to be circulated and consumed indefinitely on social media sites.

Social media and the spatiality of mediated erotics

Performance poetry's repeated incantations of outrage far transcend the 'private' boundaries of the open mic stage and venue, and have very successfully migrated into more 'public' arenas of popular culture, especially social media where they can circulate and be consumed indefinitely. Each of the poems detailed earlier was uploaded into YouTube on the UnErase Poetry channel and gathered over a million views, with Johar's (2017) 'A Brown Girl's Guide to Gender' hitting one million views within two days and Kaur's (2019) 'I Am Not a Virgin' gathering more than four million views in little over a year. Such circulations of recorded spoken word performances from urban India on a national and transnational scale have enabled the reconfiguration of certain spatialities and temporalities within media discourses. Concerned with how such 'mediated erotics are both embedded within and constitute sociality at the present historical moment', Mankekar and Schein (2012, 4) also explore 'to what end … desire [is] actively incited and sustained by media in conjunction with other social institutions such as the state, structures of family and kinship, and the demands of labor and capital'.

One such sociality that the circulation of performance poetry (re)constitutes virtually is linguistic, specifically the disjuncture between English and Hindi-language cultural spheres. Many of the previously mentioned English-language poems deploy a lexicon that could be considered 'obscene' in the Indian context; they contain words such as 'fuck', 'vagina', 'breasts', and 'orgasm', and even sexual moans are incorporated into their performative modes. Few of the most popular English-language poems on UnErase Poetry's or Kommune India's YouTube channels centre exclusively around desire and romance – as opposed to centring experiences of sexual violence. Instead, it is in a handful of highly popular Hindi–Urdu language poems (only four of which have gathered more than one million views) where articulations of romantic love, following the literary conventions of the genre, function as a placeholder for a more straightforward poetics of sexual want and need. Priya Malik's poem (2020) 'Mujhe Pyaar Nahin, Ishq Chahiye', in fact, presents a conundrum for translatability, highlighting her privileging of an Urdu word for romantic/passionate love [*ishq*], rather than the Hindi word for a more universal love [*pyaar*] that includes the romantic but subsumes more varieties of love in its semantics. Translators for YouTube's close-captioning function translate the title of her poem into English as 'I want love, not infatuation', inevitably modifying the sentiment *pyaar* in the process. The poem itself outlines the demonstrations of *ishq* its subject seeks, a kind of unparalleled, unmatched, unadulterated thirst or yearning, a kind of *ishq* that belongs in novels, and other descriptions of *ishq* implying a long-term heterosexual relationship. Malik enunciates in her conclusion 'Maang nahi rahi hoon, haqdar hoon iski' [I am not asking for it, I am deserving of it] (Malik 2020).

Despite the occasional Anglophone reference in her verse, Malik's distinctly Hindustani registers in her poetry call upon the aesthetics of love poetry in a South Asian linguistic and literary tradition while located within the modern mediatized format. In Hindi and Urdu literary traditions, sexual desires are often woven into the elaborate metaphors of spiritual imagery and a register of elevated emotions, emerging in Malik's poem in a verbal excess that sometimes seems to be in stark contrast to her more staccato delivery of her English-language verse – with lines like ' … jo bemisaal, benazeer, belaus ho, mujhe I pyaas chahiye … bebaak bekhauf betakalluf bandagi chahiye … mujhe pyaar nahin ishq chahiye' [That which is peerless, unmatchable, unadulterated, I want that thirst … I want an expressive, fearless, effortless devotion … I want love, not infatuation] (Malik 2020). Malik recites these alliterative lines, her eyes closed and her body swaying to the acoustic electric guitar strumming in the background, as the recorded performance avoids any overtly sexual or 'obscene' impulse catering to a much more conservative style of romantic poetry that is culturally recognizable for both the immediate and the digital audiences. The mediated erotics of Hindustani spoken word thus fall within the morally acceptable and respectable parameters of chaste upper-caste femininity.

Another configuration of sociality that digital media destabilizes is that of region and space, of urban sexual cultures located in metropolitan Indian cities such as Delhi and Mumbai that are translated through digital media for social media audiences in non-metropolitan cities (also known as tier-2 and tier-3 cities) or perhaps even more peripherally, in *mofussil* [provincial or rural] towns and rural districts. In Moira Rajpal's (2018) performance of 'Hookup Culture', an English-language poem, Rajpal's poetic narrator expresses disenchantment about the casual violence of urban hookup culture and bemoans a generation that has forgotten the romance of what it is like to simply hold someone's hand or talk long hours into the night. One might expect that such a feminine return to modesty in rejecting hookup culture would resonate with the large non-metropolitan YouTube audiences in India. However, the YouTube video's 'Comments' section contains a litany of responses from Hindi-speaking Indian users who reject the idea of hookup culture as being ubiquitous across India and specifically assign it to be a subcultural issue for the metro cities. As one commentator going by the name 'mukcool arora' says in Hindi: 'Hookup wagarh bade cities k lafde hai. Yaha toh pure time engineering k exam clear mein he chla jata hai [*sic*]' [Hookups etc. are problems in big cities. Here, all our time goes into clearing engineering exams] (Rajpal 2018). With this comment having gathered 738 likes, another commentator responds, saying 'Bade citites [*sic*] Mein Bhi aisa kuch nai hota. Yeh Sirf 10% of ppl on whole city hai joh Yeh karte hai. Us 10% ke Liye isne purey generation ko badnam kar diya' [Even in big cities, this doesn't happen. There is just 10% of the whole city who do this. For that 10% she has badmouthed a whole generation] (Rajpal 2018). Another commentator 'LolGuy' reiterates this opinion, saying:

> I am not familiar with this culture. Maybe it happens with rich kids of metros. From where I am from people are desperately trying to clear IBPS clerk exam. Lol. Or trying to get into any government job. No time for hookups for us. Just a few days back I gave an exam of ECGC PO,

which is an average middle class job with hardly 10 seats and at least over a lakh people competing. This is my reality. (Rajpal 2018)

These discursive rejections of hookup culture and sexual excess as irrelevant to any collective beyond a small privileged urban elite ignore Rajpal's articulations of not-so-sexual romantic desires that could be considered relevant to conservative or middle-class sexual experience. The incongruity between her fluent English-language verses and the Hindi-language comments also underscores how the unspecified 'here' of these commentators imbricates them in a predominantly non-metropolitan geography that is also classed and cultured in different registers. More critically, these accentuated differences of region, language, and culture are heightened by circulation of performance poetry as YouTube media text far beyond its immediate audience, as non-metropolitan audiences have little by way of access to upscale performance venues in suburbs like Bandra and Khar in Mumbai to engage with the performance in person. Rather than mark the typical 'West' as the site of sexual freedom then, it is upper-caste elite metropolitan sexual subjects who are constructed by their less-urban counterparts as distant – both literally and figuratively – privileged citizens against whom a discontinuity of provincial middle-class desires and pleasures can be articulated. This demarcation of desire/lack through articulations of a difference of spatiality echo what Baishya (2017, 62) has noted is a spectatorial desire to map and locate space in circulating digital media texts for audiences to form a sense of identity – an emplaced identity – connected to that space and place, or as in the case of women performance poets, distanced from the cosmopolitan urban centres of India.

Perhaps the best example for the power of the YouTube video to confound assumptions about regionality and audience is Aranya Johar's assimilation into a culture of transnational celebrity with her poems 'A Brown Girl's Guide to Gender' (Johar 2017) and 'A Brown Girl's Guide to Beauty' (Johar 2017) going intensely viral. Johar's deployment of 'brown' as a self-descriptor is unusual in the Indian context, where it is region, language, caste, and class that are often indexed in people's surnames and cultural habitus, but not race. Furthermore, in urban India's highly colourist popular culture, where being fair-skinned is considered to be a significant marker of beauty, self-describing as 'brown' is not common practice. Johar's choice to title her poems as and self-identify as 'brown' to her immediate Indian audience therefore indicates an awareness of a wider global audience already undergirding the poem's composition. Johar is far from alone in referring to herself as brown; several poets such as Taranjit Kaur and Ishmeet Nagpal also make references to their 'brown skin' in their poems.

Significantly, Johar's viral popularity was reported in two America-based publications covering youth and millennial issues, *Teen Vogue* (Wu 2017) and *Mic* (Lubitz 2017), with a link to her poem 'A Brown Girl's Guide to Beauty' (2017). Both articles cover the critique of colourism that Johar's poem offers, reflecting American media's increased awareness about topics of racism, diversity, and representation. However, her celebrity in American media expanded to include an opportunity to feature as a Bill & Melinda Gates Foundation's 2018 Goalkeeper, a nominated young leader who meets other global Goalkeepers in New York City to discuss innovations and approaches to achieve the UN's Sustainable Development Goals ('Three Young Leaders Honored: "Saving the World is Child's Play"' 2018) and an invitation to the G7 Gender Advisory Council (Johar 2019).

The rise of the microcelebrity and the mainstreaming of internet culture has meant that as the American media empire continues to target transnational markets in the Global South, an apolitical multiculturalism peppers their media discourse creating spaces where subjects can enter the American discursive imagination by marking themselves as 'brown', speaking to white American logics of race and nationality.

Such a socially aware celebrity culture where gender and sexuality can discursively mobilize vectors of race and nation brings us to a crucial aspect of performance poetry and its mediatized proliferation in the current moment – the hypervisibility of identity. Somers-Willett (2009, 4) observes that the roots of the slam poetry movement in the USA situate themselves within working-class neighbourhoods and their bar rooms, with working-class poets expressing 'frustration over the academic monopoly on poetry readings and the attending high brow airs of these events'. This combined with an open-door policy where anyone was welcome to participate either as a poet or in the audience lent a democratized air to slam poetry events, ultimately coming to be dominated by youth demographics (2009, 6). Hoffman (2013, 205) also notes that 'spoken word in the United States in recent decades has been tied up in powerful social movements that have reframed – and validated – cultural identities of minority citizens'. The Western roots of performance poetry culture thus evolved through such modalities of class, age, and spaces but also the successful circulation of identitarian scripts.

In the Indian context, gender and sexuality have emerged as critical discursive categories in the context of spoken word poetry, mobilizing popular feminist logics of representation and visibility. Sarah Banet-Weiser (2018, 22–23) examines popular feminism through such circuits of visibility, arguing that '[e]conomies of visibility fundamentally shift politics of visibility so that visibility becomes the end rather than a means to an end', and that the goal thus remains trapped within neoliberal logics of empowerment. Relying upon profit-seeking mainstream and social media also means that continual visibility is informed through mechanisms of surveillance and control (2018, 25). In contrast to these urban high-return economies of visibility are the more regional and vernacular performance spaces, where it is not often spoken word poets but comedians, singers, and musicians, with localized registers, aesthetics, and cultural traditions, who are spotlighted. Unlike their elite counterparts, however, these texts circulate through smaller economies of visibility, often through community networks and local media platforms that may not reach pan-Indian Anglophone audiences but circulate easily amongst millions of vernacular users.

Indeed, as urban and cosmopolitan women poets claim the spotlight of the stage to articulate their own gendered and sexual subjectivity, media processes imbricate them within wider neoliberal techniques of self-representation so that discourses of trauma, marginalization, and disenfranchisement accumulating likes and shares seem to become the end goal in themselves. Lauren Berlant (2001, 42) has noted that the circulation of media texts of trauma is likely to enable a kind of sentimentalizing of public culture, where 'proximity to trauma' influences how a subject can be formed in sexuality discourse, and then scripting a narrative of sexual self-transformation also potentially becomes imbricated in neoliberal triumph, less emancipatory, and 'more like "empowering"' (2001, 47). Harrington (2019, 1182) further notes that social media logics drive incitements to speak out about sexual violence, so that rape survivors are caught within the performative scripts of social media forms and genres. Johar's mediatized celebrity status perhaps best demonstrates the entanglement of performance poetry with these neoliberal scripts of transformation and triumph, qualifying her ability to speak for 'brown' women as a whole, if not 'women' themselves as a whole.

However, if American slam poets have made it clear that their articulations of marginalized identity are 'a challenge to the relative lack of diversity they feel in the academy, the canon and the dominant culture' (Somers-Willett 2009, 7), then spoken word poetry's cultural circuits in India speak to a fairly different demographic where academic concerns about poetry remain secondary or perhaps even irrelevant to feminine concerns over self-expression and identity. One could even deem these spoken word poems as demonstrating mediocre craft – as several comments do – which is perhaps secondary to this poetry's function for the poets, of being able to circulate widely through digital media technologies and participate in microcelebrity and influencer culture. Avenues of upper-caste urban performance culture and digital media content stretch far beyond spoken word poetry, with stand-up comedy and open mic events emerging as spaces where social taboos against sexual discourse and profanity have been loosened, but which ironically nonetheless emerged as sites where sexual assault and gender-based violence were rife, as #MeTooIndia exposed (Kanga, Kappal, and Sharma 2018).

Perhaps more significantly, as the next section explores, in contrast to these Anglophone metropolitan spaces with globalized universal registers of sexual speech are several regional arts and culture festival spaces, where localized vernacular performances of gender and sexuality are articulated. As Tamil, Kannada, Telugu, and Malayalam arts and culture festivals gain traction in state-sponsored urban cultural event spaces, these new avenues of popular culture situate their gendered operations in the terrain of the regional rather than the national, the vernacular rather than the Anglophone cosmopolitan, the masses rather than the markets. The particular case of the Casteless Collective is useful to contrast how the 'castelessness' of the urban upper caste is problematized through a very different semiotics of the 'casteless' – one voiced by musical artists whose politics is explicitly framed through anti-caste and feminist histories of liberatory struggles.

Castelessness in regimes of gender and sexuality

Brahmin-savarna women dominate spoken word performance circuits in urban India, yet as in much of mainstream Indian popular culture, their caste identity often goes completely unmarked in their own poetry and its commentary. This unmarked aspect of upper castes has socio-political genealogies in the public sphere, with the Indian state withdrawing from naming or acting against caste-based advantages held by the upper castes 'so long as they wore the garb of secular modernity', while legislating against caste-based disadvantages borne by the lower castes (Deshpande 2013, 37). M. S. S. Pandian (2002, 1737–1738) has also traced 'the intimacy between [postcolonial] modernity and the desire to keep caste out of the public sphere' by modern Brahmins, who expended efforts to efface their own caste identity while producing 'caste by other means'. The effects of caste – particularly its most advantageous outcomes – have thus been rendered invisible in upper-caste lifeworlds and discourses, while the effects of caste in lower-caste lifeworlds have only recently become more visible as caste violence.

In historicizing the emergence of the woman subject in particular, feminist histories have produced an unmarked woman as the liberal subject of feminism, whose struggles for agency and autonomy have been appropriated into nationalist agendas around the 'women's question' (Sreekumar 2017). Incidents of sexual assault and violence in the 2000s, such as the Mangalore 'pub-slapping' incident of 2009 or Pandey's rape and murder in December 2012, generated popular outrage against India's rape culture. However, mainstream and digital media commentaries as well as feminist studies that analyzed the protests maintained silence around the victims' dominant caste positionalities, even when class and region emerged as analytics. When class has featured in feminist scholarship on campaigns such as 'Why Loiter?', 'Take Back the Night', and the Blank Noise initiative, the recognition of the women participants as 'middle-class' tentatively acknowledges the presence of caste difference (Roy 2016) but offers little analysis of the caste and sexual economies these participants are subjected to – for instance, whether caste logics of land and urban real estate influence middle-class women's freedoms in public spaces such as city centres or 'dangerous neighbourhoods'. Or, also, if the political economy of caste is critical in constructing the 'public' and the 'private' spheres through which middle-class women must negotiate risk and safety. Navaneetha Mokkil (2018, 160) has suggested that in contrast to lower-caste women's public visibility as sexual subjects – through contentious professions such as bar dancing and sex work – upper-caste women's sexuality has been afforded an enclosed 'private' character that then has to be cast off to embrace free public expression of pleasure and desire. The sexual freedoms and liberatory visibility that upper-caste women stake a claim to thus serve to exclude lower-caste women, whose vexed histories with publicness and visibility remain unresolved.

Contradictions between family, marriage, and property dictated through endogamous conjugality in the private sphere, and the sexual and political freedoms for bodily autonomy fought for in the public sphere, highlight some of the yawning gaps that continue to haunt Indian theorizations of sexuality. Uma Chakravarti's (2003, 1–2) observation from the anti-Mandal agitations of 1990, where upper-caste women opposing caste-based reservations carried placards saying 'We don't want unemployed husbands', has been one instance where upper-caste women's enthusiastic participation in the sexual economy of endogamous marriages was made transparent by the women themselves. Indeed, in a social order where caste's most egregious forms of violence were legislated through a politics of touchability and untouchability – an entire epistemology built around who we can touch, where we can touch, when we can touch – caste and its epistemologies of touch have featured in feminist frameworks for sex and sexuality in feminist scholarship. Anupama Rao (2005, 6) has noted that the symbolic dispossession of Dalitbahujan women emanating from their material dispossession 'are mediated by the regulation of sexual and gender identity through the rules of kinship and caste purity' (2005, 7). Such a critique of casteless feminism(s) demands a 're-examination of gender relations as fundamental to the broader ideologies of caste' (2005, 5).

In the context of such complex layering of identities within popular culture, our reading strategies for spoken word poetry need to attend to the poetic discourse of sexuality that produces a set of effects in the bodies, behaviours, and the social relations of sexual subjects. Revisiting these texts, several gestures towards 'castelessness' made by the poems' discourse become obvious. For instance, Kaur's (2019) framing of virginity in 'I Am Not a Virgin' remains firmly ensconced within the biological, where it is the act (or lack) of bleeding that shapes the experience of a 'purity test', and not the social construction of virginity within the sociality of caste and its convoluted codes of honour, implicating bloodlines, inheritance, and property. Critically, the institution of caste-based arranged marriage goes uninterrogated in Kaur's critique of 'purity tests', as endogamous marriages remain foundational as an institution enforcing compulsory heterosexuality within the bounds of caste. In a similar vein, Johar's (2017) poem 'A Brown Girl's Guide to Gender' also references the hymen, framing virginity as a kind of biological purity test. She concludes by thanking the men in the room, stating 'we're all collectively reaching out for you'. The poem's appeal and gratitude to a redemptive masculinity begs the question of which men can occupy this room at The Habitat venue in Khar, Mumbai, and what investments enable poets from dominant castes to safely call upon their moral 'goodness' to redeem themselves.

Our reading strategies for spoken word poetry also need to attend to the fact that the effects of sexual discourse are produced unevenly across castes, so that similar spoken word poetry about sexual pleasure, desire, and agency are muted in the spoken word scene from Dalit, OBC, or Adivasi subjects who remain absent in Anglophone popular culture. This mirrors women's visibility in parallel spaces overlapping with performance poetry, such as in stand-up comedy, where Aju James has noted that an empowered upper-caste femininity has become:

> a characteristic associated with the new middle class and therefore part of the global Indian identity. The 'undesirable' lower caste and working-class characteristics, on the other hand, are coded as a virulent male threat to the safety of these spaces. (2020, 12)

The absent lower-caste feminine subject in popular culture gains even more salience when considering how Dalit women have become reified objects of sexual violence in the news, from caste atrocities like Khairlanji in 2006 to Hathras in 2020, so that scripts of sexual violence, victimhood, abjection, and death define the contours of their existence.

In her essay 'Swipe Me Left, I'm Dalit', Christina Dhanaraj (2020) describes what it is like to navigate dating as a Dalit woman, saying 'we are not seen as being capable of desire, love, or happiness; we don't seem to exist as individuals outside of violence'. Dhanaraj (2020) also remarks upon how a 'non-Dalit' femininity aligns with hierarchies of skin colour, a pigmentocracy, observing that 'the Dalit woman is perceived mostly in comparison to her non-Dalit counterpart: the lighter-skinned savarna woman who is pure, quiet and delicate, versus the dark-skinned Dalit woman who is polluting, loud and tough'. When contrasted with Johar's self-proclamation as a 'brown girl', Dalit feminist critique suggests that ascribing 'brownness' to savarna women's identity for a globalized audience can only be a productive function of sexual discourse for savarna women. Dhanaraj's essay also offers an articulation of difference for Dalit women whose experiences of sex, dating, and love do not adhere to the cis-heteronormative Brahminical scripts for romance. Elaborating upon how being Dalit complicates relationships with non-Dalit partners, she notes that:

> ... in most cis-hetero relationships, the price paid by a Dalit woman (stereotyped as angry and unfeminine) towards its success is far higher than that required of a non-Dalit woman. The latter can retain her political self and still be perceived as feminine, while the former will

> have to keep proving her femininity by choosing to not voice her political opinions, which are typically deemed as irrational. (Dhanaraj 2020)

This framing of a Dalit woman's political and politicized identity calibrating her performance of femininity has deep histories within academic caste–sexuality discourse as well as anti-caste activism, where Dalitbahujan figures such as the devadasi, the jogini, nautch girls, and more recently bar dancers have been labelled as engaging in 'obscene' occupations and remain stigmatized for residing outside the norms of feminine respectability. Writing for the anti-caste platform Round Table India, Jenny Rowena (2012) has pointed out that savarna feminist theory 'has constructed a hegemonic feminist politics for us, which is completely monopolized by upper caste women's concerns with regard to sexuality' and that:

> even when referring to issues of caste differences, sexual control of women etc, still manages to locate the Brahmin and upper caste women as more sexually oppressed than other subaltern women, whose exploitation (in sex work, devadasi system, etc) is often viewed as sites of agency, subversion and resistance. (Rowena 2012)

Feminist articulations that foreground sexual freedom (as opposed to other freedoms) from the upper-caste end of the spectrum without addressing how Dalitbahujan women remain materially exploited through the (de)legitimizing power of the caste-gender discourse of sexuality illustrate the limits of current sexual discourse. Indeed, the emergence of sexual modernity in late colonial India in the early twentieth century is entangled in caste logics, and as Shrikant Botre (2017, 309) argues, epistemologies of the obscene in sexual discourse consisted of a 'caste-sexual core', scripted as they were by Brahmin sex-educators who methodically constructed lower-caste lifeworlds and social practices as the obscene Other.

Within such repressive apparatuses of caste society, will a Dalit performance poet articulating a history of surviving sexual assault risk herself being reproduced in discourse as the indecent and obscene woman subject of history? The case of Isaivani in the indie Tamil music band the Casteless Collective proves to be a contrasting yet illustrative phenomenon in thinking about the performative boundaries of caste and gender, as a Dalit woman performer in a band with predominantly Dalit male band members performing in live events across Chennai in Tamil Nadu that are then circulated as WhatsApp and YouTube clips. Specializing in *gaana*, a form of urban folk music made popular by Tamil cinema, along with rock, hip-hop, and rap influences, the band – usually dressed in Ambedkarite-blue suits – composes original music advocating messages of social justice, equality, and Dr Ambedkar's call for the annihilation of caste. Isaivani appears in several recordings of these live events, also dressed in their trademark blue suit, with a long ponytail or her hair loose, singing about Dalit-Ambedkarite politics. In her rendition of the popular song 'I am sorry Ayyappa' (referring to the deity of the Sabarimala temple that bans women devotees to preserve the celibate mythology of Ayyappa), she sings about a liberatory politics of women's independence and agency, arguing that whether to wear jeans or a saree, to work as a nurse or doctor, to remain single or commit to a relationship, the choice should be hers alone ('I Am Sorry Ayyappa' 2019).

Isaivani's presence in a band terming itself a 'casteless' collective foregrounds a radically different imagination of castelessness from Deshpande's (2013) outline of the castelessness of upper castes, one that is driven by anti-caste histories and imaginaries of resistance and liberation. In songs reclaiming women's bodily autonomy intimately connected with the vision of an egalitarian society across caste, class, gender, and sexuality, the Dalit woman's desire is scripted away from the individualized erotics of her own body (in language that evades being slotted as obscene) and towards material freedoms for women collectively. Castelessness as articulated here is Ambedkarite and futurist, what Dickens (2019, 51) describes as 'a caste-less community for anti/post-caste possibilities'. While I do not imply that aspiring for castelessness allows the members of the Casteless Collective to have succeeded as such, the circulated clips of their live performances in digital economies of visibility suggest new discursive possibilities for caste and gender, where Dalits and particularly the Dalit woman are not constructed through popular trauma narratives but that her markedly Dalit identity and presence in vernacularized and subordinated performance cultures differentiates her from her savarna counterparts. Crucially, as long as she remains recognizably Dalit in the spectatorial gaze, then spoken word poets should remain recognizably savarna despite their omissions of caste identity. However, as the mediated erotics in digital spoken word culture remain mired in savarna-casteless feminist media discourses, perhaps the Casteless Collective's live performances signal that rare heterotopic other-space that has yet to be realized in Anglophone media culture which speaks to the political histories of the English language itself in India.

Anti-caste vernaculars for the erotic in digital media spaces must be highlighted here as operating in the fraught cross-currents of anatomy and obscenity, what Botre (2017, 289–290) notes have been 'mutually constitutive phenomena, fundamentally linked with the epistemic politics of caste'. As one of the few Bahujan women writers in English, for instance, Meena Kandasamy's use of erotics and profanity in her 2011 poetry collection *Ms. Militancy* was met with outrage by conservative audiences on its publication and – unlike the upper-caste women poets on YouTube – her published work continues to draw the ire of Brahminical social forces and the threat of legal action to date. For now, upper-caste performance poets still remain under the radar of the state's censorial apparatus while tenuously staking their spaces in Mumbai's performance venues and on digital platforms. However, the persistent debates about regulation of online media platforms and their liberal hosting of anti-establishment content, whether sexual, feminist, anti-caste, or critical of the state in any way, suggest that their performances remain vulnerable to accusations of being pornography. These fissures are further compounded by popular feminist frameworks of visibility as liberatory and the messy processes through which marginalized women subjects can purportedly claim more power in visibility. The disparate power stakes in mediated erotics suggest that marginalized caste subjects have more to lose if labelled obscene than their upper-caste counterparts.

Conclusion

In light of these fraught discursive histories, performance poetry and digital media's attempts at a sexual discourse that (re)imagines sexual futures beyond patriarchal control remain trapped in a casteless politics and aesthetics of disavowal. If spoken word poets' attempts to claim a universally appealing feminism expose the limits of metropolitan, Anglophone, and savarna imaginaries of emancipation, then the Tamil-Ambedkarite vernacular articulations of women's rights enmeshed in anti-caste struggles suggest the potentiality of the regional-urban, language, and the local as alternative sites for animating women's freedoms and desires, but perhaps never completely escaping the boundaries of the nation (Sreekumar 2017, 62). Along with savarna performances marking their emerging feminist subject as a 'casteless' middle-class everywoman, she is also, as transfeminist critics will point to, markedly cisgender, navigating and cautiously resisting chaste caste-femininity and operating within hegemonic frameworks of gender and heteronormativity. Her sexual freedom is also delimited by its reliance on cis-heteronormative institutions such as dating, hookup culture, and marriage. As Tharu and Niranjana (1996, 99) remind us, in India 'the marking of "women" as middle class and upper caste has a long genealogy' and while nationalist ideology hovers in the backdrop of most of these performances, they inevitably rear their head through regulating mechanisms such as transnational media cultures or, more institutionally, in obscenity laws.

In 2015, Mumbai-based comedy collective All India Bakchod organized a Hollywood-style comedy roast (called AIB Knockout) of two prominent Bollywood stars in Mumbai to a live audience of around 4000 people, and within the week it was uploaded to their YouTube channel. The roast format involved insults and jokes about the participants' appearances and professions but also sexual orientations, orgies, sex addiction, and choice of prior sexual partners – and media commentators summed up the show as 'filthy' and 'rude', but nonetheless entertaining (Bhattacharya 2015). The nearly two-hour-long video was met with 'a wave of public outcry over its perceived indecency and an order for a government probe' with a member of the film censor board referring to it as 'a porn show on stage' (Bhushan 2015). With persistent social condemnation followed by a legal investigation into the show due to accusations of obscenity, AIB pulled the show from its YouTube channel and made public apologies for its content rife with sexual innuendo, insults, and profane banter.

The AIB Roast debacle remains emblematic of the many performative and mediated forms of affect emerging out of sexuality discourse that can call upon repressive state apparatuses to reinscribe dominant notions of community, identity, and nation over rebellious subjects. Despite the roast's agenda being primarily embedded in a Western humour format – that is, not a typically erotic or pornographic format – that was new to urban India, its use of explicit language and references to sexual acts marked it as indecent and obscene, leading to its withdrawal from YouTube. Spoken word poetry overlaps with the very same spaces as Indian stand-up and comedy culture, as similarly mediated content that is performed in urban performance venues and hosted on YouTube for online dissemination and consumption. YouTube thus brings together different genres of content all of which have the potential to be labelled obscene, because as Shah (2007, 33) observes, they not only threaten to disrupt India's conservative sexual culture, they also imply easy access to the 'pornographic' through the web.

The attribution of indecency, obscenity, and pornography to any content deemed transgressive of a Brahminical social order has imbricated genres such as performance poetry in persistent debates in the public sphere, which are concerned with the regulation of online content and platforms. It must be stressed that the women performance poets have also confronted harassment and rape and death threats as their performances went viral (Joshi 2017), but none of the YouTube channels or performance organizers have buckled to social pressure. The government's recent decision to bring over-the-top streaming content providers under the direct purview of the Ministry of Information and Broadcasting (*The Hindu* 2020) now raises questions about how far the state's regulatory approach will affect YouTube content, especially as calls to boycott over-the-top platforms over their more sexually and politically liberal content become more commonplace.

Spoken word poetry's uneasy position in urban India's public culture today thus maps the terrain of sexual subject formation in a complex terrain between distance and intimacy, physicality and virtuality, resistance and recuperation, ideology and affect. As such a mediatized culture demands more affect-generating texts circulate among audiences near and far, the popularity of sexually charged popular feminist discourses in the wake of #MeToo articulating what it is to desire in this cultural moment is far from likely to dissipate. Examining the construction and evocation of desire and erotics in its multifarious avatars and its refractions through unequal social formations of caste, class, gender, and race, however, can better animate our understanding of mediations of desire in India today through the visibility of various women subjects.

Note

1. The Hive and The Cuckoo Club are performance venues located in Khar and Bandra, respectively – two prominent affluent suburbs in central Mumbai. Founded and owned by businesspersons Sharin Bhatti and Sudeep Nair, both spaces are intended for performances and screenings, as well as potentially a co-working space for members of Mumbai's arts and culture scene. Both spaces have previously hosted poetry, theatre performances, stand-up comedy, workshops, and open mic events.

Disclosure statement

No potential conflict of interest was reported by the author.

ORCID

Pallavi Rao http://orcid.org/0000-0001-6693-5069

References

Baishya, Anirban K. 2017. 'Pornography of Place: Location, Leaks and Obscenity in the Indian MMS Porn Video.' *South Asian Popular Culture* 15 (1): 57–71.

Baishya, Anirban K. and Darshana S. Mini. 2020. 'Translating Porn Studies: Lessons from the Vernacular.' *Porn Studies* 7 (1): 2–12.

Banet-Weiser, Sarah. 2018. *Empowered: Popular Feminism and Popular Misogyny*. Durham: Duke University Press.

Berlant, Lauren. 2001. 'Trauma and Ineloquence.' *Cultural Values* 5 (1): 41–58.

Bhattacharya, Ananya. 2015. 'AIB Knockout: 25 Filthy, Rude, Offensive Jokes That Had Us ROFL-Ing.' *India Today*, January 29. https://www.indiatoday.in/movies/bollywood/story/aib-knockout-roast-ranveer-singh-arjun-kapoor-karan-johar-gay-filthy-rude-offensive-jokes-237895-2015-01-29.

Bhushan, Nyay. 2015. 'Bollywood's First Celebrity Roast Slapped With Obscenity Probe | Hollywood Reporter.' *The Hollywood Reporter*, April 2. https://www.hollywoodreporter.com/news/bollywoods-first-celebrity-roast-slapped-770070.

Botre, Shrikant. 2017. 'The Body Language of Caste : Marathi Sexual Modernity (1920–1950).' Ph.D., University of Warwick. http://wrap.warwick.ac.uk/110543/.

Chakravarti, Uma. 2003. *Gendering Caste Through a Feminist Lens*. New Delhi: Popular Prakashan.

Chowdhury, Aniruddha Roy, dir. 2016. *Pink*. India.

Crown, Kathleen. 2002. "Sonic Revolutionaries': Voice and Experiment in the Spoken-Word Poetry of Tracie Morris.' In *We Who Love to Be Astonished: Experimental Women's Writing and Performance Poetics*, edited by Laura Hinton and Cynthia Hogue, 213–226. Tuscaloosa: University of Alabama Press.

Deshpande, Satish. 2013. 'Caste and Castelessness: Towards a Biography of the "General Category".' *Economic and Political Weekly* 48 (39): 32–39.

Dhanaraj, Christina. 2020. 'What Do Dating, Romance and Love Really Mean for a Dalit Woman in India Today?' *Scroll.In*, July 31. https://scroll.in/article/969032/what-do-dating-romance-and-love-really-mean-for-a-dalit-woman-in-india-today.

Dickens, Leonard. 2019. 'Towards a Caste-Less Community.' *Economic and Political Weekly* 54 (21): 47–54.

Foucault, Michel. 1978. *The History of Sexuality, Vol. 1: An Introduction*. New York: Vintage.

Goldstein, Lynda. 1999. 'Raging in Tongues: Confession and Performance Art.' In *Confessional Politics: Women's Sexual Self-Representations in Life Writing and Popular Media*, edited by Irene Gammel, 99–116. Carbondale: SIU Press.

Harrington, Carol. 2019. 'Neo-Liberal Subjectivity, Self-Branding and "My Rape Story" YouTube Videos.' *Critical Sociology* 45 (7–8): 1181–1194.

Hoffman, Tyler. 2013. *American Poetry in Performance*. Ann Arbor: University of Michigan Press.

"I Am Sorry Ayyappa அய்யப்பன் கோயிலுக்கு பெண்கள் செலவோம். - பா ரஞ்சித் நீலம் பண்பாட்டு மையம்." 2019. YouTube. https://www.youtube.com/watch?v=SkG1rTA4ris.

James, Aju. 2020. 'Caste, Gender, and "Global Indian-Ness": Spaces of Safety in Stand-up Comedy in Global Mumbai.' *Feminist Media Studies*, 1–17. doi:10.1080/14680777.2020.1815230.

Johar, Aranya. 2017. '"A Brown Girl's Guide to Beauty" - Aranya Johar.' *YouTube*. July 7. https://www.youtube.com/watch?v=ZX5soNoPill&ab_channel=UnErasePoetry.

Johar, Aranya. 2017. '"A Brown Girl's Guide to Gender" - Aranya Johar (Women's Day Special).' *YouTube*, March 10. https://www.youtube.com/watch?v=75Eh5OnNeoY&ab_channel=UnErasePoetry.

Johar, Aranya. 2019. 'So Honoured to Share That Your Brown Girl Is the Youngest Member of the Gender Equality Advisory Council for the G7 This Year Taking Place … .' *Instagram*, May 13. https://www.instagram.com/p/BxZWTgZJUVy/?hl=en.

Joshi, Sonam. 2017. 'Women vs Sexism, One Verse at a Time.' *The Times of India*, November 19. https://timesofindia.indiatimes.com/home/sunday-times/women-vs-sexism-one-verse-at-a-time/articleshow/61705578.cms.

Kandasamy, Meena. 2011. *Ms Militancy*. New Delhi: Navayana Publishers.

Kanga, Surabhi, Bhanuj Kappal, and Arnav Das Sharma. 2018. 'How Only Much Louder Failed the Women in Its Ranks.' *The Caravan*, November 1. https://caravanmagazine.in/gender/how-oml-failed-women-ranks.

Kaur, Taranjit. 2019. '"I Am Not A Virgin" - Taranjit Kaur Ft. Siddhant | UnErase Poetry.' *YouTube*, April 27. https://www.youtube.com/watch?v=eywbtzSApZl&ab_channel=UnErasePoetry.

Kumar, Omung, dir. 2017. *Bhoomi*. India.

Lubitz, Rachel. 2017. 'Don't Think Representation in the Beauty Industry Really Matters? Hear This Teen's Poetry.' *Mic*, July 11. https://www.mic.com/articles/181926/dont-think-representation-in-the-beauty-industry-really-matters-hear-this-teens-poetry.

Malik, Priya. 2017. '"Right To Pleasure" - Priya Malik | #MyBodyIsNotATemple.' *YouTube*, September 25. https://www.youtube.com/watch?v=-KqwPcBub3o&ab_channel=UnErasePoetry.

Malik, Priya. 2020. '"Mujhe Pyaar Nahin, Ishq Chahiye" – Priya Malik Ft Samuel | Valentines Day | UnErase Poetry.' *YouTube*. February 12. https://www.youtube.com/watch?v=5gD1CWE3dpA&ab_channel=UnErasePoetry.

Mankekar, Purnima. 2012. 'Dangerous Desires: Erotics, Public Culture, and Identity in Late Twentieth-Century India.' In *Media, Erotics, and Transnational Asia*, edited by Purnima Mankekar and Louisa Schein, 173–202. Durham: Duke University Press.

Mankekar, Purnima and Louisa Schein. 2012. *Media, Erotics, and Transnational Asia*. Durham: Duke University Press Books.

Mini, Darshana Sreedhar. 2019. '"Un-Sound" Sounds: Pornosonics of Female Desire in Indian Mediascapes.' *Music, Sound, and the Moving Image* 13 (1): 3–30.

Mokkil, Navaneetha. 2018. 'Visual Practices, Affect, and the Body: The Story of a Night-Vigil in Kerala, India.' *Women's Studies Quarterly* 46 (3 & 4): 158–174.

Mowlabocus, Sharif and Andy Medhurst. 2017. 'Six Propositions on the Sonics of Pornography.' *Porn Studies* 4 (2): 210–224.

Pandian, M. S. S. 2002. 'One Step Outside Modernity: Caste, Identity Politics and Public Sphere.' *Economic and Political Weekly* 37 (18): 1735–1741.

Rajpal, Moira. 2018. '"Hookup Culture" – Moira Rajpal | UnErase Poetry.' *YouTube*, February 9. https://www.youtube.com/watch?v=O_whGoi_Q8Y&t=78s&ab_channel=UnErasePoetry.

Rao, Anupama, ed. 2005. *Gender & Caste*. London;New York: Zed Books.

Rowena, Jenny. 2012. 'The "Dirt" in The Dirty Picture: Caste, Gender and Silk Smitha - Part 2.' *Round Table India*, October 8. https://roundtableindia.co.in/index.php?option=com_content&view=article&id=5822:the-dirt-in-the-dirty-picture-caste-gender-and-silk-smitha-part-2&catid=119:feature&Itemid=132.

Roy, Srila. 2016. 'Breaking the Cage.' *Dissent Magazine*. https://www.dissentmagazine.org/article/breaking-cage-india-feminism-sexual-violence-public-space.

Sarkar, Pradeep, dir. 2014. *Mardaani*. India.

Shah, Nishant. 2007. 'PlayBlog: Pornography, Performance and Cyberspace.' In *C'lick Me: A Netporn Studies Reader*, edited by Katrien Jacobs, 31–44. Amsterdam: Institute of Network Cultures.

Shandilya, Krupa. 2015. 'Nirbhaya's Body: The Politics of Protest in the Aftermath of the 2012 Delhi Gang Rape.' *Gender & History* 27 (2): 465–486.

Shetty, Rohit, dir. 2018. *Simmba*. India.

Somers-Willett, Susan B. A. 2009. *The Cultural Politics of Slam Poetry: Race, Identity, and the Performance of Popular Verse in America*. Ann Arbor: University of Michigan Press.

Sreekumar, Sharmila. 2017. 'Equivocations of Gender: Feminist Storytelling and Women's Studies in the Contemporary.' *Indian Journal of Gender Studies* 24 (1): 47–68.

Tharu, Susie and Tejaswini Niranjana. 1994. 'Problems for a Contemporary Theory of Gender.' *Social Scientist* 22 (3/4): 93–117.

The Hindu. 2020. 'Government to Govern Netflix, Amazon Prime and Other OTT Platforms.' November 11. https://www.thehindu.com/news/national/netflix-amazon-prime-other-ott-platforms-now-under-govt-regulation/article33072710.ece.

'Three Young Leaders Honored: "Saving the World Is Child's Play"'. 2018. *SDG Knowledge Hub - A Project by IISD* (blog). September 27. https://sdg.iisd.org:443/news/three-young-leaders-honored-saving-the-world-is-childs-play/.

Udyawar, Ravi, dir. 2017. *Mom*. India.

Wu, Sarah. 2017. 'Slam Poet Aranya Johar Performs "A Brown Girl's Guide to Beauty".' *Teen Vogue*, July 11. https://www.teenvogue.com/story/slam-poet-aranya-johar-brown-girls-guide-to-beauty.

'I am a porn star!' Sex and Sunny Leone unlimited in Bollywood

Tupur Chatterjee

ABSTRACT

Located at the intersections of international porn studies, celebrity studies, gender, sex and globalization, this article looks at the recent and unusual case of Sunny Leone, an Indo-Canadian bisexual pornographic actress who successfully crossed over to Bollywood. By examining her many lives and avatars – as an international porn star, a reality TV contestant, a Bollywood celebrity and now a show host on MTV India, who maintains an active presence on social and digital media – I suggest that the unprecedented situation Sunny Leone has engendered in India presents us with a form of transnational onscenity: in other words, it brings to the fore the centrality of porn in the economies of global cross-cultural exchange and forces us to rethink previous paradigms of both 'pornography' and stardom, two domains that have more or less remained mutually exclusive of each other in the sub-continent. Leone's case brings to the fore economic, social and cultural exchanges between two mammoth entertainment industries, Bollywood and American pornography, which had not encountered each other in these ways before. The capital gains from these exchanges seem to overshadow concerns about preserving the nation's 'moral' fabric and have concurrently given way to newer spaces for accommodating a celebrity like Leone. Given that her crossover from porn presents an absolute rupture from all previous paradigms of female stardom in the Indian context, I place the discourses surrounding her within the tangible anxieties and fantasies of both desire and control over her 'Indian but foreign' and 'pornographic' body. Highlighting Leone's agency through the entire process, which is unique in many regards, this article attempts to further rethink and complicate overarching notions of 'objectification' that often dominate the field.

Introduction

Karenjit Kaur Vohra, better known as Sunny Leone, is an Indo-Canadian adult actress who crossed over from North American pornography and joined Bollywood in 2012. In the four years that she has now spent in India, she has acted not only in Hindi films but also in Kannada and Telegu films. Before moving to India, Leone had an immensely successful career as an adult actress in the United States. Born to Sikh parents in Ontario, Canada, Leone started off as a nude model in California before being discovered by *Penthouse* magazine, and eventually became a contract star with American porn giant Vivid Entertainment, transitioning to hardcore pornography. She has also produced, directed and acted in adult content made by her own production company, Sun Lust Pictures, which she co-owns with her husband and manager, Daniel Weber. She was chosen as a participant on the fifth season of the immensely popular Indian reality show *Bigg Boss* (modelled on UK's *Big Brother*) in 2011, which aired on the primetime Hindi language channel, Colours. Initially, her identity was hidden from her fellow housemates and she claimed to be a model from the United States. But the audience was well aware of her real identity and the country outside the *Bigg Boss* house suddenly awoke to a porn star on their television screens for the first time in history. Following this, she trended on Twitter India non-stop for three days and overtook the Prime Minister Narendra Modi and Bollywood superstar Salman Khan as the most searched for Indian celebrity (a trend that has continued for four years in a row), a cause for concern for many. Some First Information Reports for ruining 'Indian culture' through 'obscenity' have since been filed against her.[1] During the show, veteran Bollywood director and producer Mahesh Bhatt[2] entered the house to offer her the lead role in his daughter Pooja Bhatt's[3] new film *Jism-2* [The Body - 2] (Bhjatt 2012). The audacious mainstream presence of an international hardcore pornographic actress known best for her lesbian porn work in a country that is supremely conservative, homophobic and hostile to any public expressions of nudity or physical intimacy and has only recently reconciled to heterosexual couples kissing on screen has led to considerable debate and endless scrutiny, awe and curiosity around the spectacle that is Sunny Leone.

I situate my analysis of the unusual cross-cultural and post-pornography career of Sunny Leone at the intersection of transnational porn studies, celebrity studies, gender, sex and globalization. Importantly, we need to locate the Sunny Leone scenario within the meanings and significations of 'pornography' in the current Indian context, and especially recent debates around controlling pornographic content on the internet. This in a sense represents what Linda Williams (2004, 3) has called the fundamental paradox of pornography in contemporary popular culture: 'on/scenity: the gesture by which a culture brings on to its public arena the very organs, acts, bodies, and pleasures that have been designated ob/scene and kept literally off the scene'. This article also follows Feona Attwood's (2004, 7) assertions that terms like 'pornography' and 'objectification' might be extremely limiting to the development of this field and that greater emphasis must be placed on the context of particular images (in this case, events) and the reactions they provoke as a more helpful model for understanding contemporary sexual representations. She argues that the early tendency in feminist media studies focused on anti-pornography criticism of porn as being especially sexist and violent towards women and this has tended to close down alternative ways of thinking about gender and sex. This article contextualizes the mainstream presence of Sunny Leone within the multiple meanings of 'pornography' in India and the increasingly disintegrating borders between the 'real and representational, public and private, high and low cultural forms and acceptable and unacceptable sexualities' (Attwood 2004, 17) in a situation where media proliferates and circulates with dizzying rapidity.

Moving away from the familiar narrative of the 'objectification' of a female adult actress, I argue that Leone has registered in the country's collective psyche in multiple ways and more often than not has disrupted the dominant discourse. I suggest that the unprecedented situation Sunny Leone has engendered in India presents us with a form of transnational onscenity: in other words, it brings to the fore the centrality of porn in the economies of global cross-cultural exchange and forces us to rethink previous paradigms of both 'pornography' and stardom, two domains that have more or less remained mutually exclusive in the sub-continent. Leone's case brings to the fore economic, social and cultural exchanges between two mammoth entertainment industries, Bollywood and American pornography, which have not encountered each other in these ways before. The capital gains from these exchanges seem to overshadow concerns about preserving the nation's 'moral' fabric and have concurrently given way to newer spaces for accommodating a celebrity like Leone. Given that her crossover presents an absolute rupture from all previous paradigms of female stardom in the Indian context, I place the discourses surrounding her within the tangible anxieties and fantasies of both desire and control over her 'Indian but foreign' and 'pornographic' body. How is the present situation different from previous or comparative instances? Highlighting Leone's agency through the entire process, which is unique in many regards, this article also attempts to further rethink and complicate overarching notions of 'objectification' that often dominate the field.

India has had a long-standing history of depictions of sex, sexuality and eroticism in art, architecture and literature, prime examples of which are ancient temple architectures,[4] a fascinating manual on sexual arousal, erotic love and pleasure – the Sanskrit *Kamasutra*[5] [A Manual of Sex] – and Mughal and Rajput miniature paintings. Hindi-Urdu cinema, originating in Bombay, however, has long chosen to restrict sex to the heteronormative domain of Hindu marriage (although any actual expressions of physical intimacy are extremely rare) and sexual energy among heterosexual couples is often presented through suggestive song lyrics and sexually charged dance numbers, in which censorship has played a huge role.[6] Such iterations have become safe and commonplace through the decades and audiences are still encouraged to find pleasure through repression on screen. Frequently, overt expressions of sexual desire or sex have been immediately labelled as 'vulgar' and 'dangerous', leading to moral panic and debates about maintaining the purity of 'Indian culture'.[7] Long kissing scenes or female actors in bikinis in Indian films have been the subject of speculation and conversations in the media because of their 'boldness'. These were some of the early expressions of moral panic directed against the forces of globalization 'and the paraphernalia that it carries with it; arguments which were eventually mapped onto the arrival of the Internet and easy access to "pornographic" material that it provided' (Shah 2008). Although it might seem dated two decades later, pornography still represents a scandalous extreme, which when not confined to illegal circuits can be 'dangerous'.

Leone has repeatedly claimed in interviews that she is a former pornographic actress and has no plans of returning to the American adult industry. However, her image is entirely consumed and saturated by pornographic sex – it is impossible to imagine her outside it and nobody seems to be in a mood to do so, but Leone exercises considerable agency in producing, managing, packaging and distributing this image. This control, coupled with the literal and metaphorical 'excess' of the nature of her work and finally, her position as an Indian but 'American import' makes her case entirely novel in cross-cultural and transnational porn studies.

Contextualizing pornography in India: debates, definitions and pornophobia

The production and distribution of hardcore pornography is illegal in India and only exists clandestinely. Local pornographic films (mostly softcore) are openly screened in small-time 'blue film' cinema halls primarily meant for working-class men all over the country, but this has inexplicably escaped the law's radar for decades. While some efforts have been made to examine and study these local industries, we still need to contend with the widespread circulation of American and international porn through the web and mobile phones in India post-globalization and the apprehensions they have unleashed in their wake. It is here that we must also make the important distinction between pre-existing forms of visual pornography and erotica (boundaries between which are blurred beyond recovery in India) and internet pornography. In this case, I am concerned primarily with the latter. A recent study by the portal Pornhub (2014) on India's porn-watching habits positioned the country as the fifth-largest consumer of porn globally. Unsurprisingly, the most searched for porn star in India was Sunny Leone, followed by Priya Rai, another Indo-American adult actress, revealing a dominant taste for *desi* (a colloquial term for Indian or Pakistani) porn stars over the plethora of international sensations, especially white adult performers, on offer.[8] Although beyond the scope of this article, Leone has also racially been read as 'Latina' in some of her adult videos, which may have also contributed to her being the top porn star in Spain. Commonly searched for terms in India were: 'Indian wife' and 'Indian *bhabhi*' (sister-in-law), a reference to the infamous pornographic comic strip - Savita Bhabhi - chronicling the escapades of a married Hindu housewife named Savita, with an insatiable appetite for sex. The government promptly banned this website, although it is still available through proxy servers.[9] Pornhub (2014) also revealed that 25% of all porn consumers in India were women, and that 50% of the traffic came from mobile phones and 47.5% from desktops. Interestingly, when Sunny Leone became a participant in *Bigg Boss*, the Information and Broadcast Ministry was inundated with complaints that the TV channel Colours was indirectly promoting and encouraging 'pornography' in India, in a show meant for 'family audiences', and this was illegal (*Daily Bhaskar*, 29 November 2011). It was alleged that after seeing her on the show, 'thousands of youth' were driven to search for her on Google – thus finding hardcore explicit materials. Moreover, Leone's site had the audacity to say 'you can watch her on *Bigg Boss*'. Given that the mere presence of an adult performer did not amount to 'pornography' per se, the channel promptly moved the telecast of the show from 10:00 to 11:00 pm to assuage offended viewers and left it at that.

Crucial to our current concerns is this slippage between 'obscenity' and 'pornography' in the Indian legal system and a severe blurring of boundaries between 'high art' (like ancient temple architecture), erotica, softcore and content that can be considered 'lascivious', all of which has been complicated with the arrival of cyber porn. What is rampant is a pornophobia that seemingly engulfs all manner of things from Hollywood films with sex scenes screened on HBO and Star Movies to sexually suggestive lyrics in film songs to the aforementioned *Savita Bhabhi* comic strips. In 2014, the government asked the Internet and Mobile Association of India for assistance to suggest a plan to block all offending sites. In a closed-door meeting the 'porn problem' (another example of what Williams has called the 'on/scenity' of porn in politics and policy) was discussed at length and the IT minister Ravi Shankar Prasad stated that despite porn being legal in other countries, in India the supreme concern was 'culture and moral obligation to society' (Jayadevan and Alawadhi 2014). The internet service providers, in no mood to toe this line, in turn asked the Supreme Court to clarify the term 'pornography' and whether the ancient erotic sculptures at Khajuraho could be defined as such (*Hindustan Times* 28 January 2015). Rape, molestation and harassment of women were all said to stem from the 'ill-effects' of porn, 'redolent of the pornophobia which had gripped the puritanical English legal system in the Victorian era' (Dutta 2014). These problematic and untenable linkages between pornography and violence against women often suggest that 'it is pornography we must fight, not rape' (Williams 2004, 17) and have also occurred in other parts of the world. Such assertions have been steadily discredited and criticized (see Dworkin 1981; Williams 2004, 11–13). The Indian government has also acknowledged that it lacks the infrastructure to establish the kind of internet control that countries like North Korea and China have done,[10] while other ministers have raised questions about whether or not that should be the goal at all. Further, blocking 40 million porn sites that exist worldwide with servers operating out of countries where porn is legal is also at odds with the government's eagerness to position India as an economic superpower. India's internet speeds are already below average compared with several countries and such a move will only increase the latency of the web (Telecom Secretary Rakesh Garg, in Jayadevan and Alawadhi 2014). This puts the current ruling party, the Bhartiya Janta Party, vocal Hindu right-wingers and against everything 'anti-Indian' and 'western' but champions of economic privatization, shopping malls, 'smart cities' and Special Economic Zones, in a serious predicament – no 'superpower' can run on slow internet.

It is within these contexts and intersections of pornography, pornophobia, cyber porn and gender that we must understand the arrival of 'American import' Sunny Leone. The government's approach towards online pornography has been one of 'reactive resistance', taking measures only when particular things offend people and they report it to the state (Shah 2008). The cyber laws 'blame only the consumer of pornography for his/her (generally his) access to the pornographic material, thus creating a category of a consuming citizen who is responsible, law abiding and "morally chaste"' (Shah 2008, 5). Sunny Leone, as the active producer, entrepreneur, distributor and star of hardcore pornographic material, both lesbian and heterosexual, destabilizes the approach to 'pornographic materials' that have so far existed in the country. If her very presence is equated with 'pornography' then it turns all of us into porn consumers, and since she is a real person and not a website or a mobile phone, she cannot be 'technically' shut down. Leone, 'well in control of her meta-data and meta narrative' (Friese 2015) has acknowledged the illegality of creating adult content in India and as a law-abiding person of Indian origin has refrained from making any of it while in the country. But the internet has given us full and free access to everything she has filmed in the United States. Herein lies the fascinating paradox of renewed anxieties around globalization and this explains the confusion that marked her arrival in *Bigg Boss*: what do we do with Sunny Leone?

It is Sunny in Bollywood!

Leone made her Bollywood debut after her stint at *Bigg Boss* with *Jism-2*, the sequel to the erotic thriller *Jism* (Saxena 2003), which had met with moderate commercial success and critical acclaim. There is no narrative continuity between the two films. The producer of the earlier film, Pooja Bhatt, is the director of its sequel. *Jism* was a rehash of two Hollywood films: *Body Heat* (Kasdan 1981) and *Double Indemnity* (Wilder 1944). *Jism-2*, however, was a comically bad film with its only Unique Selling Point being Sunny Leone. She was cast as Izna, an ex porn star, although this had absolutely no bearing or connection to the plot of the film, a loophole-ridden thriller about an intelligence officer hiring an ex porn star to entrap her old boyfriend. The dialogue was unintentionally funny and contrived. Critics particularly slammed Leone's acting; as one female reviewer wrote:

> Why would any self-respecting woman (so what if she's a porn star in and outside the movie) romp about in provocative, barely-there lingerie while sharing space with a sort-of employer she's getting paid by to spy for? (Rediff 2012)

Jism-2 must be read through its porn-saturated promotional posters and interviews with the directors, producers and cast as the first instance of handling an American adult star's transition to mainstream Bollywood films. The poster shows a wet, naked woman lying on the floor with an arched back covered in a flimsy white sheet. Her face is not visible. Since we know that the film stars Sunny Leone, we assume this woman must be her. Considered 'obscene' and 'too excessive' to be displayed on the city billboards, the Bombay Municipal Corporation ordered the posters to be removed (Dubey, *Hindustan Times* 2012). The second poster shows Leone in a hot-pink bikini in the shower with her co-star Randeep Hooda, who is bare chested, both locked in an intensely passionate pose. Here, we see her face, and the expression of arousal is instantly recognizable: it is Sunny Leone, our laptop fantasy now on our movie screens! When the posters of *Jism* and *Jism-2* are compared, we can see that the representation has moved from a promise of 'soft' erotica to 'hard' porn, although the actual film delivers neither.

Jism-2 was known only for its casting coup. Even before Mahesh Bhatt had met Sunny Leone in person to offer her the role in the film, he held forth at a press conference on the issue:

> We are going there [to the Bigg Boss house] to see if Sunny can pull off the lead role in *Jism-2*. Behind the image of a beautiful, magical porn star, there is a person that has gone through the trials and tribulations of life, and dealt with shame and insults. Is she interested in revealing the hidden side to Sunny Leone? (November 2011, translation by author)

Similarly his daughter, the director Pooja Bhatt, remarked:

> I think when she came into our living rooms and our television sets through *Bigg Boss*, there is no denying that everybody was quite floored by her charm, and nobody quite had the audacity to go and bell the cat. So we did and the rest is history. (*Hungama Bollywood* 2012)

Further, Pooja Bhatt also revealed in a newspaper interview that her biggest challenge was 'humanizing Sunny Leone' and the reasoning for her casting decision was:

> Sunny Leone has a kind of innocence stamped on her face. Seeing her makes people think twice about her profession – whether or not she really is a porn star. Sunny too has got some very traditional values, the yearning to be accepted into mainstream industry. (Battacharya, *Zee News* 2012)

As is apparent from this dialogue, the initial tendency by the filmmakers who chose to cast her was to dictate her larger narrative through the conventional gendered tropes of rehabilitating a porn star into mainstream Indian society by foregrounding her 'innocence' and 'hidden persona', talking about her 'traditional values', touching upon her 'anguish' while paradoxically failing to actually depict her as anything but a rather meaningless 'sexy girl' in the film. This narrative, however, was disrupted by Leone's own assertions about her choices and decisions. Stating that she was 'very much a human being before I met her (Pooja Bhatt)', she also told the Indian press that her traditional Sikh parents were well aware of her profession and knew they were up against a 'headstrong and opinionated person', that her husband had supported all her decisions, and that they work together to build 'Brand Sunny' (Lalwani, *Times of India* 2013; Majumdar, *The Indian Express* 2014). She also clarified that at age 32 she had reached the peak of success as an adult actress in the United States, and thus her transition to Bollywood was a strategic career move to explore a new entertainment market: 'I choose to own a production house so I can produce, own, direct and distribute my own content and of others. It was the logical step to take to be successful in the business' (*The Indian Express* 2014). Talking about her image, she claimed complete ownership: 'I created that persona. I can't get away from it nor do I want to' (*The Indian Express* 2014). Specifically discussing the hype surrounding the 'boldness' of *Jism 2*, an amused Leone said that the film was not as provocative or novel as much as the filmmakers would like to believe, because in India:

> you can only go far. You can only push the envelope so far. And that envelope doesn't even crack open here. The film is not as crazy as you think it is, it's something parents can watch and children can watch. (Zoom 2012)

'I love everything about the adult industry!'

Another conversation that engulfed Leone was around how much and whether she wanted to dilute and shed her past porn star status, and this tended to hinge on the initial assumption that she must be attempting to 'erase' or 'forget' that aspect of her life. Such a narrative easily fits into gendered socio-cultural expectations of 'tainted women' changing themselves as the popular Hindi expression goes, *'paap dhona'* (to wash your sins away). The lines between pornography and prostitution, however, seemed blurred in the discourse. When Leone alleged that her *Bigg Boss* co-participant, popular television actor Amar Upadhyay, acted inappropriately with her in the house, his violent and conservative reaction spoke directly to the key anxieties that her presence invokes for sections of the Indian audiences. He said:

> What the hell have I done to her? I merely kissed her hand in a task! ... Bringing her in a family show like Bigg Boss doesn't augur well for Indian culture. She is ruining the psyche of 12-year-old boys in India ... I wonder why has Sunny come to India? Kya woh yahan apne paap dhone aayi hai? [Has she come to India to wash way her sins?] ... I didn't want to disrespect a woman on national TV, *even if she is a porn star* [emphasis added]. (Chaturvedi, *Times of India* 2012)

Here too, Leone refused to position her 'return to the homeland' as an act of 'purification' and 'purging of sins'. Initially, for the press, her Indian origins and porn star status seemed thoroughly incongruous. She was repeatedly prodded about her family's reaction to her profession. In an interview with a leading English daily, Leone said:

> When my father realized what I did, he said, 'you didn't even ask us before you did this! But whatever you do, make sure you do it well.' My mother was also stunned when she found about my lesbian lovemaking videos, but she accepted it. And the fact that my work didn't change me as a person worked in my favor. So there was never any question of being disowned by my family. (Pall, *Times of India* 2011)

The press also seemed uninhibited and unhesitant in asking Leone for details about her sex life. Such an approach is seldom taken with celebrities in India, especially those who are female, but her status as an adult actor seemed to make her 'accessible'. She was asked about when and to whom she lost her virginity and whether her parents had ever watched any of her hardcore videos (to which Leone responded: 'Of course not! Whose parents would do that?') (*Times of India* 2011). Time and again Leone stressed the labour involved in pornography as a profession and the active role she took it in:

> I think India does not have an adult entertainment industry – that's why people have no idea what it is. I ran a company that took care of the deals I sealed with firms to sell and share my content online and to other media. Running a company was hard work. I'd work for about 60-70 hours a week. It wasn't a party. I don't regret anything that I have done so far. I have no regrets about who I am. (*Times of India* 2011)

Leone broke it down further for the Indian audience:

> Ours [the American porn] is a huge industry, yet a small one. Also every woman has the right to say yes or no to the job. Our blood and urine is tested every three weeks. And everything is recorded in a database. Let's say your HIV +ve tomorrow it gets documented and you're barred from doing porn. What I do as a profession is illegal in India. But I love my job! I love my life! I love everything about the adult industry! (Kandpal, iDiva.com 2012)

As Indians, we are a nation obsessed with sex, but brought up on a potent cocktail of guilt, shame and repression around it. This manifests itself through expressions of panic and insecurity whenever anything 'ob/scene' threatens to become 'on/scene' and, as Kipnis (1996, 164) writes, 'a culture's pornography becomes in effect a very precise map of that culture's borders'. The knee-jerk reactions to Leone's sudden presence in the country thus unsurprisingly ranged from rage to befuddlement to anxiety. Leone's arrival and success has made the country confront the varied repercussions of the transnational onscene: pornography and Bollywood now collide head-on via Sunny Leone's body, leading to new collaborations, new identities and possibilities for new sexualities.

In all of her interviews and appearances Leone comes across as warm, affable and vibrant, quickly charming her interviewers with her broken American-accented Hindi. One journalist recently wrote:

> Reporters who are assigned to interview Leone bring along their visions of a porn star, only to be greeted by an attractive and intelligent woman who is not ashamed of her past and plays the game the way it's meant to be played.[11]

There are thousands of viewer comments on YouTube, several of which claim that they changed their perspectives and views about her after one or another interview video. It is through these responses that we can read the globalization narrative in Leone's crossover. She politely refuses to indulge in any Indian cultural fantasies of family shame or repentance, but speaks in a language that is thoroughly indicative of female agency in porn work. Her reiteration of the industrial and business dynamics of her work is in tandem with India's fantasies of economic globalization, except that the anxiety at the heart of it has always been the preservation of 'cultural values' mainly through the bodies of its women. It is here that Leone again completely disquiets and dislocates the narrative of non-resident Indian success, which has long centred on the Indian male and his economic gains in the West. Interestingly, most of these success stories have been tied to the professional realms of technology and entrepreneurship that Indians have excelled at abroad, very much like Leone. Of course, the irony is lost on nobody.

Ragini MMS 2: Sunny Leone as Sunny Leone

Ragini MMS 2 (Patel 2014) begins with a strange disclaimer: 'This film does not promote any illegal activity of girl kissing or any anti-scientific activity.' It remains unclear whether 'girl kissing' is an 'anti-scientific' activity. Whatever the case may be, before the film was released we already knew that Sunny Leone would kiss a girl in this movie (a fleeting few seconds), besides being chased by a witch in a haunted house at night when she is roaming around in her lingerie, and would also dance to the foot-tapping smash hit 'Baby Doll' whose previews had already garnered over four million views on YouTube. Borrowing heavily from the cinematic styles and tropes of *Paranormal Activity* (Peli 2007) and *The Blair Witch Project 1* (Myrick and Sánchez 1999) and *2* (Berlinger 2000), *Ragini MMS 2* is a comically self-referential film within a film, a sequel to the 2011 *Ragini MMS* (Kripalani 2011). In the previous film, a couple's plans for a 'dirty weekend' go horribly awry when the abandoned house they choose for their escapades turns out to be haunted by an ancient evil witch and her dead children. Unknown to Ragini, her boyfriend Uday has planned to film their sexual encounters in the hopes of becoming an actor by circulating the clip as an

MMS. Uday is tortured and killed by the witch and Ragini ends up at a mental asylum traumatized and insane. The clip survives and circulates among young men looking for titillation.

In the sequel, sleazy director Rocks (Parvin Dabbas) decides to recreate the 'Ragini MMS Scandal' in the same haunted house where the previous incidents took place. This time he has cast porn star Sunny Leone to play Ragini. In the opening scene of the film, he declares that this film will be a 'horrex' (horror + sex) and after watching it 'the viewer won't know whether to be terrified or aroused', thus spelling out the classic tropes of the erotic-horror genre. We are then introduced to the lead in the film: porn star Sunny Leone as Sunny Leone – she rises out of a bathtub and magically changes into a glittering goddess in a gold dress to lip-sync to the now iconic song: *'yeh duniya, yeh duniya pittal di/baby doll mein sone di'* (this world is all brass/I'm a baby doll made of gold).

The film was a commercial success and Leone even managed to garner some critical acclaim for her acting. It is classically campy, an almost B-horror film in its plot and narrative treatment. A film crew shoots in a haunted house and, finally, the witch decides to possess Leone who then entices the cast and crew to have sex with her. I suggest that this film effectively maps the nation's fascination and desire for Leone by casting her as herself and representing the cultural anxieties around her 'pornographic body' through the tropes of supernatural possession. Linda Williams has pointed out in *Hard Core* (1999) and elsewhere that pornography and horror are genres of excess because they provoke the audience to mirror the bodily responses and actions on screen. Suhani Kanwar, credited for the film's story and screenplay, admits that she initially began work without Sunny Leone in mind ('I don't care if she's a porn star, how does it matter?') but gradually realized that it was the only thing on the producers' mind. She explains:

> Because she has been a porn star she cannot connect with an Indian audience as a character anymore. That persona obliterates everything else that might happen in the future. I have reason to believe that she charges a fairly high fee; it's not like any other actor who is just one film old. So technically it's nothing over the top ... because when an Indian actress wears a bikini on screen it makes the news, when they ask Sunny to wear a bikini ... she asks, what's the big deal? Because we are so repressed as a society, people ask for really banal things. So her life's conflict between porn and Bollywood overshadows any film she might be in. Then I began to write around that ... which was odd. Of course the scenes are written for a male audience, scare the women, titillate the men. A woman who is fearsome and sexy at the same time – the ultimate male fantasy. (Personal interview 2013)

In a memorable scene from the film, Leone parodies herself by faking an orgasm. It commences when Leone overhears her co-actor (television actor Maddy) tell the director that 'blue film' actors do not have much to do and lack 'real' acting skills, referencing the actual criticism Leone faced after her first couple of acting attempts in Bollywood. She decides to prove him wrong by giving the cast and crew a 'porn performance': body writhing, voice trembling and moaning, Leone loudly climaxes into a full-blown fake orgasm, leaving everybody (the director, cinematographer, co-actors and actresses, and assistant directors) stunned, shocked and aroused. It is clear that we are meant to mirror the reactions of what the film-crew-in-the-film is experiencing. What is profitable, enticing and ironical about inviting the Indian audience to watch Sunny Leone enact a fake orgasm when they have already seen the real deal elsewhere is the medium: it is not an American porno to be consumed clandestinely but a regular Bollywood film shows a porn star fake an orgasm with all her clothes on. The film was heavily promoted as the 'hottest date film of the year'.

Sunny Leone unlimited!

In India, Leone is deemed equivalent to 'pornography', an example of 'pornographizing': a transgression of borders and a spill over of something that should have been contained in a particular location and context only. But 'pornification' alone cannot delineate the peculiarities of this scenario, and thus I use another phrase: transnational onscenity. Let us consider the following example: keeping within the larger tendency of Bollywood song-and-dance numbers to take on different lives and trajectories outside the film text, Sunny Leone's 'Baby Doll' became a particularly popular performative number for women in different spaces: offices, fitness studios, weddings, parties and so forth. The song was played and replayed on the radio, at discos, clubs and bars, at house parties, at the gym, in auto-rickshaws and in beauty parlours. A simple search on YouTube reveals several clips of women dancing to this song, among which one called 'Sunny Leone Dance Fever: Baby Doll Employees at Office' where the female workforce of a multinational firm in Bangalore in formal and conservative corporate office wear are seen gyrating in their cafeteria, choreographed like a flash mob. Similarly, a journalist recounts:

> Earlier this year a culturally conservative Hindu friend of mine was insisting that her son's wedding ceremony would include a joint family re-enactment of the famously sexy Sunny Leone song-and-dance sequence 'Baby Doll', from the 2014 film, 'Ragini MMS 2'. I have also seen 'Baby Doll' performed with some gusto at the anniversary party of a feminist human rights organization in Delhi. (Friese, *The New York Times*, 2015)

While the song-and-dance sequences are often divorced from the film context, they are rarely disassociated from the performer.[12] The appropriations of 'Baby Doll' might be read as one instance of transnational onscenity and the new spaces that it is creating, both conscious and unconscious. It must also be kept in mind that 'Baby Doll' is a Punjabi song in a Bollywood film, and that the audience is well aware that Leone is ethnically Sikh (albeit Canadian and of course an American 'porn-star'). For most women, performing or dancing to 'Baby Doll' is an act of pleasurable subversion, as have other suggestive film songs in the past, but the knowledge that the song belongs to Sunny Leone, *desi* porn star, makes it an even more radical claim to female desire.

Moving away from their initial bemusement, the Indian press has recently begun to frame Leone as an empowered woman from whom we have much to learn. They have also begun to condemn and criticize the nation's hypocritical attitude towards both sex and pornography. However, this is not to suggest that Sunny Leone has finally managed a feminist triumph in India. Most top male stars have reportedly refused to work with her, possibly uncomfortable with romancing a 'dirty' American porn star as opposed to a 'clean' young heroine.[13] On 19 January 2016 she gave an interview to a leading English language news channel, CNN-IBN, as part of the promotional activity for her upcoming sex-comedy *Maastizade* [The Pleasure Seekers] (Zaveri 2016). The interviewer, a veteran male journalist, Bhupendra Chaubey, subjected Leone to a series of humiliating and offensive questions, displaying a rampant obsession with her prior career in pornography:

> Do you not sometimes get affected that your past, the past that you were a 'porn queen', will continue to haunt you? I wonder, and pardon me if I am being offensive here, how many people would think in terms of growing up to be a porn star? Is your past now literally, figuratively a thing of the past now? Is that something that you think about? I began by asking you if you had any regrets, and you spoke about your mother, and if I were to turn the clock back, would you still do what you did? (Chaubey, CNN-IBN 2016)

He did not ask any questions about her upcoming film or her post-pornography career. He wondered whether he was being 'morally corrupted' by just sitting with her (Leone responded 'I can leave, if you want me to'). Leone was able to maintain her calm and sense of humour throughout this interview. In the aftermath of this, Chaubey was severely criticized for his stance and the Indian internet exploded in an outpouring of support for Leone. Several A-list Bollywood stars have condemned the journalist and expressed public support for Leone via Twitter and Facebook. Aamir Khan[14] wrote 'Sunny, I will be happy to work with you. I have no problems with your "past" as the interviewer put it', in direct response to Chaubey's question: 'So you would want to work with Aamir but Aamir would not want to work with you. How do you feel about that?'. A female journalist angrily retorted:

> The judgment that was on display in the *CNN IBN* interview was utterly uncalled for and reeked of misogyny and misplaced moralising. But hats off to Leone for maintaining her poise and confidence through it all. If anything, she should be a role model for all women who are faced with sexism and misplaced male bravado.[15]

These examples help us delineate the multiple ways in which Leone and what she represents is currently circulating in the country. What is certain is that the dialogue surrounding her has been relentless. I do not read any post-feminist tendencies of 'progress' in the arrival and depiction of explicit female sexual pleasure in the mainstream through Leone. I do, however, argue for Leone's agency and control over the production and distribution of her image.

What I suggest is that Leone and her situation in India has engendered a space that is different from the one usually occupied by female actresses and celebrities. Female stardom in Bollywood has been an intense and constant negotiation of the boundaries between public and private, between domesticity and career success.[16] The appeal and attractiveness of the Indian actress and heroine has been framed through her sexual innocence and apparent virginity. For decades, this was the primary reason female actors retired from successful careers immediately after marriage and retreated into the private domains of domesticity and motherhood. Bollywood actor Shilpa Shetty, who participated in the UK's *Celebrity Big Brother UK* in 2007, provides a counter-narrative to Leone's presence in *Bigg Boss*. Shetty emerged from that show portraying herself to the Indian and British media as a 'modern-yet-traditional' Indian woman. She refused to react to the racist comments made against her by fellow participant Jade Goody to maintain her 'Indian' poise, calm and dignity (Mitra 2012). Sunny Leone, on the other hand, has already taken off all her clothes and had sex with multiple people multiple times on camera and distributed that content as widely as she could. She leaves nothing to the imagination of the Indian audiences. She cannot offer them pleasure through repression; she is unable to feign sexual innocence. She has reached a point of no return, or what Linda Williams has called the primary aesthetic of pornography: 'maximum visibility'

(1999, 49). She is unlimited. It is for these reasons that we cannot situate her celebrity persona within the same discourse as other Bollywood female actors. Her persona, image construction and media texts must be read as events that share a somewhat relational link to the narratives of female stardom, but concurrently remain outside and independent of it. Leone therefore occupies a unique position in the global circulation of capital and the exchanges between entertainment industries. She cannot be ignored by a film industry that is driven by the logic of profit and hard capital gains because of her net worth and international popularity as an adult star (she was recently placed 45th on the Forbes India list of Indian celebrities). At the same time, Bollywood seeks to maintain its position as a culture industry with 'Indian sensibilities', and thus it is unable to do much with her on screen due to both the Censor Board[17] and its own limited tropes of narrative organization. Neither can it grant her the usual off-screen space of benign acceptance in its cultural story as it has to other 'foreign imports' such as Katrina Kaif[18] and Jacqueline Fernandes.[19] Sunny Leone in Bollywood thus perfectly exemplifies the contemporary paradoxical complexity of economic globalization and its relationship to pornography: capital reigns supreme over rampant cultural anxieties, which are then slowly managed, assuaged, negotiated and placated as they surge from time to time.

Notes

1. Several newspapers and websites reported on Sunny Leone's popularity on Google India (NDTV 16 December, 2014; *Zee News* 17 December, 2014; *The Indian Express* 2 January, 2015). For a full list of First Information Reports so far filed against Leone, see The New Indian Express 27 May, 2015. The charges are the Indian Penal Code sections 292 (Obscene and indecent advertisement and display), 292A (Printing of grossly indecent or scurrilous matter) and 294 (Performing obscene act in public place), the IT Act's section 67 (Publishing or transmitting obscene material in electronic form) and the Indecent Representation of Women Act's sections 3 (Prohibition of advertisements containing indecent representation of women) and 4 (Prohibition of publication or sending by post indecent representation of women) (in *Times of India* 16 May, 2014). The Cyber Crime Cell is currently investigating the case. The police have stated that they cannot block the website because it does not operate out of India.
2. Mahesh Bhatt is a veteran director, producer and writer in the Bombay film industry. He has made several critically acclaimed films that have often dealt with issues considered 'unusual' or especially 'bold' for commercial Hindi cinema.
3. Pooja Bhatt is an actor, producer, writer and director. She is also Mahesh Bhatt's older daughter. She was a commercially successful actor in the 1990s. Besides her film career, she has courted some controversies in her day. She appeared on a magazine cover lip-locked with her father, which drew much flak and criticism for being 'incestuous', and then followed it up by posing only in body paint, inspired by Demi Moore's *Vanity Fair* cover of 1992.
4. Several ancient India temples like Khajuraho in Maharashtra, Padawali in Madhya Pradesh, Ranakpur in Rajasthan, the Sun Temples in Orissa and Gujarat and the Virupaksha Temple in Karnataka are famously filled with carvings and sculptures depicting nudity, erotic art and people engaged in acrobatic sexual positions with multiple partners, and even animals. For a historical account of erotic temple architecture, see Harle (2004).
5. See O'Flaherty (1986).
6. For a full account of censorship and sexuality in Bombay cinema, see Monika Mehta (2001, 2012).
7. Several examples of public concerns over 'obscenity' can be recalled since the early 1990s coinciding with anxieties around globalization. In 1993, major superstar Madhuri Dixit was

accused of propagating 'vulgarity' and 'obscenity' through her hit song-and-dance number inundated with sexual innuendos '*choli ke peeche kya hai?*' (What's behind the blouse?). In 1996, supermodels Madhu Sapre and Milind Soman posed nude with only a python wrapped around them for a shoe brand. The film *Kama Sutra: A Tale of Love* (Nair 1997) went through endless rounds of banning, censorship and shunning. For a complete list, see Nishant Shah (2008).

8. This is interesting because the white female body has traditionally been the site on which Bombay cinema has sought to deflect the Indian male sexual gaze. White women have been depicted in stark contrast to their Indian counterparts, often as the villain's moll, or a bar or cabaret dancer. For more, see Ranjani Mazumdar (2007), Jyotika Virdi (2003), Ajay Gehlawat (2015) and Neepa Majumdar (2009). From the 1980s, the mainstream heroine has encroached upon the space of the white vamp's dancing by performing those numbers herself. The songs have also become especially innuendo-laden, as have the dance steps, like the famous Bollywood 'pelvic thrust'.
9. For an insightful piece on *Savita Bhabhi*, see Shohini Ghosh (2009).
10. Production and distribution of pornography is illegal in North Korea and China, much like in India, but the government infrastructure very effectively supports these laws. In 2010, 60,000 websites were shutdown in China and 5000 people arrested in the process. Regulation and censorship is widespread and brutal.
11. http://thereel.scroll.in/802011/she-is-nice-she-is-not-like-her-videos-sunny-leone-charms-the-media-ahead-of-mastizaade. Accessed 18 January, 2016.
12. For an excellent account of how Bollywood song-and-dance numbers by iconic dancing divas of the 1980s and 1990s, Madhuri Dixit and Sridevi, have been used to express queerness and identity by *desi* youth in Bangalore and Chicago, see Kareem Khubchandani 2016.
13. In Bombay Cinema, male actors have far longer lasting careers their female counterparts. Women aged over 35 and/or married are considered 'too old' and film offers for them start to peter out. A few years later, we might see the leading ladies transition to elder sisters or mothers much quicker than the men, who continue to retain their roles as heroes well into their 50s, consistently romancing actresses as young as 21 on screen.
14. Aamir Khan is one of the industry's biggest A-list male stars. Along with Salman Khan and Shahrukh Khan, he is one of the 'Khan trio' who rule the box-office and enjoy immense clout in the industry. All of the Khans have been around for nearly two decades.
15. http://www.livemint.com/Opinion/Q7mlCmqClnA3F0dpkMysYK/Judging-Sunny-Leone.html. Accessed 19 January, 2016.
16. See Neepa Majumdar (2009).
17. The Indian Censor Board refused to give Leone's upcoming film *Maastizade* (The Pleasure Seekers) (Zaveri 2016) an A-certificate and banned it entirely, stating that the content is 'unsuitable' for Indian audiences. This film was finally released amid great controversy on 22 January, 2016.
18. Katrina Kaif is a British-Indian Bollywood actress who managed success and fame in the industry despite being unable to speak Hindi, the primary language of Bollywood films. She debuted with *Boom* (Gustad 2003), a commercial and critical failure. Kaif has since said that this film was a mistake she made when she knew nothing of the Indian audiences or Bollywood films. Because of her poor acting and language skills, her success in the industry is often attributed to support from powerful male actors. She had delivered a number of commercial hit films, but mostly those that heavily focus on the male lead. One important skill she does possess is dancing and several of her song-and-dance numbers have been hits that have circulated across spaces outside film texts. Some of them have also been very sexually suggestive, like '*Sheila ki Jawani*' (Blossoming Sheila) and '*Chikni Chameli*' (Slippery Chameli).
19. Jacqueline Fernandes is a multi-racial Sri Lankan actor and model, moderately successful as a Bollywood actress. She too is known primarily for her seductive dance numbers and limited acting skills.

References

Attwood, Feona. 2004. 'Pornography and Objectification.' *Feminist Media Studies* 4 (1): 7–19.

Attwood, Feona, and Clarissa Smith. 2014. '*Porn Studies*: An Introduction.' *Porn Studies* 1 (1-2): 1–6.

Battacharya, Ananya. 2012. 'Humanizing Sunny Leone was the Biggest Challenge: Pooja Bhatt.' *Zee News*, August 7. Accessed June 1, 2015. http://zeenews.india.com/entertainment/celebrity/humanising-sunny-leone-was-the-greatest-challenge-pooja-bhatt_116736.html.

Berlinger, Joe, dir. 2000. *Book of Shadows: Blair Witch 2*. USA.

Bhatt, Pooja. 2012. *Jism-2*. India.

Chaturvedi, Vinita. 2012. 'Sunny Leone is Trying to Fool the Indian Public: Amar Upadhyay.' *The Times of India*, January 12. Accessed June 3, 2015. http://timesofindia.indiatimes.com/tv/news/hindi/Sunny-Leone-is-trying-to-fool-Indian-public-Amar-Upadhyay/articleshow/11448192.cms.

Chaubey, Bhupendra. 2016. 'Hot Seat: Sunny Leone.' *CNN-IBN*, 19 June. Accessed June 20, 2016. https://www.youtube.com/watch?v=PA66yrZt6FY.

Correspondent, *Daily Bhaskar*. 2011. 'Big Boss 5: Complaint Filed Against Sunny Leone.' *Daily Bhaskar*, November 29. Accessed June 3, 2015. http://daily.bhaskar.com/news/ENT-bigg-boss-5-complaint-filed-against-sunny-leone-2601504.html.

Correspondent, *Hindustan Times*. 2015. 'Internet Providers to SC: Are Khajuraho Sculptures Pornographic?' *Hindustan Times*, January 28. Accessed June 4, 2015. http://www.hindustantimes.com/StoryPage/Print/1177243.aspx?s=p.

Dubey, Rachana. 2012. 'Removal of Obscene "Jism 2" Poster Angers Mahesh Bhatt.' *Hindustan Times*, August 3. Accessed June 3, 2015. http://www.hindustantimes.com/bollywood/removal-of-obscene-jism-2-posters-angers-mahesh-bhatt/story-8fiuL0c0hTd1oG2YQExfLI.html.

Dutta, Saurav. 2014. 'Indian Courts Caught in Pornophobia.' *Index on Censorship*, February 14. Accessed June 3, 2015. https://www.ifex.org/india/2014/02/14/pornophobia_takes_over/.

Dworkin, Andrea. 1981. *Pornography: Men Possessing Women*. New York: Putnam.

Friese, Kai. 2015. 'The Porn Star Sunny Leone's Bollywood Makeover.' *The New York Times*, May 8. Accessed June 3, 2015. http://www.nytimes.com/2015/05/09/opinion/the-porn-star-sunny-leones-bollywood-makeover.html.

Gehlawat, Ajay. 2015. *Twenty First Century Bollywood*. New York: Routledge.

Ghosh, Shohini. 2009. 'The Pleasures and Politics of Pornography.' *Himāl Southasian*, September. http://old.himalmag.com/component/content/article/617-the-pleasures-and-politics-of-pornography.html.

Gustad, Kaizad, dir. 2003. *Boom*. India.

Harle, J.C. 2004. *The Art and Architecture of the Indian Subcontinent*. New Haven: Yale University Press.

Hungama, Bollywood. 2012. 'Pooja Bhatt on Sunny Leone.' YouTube. Accessed May 25, 2015. https://www.youtube.com/watch?v=XzyLnt-_CyA.

Jayadevan, PK, and Alawadhi, Neha. 2014. 'Government Asks ISPs to Block Pornography Sites, Upgrade Systems.' *ET Telecom*, November 11. Accessed June 3, 2015. http://telecom.economictimes.indiatimes.com/news/internet/government-asks-isps-to-block-pornography-sites-upgrade-systems/45105762.

Kandpal, Kartika. 2012. 'Sunny Leone: I Love the Adult Industry.' *iDiva.com*, August 24. Accessed June 3, 2015. http://idiva.com/news-entertainment/sunny-leone-i-love-the-adult-industry/15028.

Kasdan, Lawrence, dir. 1981. *Body Heat*. USA.

Khubchandani, Kareem. 2016. 'Snakes on the Dance Floor: Bollywood, Gesture, Gender.' *The Velvet Light Trap* 77: 69–85.

Kipnis, Laura. 1996. *Bound and Gagged: Pornography and the Politics of Fantasy in America*. New York: Grove Press.

Kripalani, Pawan, dir. 2011. *Ragini MMS*. India.

Lalwani, Vicky. 2013. 'People in India are Conservative: Sunny Leone.' *Times of India*, October 8. Accessed June 3, 2015. http://timesofindia.indiatimes.com/entertainment/hindi/bollywood/news/Sunny-Leone-Jism-2-Teena-and-Lolo-Ragini-MMS-2-Jackpot/articleshow/23691999.cms?

Majumdar, Anushree. 2014. 'Heat of the Moment: Sunny Leone Says She Is Different From What People Think Of Her.' *The Indian Express*, June 23. Accessed June 3, 2015. http://indianexpress.

com/article/entertainment/bollywood/heat-of-the-moment-sunny-leone-says-she-is-different-from-what-people-think-of-her/99/.

Majumdar, Neepa. 2009. *Wanted Cultured Ladies Only!: Female Stardom in India 1930s-50s*. Champaign: University of Illinois Press.

Malhotra, Namita. 2009. 'Negative of Porn.' Centre for Internet and Society, September 12. Accessed June 3, 2015. http://cis-india.org/raw/histories-of-the-internet/blogs/law-video-technology/looking-closer-at-porn-with-x-ray-spectacles-savita-bhabhi-mms-video-and-others.

Mazumdar, Ranjani. 2007. *Bombay Cinema: An Archive of the City*. Minneapolis: University of Minnesota Press.

Mehta, Monika. 2001. 'Selections: Cutting, Classifying and Certifying in Bombay Cinema.' Ph.D diss., University of Minnesota.

Mehta, Monika. 2012. *Censorship and Sexuality in Bombay Cinema*. Austin: University of Texas Press.

Mitra, Shreya. 2012. 'Screening the Nation: Producing the Bollywood Star in Contemporary India.' PhD diss., University of Wisconsin-Madison.

Myrick, Daniel and Eduardo Sánchez, dirs. 1999.*The Blair Witch Project*. USA.

Nair, Mira, dir. 1997. *Kama Sutra*. UK, USA and India.

O'Flaherty, Wendy Doniger. 1986. *Siva: The Erotic Ascetic*. Oxford: Oxford University Press.

Pall, Divya. 2011. 'Porn Star Doesn't Mean Prostitute: Sunny Leone.' *Times of India*, May 20. Accessed June 3, 2015. http://timesofindia.indiatimes.com/tv/news/hindi/Porn-star-doesnt-mean-prostituteSunny-Leone/articleshow/10792373.cms.

Patel, Bhushan, dir. 2014. *Ragini MMS 2*. India.

Peli, Oren, dir. 2007. *Paranormal Activity*. USA.

PornHub. 2014. '2014: Year in Review.' January 7. Accessed June 4, 2015. http://www.pornhub.com/insights/2014-year-in-review.

Saxena, Amit, dir. 2003. *Jism*. India.

Shah, Nishant. 2008. 'PlayBlog: Pornography, Performance and Cyberspace.' Centre for Internet and Society. Accessed June 3, 2015.

Varma, Sukanya. 2012. 'Jism 2 Makes Even Sex Look Boring.' *Rediff*. Accessed June 1, 2015. http://www.rediff.com/movies/review/review-jism-two/20120803.htm.

Virdi, Jyotika. 2003. *The Cinematic ImagiNation: Indian Popular Films as Social History*. New Brunswick: Rutgers University Press.

Wilder, Billy, dir. 1944. *Double Indemnity*. USA.

Williams, Linda. 1999. *Hard Core: Power, Pleasure and 'Frenzy of the Visible'*. Berkeley: University of California Press.

Williams, Linda. 2004. *Porn Studies*. Durham, NC: Duke University Press.

Zaveri, Milap Milan, dir. 2016. *Mastizaade* [Fun Seekers]. India.

Zoom. 2012. 'Sunny Leone: India can Never have a Thriving Adult Film Industry.' Zoom TV, August 28. Accessed May 25, 2015. https://www.youtube.com/watch?v=a0Oc_di6D2c.

'We give sex a good name': an Interview with Paromita Vohra

Darshana Sreedhar Mini and Anirban K. Baishya

ABSTRACT

In India's censorial climate where debates about pornography exist only in terms of criminality, illegality, and the underground circuit, a feminist and pleasure-positive space has emerged under the aegis of (non-state-sponsored) sex education. In this playing field, the multimedia project and website Agents of Ishq (AoI) has emerged as a major voice in normalizing conversations about sex, pleasure, and even porn. Founded by the feminist filmmaker, artist, and curator Paromita Vohra, AoI carries essays, videos, and images that focus on fostering a community of readers/interlocutors that talk, teach, and learn freely about sex. In a sense, AoI approaches these matters in the same spirit as Vohra does in her filmmaking and her other work. In this interview, Paromita Vohra speaks to us about her films, artwork, AoI, and the effort to create a stigma-free 'private public' where people can talk about their desires, pleasure and sexuality.

Introduction

Speaking about sex, pleasure, and porn is not an easy task in India, let alone South Asia more broadly considered. When conceiving the two issues of 'South Asian Pornographies' for *Porn Studies*, we were hard pressed to find any figures that spoke from the world of porn – quite frankly, we did not have a Candida Royalle or a Tristan Taormino to turn to. What scant voices we did find were all from the world of academia, with one exception – Paromita Vohra.

An eclectic filmmaker, writer, curator, and sex educator, Paromita Vohra's body of work resonates with an energy almost unparalleled in the South Asian context. As a filmmaker working in the documentary mode, her work is exemplary for bringing in a fresh, feminist vocabulary, as well as a welcome touch of intelligent humour at a time when documentaries in India were usually deemed serious (men's) business. While her documentaries are not directly about pornography, she has made it her mission to talk about pleasure, desire, and sex through it – and in a language that is accessible to the masses. Blending a focus on feminist art and thought with references to popular culture, Vohra's work offers a sharp, incisive look into the otherwise repressed realm of desire and pleasure in contemporary India.

Her films include *Partners in Crime* (2012), a documentary on culture, markets, and the arts (Best Documentary, Ladakh International Film Festival, 2012, Special Jury Mention, SIGNS 2012); *Morality TV and the Loving Jehad: A Thrilling Tale* (2007), a documentary on tabloid TV news and moral policing (Best Short Documentary, Int. Video Fest, Trivandrum); *Q2P* (2006), a film on toilets and the city (Best Documentary IFFLA and Bollywood and Beyond, Stuttgart); *Where's Sandra?* (2005), a playful exploration of stereotypes of Catholic girls from a Bombay suburb; *Work In Progress* (2004), an impressionistic portrait of the World Social Forum held in Mumbai; *Cosmopolis: Two Tales of a City* (2004), a short film which explores Bombay's cosmopolitan self-image through land and food politics, which won an award for mixing fiction and non-fiction at the Digital Film Festival, UK; and *Unlimited Girls* (2002), a personal take on engagements with feminism in urban India (Feminist News Award, Women's Film Festival in Seoul; Best Film Award, Aaina Film Festival, India).

Apart from making films, Vohra is also a frequent contributor of articles on subjects of feminism, sexuality, porn, and desire in popular venues such as *Outlook*, *The Ladies' Finger!*, *Time Out Mumbai*, and the *Times of India*. Vohra is also the founder and creative director of Agents of Ishq (AoI), a 'multi-media project about sex, love and desire' alternatively described as a website that creates 'cool video, beautiful images and great audio about sex, love and desire in India'.[1] Like Vohra's approach to filmmaking (and life), AoI is marked by a uniquely pleasure-positive and sex-positive, as well as intersectional, way of talking about topics as wide ranging as mental health and masturbation. Combining the written word and visual forms such as illustrations, memes, GIFs, and digital video with the reach of platforms such as Instagram, Facebook, and Twitter, AoI has become a major force in normalizing conversations about love, sex, and desire (and everything in between) in India. In this interview, Vohra gives us a detailed insight into her own work and philosophy, as well as that of AoI.

Darshana Mini and Anirban Baishya, Guest Editors (GE): Can you tell us a bit about your journey as a filmmaker and a feminist educator interested in questions of sex and desire? Where do you see conversations on pornography fitting into the existing discourses on sex and desire in contemporary India?

Paromita Vohra (PV): From early in my work life, the landscape of desire, intimacy, and sexual-ness (which I think is different from sexuality) seemed fertile for feminist exploration of a kind that was not neat, easy to categorize, and so, easy to tame or domesticate into 'women's issues'. I think there were many reasons for this. Within the documentary film tradition, particularly in India, the sexual was a missing element on the whole, primarily showing up only in terms of violence. Even within the feminist space, people did not really talk about these things. This made it an open space, not weighed down with the baggage of pre-existing schemas, because for an artist, a feminist, or a person in general, the worst thing is having to constantly say 'no, that is not what I meant at all', to wade against the tide of misperception. It allowed the political to be understood and interpreted in heterogeneous ways, but it also allowed for the full spectrum of the self to be interpreted and understood politically. I think the fact that I came from an atypical middle-class family – mixed parentage through a couple of generations, many migrations, and also, grandparents in the movie industry – made it possible and important for me to find a political language that felt informed by what I had grown up with. And I came to the realization that respectability, as an idea, is highly disciplining and maintains elite power status. The sexual unmoors that respectability and allows us, then, to make new and different political and personal journeys, and establish new genealogies of being. For instance, when I first went to a photographic exhibition of women achievers from the nineteenth and early twentieth centuries, I felt that a strange sobriety informed it which left out multiple journeys of women – including the women of my own family – and especially in terms of their passions, their emotions and relationships which had determined their professional and social, even economic journeys, definitely their intellectual ones – as much as being determined by those factors (Figures 1–7).

It seemed too, that to talk about sexual-ness bypassed heteronormative and binary assumptions (which can easily enter the rights discourse too), because it was rooted in experience, metaphor, affect, excess, and naughtiness – it refused sobriety and the pre-existing power equations it carried. It was also a way to have conversations about feminism – not conversations about the patriarchy purporting to be about feminism. So, the critique of straightness or men happens very fluidly in this context, and by decentring

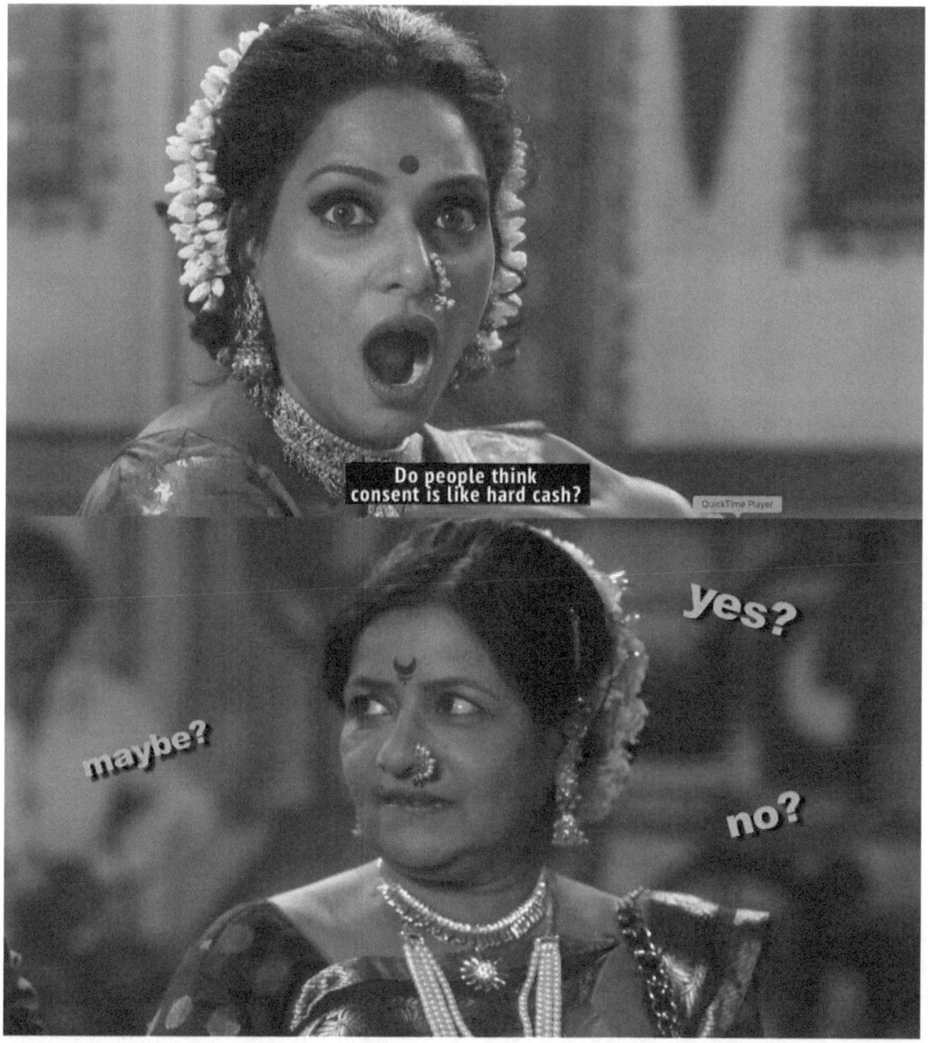

Figure 1. Two moments from the AoI video *A Lavni About Consent: The Amorous Adventures of Megha and Shakku* (Dir. Paromita Vohra, Performers: Shakuntala Nagarkar, Megha Ghadge, 2016). Image courtesy: Agents of Ishq.

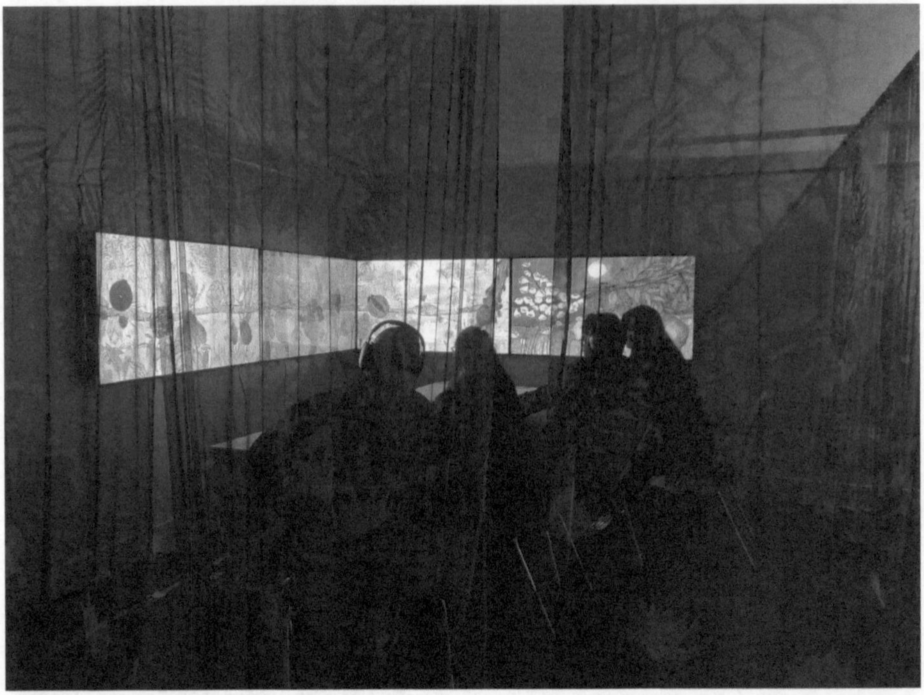

Figure 2. Members of the audience interact with the installation in the 'public privacy' of *Love Latika*. Image courtesy: Paromita Vohra.

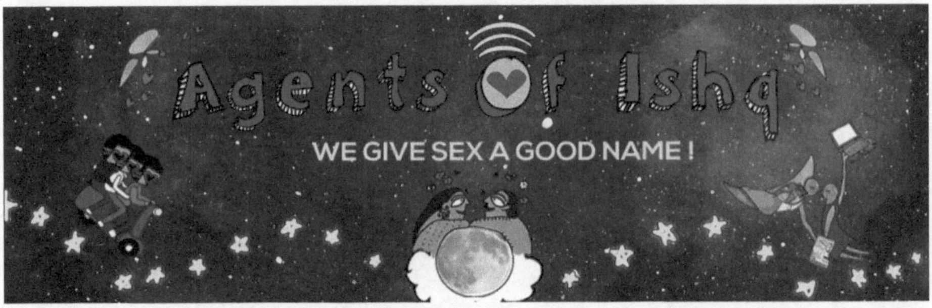

Figure 3. AoI homepage header image with the tagline 'We give sex a good name'. Image Courtesy: Agents of Ishq.

those things, it allows for something new to be perceived and discussed. It can create a language and tone where people could speak of themselves, without being boxed into a representative version of who they are, only as examples of their identity and not implying their wholeness.

So, from an early time in my work I was intuitively reaching for that tonality, and it existed not so directly or topically but always as a quality, a feeling in the work. It would emerge sometimes as a metaphor – for instance in *Partners in Crime* (2011), a film about art, copyright, piracy, and capitalism, where love became a conceptual frame of value counter to the logic of capitalism. On the whole, it was present as a

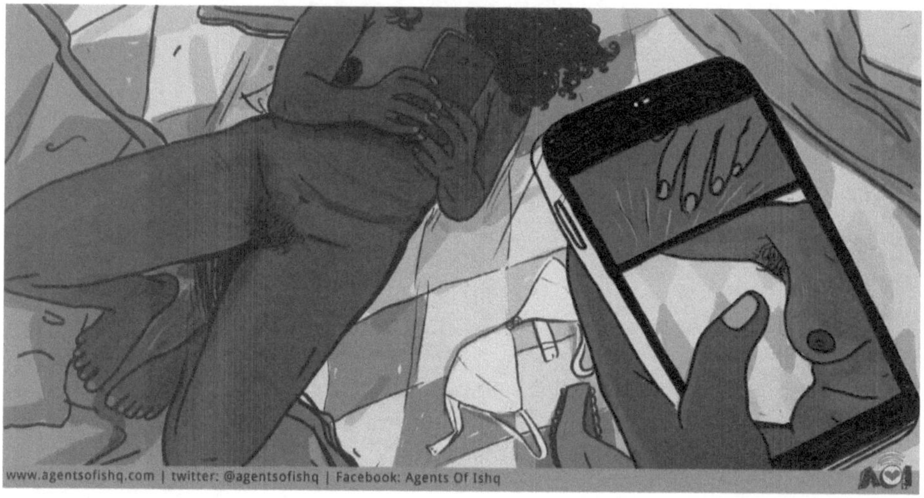

Figure 4. Illustration accompanying the article 'I Took a Nude Selfie. It Changed My Life' on AoI. Illustration by Harjyot Khalsa. Image courtesy: Agents of Ishq.

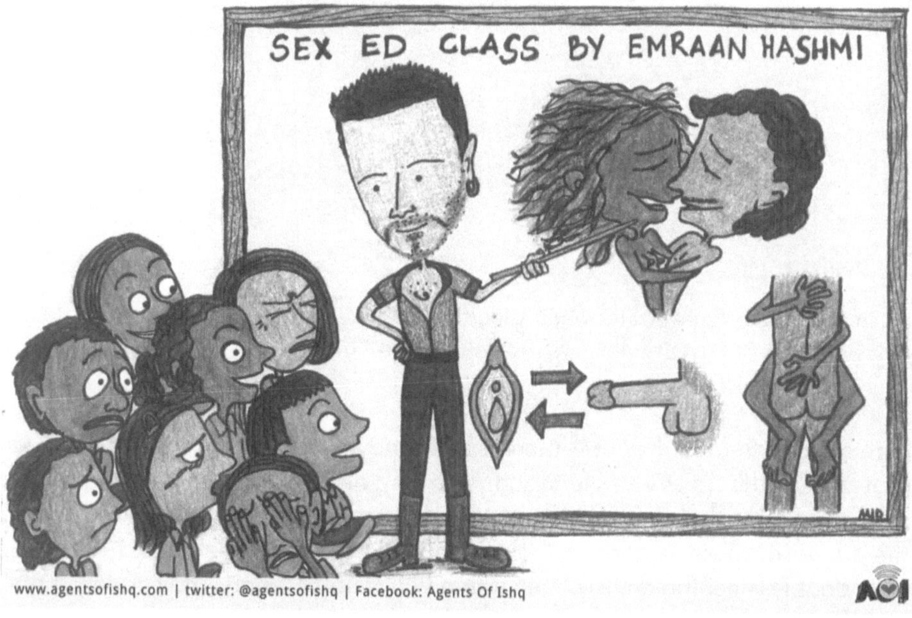

Figure 5. Illustration accompanying the article 'What Emraan Hashmi Couldn't Teach Me About Dhichak' on AoI. Illustration by Maitri Dore. Image courtesy: Agents of Ishq.

pronounced engagement with pleasure and pleasurable viewing that was sensual and often naughty, full of similar pleasures to Bollywood films – music, visual puns and saturation, jokes about things like bras and orgasms. In earlier films like *Unlimited Girls* (2002), which deals with feminism and urban India, and *Where's Sandra?* (2005), dealing with the stereotype of the Christian girl from Bombay, it drew to an extent from popular culture, sometimes referencing something 'sleazy', like music videos which drew from the visual

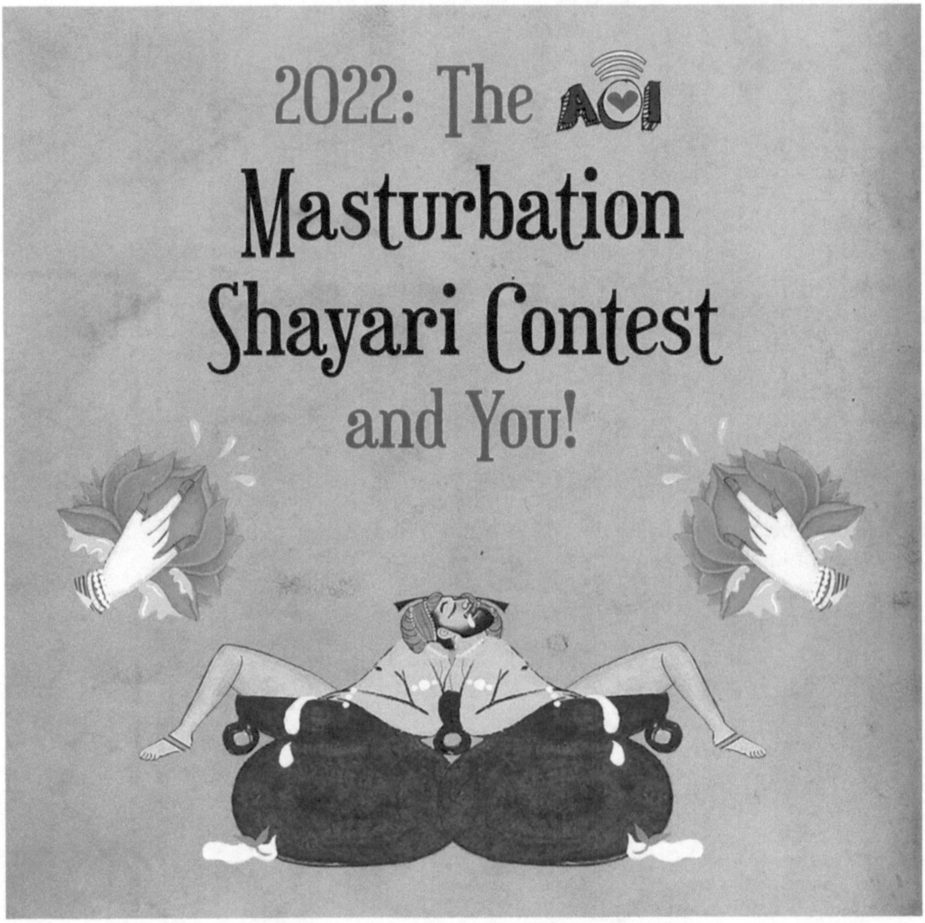

Figure 6. Image on the AoI website announcing the 2022 'Masturbation Shayari' contest. Design: DebasmitaDas and Anshumaan Sathe, Courtesy Agents of Ishq.

repertoire of porn. In *Unlimited Girls* there is a fake advertisement where three women in short, hot-pink clothes promote the Misognenie Feminist Detector, quite like the women on American sex channels of the 1990s. *Where's Sandra?* re-enacted a Bollywood song with the suggestiveness ramped up. The title *Unlimited Girls* itself was full of what I shall call a double-meaning energy, preventing you from entering with sobriety, nobility, and respectability in your affect. You had to enter with that uneasy feeling that this might be a serious documentary, or a peep show, and well, maybe it was a bit of both, featuring the director too. You had to enter and undress intellectually and watch the film with your whole body. The film in fact begins with a young woman reading a romance novel in bed, then looking for love on the internet only to stumble upon a feminist chatroom (and perhaps porn plots are not dissimilar, with pizza deliveries leading to sex!). Even now many universities will not let you access web pages which mention this film because it is assumed to be porn.

In 2007, though, I made a film called *Morality TV aur Loving Jehad: A Thrilling Tale*. It was about an incident of moral policing that took place in the northern town of Meerut and

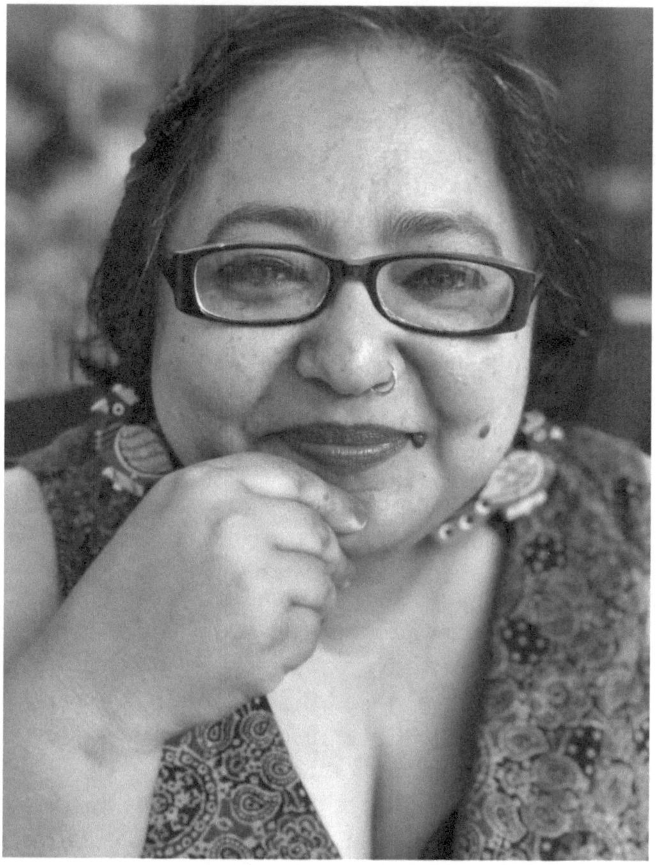

Figure 7. Paromita Vohra. Photograph by Abhijit Dutta. Image courtesy: Paromita Vohra.

the manner it had been played out on national television news. It had been preceded by an incident with a Hindi film actor who played villainous characters (Shakti Kapoor). A channel called India TV had apparently done a sting operation of him propositioning a reporter posing as an aspiring actor, to prove the casting couch is rampant in the film industry. As I understood then, this idea of the sting operation, the 'exposé', became a mainstay of television over time and it always hinged on something being designated obscene, or shall we say designed and then designated as obscene. So, for instance, sting operations would be rigged to be carried out in massage parlours or dance bars and the women caught, paraded on television along with an overheated pulp fiction style commentary, describing the 'obscene acts' with relish and then denouncing them. This televised format drew from the language of true crime magazines like *Manohar Kahaniyan* [Thrilling Tales] and pulp detective fiction to create a landscape of scrutiny for women and a control of their sexual expression and even their economic freedom or mobility for work, by constantly rendering it in terms of obscenity, vulgarity, sexual excess. At the same time, it was effectively creating a kind of non-consensual pornography of its own, where conversations about sex and images of sexual-ness were present right there on national television.

Now, it is very easy to of course label this hypocrisy, which is the classic reading by liberal elites, but it seems to me it is more complex and there is a double-ness involved. A desire to speak of sex that is simultaneously expressed and repressed even while anxieties about class and caste are quelled through talk of respectability. This is a kind of double-meaning energy. I am quoting from an essay I wrote in *Outlook* here:

> Why does the double entendre cause such discomfort? For the simple reason that it disturbs a line of control – respectability. Respectability implies that being rich and being good are the same thing. That being tasteful and being noble mean one thing. That being elite and being meritorious mean one thing. The double entendre disturbs these conflations by its very mischievous Looking London, Talking Tokyo nature. We say one thing, but mean another—and everyone knows this to be so. In this way we defy the line of permissibility, but also toe that line, thus mocking the powerful who impose and maintain this line. The double meaning by its very form communicates that one person's opportunity is another person's oppression; or, that one person's erotica is another's porn. We imply that there is nothing naturally good about this line, but that it has been put in place by those who control our intimacies and our possibilities. In part, this is what is disturbing about double meanings. And from colonial times, the effort to separate things into singular meanings has been consistent.[2]

What was also very interesting to see at the time was that there would occasionally be narratives that queered this tendency, or this binary. An example is the story of Julie and the Professor – a relationship between a professor (Matuknath Chaudhary) and his student that hit the headlines for a while.[3] But their language, which refused to buy into the notions of respectability – either to defend it or decry it – but simply shrugged it off as a construct, made it difficult to pin them down and you saw the entire narrative about 'obscene relationship using studies as the excuse' suddenly run out of steam. And often, these '*manohar kahaniyan*' are based on true stories and experiences which means that many people are eloping, having affairs, or involved in some form of sex work of their own volition.

I understood with a kind of striking clarity, then, that the domain of love and sex is where numerous political disruptions occur, which are intersectional in nature, which rescue feminism from disciplined, well-behaved instrumentality, which are messy in nature but also potent. And the important part of it is that it resonated for me personally, in terms of my own life and experiences as a young woman in Bombay. It was also very clear in the film – which as it happens is the first public documentation of the term 'Love Jihad' – that this was a domain that would be increasingly used to control young people.[4] As long as the concept of Love Jihad operated in this 'porn' world of moral policing, the liberal left paid little or no attention to it. It is only when it entered the overtly political domain that they noted it, by which time there was no real response to be made – the legal one being insufficient in today's context. The fact that the sexual gets spoken of always in terms of violence translates into a language where women must be protected, rather than engaging with their freedoms and their desires; the fact that it is spoken of only as rights means that often the queer must present normatively (marriage equality) – singular meanings, which make intersectionality elusive. So, eventually, this domain of sex is where a different (I want to say more meaningful) politics seems possible – it is fertile with meanings, and it is an inclusive frame. It evades the linearities and binaries of tradition versus modernity, East versus West, left versus right, violence and protection to create a politics of the possible and includes more types of people.

From then on love and desire became a more central exploration in my work and I wrote a column about modern love for a few years as well as several pieces on pornography-adjacent ideas like Sunny Leone's Bollywood career[5] and the idea of the selfie,[6] as well as bodies, dance, and desires in Bollywood films. In 2015, I created Agents of Ishq (AoI),[7] a multimedia project on love, sex, and desire (which I currently run) in which of course sex is more directly spoken of, but in which I also made some films in collaboration with *lavani* artists (a Maharashtrian song and dance form performed by women, and noted for its sexual innuendos) and more directly worked with this double-meaning energy.

In India, I think conversations on pornography seem to hinge on ban or not ban, but we must understand that porn is a very routine part of a young person's life today, thanks to the internet. It is the first sex education most people get, and it also massively shapes the experience of sex even for adults. The conversation on banning or not banning is feeble. I think young people have moved on from that conversation on the one hand. They are relieved to find spaces where they may speak of sex without stigma. At the same time their lived experience of eroticism is limited because porn might make sex familiar but it does not always make sex intimacy-ready.

GE: Your work involving sexual-ness and eroticism clearly moves beyond just films. Can you talk about the electronic installation that you have curated as a part of Goethe-Institut's 'Five Million Incidents' and the sensory pleasures that it works with? The installation includes erotic poems – in today's political climate in India, do you see a work like this being tagged as 'pornographic' (not that it is a bad thing, but perhaps as a way of delegitimizing the heterogenous sexual cultures that preceded and even now co-exist with ours)?

PV: The installation 'A Love Latika' was part of Five Million Incidents, a series of art events organized by Goethe-Institut/Max Mueller Bhavan, New Delhi and Kolkata.[8] I describe it as an electronic forest of erotic poems. It featured four screens with flora and fauna that were uncontrolled, the colour of fever dreams, and often imaginary. If you clicked on a flower it would bloom – or animate into something, a leaking breast, a carnivorous fruit, a frog with a long tongue – and simultaneously play an erotic poem on the audio track. The poems were from all over the world but with a focus on Indian ones. Four people could listen to the installation at one time and the entire installation was enclosed in a net curtain with a forest printed on it.

The installation played with the senses, flooding the eye, the ear, and even the skin with eroticism and sensuality. It played with the idea of translucence and a concept I like to call 'public privacy' – where people were sitting together doing something very private. Reading erotica or porn is something people are expected to do alone, but here it was a double-meaning energy – they were alone with their headphones, yet side by side with others. Enclosed in a curtained space, but a translucent one, being made of a netted fabric, covered in print – so they could in fact be seen, their blushes, their intensity, everything visible to those sitting outside. After they listened, they were invited to write an erotic poem of their own and a remarkable number of people did.

The installation aimed to represent the heterogeneity of desire, to muddle the porn versus erotica hierarchy – the poems were tender, carnal, arch, voracious, dreamy, yearning, explicit, oblique, and dwelt on different sexual acts – kissing, anal sex, fucking, cuddling, oral sex. I asked different kinds of 'regular people' to read them, but some of these people were famous with recognizable voices (Sanjana Kapoor, Devdutt Pattanaik, Dhruv Sehgal), which also added frisson of a different kind.

With that experience, a kind of saturated silence ensued (perhaps the kind of velvety dark or '*makhmali andhera*' mentioned in seductive Bollywood songs) where people connected deeply with their own sexual self, emotionally, with beauty and emotion. Many people cried – for their own locked up selves maybe. This catharsis, which was both emotional, sensual, and creative, is what I think of as erotic. It may come through any means, but of course in art it allows our many selves to co-exist, to embrace each other – which can also be thought of as a different kind of orgy, I guess.

There is a political suggestiveness to such a work which refuses to put its politics into words, but everyone leaves knowing for sure what that politics is, and it cannot be constrained by anything literal – not academic sorting, nor capitalist imperatives to speak, nor mealy-mouthed left-liberal rebellions. It is deeply private, a thick river of meaning inside people setting off other meanings and ideas. To me, this is the political power of eroticism. I suppose if someone wanted to tag it pornographic – they could. But the fact that it is poetry and such fluid imagery makes it harder to do so.

I think there is a discourse – the sexually backward India full of toxic masculinity versus the enlightened urban India that knows how to treat 'its' women. I think you can see how it is a colonial discourse mapped onto a caste and class context, to put it a bit simplistically. I do think that putting things in that binary generates a confrontation and then the conversation becomes reactive and violent. It is in itself a censorious position, which meets an answering censorship. It is not a conversation about sex, but about power. I think there are other culturally resonant ways in which one can talk of desire, sex, and feeling, and not be waylaid and sidetracked by the censorious forces. These become inclusive frames which allow for engagement and mutuality, rather than conformity of any kind (progressive or conservative), and so are less likely to confront force.

GE: Speaking of the censorial, in the heavily censored climate of India, what are the challenges faced by feminist collectives and sex educators in facilitating conversations on safe sex and pleasure?

PV: As of now, I think as a woman sex educator the resistance you face is not so much from the contemporary political context as this theme is still a bit under the radar – it is from the old morality of not 'putting ideas in children's heads and corrupting their innocence' and not 'misleading women'. The government has made official programmes difficult – rerouting sexuality education into 'life skills' and the idea that there should be sex education without using the word sex. This resistance has always existed, but it may be more stated through the system now than before. It is not as if the right-wing alone have been using the idea of *sanskar* [sacred, traditional, or relating to morality], Indian culture, and so on. With the coming of digital media, communities are ever more anxious about what women are exposed to and want to control conversations about sex. I think from time to time censorship and backlash does surface with the language of 'disgusting un-Indian acts', but the backlash is stronger to women being seen as free and assertive. I think the climate is one where women's political opinions invite verbal sexual violence.

For influencer type of sex-education content producers, who, as women, speak openly about sex, there is more direct violence in terms of unsolicited dick pics and accusations of destroying Indian culture. But it has not reached a place for extreme censorship yet. That is partly because the real censorship is from social media platforms themselves, which, in the six years I have been running AoI, has gotten more and more constricting. For instance, promotions of sex-education posts are denied because they are seen as porn, soliciting, or adult content of some kind. Notices that deny promotion also say things like 'we do not allow promotion of posts about sexual health which promote pleasure'.[9] So, these so-called community standards do the work of censorship very effectively and see sex education as porn-adjacent or sex-work-adjacent in practice even though they may not do so in speech. This itself is an interesting subject of study – should it not be seen in that way? Should sex education see itself as a different 'respectable' caste? Any serious engagement with sexuality constantly brings us up against this central idea of respectability versus respect and the necessity of dismantling it. The other thing is that so many people, irrespective of political leanings, really do have a need for sexuality education – they have questions, they have confusions, and they have a lot of emotional turmoil and shame they are dealing with, and they are seeking this for now, where they can get it. So at least online, there is a push and pull in that sense.

However, the word feminist does now frequently crop up in the list of anti-national characters and it is a matter of time before these conflicts become more edgy. Also, on AoI one of the things we have seen some trolls come in on more recently is our use of popular culture imagery, for instance Raja Ravi Varma, which has got demarcated as Hindu ('you are insulting our *rishi munis* [sages or saints]'). The conflict of sex and culture keeps taking different shapes, telling us something about the importance of sex.

GE: Can you tell us about the genesis of AoI? How did you arrive at using the platform of AoI for sex education? As a multi-media project about sex, love, and desire, what were the immediate challenges and lacunae that the project was attempting to fill?

PV: I thought of creating AoI in 2014, as a response to the kind of discourse around women's sexuality that had grown following the Delhi gang rape of 2012.[10] It is true that sexual violence was finally on the front page – but two things were happening. The only 'women's issues' being discussed were sexual violence. And the only way we were discussing sex was in terms of violence, a negative thing. This resulted in several protectionist responses over the years which also de-sexualized women: 'Selfie with Beti',[11] 'He for She',[12] and so on. In a way it was a more sophisticated *Manohar Kahani* – telling the story of how the outside world was rife with sexual danger for women and that you could prove how liberal you were by saying how you cared for, respected, or protected women from an obscene gaze (that gaze somehow often belonged to men of marginalized identities). Conversations on consent emerged that seemed to be helpful but were in fact binary and did not engage with the granular complexities of sexual interaction. They repeatedly presented women as passive figures – men desire sex, and women either agree or disagree aka consent. The government then asserted a ban on sex education in several states and this too resulted in an odd public conversation which was rooted in caste and class – where it was always the provincial man who was a hypocrite, reading porn, while skipping the chapter on reproduction, and the woke-bro who was sexually open. An example of this is AIB's *Creep Qawwali* (2015), where the man in the 'others' inbox was a creep, and, by implication, English-speaking liberal men were not.[13] Many internet videos mocked sexual ignorance, usually of provincial or 'vernie' men.[14]

Alongside this, one knew that young people are dating online, watching porn online, and do not have sex education or a genuine culture of sexual conversation. They were turning to Western sources which were helpful with information but were not culturally helpful and were full of Americanisms like 'vajayjay' and 'coochie'. So, it created a kind of fake cool which was unrelated to people's own context. Third, there was constant conversation about agency and the sexual revolution (which is apparently always arriving), and a greater commonality of hook up culture and casual sex. This created a kind of double shame where people did not want to admit they were sexually ignorant, while also dealing with the usual sexual shame and did not want to talk about emotional hurts or expectations for fear of seeming old-fashioned.

So, I decided to create a project that would try to address this very knotted-up gap. That would talk about sex and love not as different things but as part of a continuum. That would give information in a culturally relatable language, and an enjoyable form, like film songs do, that would work to co-create – not simply dole out – an Indian language of sex, that would centre the experiences of women and queer people and reframe the terms of the discourse around sex. It would be a universe of pleasure – pleasure positive over sex positive, which would be inclusive and let people enter on their own terms to deal with their confusions in a loving and friendly atmosphere. It would be beautiful and friendly and inviting. It would give sex a good name – whatever that good name might be. We did not define what it meant but, rather, we would invite numerous definitions. It would be a non-hierarchical, non-prescriptive project about sex and also about education, which we see as co-created and dynamic. AoI was one of the first such projects in India. I am happy to say that I think it achieved many of the goals it set out to achieve and opened the portal to so much online sex education.

GE: In AoI, there seems to be a concerted effort to normalize the conversation on sex – from the phrase that appears on the homepage 'We give sex a good name', to tags such as 'Sex ki Baatein-Sex Ke Khayaal' [Sex Thought, Thoughts on Sex], to sections such as 'Doing it Right' that features articles on orgasm and masturbation. In what ways does AoI extend the sex-expert advice columns that were part of the print culture of yesteryears?

PV: To normalize, one must act as if something is normal, as one might in a dance party, not simply exhort others to say it is normal, as one might in a religious gathering.

This is why AoI uses a language that is both celebratory and mundane. I do not believe in using the emergency mode of politics – that is to say pinpointing a crisis (sexual oppression) and then saying we can be 'saved' from it. That results in evangelism and then, the idea of sex and pleasure become instrumental, rather than acknowledged as a domain of life on its own terms. This only repurposes normativity.

If it is considered shameful to talk about sex, then it will be countered by talking 'openly' about sex. If heterosexuality is designated the regressive norm, then homosexuality gets held up as the idealized norm. If monogamy is decried as restrictive then its opposite, polyamory, gets notified as liberated. Hence all you do is replace old norms with new norms and keep enforcing a conformity and a silencing. It is as if sex has to be justified on the basis of some 'higher' purpose (progress and to establish one's enlightened identity rather than be present as itself). And the question arises, to whom are we justifying it? To the existing authority or normative community, right? So, in a way, our efforts to speak for sexual freedom or equality all end up acknowledging the existing power as the real power, if inadvertently, and asking to be 'included' in their framework, without dismantling that framework. Which means you also always exclude someone or something (for instance, you may eventually include sex education, but not, say, porn; or set up porn/erotica, courtesan/prostitute hierarchies).

While this seems to signify change, it in fact merely refreshes a status quo because the terms of engagement are always in binaries. Liberation from binaries does not have a fixed destination. Rather, it is the possibility of constantly moving forward into experience and ever new understandings, fluid insights, and the constant possibility of changing – or change with a capital 'C' – and movement, with a small 'm'. It cannot be guaranteed that this will be purely progressive or useful. But it could be radical in all sorts of ways, we do not yet know. Erotics – creativity, sexual-ness, pleasure, play – in that sense release something moist into the air which keeps life going. These things are the opposite of pure, neat, and disciplinary. That is why, for me, in all my work the starting point is always as if it is perfectly normal to be talking about sex, or feminism, or whatever theme I am working with – making that the compass which guides us in unmapped territory.

So, AoI was created with a built-in aesthetic or tonal assumption: sex is there, it is normal to talk about it not in some performative or declarative sense, but as it is normal to talk about life itself. Perhaps ordinary is a better word to use than normal – it is ordinary to talk about sex. It is special to talk about yourself, but everyone is special, therefore it is also ordinary – it is just something we do. The aesthetic, the language and tone, the questions and information are all crafted for that. The questions we ask before we create any content are as follows:

1. Is this helpful? Will people be able to use this information to help themselves?
2. Is this answering a question people have in their heart, but may not even have articulated yet?

I think the relationship to the 'sexpert' columns is accurately noted. Sexpert columns were the only place that sex was spoken about on its own terms and also as if it was a part of life. Only sexpert columns had the compassion for people's sexual doubts – and even in the most *'nichle sthar ki'* [low-end] versions of *Manohar Kahaniyan*, there were sexpert/agony aunty columns (I myself have written three agony aunty columns in my career: 'Extc Aunt' at *Time Out Mumbai* for three years, 'Ask the Billi' on *The Ladies Finger!* for a year or two, and then the 'Sex Ett' comic on AoI). These columns never laid down norms so strongly for sex, but somewhat dealt with each question on a case-by-case basis. They fluidly considered and braided the private, the public and the personal – the social, the ethical, and the individual. This braiding is something that rarely happens in more public politics which are unable to accommodate emotion and desire, and so, remain partial and always potentially exclusionary while imagining they are inclusive. So yes, we (AoI) are part of a continuing legacy of that idea, but through art and creativity – and this creates an interesting difference.

As soon as we launched, a lot of people began writing to us saying 'I too want to be an "*agent of ishq*"' (and in fact, *'ishq'* means love, or passion) – and often this meant they wanted to recount a sexual experience of their own, the impact on their lives and beings and their learning from it. We worked with these accounts to create readable, reflective pieces and what it turned into is a repository of lived sexual wisdom of people, a community of wisdom so to speak. Here are a couple of excerpts:

> Even when I was very young, I understood in an inarticulate way that my body was capable of eliciting desire, but not the wholesome kind that runs cursive in rose day cards, smiling in living room photographs, and is given a U certificate. Bodies like mine, it was indicated in several different, deliberate ways, were suited for a different kind of desire – one that was between sheets, either on the bed or in a magazine. And in a world spun into a digital web, this other kind of desire was the lifeblood of its most profitable industry, porn. And so, the word best suited to my body was not just illegitimate, it was also illicit.[15]

> Finally, somehow, one of my friends got a cellphone with an Internet connection after trying to convince her parents for more than a year. And that was our ticket to watching actual porn. I was in the 9th standard at that time. Back then, we didn't think about pleasure or pain, just the idea of a penis entering into a vagina was too much (especially because until then, I imagined sex as two people lying together under a blanket, and only smooches were involved). We discovered that the actors were actually enjoying (or pretending to enjoy) the things that they were doing. It was surprising – seeing that sex could give you pleasure. And while mainstream movies only seemed to show us one position in which people had sex, we were suddenly seeing that sex could be had in various kinds of positions. The desire and lust shared by the couple we were watching seemed mutual. After that, our attitude towards sex began to change, and we began to realise that it could be a fun and pleasurable activity shared by two people.[16]

Such personal accounts are examples of people learning from their own lives and sharing it and learning from each other and then sharing some more – people being able to articulate what works for them outside the norms – old or new – of what is considered acceptable or cool. So, in a way, the project is a deconstructed sexpert column where there are several sexperts including the contributors – although primarily they are the sexperts on their own lives. The digital as a form is a lot about this idea of remixing and deconstructing concepts and forms to recuperate what is meaningful from the 'past' and link it to the new, the incoming, the ongoing – aka create new genealogies outside the logic of social identity alone, a third or fourth domain of being and power. I think where AoI takes forward the sexpert columns is in being deeply aware of context and intersectionalities and trying to constantly craft formats and contexts that will energize the intersections and create a new sexual politics. Where it expands the role of the column is breaking the idea of an expert versus the sufferer and makes a space for people as experts in some way.

GE: Fascinating! Do you find any resistance to the kind of work that you and AoI are trying to do? If so, how do you negotiate such roadblocks?

PV: On the contrary we have not faced any resistance – I think because we do not take the tone of confrontation or upliftment. But that is not a coincidence. We use a language that is cheerful, that is not calculated to shock, that is an invitation to play, and we create a frame that is emotional as well as sexual/informational so that people of diverse backgrounds may enter on their own terms. You do not need a pre-existing ideal identity to partake or participate. This creates a comfort and there may be many in the AoI community who might disagree with each other if mainstream political topics were discussed.

The roadblocks we do confront are mostly with regards to the protectionism that comes through community standards – which deem posts acceptable or not on social media – the internet's structure right now which is highly based on social media and its algorithms (so, in a nutshell corporate capitalism).

GE: The Instagram and Twitter pages of AoI make use of popular culture through memes and GIFs. What is the target constituency that AoI caters to in these posts?

PV: I think I want to answer 'everyone' but perhaps it is more 'potentially everyone'. The use of memes and GIFs and pop culture is in order to make it part of the culture of young people and their lingua franca. But in a way this very *desi* [South Asian] treatment is also to appeal to the kind of audience that is not doing the usual woke performance of sexual politics through terminology and discussing 'problematic tropes' [eye-roll]. It is to appeal to an audience that might want to talk about love and sex and have doubts and questions but feels a little culturally uncertain. There is such an identification with English when it comes to talking about sexuality and by extension elite metropolitan or Western culture. But we want to reach an audience which is not just a part of that space – rather one that is quite rooted in India and wants a language to talk about sexuality as Indians. They could be located anywhere, their first language may not be English.[17]

The assumption that sophisticated thought about these issues resides in English is something that one still (surprisingly) has to counter and visuality allows for a certain inclusiveness. Proof of that is also that we receive submissions in Hindi – and when we do our annual masturbation *shayari* [poetry] contest, in several languages.

GE: In AoI, you also work with very locally specific idioms of sex and desire. How do you see conversations of globalization fitting into such themes and concerns, especially as we are at a juncture where populist politics is trying to homogenize even sex and desire under the sign of some primordial civilizational culture?

PV: In continuation with the earlier answer – one might say the mission of AoI, politically speaking, is to recuperate a meaning of Indianness that is far more heterogeneous, far more lived, and encompassing. It is to avoid the 'India is the land of the Kama Sutra' pablum, which locates Indianness in a glorious liberal past, and to ignore the 'sex is a Western import' notion and enter a third space, where people remix many cultures and influences to constantly create numerous renditions of what it means to be Indian.

To me it seems very important to hold on to it in the face of globalized culture which also does what populism in a way is doing – encourages binaries of 'backward' and 'progressive' cultures which leave people excluded and behind. This also leads people to conform to a homogeneous idea of the cool, the 'progressive' or the modern. Influencer culture is a sign of that, some critiques of Pride touch on this. Such tendencies disallow the fecundity of sexual life, its bio-diversity so to speak, to grow and develop and transform our culture and politics.

Notes

1. See the 'About Us' page on AoI. https://agentsofishq.com/about-us/.
2. See Paromita Vohra, 'Tumhara Ishq Ishq…? The Double Meanings Of Desire, Porn And Erotica', Outlook. August 13, 2021. https://www.outlookindia.com/magazine/story/entertainmentnews-tumhara-ishq-ishq-the-double-meanings-of-desire-porn-anderotica/304872.
3. For a contemporary report of the incident, see 'Love in the Time of Media' in the *Times of India* (2006).

4. Charu Gupta describes this as an Islamophobic conspiracy theory floated by the Hindu right wing. Love Jihad is 'supposed to have been launched by Muslim fundamentalists and youthful Muslim men to convert Hindu and Christian women to Islam through trickery and expressions of false love' ('Hindu Women, Muslim Men: Love Jihad and Conversions,' *Economic and Political Weekly*, 2009, 44 (51): 13–15, at 13).
5. See Paromita Vohra's 'What Sunny Leone's Success Tells Us about Indian Society' in *The Ladies' Finger!* (June 24, 2015 http://theladiesfinger.com/the-baffling-success-of-sunny-leone/#:~:text=She%20owns%20her%20work%20completely,themselves%20apart%20from%20other%20natives.).
6. See Paromita Vohra's 'Sexist ya feminist? Whose selfie is it anyway?' in the *Times of India* (July 5, 2015, https://timesofindia.indiatimes.com/home/sunday-times/all-thatmatters/Sexist-ya-feminist-Whose-selfie-is-it-anyway/articleshow/47940649.cms).
7. For the AoI website, visit https://agentsofishq.com/.
8. For a description of the project on the Goethe Institut Indien website, see https://www.goethe.de/ins/in/en/kul/art/fmi/pav.html.
9. For instance, Facebook's advertising policy puts it as: 'Ads must not promote the sale or use of adult products or services. Ads promoting sexual and reproductive health products or services, such as contraception and family planning, must be targeted to people aged 18 and older, and must not focus on sexual pleasure.' See https://www.facebook.com/policies/ads/prohibited_content/adult_products_or_services.
10. The Delhi gang rape of 2012, often called the 'Nirbhaya' case (after the media-endowed moniker meaning 'fearless'), involved the brutal rape and murder of a young woman on a bus at night in Delhi, and sparked off a series of conversations about women's safety (and later the death penalty) in India, particularly in the city of Delhi. The event also saw the outbreak of major public protests in Delhi which were met by repression and violence by the police. For more details see, Esha Shah's 'Delhi Gang Rape – Understanding the Structure of Violence' in *Kafila* (February 2, 2013, https://kafila.online/2013/02/01/delhi-gang-rape-understanding-thestructure-of-violence/).
11. Paromita Vohra, 'Sexist ya feminist? Whose selfie is it anyway?' (2015).
12. See https://www.heforshe.org/en/wheels-change.
13. AIB or 'All India Bakchod' is a comic collective. The *Creep Qawwali* video was created with the Indian mobile phone dating app, Truly Madly, which promoted itself as a 'safe' dating app for women, drawing on the discourses of safety after the 2012 Delhi gang rape and murder. For more details see, Vishnupriya Das's 'Dating Applications, Intimacy, and Cosmopolitan Desire in India', in *Global Digital Cultures: Perspectives from South Asia*, edited by Aswin Punathambekar and Sriram Mohan, 2019, Michigan: University of Michigan Press, 125–141.
14. Clearly making an implication that the 'vernacular' is a lower-class space rife with danger – an idea that this special issue of *Porn Studies* and the one preceding it actively push against.
15. See Ini's 'I Took a Nude Selfie: It Changed My Life' on AoI (13 July 2020).
16. See Ankita Salian's 'What Emraan Hashmi Couldn't Teach Me About Dhichak' on AoI (19 August 2019).
17. Which brings us back squarely to the question of the vernacular.

Disclosure statement

No potential conflict of interest was reported by the authors.

Confluences: of war porn and nationalism, at the limits of memory

Ricky Varghese

ABSTRACT

This short article explores the suggestive and complicated genre of 'war porn' as first described by Jean Baudrillard in his now-famous essay from *Libération*. I attempt to situate the genre within the context of South Asia, and specifically of India, to undergird a conversation regarding nationalism and the ways by which violence – its production, mediation, circulation, and subsequent consumption – becomes promulgated, particularly when we consider the violation of others. How does understanding its mediation become central to an understanding of how this violence becomes enacted and how does a discussion about 'war porn' facilitate a better comprehension of such conceptual frameworks as nationalism, religious fundamentalism, historical memory, and the problematic construction of the figure of the other – these are some of the queries that will be examined here. Furthermore, I also explore how the virtual mediation of violence participates in the ongoing perpetuation of the violation of others as much as the very real acts of violence themselves.

> Our mortification and our painful disillusionment on account of the uncivilized behavior of our fellow-citizens of the world during this war were unjustified. They were based on an illusion to which we had given way. In reality our fellow citizens have not sunk so low as we feared, because they had never risen so high as we believed. (Freud 1957, 285)

I write as someone interested in the interstitial or liminal space that can be conceived of as existing between porn/sex studies and ruin/memory studies.[1] When invited to contribute a text to the Forum section of this issue on 'South Asian Pornographies' I had initially wanted to write about the subject of boredom. I had specifically wanted to address the affective registers of boredom and how they manifest/materialize in relation to the genre of war porn and its consumption. Jean Baudrillard ([2004] 2005) popularized the phrase in his now-famous essay 'Pornographie de la guerre' ['War porn'] published in *Libération* in the immediate aftermath of, and as a critical response to, the release and circulation of the shocking images from Abu Ghraib. Perhaps he was thinking alongside Freud (who was, himself, reflecting on the consequences of the Great War) when he wrote the following of the images under this heading and the general category of war porn:

> The worst is that it all becomes a parody of violence, a parody of the war itself, pornography becoming the ultimate abjection of war which is unable to be simply war, to be simply about killing, and instead turns itself into a grotesque infantile reality show, in a desperate simulacrum of power. (Baudrillard [2004] 2005)

Both Freud and Baudrillard seem to be concerned with a kind of structural desperation in how we attempt to contend with violence and the virulent nature by which it gets mediated – simply put, Freud suggests 'we' were never as good as we thought we were, no amount of a claim to being disillusioned can disabuse us of this; and for Baudrillard, it appears that he is attending to a desperation in the very nature of the violence that is both produced and then its (re)presentation disseminated, that this violence desperately wants to exceed itself, become its own excess, foment a power that exceeds the very nominal, and perhaps even the notional, value of power itself.

The quote from Freud's 'The Disillusionment of the War' that forms the opening epigraph to this article and the quote from Baudrillard's own 'War Porn' can both be found in and seen to form the central theses expanded upon by Prabha Manuratne (2014) in her rigorous essay 'Parody of War: Pleasure at the Limits of Pornography', which appears in the anthology *Porn Archives* edited by Tim Dean, Steven Ruszczycky, and David Squires. Manuratne's own focus was on conducting an exegetical reading of viewer/consumer responses that can be found in online forums which are a part of websites that showcase/display war porn – video and surveillance footage, often edited, tweaked, and redone, that depict the violence which takes place on the frontlines during wartime. In reading, analyzing, and theorizing about these responses, found on sites like LiveLeak.com or the now-defunct Ogrish.com and Nowthatsfuckedup.com, Manuratne brilliantly connects the racial and neocolonial logics at play in how war porn, or the dissemination of wartime violence, becomes consumed, sexualized, and talked about, primarily by subscribers and users in the Global North/West. War porn, it would seem, as such provides the site for a confluence of two precisely Freudian and psychoanalytic investments – that in the study of aggression and that in the study of sexuality. Much of what Manuratne assessed revealed the racist ways by which war porn became consumed because it showcased violence enacted in the service of dominating others, specifically those others marked as racialized or other than. The charged language of domination, here, that Manuratne discovered on these forums, in the form of comments users left about the videos posted on these sites, was often highly sexualized. My own intention is to resituate Freud' s remarks on disillusionment – which notably might differ from anything resembling boredom – and Baudrillard's own observations regarding war porn to a different geography and a different socio-political and historical context.

The date December 6 1992 in the contexts of both the history and the contemporary politics of India is particularly charged. This was the date on which Hindu Kar Sevaks (Hindu nationalist right-wing activists) organized together to demolish a sixteenth-century mosque, the Babri Masjid, in the city of Ayodhya. The centuries-old mosque had long been part of the famed Ayodhya dispute – the dispute makes the claim, a claim made by Hindu right-wing outfits, that the mosque stood at the site on which a temple once stood, one that apparently marked the precise place of the birth of the Hindu god Ram. The history, the intricate details, and the longstanding political debates surrounding the Ayodhya dispute are well-worn and well-trodden terrains. These are too elaborate to detail in the context of this very brief article and would veer us away from the subject matter at hand. Suffice it to say, the event radically changed and shifted the political landscape of India, and in the ensuing 25 years since, the rise of Hindu nationalism has been constant, and a particular cause for alarm for India's many communities of religious minorities and those marginalized on the basis of caste. At the time of writing this Forum piece, the Hindu right-wing Bharathiya Janata Party is in power at the federal level and at the state level in 12 out of India's 29 states. Violence against religious minorities – in the form of public lynchings and mob violence – has increasingly, in a sense, become commonplace, undisputed, and even, in some cases, encouraged either passively or actively. Justice for victims and survivors alike is often hard-fought, distant, and/or elusive. In what space remains, I want to offer an account of an instance in which such a scene of unthinkable violence took place, was captured on camera, and then was disseminated and shared over various forms of social and mainstream media as a way to showcase that the violence does not merely reside in the brutal acts themselves, but in their continued perpetuation and ongoing bolstering vis-à-vis their mediation, circulation, and consumption.

On December 6 2017, the 25th anniversary of the demolition of the Babri Masjid – one cannot emphasize enough the precise significance of the date, a date which in India is celebrated by extremist Hindu groups and mourned by Muslims – a Muslim migrant worker, Mohammed Afrazul, in the Rajsamand district of the state of Rajasthan, originally hailing from the state of West Bengal, was hacked to death and his body set on fire. The perpetrator of this murderous act, a Hindu man by the name of Shambulal Regar, made his 14-year-old nephew capture the event on his phone, the video of which began to be shared shortly thereafter on local Rajsamand Whatsapp groups. Towards the end of the day, more videos started to appear on social media, wherein Regar was shown ranting away a justification for the brutal act – he claims that he committed the murder to protect a local Hindu woman from 'love jihad', the hate-mongering myth or fantasy structure created by extremist Hindus wherein Muslim men are cast as ghastly figures who force Hindu women to fall in love with them, marry them, and convert to Islam. The false myth, a myth in which the other is constructed as a figure to be feared and abhorred, perpetuates the idea that 'love jihad' is a covert operation of gradual Islamic takeover of the predominantly Hindu society of India. As reported in an article in *The Wire*, '[in] one of the videos, Regar is seen warning Muslims by bringing up the bogey "love jihad" and saying: "This is what will happen to you if you do love jihad in our country"' (The Wire Staff 2017). Suffice it to say, the videos have been shared extensively and watched by millions across the country. Extremist Hindu outfits have hailed Regar a hero and his act a clarion call to wage war against the threatening figure of the Muslim other. Within days and weeks of the incident taking place and its video being disseminated, Muslim migrant workers, fearing for their personal safety, started clearing out of Rajsamand and the neighbouring areas, and religious minorities in the state and across the nation have started to wonder what the implications of this event might be and what sorts of repercussions may be produced as a result of it.

Violence against religious minorities and those marginalized on the basis of caste are not in the least bit a new phenomenon in India. Further to this, something about the way in which these acts are conducted, captured, and circulated depicts the alarmingly hyper-mediated viral and virulent ways by which violence against the other or perceived others comes to be normalized within the fabric of everyday life. Megha Anwer, in writing about lynching photographs in the Indian context, has already suggested that 'the imagistic vocabulary of lynching has [taken] a touch of the mundane inevitability in caste and communal violence' (Anwer 2016). Once might hear in Anwer's claim echoes of the Arendtian sense of the banality of evil. For the marginalized, violence and its commodification in the form of the image has become uncannily commonplace, even banalized as the case may be. While the act here in this specific case and the recording that captured it do not arrive at its viewers/consumers from the frontlines of a battlefield or war, they do, however, reproduce the central premise which is constitutive of war porn: the mediated violation of others, the mediated waging of war upon others, and the circulation of that mediated violence for mass consumption. Such mediation and its subsequent consumption – the mediation and the consumption of the image, so to speak, in its totality as an object produced precisely for consumption – has become as much a part of the violence as the violent acts themselves, and this is precisely why Baudrillard views such imagistic violence as having a notable virtual and pornographic quality to them:

> For images to become a source of true information, they would have to be distinct from the war. They have become today as virtual as the war itself, and for this reason their specific violence adds to the specific violence of the war. In addition, due to their omnipresence, due to the prevailing rule of the world making everything visible, the images, our present-day images, have become substantially pornographic. Spontaneously they embrace the pornographic face of war. (Baudrillard [2004] 2005)

The pornographic quality of this violence thrives not so much on its capacity to be possibly sexualized, as much as it does on the seemingly unrelenting fidelity to the scopic nature of mediation itself, on the commitment to make visible vis-à-vis mediation the capacity of perpetrators to both virtually and metaphorically denude the other. As Baudrillard himself has suggested, in such cases 'the other will be exterminated symbolically. One sees that the goal of war is not to kill or to win, but to abolish the enemy, extinguish the light of his sky' ([2004] 2005). I would argue that while there is a symbolic aspect to this violence, there is, as well, a materiality, realistically speaking, to the violence being represented and mediated in such instances.

What is made visible here in the virtual mediation of real violence – in the sense that it was committed and then mediated – are a set of confluences, affectively charged registers, that are as significant as the date upon which the violence against Afrazul was perpetrated. Earlier I noted that the date – the 25th anniversary of the demolition of the Babri Masjid – cannot be disregarded as bearing any significance to the date on which Afrazul was murdered. The figure of the Muslim other comes to stand in, here, both literally – materially, as the case may be – and symbolically for the demolition itself. Further to this, that a minor, Regar's nephew, was tasked by his uncle with the responsibility of documenting the murder makes visible, lays bare, the ways by which children themselves are indoctrinated in the rhetorical and material violence implicit in the logic of Hindu nationalism and nation-building in the context of India. Still further, that gender – the self-proclaimed protection of a Hindu woman, or Hindu women in general, from the fantasized other that is constructed as a threat and as one to be feared – was utilized as a rationale for the murder reveals how gender becomes the justification for nationalist forms of violence and their promulgation. It reveals how the logic of patriarchal protectionism, a protectionism that refuses to recognize women's agency or rather actively denies women their agency, becomes confluent with the rhetoric of nationalism. There appears even a confluence in the aesthetic choices made in both the production of lynching videos and of MMS (Multimedia Messaging Service) pornography so prevalent within the South Asian context. The hazy quality seems to, at once, both reveal something while appearing to obscure what is being captured. There is a voyeuristic quality to the aesthetics, as though what is captured on video appears to be done so by a bystander, a figure outside the frame, a wandering set of eyes that land their focus on something sinister in the case of the lynching video or seductive and sultry in the case of a MMS video. There appears to be, simultaneously, a desire to represent while also have the scene remain cached, even a bit somewhat hidden from view, under the radar as it were.

What, then, are the limits of and for historical memory here? While it can be argued that we have come to inhabit a time in history, wherein the culture we find ourselves in appears to have become thoroughly desensitized to violence and its seemingly endless mediation, the point that I hope I have made is to situate the incidence of violence that took place in Rajasthan within the larger socio-political and historical context mired by the significance of the date of December 6 and the demolition of the Babri Masjid. Perhaps the limits can be unravelled precisely as we, in a nuanced manner, observe and assess the scenes revealed in such confluences. Here, Freud warned us against being disillusioned when it came to the limits, or rather the limitlessness, of the human capacity for violence. As the speed of mediation ramps up, the speed of our responses to such violence, to remembering the anxious history, memory, and present that this violence might signify, cannot be hindered or slowed down by a claim to being disillusioned or, even, perceptually distant from what we are made to bear witness to.

Note

1. In *Pornographies: Critical Positions* (Harrison and Ogden 2018) I have a chapter titled 'Barebacking and Historical Time', wherein I make a similar move pulling together the fields of porn/sex studies and ruin/memory studies to consider the present-day proliferation of queer/gay male bareback pornography alongside the history, memory, and present of the AIDS crisis.

Disclosure statement

No potential conflict of interest was reported by the author.

References

Anwer, Megha. 2016. 'Three Photographs, Six Bodies: The Politics of Lynchings in Two.' Kafila, June 5. Accessed July 15 2018. https://kafila.online/2016/06/05/three-photographs-six-bodies-the-politics-of-lynching-in-twos-megha-anwer/.

Baudrillard, Jean. [2004] 2005. 'Pornographie de la guerre.' *Libération*, May 19. Also published as 'War Porn.' Translated by Paul A. Taylor. *International Journal of Baudrillard Studies* 2 (1). https://www2.ubishops.ca/baudrillardstudies/vol2_1/taylor.htm.

Freud, Sigmund. 1957. 'The Disillusionment of the War.' In *The Standard Edition of the Complete Psychological Works of Sigmund Freud, vol. 14, 1914–1916*, translated by James Strachey, 273–300. London: The Hogarth Press.

Varghese, Ricky. 2018. 'Barebacking and Historical Time.' In *Pornographies: Critical Positions*, edited by Katherine Harrison and Cassie Ogden, 242–263. Chester: University of Chester Press.

Manuratne, Prabha. 2014. 'Parody of War: Pleasure at the Limits of Pornography.' In *Porn Archives*, edited by Tim Dean, Steven Ruszczycky, and David Squires, 356–372. Durham: Duke University Press.

The Wire Staff. 2017. 'As Filmed Murder of Muslim Man in Rajasthan Goes Viral, Official Culture of Impunity Towards Hate Crimes Blamed.' The Wire. December 7. Accessed December 20 2017. https://thewire.in/202831/rajasthan-muslim-man-hacked-to-death-video/.

Porn, sexuality and expression in Sri Lanka: feminist debates and interventions

Subha Wijesiriwardena

ABSTRACT
This article explores the engagement of feminists in Sri Lanka with the question of pornography. The article looks at some of the ways in which feminist scholars in Sri Lanka have written about sexuality, sex work and freedom of expression, as a way of engaging with the gaps and nuances in Lankan feminist discourse and debate, if any, about pornography. The article explores how state prohibition and social stigma about sexuality inform the conditions within which expressions of sexuality and the production and dissemination of erotic material takes place in Sri Lanka, and how, at times, feminist and/or women's rights interventions themselves support or impede the process.

In search of 'Sri Lankan' porn

My first experience of pornography was about at the age of 12 or 13 years as a young girl-child growing up in Colombo, with dial-up internet. At this time, when I first discovered porn through glimpses of pictures, it was not yet a major revelation. We had a shared computer, and the sound of dial-up tones became everyday, ringing in my ears; I would have very little private time, perhaps 15 minutes a day, here and there. At this time, it was, at most, a glimpse of images of nude bodies (and not always because I was even looking). Mostly, they were white women with big breasts. This was about it. When I was about 16 years old, our ability to use the internet had grown more advanced. Concurrently, I also learnt to 'look', and what I found were mostly images of people having sex. By then, the glimpses were not always accidents anymore. And by 'people having sex', I mean white men and women having sex with each other. I rarely saw anything else at this time, perhaps because I was not so good at navigating the space, or because the landscape in itself was still limited at the time; more likely, it was a combination of both.

Nonetheless, as a young person, in a world where most signals coming my way told me my sexuality was somehow dangerous (to me and others), porn was a formative encounter with sexual pleasure and affirmation. It was my first real encounter with diverse bodies and sexualities; I learned that trans, intersex, disabled, fat, black, brown and old people are all sexual beings – before I knew it politically, and experientially, I knew it viscerally through watching other people have sex on screen. As my own awareness of my sexuality and eventually, an awareness of my queerness, has grown (and continues to grow), my ability to navigate the world of porn has too. Today, I will admit that porn is inextricable from my sexuality and my queerness. I think porn is queer; not just 'queer porn' but just porn itself. It subverts all kinds of norms and is fuelled by people seeking pleasure (on both sides of the screen).

When I began to write this article, I wanted to go in search of the porn industry in Sri Lanka. I started to scour local and global porn websites for 'Sri Lankan' porn, hoping something might give me access to those in the scenes. I also scoured local escort sites, hoping to connect with in-person sex workers in Sri Lanka who might have some insights into how porn gets produced. I wrote to a number of people (women, I assume), on a number of sites, and got responses from some, but found none who were willing to be interviewed about making porn itself. I must also admit that when I looked for 'Sri Lankan' porn, I had never really done it before. At least, not with any real intention.

What I found was a lot of the 'home-made' variety. In some clips, the face of the woman is deliberately obscured (through the placement of an emoji, for example). In some, the camera is angled in such a way so you cannot see the man's face; in some, both faces are out of view. Platforms like Jillhub seem to aggregate what largely appears to be local content. On Pornhub, some accounts which identify themselves as Sri Lankan have thousands, if not tens of thousands, of followers. It seems apparent that local content producers also tactically use the tag 'Indian', where convenient, to boost views on Sri Lankan porn. Some verified accounts on Pornhub, which identify themselves as 'Sri Lankan', have a considerable amount of views; for example, Kuweni Devi has 2.8 million, and Shani Akka has about 5000 subscribers and also about two million video views (for content mostly of the BBW, or Big Beautiful Women, variety). Princess Alekhshi has almost 15,000 subscribers and more than 20 million video views.

Of course it is impossible to know whether they are actually run by the person seen in the profile image(s) and who is described in the brief bio; if we are to believe they are, then these accounts, like many, many others on Pornhub, belong to young Sri Lankan women. It is also impossible to tell whether all of the content hosted by these accounts feature the same person/people (especially because faces are not always visible). They could be hosting their own content or be aggregating others' content, or both. Many sex workers in Sri Lanka who use online spaces (such as escort sites) also typically seem to blur or obscure their faces. It is easy to understand why (as I explicate a little later) – both the criminal law and the social contract in Sri Lanka require them to engage in their pursuits while 'hiding'.

In the interim period, I interviewed some internationally renowned porn workers (such as Sinn Sage), who I was luckily able to reach thanks to OnlyFans, to understand better how a well-developed industry works. Where this path eventually led me was interesting in itself, although it was not where I expected to end up: I began to read various Lankan feminist writings on sexuality, and on sex work.[1] I believe this gives me some clues with which to understand better how we have (or have not) engaged with the area of pornography as a field for feminist inquiry in Sri Lanka, in terms of labour, pleasure and expression. In what follows, I lay out a map of this field through an analysis of media discourses, feminist approaches and interviews with feminist researchers and activists working on sexuality, sexual expression and freedom of expression (including on the internet).

Pornography, obscenity and feminism in Sri Lanka

Porn, is of course, effectively 'banned' in Sri Lanka. But the broad lack of consensus on what constitutes pornography, on the part of the state, society and even within the women's movement, is one of the often unnamed yet defining features of the debate. In response to a question I posed about a well-publicized 2010 'crackdown' on porn (including mass arrests of people who were called 'pornographers') in Sri Lanka, Paba Deshapriya, co-founder of The Grassrooted Trust and an advocate for comprehensive relationship education, said that while such incidents were reported, it was not possible to know what had really transpired: 'They [law enforcement] will say "obscene publications", but who knows what they mean'.[2] As elsewhere in South Asia, pornography and obscenity are inextricably bound together in Sri Lanka, and this is a historical relationship. The Obscene Publications Ordinance No. 4 of 1927 (as amended) makes it an offence to produce, possess, import, export, carry on, take part in a business or advertise the availability of obscene publications, but of course does not define 'obscenity'. The impact of this legislation is compounded by the continuing criminalization of same-sex sexual relations in Sri Lanka (under Penal Code Articles 365 and 365A, which prohibit 'unnatural acts' and acts 'against the order of nature'), the continuing criminalization of several aspects of sex work, including of those who own brothels (the Brothels Ordinance of 1889), and, of course, decades of state and state-sanctioned attacks on speech and expression in Sri Lanka. About three months before the aforementioned crackdown in 2010, Sri Lankan authorities had sought to block public access to about 100 websites through the national Telecommunications Regulatory Commission, claiming that people were accessing pornography on their mobile phones through these websites (Reuters 2010). On 4 November 2010, AVN (originally the Adult Video Network), the US leader in adult entertainment industry news and business, reported that 'Sri Lanka's Telecommunication Regulatory Commission (TRC) has announced plans to install ISP-level software that will filter out pornographic websites, according to local news reports' (Hymes 2010). The crackdown must be read in this context.

On 5 November 2010, a Sri Lankan court ruled that it was permissible for the police to publish faces of suspected 'porn stars' in their efforts to 'break up a porn ring' (Natarajan 2010). Media reports also revealed a wide range of problematic and unsubstantiated assumptions made by the authorities in justifying these arrests. 'Most of these people are Sri Lankans. We know this from their features', a police spokesperson was reported saying (Swaminathan 2010). Some other reports stated: 'The authorities say pornography leads to sexual crimes, including rape' (Haviland 2010). Subsequently, the police released photographs of about 80 people to be published; local paper *Lakbima* at the time published photographs of 27 people, alleged 'porn stars' (Swaminathan 2010). Similarly, in 2017 a young couple in the south of Sri Lanka were detained for a short while, for watching pornographic films on a phone, in private. The police raided a bedroom of a private residence and detained this couple, searching their phones for porn, acting on a neighbour's report. The whole thing was under-reported; I myself was unable to find any English language reporting on this incident. I contacted a lawyer, Thishya Weragoda, who made some public statements at the time, insisting that the police had no right to raid a private residence nor to arrest consenting adults for watching porn in private. He said:

> The archaic law on obscene publications ordinance only prohibits possession of pornography for purposes of sale, distribution or public display or for purposes stated or otherwise. However, the issue is, could the words 'or otherwise' be interpreted to encompass private possession for personal consumption? This was the issue in 2017 [in this case].[3]

As Weragoda noted during our conversation, the experience for this couple was mired in various manifestations of gendered stigma by law enforcement which ended up violating the couples' privacy while playing the moral police (e.g. the woman was subjected to an arbitrary STD test; the man was not).

Questions of obscenity, pornography and sexuality have also found their place in feminist engagements in Sri Lanka. In the 1990s, feminists in Sri Lanka began to postulate that we must understand the repression of women's sexuality in conjunction with intensifying communalism in South Asia (Jayawardena and de Alwis 1996) and ask whether the sexual can be 'part of a nation's heritage' (de Alwis 1996, 103). Feminists such as Sunila Abeysekera (1999) addressed the dichotomy created between 'good woman' and 'bad woman' in society as a tool to shame women into not enjoying sexuality, as well as addressing the issue of 'control', related to abortion and reproduction (Abeysekera 1997), while others have studied and documented feminists' own articulations of their role in advocating for the rights of lesbian women, bisexual women and transpersons, or LBT persons (Wijewardene 2018).

Lankan feminist engagement with expression and censorship contains diverse and sometimes seemingly contradictory approaches and political positions. Many leading women's rights organizations and activists often join other civil society organizations and human rights defenders in publicly objecting to arrests, assassinations and abductions of journalists and dissidents over the years, through signing petitions and statements (e.g. the case of Shakthika Sathkumara, who was arrested for the online publication of an erotic short story).[4] There have also been many Lankan feminist interventions which have supported women's freedom of expression (even if this is not always overtly stated as a politics); for instance, the Women and Media Collective, which emphasizes control of technologies of production and communication (Ganesh and Shah 2020, 338), or *Minmini Seithihal*, an SMS-based feminist news service, which was launched in 2010 with a desire to centre women's rights to information and expression (Kottegoda et al. 2012). However, according to Sanjana Hattotuwa, a researcher who has been studying and collecting data at the intersections of politics and digital media in Sri Lanka: 'there is no critical approach to the question of expression, feminists haven't substantially engaged with this question [and] Lankan civil society interventions in general, on the issue of freedom of expression, are rudimentary at best'.[5]

As elsewhere, in the Sri Lankan context too there is great anxiety about porn's perceived link to violence. For example, in a 2018 article in the *Daily News*, a Sri Lankan sexual health advocate wonders whether there is a link between porn and violence, making an assumption that not only can some acts we see in porn naturally be considered 'rape', but they are also shown to be 'enjoyable all the time' (Daily News 2018). This article talks about high rates of Sri Lankan viewership on Pornhub, shown by statistics released by Pornhub in 2018. In 2017, bakamoono.lk[6] (a website run by The Grassrooted Trust) released a landmark study of 800 respondents about watching porn in Sri Lanka. On the bakamoono.lk site, in a blog titled '800 Odd Criminals: A Reflection' (Sekaram 2017), the writer (who identifies as a feminist, going by this excerpt and others) noted:

> There were a couple of key stats that caught my eye – and spurred on questions I have been asking about the objectification of women, gender binaries and role, and of course the equality of the sexes – *feminist questions*. What role does porn (if any) play in these arbitrary, hotly debated upon, ideas? What link does a schoolboy masturbating to a video of a girl having sex with several men (filed under 'gangbang') have to do with catcalls and rape? (Sekaram 2017; my emphasis)

Here we see some dominant ideas surface, such as the one about 'objectification'. In her own self-described feminist column, 'The F Word', the same author also writes: 'What does this mean for young people with easy access to porn coupled with little to no sex education?' (Sekaram 2019). The author also points out that, as per the report, 'pornography has the potential to create misconceptions about sexual orientation, non-conforming sex acts, gender identity, sex, sexual preferences, sexual violence, and relationships' (Sekaram 2019), not taking into account that the exact opposite has also been true for many.[7] The authors of the bakamoono.lk report, however, were themselves cautious about drawing direct correlations with the findings and respondents' sexual behaviour because, due to the anonymity of the report, 'it was not possible to distinguish if the respondents were being honest' (Daily News 2018). These diverse positions reflect the complex and contradictory nature of feminist debates on pornography.

Sometimes stigma and shame around porn and other sexual acts are reinforced by 'women's rights' campaigns. Campaign videos on the website for 'Women in Need', a large, national women's rights non-governmental organization, are a good example. In one of them, there is a mention of pornography as related to violence, the term 'lewd phone conversations' is used to describe some manner of phone sex between two consenting adults, and there is an implied advocacy for the use of the Obscene Publications Act to indict perpetrators.[8] In one video, the 'innocent' is posited as oppositional to 'sexual' – as per the script, 'their innocent affair developed into something sexual'. Other non-governmental outfits, like the think-tank LIRNEasia, seem to have stated caution about regulation. LIRNEasia published blogs about the Telecommunications Regulations Commission's attempts to block websites, on the basis of blocking porn, stating that strict enforcement can even go on to justify blocking of email services, as porn videos can also be distributed via them (LIRNEasia 2008).

However, there is an emerging contemporary body of work by feminists in Sri Lanka which addresses sexual expression and pornography, perhaps for the first time, directly through a feminist lens that accounts for the intersection of gender, sexuality and the internet. In 2019, two Lankan feminist researchers – Sachini Perera and Minoli Wijetunge – wrote about TikTok in the Sri Lankan context, exploring how sexual expression online can challenge and shift hierarchies of sexuality, behaviour, class as well as the public/private divide (Perera and Wijetunge 2019). Zainab Ibrahim and Sachini Perera have conducted research in Sri Lanka (Perera and Ibrahim 2021) as a part of EROTICS (Exploratory Research on ICTs and Sexuality) by the Association for Progressive Communication. EROTICS is an ongoing project by feminists to regionally and globally map internet use in its intersections with gender and sexuality. Sri Lanka has been a part of the EROTICS study network before, in 2017, when the Women and Media Collective produced 'Disrupting the Binary Code: Experiences of LGBT Sri Lankans Online'.[9] Ibrahim and Perera's research will take the EROTICS methodology further, creating a more comprehensive and nuanced study of people in Sri Lanka (including communities and people on the margins, such as sex workers) using the internet for work and livelihoods, pleasure and play.

Cat's Eye, a collective of feminists writing anonymously on Sri Lankan, regional and global current affairs (in English), has been in circulation in some shape or form since the 1990s.[10] With the tagline 'a feminist gaze on current affairs in Sri Lanka and beyond', Cat's Eye articles are now archived online on a WordPress blogsite.[11] In perusing some recent Cat's Eye articles, I found one on women in the media, which takes a different approach than looking at 'representation' or 'portrayal' of women in the media: instead, this article asks why women's opinions are so rarely sought in news reports and coverage in the mainstream media in Sri Lanka. Although there is a section on 'portrayal', this section does not veer into the territory of 'objectification'; instead, its arguments rest on a solid foundation of drawing attention to the very different standards applied when writing about women and men, and how women's activism is written about in the local news (Cat's Eye Collective 2018b), in a way which discredits and makes light of it. Another article in Cat's Eye goes more directly into the territory of pornography, sexual expression and erotic content. In an August 2018 discussion about a popular Sinhala rap music video, the article states that the video's self-conscious framing to invoke pornographic genres also meant that there was much moral outrage with a popular narrative of the '"exploitation" and "objectification" of the women in the video' being imposed on it (Cat's Eye Collective 2018a). The article also goes to challenge this 'objectification' narrative by stating that while some responses to the video veered on protectionism, the women who performed in it asserted their own agency by framing it as a professional choice that they were comfortable with, rather than some kind of exploitation (Cat's Eye Collective 2018a).

Pornography, pleasure and consent

Part of the anxiety around porn in Sri Lanka is a result of the murky waters around the question of consent in all kinds of erotic or intimate videos. While this sometimes manifests in stigmatization of sex, more nuanced views have also begun to emerge. For instance, Sachini Perera, Jayanthi Kuru-Utumpala and Zainab Ibrahim are building a platform online called Delete Nothing.[12] In our interview, they told me Delete Nothing will be queer-friendly, and will be partly a place to document instances of consent violations and gender-based violence online in a systematic and safe manner, and partly a resource for survivors seeking support outside of normative frameworks of criminal justice. They said they want to take an affirmative approach unlike the stigmatizing, prohibitionist approach taken by some others, including some who work with survivors of online violence.[13] When I asked them about pornography (both whether they encountered people who are making porn and whether they spoke to people about watching porn), Perera said that they spoke to a number of sex workers who started taking their work online – not necessarily performing sex acts online, but using online spaces to connect with clients.[14] Perera also said they encountered some young queer folks who wanted to open OnlyFans pages to supplement their income and were currently navigating their way through this decision. Their key concerns were about becoming criminalized or penalized.

Ibrahim and Perera also noted two issues when talking to people about watching porn and using the internet for pleasure. One was that 'pleasure' did not really seem to be a part of their vocabulary, and the other was that not all respondents directly related porn to pleasure. Ibrahim stated: 'There was one interview, for example, where someone spoke about watching porn, but they also said they never use the internet for sexual pleasure.' For instance, Ibrahim noted that most of their respondents reported the pleasure derived from the internet as being 'kind of average',[15] while Perera stated that the word 'pleasure (the local language equivalent for it)' did not even form part of the daily lexicon of most people.[16]

In 2018, the advocates who run The Grassrooted Trust in Sri Lanka wrote an article titled 'Sri Lanka's Nude Culture Revisited: Responding to Homemade Porn'. This was a follow up to a somewhat explosive article published by Grassrooted in 2017, titled 'Investigating Sri Lanka's Nude Culture' (Billimoria 2017), which looked closely at a subculture of taking and sharing nudes among young people in Sri Lanka, using internet-based technologies. What it revealed was the underbelly of an otherwise seemingly harmless adolescent practice: an entire economy based on sharing nudes of young people publicly without their consent. 'Nudity is now inextricably linked with shame', writes Billimoria (2017), who, through The Grassrooted Trust, works with young people to address situations where their consent has been violated. In the article Billimoria wonders:

> what it would take to arrest the homemade porn entrepreneurs of Sri Lanka. Those who have convinced lodge owners to affix spy cams in rooms sold by the hour; convinced boys and men to set up spy cams in bathrooms, shower cubicles and outdoor baths, sheltered by cement walls, corrugated iron sheets, or dried coconut and/or Palmyra fronds, but still broadcast her wet soapy nudity to thousands of Sri Lankans. (Billimoria 2017)

It may be worrying that those like Billimoria would advocate for the arrest of 'home-made porn entrepreneurs', but this is because they are faced with a unique challenge. In my interview with Deshapriya, co-founder of The Grassrooted Trust along with Billimoria, she talked with me about the primary conflict they face when doing their work. Fundamentally, the copious amounts of non-consensually disseminated erotic material out there in Sri Lanka makes it hard to distinguish that from the home-made porn that is consensually made for distribution and forms a category on porn sites, because the images share the same aesthetic qualities.[17]

Deshapriya spoke about the complex feelings she and others at Grassrooted encounter when working with young people who are facing consent violations. There is a lot of victim-blaming and stigma associated with such violations, which makes their work much harder:

> They want us to press a magic button and make everything go away, so they can go back to their 'good girl' lives. We have to re-define what it means to be a good girl. Our message is always, you have not done anything wrong.[18]

When they deal with consent violations, they write to the porn sites first, with the well-known porn sites usually being very responsive, but she also notes that there are many pathways for these videos to get out –from mobile phone shops, to WhatsApp groups, to intimate partners.[19]

Deshapriya also reflected on the analogous relationship between the internet and porn: 'For most people, the internet is porn. They conflate the two. This is actually the way a lot of people here discover the internet',[20] she said, referring to the fact that Sri

Lanka keeps appearing on the top of the list of most Google searches for 'sex'.[21] She spoke about hearing a lot of anxiety about 'the internet' from parents and educators, due to this conflation. She also said that, in their experience, access to the internet can itself be gendered: 'Boys have a lot of access in a way that girls don't'.[22]

Conclusion

While this is not a comprehensive history of porn and feminism in Sri Lanka, such discourses offer us a glimpse into the various (often conflicting) approaches to porn and sexual expression in the country. A number of factors make it difficult for a more formalized porn industry to thrive in Sri Lanka. The country routinely penalizes all kinds of non-normative sexual behaviour and sexual expression, of which porn – making it and watching it – is simply one part. After all, this is underpinned by the continuing penalization of sex work in Sri Lanka, the criminalization of same-sex sexual relations, and the heavy stigma and discrimination faced by sex workers, and lesbian, gay, queer, trans and gender non-conforming persons. The lack of a national-level commitment to comprehensive sexuality education, in policy and practice, only heightens the stigma, and the resulting silence, around conversations on sex and sexuality.

These same factors produce consent violations and make it hard for survivors, advocates and activists to fight such violations. Existing legislation and state policies have created an environment where violence and rights violations will thrive, and both those who want to engage consensually in the production of porn for public dissemination as well as those who are creating erotic imagery for intimate purposes can easily be exploited. It means porn actors and producers of erotic content most likely are better off hiding who they are and can probably never demand better if anyone within the scene is exploiting their labour. They cannot formalize the porn economy in Sri Lanka in ways which ensure their rights as workers. Coming forward to discuss grievances may increase their vulnerability to being exposed to the criminal justice system, to state violence and to marginalization in society. It also means young people who are facing consent violations online often will not seek pathways to redress and may frequently suffer in silence, because of the fear of stigmatization.

Feminist interventions in Sri Lanka on the issues of porn, sexual expression and regulation have evolved and diversified with time; with the study of the internet through a feminist lens, we see the beginnings of a strong body of feminist scholarship which is more visibly around pleasure and expression. This body of work, at long last, seems to want to begin a feminist discussion on porn. This speaks to the fact that the feminist study of technology has implications for fields and areas far beyond the visible bounds of 'technology' itself.

Lankan feminists have a number of potential pathways to explore including: more feminist inquiry on the regulation of porn as a freedom of expression issue; more feminist engagement with porn as part of sexuality and pleasure; and more feminist support for porn and sex work as labour rights issues. Of course, the most ideal feminist work would sit at the intersections of these various pathways. Such interventions are urgently needed in the Sri Lankan context. As feminists, we should consider it a part of our core mandate to debate and reject any kind of censorship. We should be prepared to defend the spaces we have created, and those we use, for our expression and for our pleasure, and, importantly, to defend the rights of those who continue to be penalized for transgressing sex, gender and sexual norms.

Notes

1. When I use the term 'Lankan feminist' I do not do this to assert national identity, but simply to add context. I refer here to a broader body of work which may include work which has studied varying Sri Lankan contexts through a feminist lens, and/or has been collaborations between researchers from other contexts and feminist researchers in Sri Lanka (who may or may not be 'Sri Lankan').
2. Interview with Paba Deshapriya, 3 November 2020.
3. Interview with Thishya Weragoda, 13 January 2021.
4. 'DROP ALL CHARGES AGAINST SHAKTHIKA SATHKUMARA', Amnesty International, 24 August 2020, https://act.amnestyusa.org/page/65823/action/1?locale=en-US.
5. Interview with Sanjana Hattotuwa, 11 November 2020.
6. An online, tri-lingual resource platform on sexuality, violence, and sexual health: http://www.bakamoono.lk.
7. 'A queer porn movie can have various porn scenes that include people who might be trans, femme, boi, fag, cisgender, queer and more. The range of diverse representations is a lot greater than in mainstream productions; in queer works, you'll find performers of all sizes, a higher percentage of people of colour, and different displays of gender expression. There's too much to categorize. Boxes fly out the window' (Lee 2013, 277).
8. See https://www.winsl.net.
9. Available on both Association for Progressive Communications (APC) and Women and Media Collective sites: https://womenandmedia.org/wp-content/uploads/2018/02/Disrupting-the-Binary-Code-_-for-web.pdf.
10. The Social Scientists' Association published a collection of Cat's Eye articles in a book edited by Malathi de Alwis in 2000.
11. See https://catseyesrilanka.wordpress.com.
12. See https://deletenothing.org/.
13. Interview with Sachini Perera, Jayanthi Kuru-Utumpala and Zainab Ibrahim, 13 November 2020.
14. Ibid.
15. Ibid.
16. Ibid.
17. Interview with Paba Deshapriya, 3 November 2020.
18. Ibid.
19. Ibid.
20. Ibid.
21. 'Google searches for sex; SL tops list again', *Daily Mirror*, 8 December 2016, http://www.dailymirror.lk/120457/Google-searches-for-sex-SL-tops-list-again.
22. Ibid.

Acknowledgements

The author thanks all who sat down for a conversation in the writing of this article: Paba Deshapriya, Sachini Perera, Zainab Ibrahim, Jayanthi Kuru Utumpala and Sanjana Hattotuwa. Gratitude also goes to Sinn Sage for the time spent talking across time zones. The author owes a debt of gratitude to all feminist academics and activists, both those named in this article and those not, who are working hard for sexuality to be understood as a critical feminist issue, who are advocating for the rights of sex workers, and for freedom of expression, including sexual expression, online and on the ground. Huge thanks to Darshana Sreedhar Mini and Anirban Baishya for making sure the author stayed the course and for their patient and thoughtful edits. Deep gratitude to Kimaya de Silva, who supported the development of this article.

Disclosure statement

No potential conflict of interest was reported by the author.

References

Abeysekera, Sunila. 1997. 'Abortion in Sri Lanka in the Context of Women's Human Rights.' *Reproductive Health Matters* 5 (9): 87–93.

Abeysekera, Sunila. 1999. 'Sexuality: A Feminist Issue?, Exploring the Reasons Why Many Women Fear Their Own Sexuality.' *Women in Action* 1.

Billimoria, Hans. 2017. 'Investigating Sri Lanka's 'Nude' Culture.' OpenDemocracy. January 27. https://www.opendemocracy.net/en/5050/investigating-sri-lanka-s-nude-culture/.

Cat's Eye Collective. 2018a. 'Where Are Women's Voices in Media?' Cat's Eye – UNCUT. October 11. https://catseyesrilanka.wordpress.com/2018/10/11/where-are-womens-voices-in-media/.

Cat's Eye Collective. 2018b. 'A Fill-T Look at Sinhala Rap Videos, Pornography, and Women.' August 8. Cat's Eye Sri Lanka. https://catseyesrilanka.wordpress.com/2018/08/08/a-fill-t-look-at-sinhalarap-videos-pornography-and-women/.

Daily News. 2018. 'Where Do Sri Lankans Learn about Sex?' Daily News. January 18. https://www.dailynews.lk/2018/01/18/features/140240/where-do-sri-lankans-learn-about-sex.

De Alwis, Malathi. 1996. 'Sexuality in the Field of Vision: The Discursive Clothing of the Sigiriya Frescoes.' In *Embodied Violence: Communalising Women's Sexuality in South Asia,* edited by Kumari Jayawardena and Malathi de Alwis. New Delhi: Kali for Women.

De Alwis, Malathi, ed. 2000. *Cat's Eye: A Feminist Gaze on Current Issues*. Colombo: Cat's Eye Publications.

Ganesh, Maya Indira, and Nishant Shah. 2020. ''Between Memory and Storage: Digital Transitions for Art Organizations.' In *Forces of Art*, edited by Carin Kuoni, Jordi Balta Portoles, Nora N Khan and Serubiri Moses, pp. 327–349. Amsterdam: Valiz together with Prince Claus Fund for Culture and Development, Hivos, European Cultural Foundation. https://forces-of-art.org/book.

Haviland, Charles. 2010. 'Sri Lanka 'pornographers' Outed in Police Crackdown.' BBC News. November 9. https://www.bbc.co.uk/news/world-south-asia-11717315.

Hymes, Tom. 2010. 'Sri Lanka Prepares to Install Porn Filters at the ISP-Level.' ABC Newsletter. AVN. November 3. https://avn.com/business/articles/technology/sri-lanka-prepares-to-install-porn-filters-at-the-isp-level-416993.html.

Jayawardena, Kumari and Malathi de Alwis, eds. 1996. *Embodied Violence: Communalising Women's Sexuality in South Asia*. New Delhi: Kali for Women.

Kottegoda, Sepali, Sitralega Maunaguru, Sachini Perera, Sarala Emmanuel and Sri Lanka. 2012. 'Women and New Media in the Margins of the Sri Lankan State.' https://www.gender-is-citizenship.net/sites/default/files/citigen/uploads/SLDraft_cover.pdf.

Lee, Jiz. 2013. 'Uncategorized: Genderqueer Identity and Performances in Independent and Mainstream Porn.' In *The Feminist Porn Book: The Politics of Producing Pleasure*, edited by Tristan Taormino, Mireille Miller-Young, Celine Parreñas Shimizu and Constance Penley, 273–278. New York: The Feminist Press.

LIRNEasia. 2008. 'Sri Lanka Pornography Regulatory Commission?.' — LIRNEasia. August 2. https://lirneasia.net/2008/08/sri-lanka-pornography-regulatory-commission/.

Natarajan, Swaminathan. 2010. 'Sri Lanka Launches Anti-Porn Initiative.' BBC News. November 5. https://www.bbc.co.uk/news/world-south-asia-11697565.

Perera, Sachini and Minoli Wijetunge. 2019. 'How Tiktok Is a Platform for Performance and Play for Women in Sri Lanka.' GenderIT.Org. May 10. https://www.genderit.org/articles/how-tiktok-platform-performance-and-play-women-sri-lanka.

Perera, Sachini and Zainab Ibrahim. 2021. 'Somewhere Only We Know: Gender, Sexualities, and Sexual Behaviour on the Internet in Sri Lanka.' https://erotics.apc.org/wp-content/uploads/2021/03/Somewhere-only-We-Know-Online.pdf.

Reuters. 2010. 'Sri Lanka Launches Porn Star Man-Hunt.' ABC News. November 9. https://www.abc.net.au/news/2010-11-10/sri-lanka-launches-porn-star-man-hunt/2330350.

Sekaram, Sharanya. 2017. '800 Odd Criminals: A Reflection.' Bakamoono. April 25. http://www.bakamoono.lk/en/article/1458/800-odd-criminals-a-reflection.

Sekaram, Sharanya. 2019. 'Let's Talk Feminism and Gender: Porn, Watching Porn, and Misogyny.' The Sunday Morning. October 20. http://www.themorning.lk/lets-talk-feminism-and-gender-porn-watching-porn-and-misogyny/.

Wijewardene, Shermal. 2018. 'Autonomous Sri Lankan Women's Organizations and Their Engagements with LBT 1 Advocacy.' In *Beyond Gender: An Advanced Introduction to Futures of Feminist and Sexuality Studies*, edited by Greta Olson, Mirjam Horn-Shott, Daniel Hartley and Regina Leonie Schmidt, 257–276. London: Routledge.